UR110

W9-AAN-172

Law

THE FUTURE OF LAW

The Future of Law

*Facing the Challenges of
Information Technology*

Richard Susskind

CLARENDON PRESS · OXFORD

Oxford University Press, Great Clarendon Street, Oxford OX2 6DP
Oxford New York
Athens Auckland Bangkok Bogota Bombay
Buenos Aires Calcutta Cape Town Dar es Salaam
Delhi Florence Hong Kong Istanbul Karachi
Kuala Lumpur Madras Madrid Melbourne
Mexico City Nairobi Paris Singapore
Taipei Tokyo Toronto
and associated companies in
Berlin Ibadan

Oxford is a registered trade mark of Oxford University Press

Published in the United States
by Oxford University Press Inc., New York

© Richard Susskind 1996

First published 1996
First published as paperback 1998

The right of Richard Susskind to be identified as the author of this work
has been asserted by him in accordance with the Copyright, Designs and
Patents Act 1988

All rights reserved. No part of this publication may be reproduced,
stored in a retrieval system, or transmitted, in any form or by any means,
without the prior permission in writing of Oxford University Press.
Within the UK, exceptions are allowed in respect of any fair dealing for the
purpose of research or private study, or criticism or review, as permitted
under the Copyright, Designs and Patents Act 1988, or in the case of
reprographic reproduction in accordance with the terms of the licences
issued by the Copyright Licensing Agency. Enquiries concerning
reproduction outside these terms and in other countries should be
sent to the Rights Department, Oxford University Press,
at the address above

This book is sold subject to the condition that it shall not, by way
of trade or otherwise, be lent, re-sold, hired out or otherwise circulated
without the publisher's prior consent in any form of binding or cover
other than that in which it is published and without a similar condition
including this condition being imposed on the subsequent purchaser

British Library Cataloguing in Publication Data
Data available

Library of Congress Cataloging in Publication Data
Data available
ISBN 0–19–826007–5
ISBN 0–19–876496–0 (Pbk)

Printed in Great Britain
on acid-free paper by
Biddles Ltd. Guildford and King's Lynn

With all my love
I dedicate this book
to my wonderful children

Daniel
Jamie
Alexandra

Preface to Paperback Edition
The Future of Law Revisited

Contents of Preface

Introduction

The world has moved on remarkably since I completed the original manuscript of this book in late 1995. At that time, hard though it is to believe today, barely a lawyer in the UK had even heard the term 'Intranet', only a few could claim to have seen the World Wide Web, and the government of the day was more or less silent on the question of IT and its impact on society. Although the revisionists would have us think otherwise, it has only been in that intervening period of less than two years that the political and legal worlds, under numerous pressures, have publicly woken up to the potential of information technology.

In 1996, in its progressively entitled green paper, 'government.direct',[1] the Conservative government put forward its important prospectus for the electronic delivery of government services, while the House of Lords Select Committee on Science and Technology set out an impressive agenda for our advance into the information society.[2] More recently, the new Labour administration has been endorsing the broad thrust of these documents and is coming to project a vision of society in which IT will play an ever-increasing role in the lives of all.[3]

As for the justice system in England, the Lord Chancellor of the new government has recently confirmed that Lord Woolf's proposed reforms for civil justice in England are to be implemented.[4] This, in turn, will require and bring about widespread and advanced use of IT by judges and practitioners. This far greater uptake of IT is also a central recommendation of the recent review of the Civil Division of the Court of Appeal.[5] At the same time, many other opinion formers and decision makers in the world of law are

---

[1] Cm 3438, Nov. 1996.

[2] House of Lords Select Committee on Science and Technology, 'Agenda for Action in the UK: Information Society', 23 July 1996, HL Paper 77.

[3] http://www.open.gov.uk/gdirect/

[4] Lord Woolf, *Access to Justice*, 2 vols (Woolf Inquiry Team, London, June 1995, July 1996).

[5] See Bowman, J. (chairman), *Review of the Court of Appeal (Civil Division)*, Report to the Lord Chancellor (Sept. 1997).

now regularly acknowledging or proclaiming that IT is vital for the future and indeed are questioning how anyone could have contemplated otherwise. And, in legal practice, thousands of lawyers across the world are using the Internet as their principal electronic mail system, while a growing number of law firms are setting out their stalls on the World Wide Web ('the Web') in the belief that it will be central to the delivery of legal services in years to come.

In short, the political and legal bandwagons are on the move, adopting IT as their own, and gathering speed. This is just as well because the last two years have also seen huge leaps in IT itself. Around the world, the Internet is being embraced with fervour in the home and at work, telecommunications technology is progressing rapidly, and processing power seems to be increasing at an even greater rate than the doubling every eighteen months which until recently was taken to be axiomatic.[6]

The main themes of the book

I am pleased to say that during this period of immense change the hardback edition of this book seems to have attracted much attention and stimulated considerable debate. As an author, it has been especially gratifying to have had the good fortune to receive a great deal of interesting and challenging feedback, in response both to the text and to the numerous presentations I have made since its publication. While the reactions, quite naturally, have been varied, the reviews and commentaries have generally been more sympathetic than I could have hoped. That said, it is not fashionable to criticise IT and those who do so today run the risk of being rejected as luddites or dinosaurs. I am under no illusions that my themes command universal support. I have no doubt, in fact, that there are closet critics in abundance because much that I have to say is threatening to the livelihoods of many practising lawyers and so unsavoury for not a few for that reason alone.

But I stand by the major arguments of the book. If I may be permitted the gall of quoting myself so early in this preface, I remain firmly of the view, as expressed in the penultimate paragraph of the book, that:

legal practice and the administration of justice will no longer be dominated by print and paper in tomorrow's legal paradigm. Instead, legal systems of the information

---

[6] Several important new publications on IT and the future have appeared since the hardback edition of this book was published. I have found the following especially helpful: Dertouzos. M., *What Will Be* (HarperCollins, New York, 1997); Gibson, R. (ed.), *Rethinking the Future* (Nicholas Brearley, London, 1996); Martin, J., *Cybercorp* (Amacom, New York, 1996); Tenner, E., *Why Things Bite Back* (Fourth Estate, London, 1996).

society will evolve rapidly under the considerable influence of ever more powerful information technologies. We will no longer suffer from the excessive quantity and complexity of legal material. There will be mechanisms in place to give everyone fair warning of the existence of new law and changes in old. Legal risks will be managed in advance of problems occurring and so dispute pre-emption rather than dispute resolution will be the order of the day. Our law will thus become far more fully integrated with our domestic, social and business lives.

The legal marketplace, I still maintain, will change beyond recognition as we progress into the information society. Just as guidance on consumer products, investment trends, trading opportunities and medical matters will be easily accessible on the Internet, so too will guidance on the law— readily available both for individuals and for small and large businesses as well. The guidance offered will be less focused than that delivered nowadays by traditional advisory service. But IT-based legal service will be vastly more useful than today's only alternative: the booklets, texts and other sources found in libraries and book stores.

The guidance made available on the information highway will more closely resemble the kind of practical pointers that a lawyer might currently pass along to a friend: a short list of key points and reminders; maybe a few pieces of standard text; and perhaps an indication of some relevant, common pitfalls. From orienting a consumer dissatisfied with some purchase to briefing a chief executive on the basics of some deal, the help on offer will tend to be punchy, practical and free of legal jargon.

Such desert island guidelines may be no substitute for the formal advice of legal specialists provided in the time-honoured, consultative fashion, but they will be an immeasurable improvement over having no access to legal help whatsoever, which is the regrettable state in which so many now find themselves.

IT-based guidance will be less forbidding to obtain, more affordable, and brought to bear far more frequently than legal advice of today. No longer will the law be meted out occasionally on the basis of billing by the hour. Instead it will become, in large part, a low cost commodity, distributed in high volumes.

Latent legal markets will be liberated by IT. These are the vast markets populated by those many millions of people who require legal help today but are deterred from obtaining it because it is too costly, complex or inconvenient. And these latent legal markets are as needy in large corporations as they are in society generally—citizens and business concerns everywhere face substantial legal risks today which they have no realistic hope of recognising and controlling.

In the language of technologists, lawyers of today are the interface between non-lawyers and the law. If a person wants to know his legal position, he will generally have to consult a legal adviser. In the future, legal information systems will become a vital interface, as legal guidance becomes one of countless sorts of information available on the global information highway. The law will no longer be the exclusive preserve of lawyers.

Although this clearly constitutes a threat to practising lawyers, it is still my position that the law is no more there to keep lawyers in business than ill health is there to provide a livelihood for doctors.

Recurrent questions

I am confident at the same time that all manner of new opportunities will arise for lawyers and those who are imaginative, creative and entrepreneurial will develop and market useful legal guidance systems. These will not only be of great use to non-lawyers but will also serve as a major source of revenue for these legal information engineers (as I call them).

I am far less confident, however, that I am sufficiently clear in the book about the many practical implications of my analysis of the future of law. In particular, there have been a number of basic recurrent questions asked of me by readers. By way of response, I thought it might be helpful to write this new preface.

The key questions have been these:

- what are the most *likely* developments in IT over the next ten years or so?
- with these developments in mind, what *possibilities* will arise for legal practice and for the administration of justice?
- what is the future of the justice system in light of IT and how should governments be reacting today?
- what is the future for lawyers and what role is the World Wide Web likely to play?

I hope that this preface answers these questions in sufficient detail to help decision-makers across justice systems and in the legal professions around the world with their long term planning for information technology. I have written the preface both for those who have read the book or are familiar with its central arguments as well as for those who are new to my various claims. The former will recognise that I have refined and developed but not changed my central themes. The latter can choose either to read the book first and then return to this preface or, as usefully I hope, to work through these latest views first and turn thereafter to the main text for the far more detailed arguments and for some theoretical analysis as well.

1 Likely developments in IT over the next 10 years

My first task, then, is to suggest what are likely to be the most significant developments in IT over the next ten years.

It might immediately be wondered whether or not it is actually possible to make reliable long term predictions about IT. Indeed, it is often argued that long term planning for IT is futile because no one can confidently predict what technological advances might be made many years hence. In support of this, it might be said that if a long term forecasting exercise analogous to the one in this preface had been conducted in 1977 it would have neglected the advent of the personal computer (which came to the market in 1981) while a similar initiative in 1987 would have had no insight into the World Wide Web (developed in 1990). Both of these developments fundamentally changed the world of IT (and the world generally) but neither could have been predicted. Should we not therefore wait and see what new technologies emerge and focus instead today on making IT work for us in the short term?

On reflection, the position today, in 1997, is significantly different from ten and twenty years ago. In particular, it is striking to note that even if there were to be no new advances in IT over the next decade as radical or fundamental as the PC and the World Wide Web have been, nonetheless the likely impact of the entirely foreseeable consequences of today's proven technologies will of itself be extremely profound both for the administration of justice and for the practice of law. This was not so ten or twenty years ago, when what was foreseeable then did not promise such pervasive and penetrating change. Thus the predictions of this preface assume no major step changes and yet begin to offer a vision of a justice system and of legal practice which would be quite different from today's. (At the same time, the possibility of some far-reaching, new technical innovations emerging over the next ten years cannot be discounted and this highlights the need constantly to monitor research activities across the world.)

In any event, pragmatic managers often harbour doubts about long term strategy, fearing that it can result in unrealistic and impractical proposals which might distract IT specialists as well as users from the basic requirements of keeping existing systems running today and in the short term. There is a danger here; but so long as long term strategy and day-to-day operational work are managed separately (even if closely linked), a strategic approach should actually support ongoing systems administration. It is surely crucial to think ahead, to choose from future possibilities and, in turn, to offer support to others who will benefit from direction when, for example, they come to be faced with a variety of options in implementation.

Finally, by way of introduction to this discussion of IT over the next ten years, the suggestion that the developments are likely within that particular period requires qualification in two respects. First, it is more responsible to claim that these developments might come to fruition some time between five and fifteen years from now, which is to say that some will be realised more quickly than within a decade while others may be more challenging than currently appears and so may take longer than the ten years. Second, and building on an earlier point, the predictions are restricted to developments which are clearly foreseeable and, of course, can take no account of radical new technologies to which we have no insight today.

As for the developments themselves, building on and bringing together various themes in the book, I am now able to identify ten.

(1) Global telecommunications

With massive and ongoing improvements in a variety of telecommunications technologies (including advances in optical fibre and compression techniques and in satellite technology as well), there will be broadband, interactive networks, across most of the world and in practically all of England, connecting all buildings and all computers to one another. If a crude analogy is drawn with the flow of water, this broadband network will be akin to a mains pipe through which water is pumped where most of today's links can be likened to encouraging water to dribble from a drinking straw.

This will mean, in due course, that there will be no practical limits to the quantities of information which can be transmitted around the world almost instantaneously. The information itself will not only be text but also sound, image, animation and video as well, so that high quality desk-top to desk-top video conferencing will come of age. There will be a huge increase in digital traffic across this global telecommunications infrastructure which will enable transmission costs to fall rapidly, eventually to a negligible level for individual transactions. A variety of techniques will be developed to ensure that transmissions can be secure, confidential and capable of authentication; and also to enable and encourage reliable payment and transfer of funds.

In summary, there will be a global telecommunications infrastructure which, for practical purposes, will enable the instantaneous transmission of seemingly limitless amounts of digital information at negligible cost.

(2) The information industries

The global telecommunications infrastructure will provide the basis for a rapidly growing range of information industries, early examples of which can be seen today in the form of Internet email and the World Wide Web (these terms are explained in greater detail in the book). Already there are said to be about 100 million users of Internet email; and most commentators believe this figure will rise to around 1 billion in the first few years of the new millennium. Soon electronic mail will be more widely used than the telephone but its use will be extended to embrace the transfer not just of text but also of voice messages, photographs, images and video as well (video conferencing to and from computers and televisions will soon be commonplace).

As for the World Wide Web, today's position offers some insight into emerging methods of providing information and entertainment across the global telecommunications infrastructure. Even now, massive amounts of conventional published materials can be accessed through the Web. However, more sophisticated forms of information service will emerge. Systems which offer guidance and not just raw data or information are already under development; and the more advanced applications are interactive, whereby users can be tracked through complex issues on a question and answer basis. Domestically, this will enable, for example, the on-line booking of restaurants and cinema tickets or the purchase and sale of cars; while in the business world many of the middlemen known or referred to as brokers, agents or intermediaries (estate agents, insurance brokers and travel agents for example) will find an equivalent of their service being delivered by other information providers on the information highway. This 'disintermediation' (a dreadful word for a vital concept) will come to pervade the service industries. Middlemen will manage to survive only if they can add value that no system can currently replicate.

As stressed later, the natural first port of call for guidance on almost any issue will soon be electronic information services. More than this, trading, transacting and business processes generally will be conducted and mediated over the information highway. Here entirely new forms of business will emerge.

(3) Virtual private networks

Although innumerable services and facilities will remain directly accessible to all users across the world, the same global telecommunications infrastructure will also support the establishment of restricted and sometimes even private networks. These will enable communities of users with shared interests to communicate easily with one another (by conventional electronic mail, voice messaging and video, for example), perhaps with enhanced security or confidentiality features as appropriate for the information and services involved. Identifying the addresses of individuals with such common interests will be straightforward and there will be common areas to visit to hold public and private, on-line and off-line, discussions and forums.

As a practical matter, participation within these private networks (sometimes referred to, somewhat inaccurately, as 'intranets') will make it far easier for users to identify information services suitable for their particular purposes. Today's World Wide Web is already rather unmanageable. Tomorrow's restricted networks will help steer users towards what they need. These private networks will support specific industry groups and professions for their members' internal purposes but will have an external face too, offering non-member users of their services limited access to parts of these networks and providing certification of the provenance and authenticity of the services on offer.

All these networks will not actually be separate systems, each with their own plumbing. They will be 'virtual' private networks—in the world of IT, the word 'virtual' has come to be used where technology is electronically creating some effect in the physical world. Thus, the networks will function as though they were discrete and separate.

Users will no doubt communicate across innumerable different private networks. I find it helpful to think of every user having a portfolio of affiliations to a range of networks, some devoted to particular projects, others to organisations to which they belong and still others to bodies of individuals with shared interests. A busy person might be affiliated to fifty or so such virtual private networks.

(4) Computing power

Although advances in telecommunications may appear to be more dramatic, the power of computers will continue to burgeon. Until recently, it was widely held that, for the foreseeable future, the performance of microprocessors could be expected to continue doubling every eighteen months and yet become thirty per cent cheaper per annum. It is now thought that performance will come to double in less than eighteen months, so that it will be less than the predicted twenty years before one personal computer will be as powerful as the sum total of all of today's machines in California's Silicon Valley.

The storage capacity of computer disks is also set to increase astoundingly (although it is arguable that the relevance of computer storage will decline with the availability of cheap, on-line systems across the new telecommunications infrastructure). Where a single compact disk (CD) of today can store a large set of encyclopaedias, emerging technologies such as Digital Versatile Disk (DVD) will offer up to thirty times that capacity. Looking further ahead, as is suggested in the main body of the book, holographic memory holds the promise of storing the entire contents of the British Library in a unit no bigger than a regular paperback book.

All the while, machines themselves will go on shrinking in size, such that credit card sized machines more powerful than any PC of today with detachable, slim-line screens are entirely conceivable within the next ten years or so. Even since this book was published in hardback, a whole array of handheld machines have arrived, some the size of a pack of cards and many with power and capacity that exceed state of the art personal computers of a decade ago. Screen display technology continues to improve steadily, to the extent that the quality and resolution of today's most polished conventional colour publications (glossy magazines, for instance) will soon be rendered on digital display units.

(5) *Convergence of computers and television*

Over one third of households in England already have home computers. The overwhelming majority also have television sets. Together, these two apparently different display units are coming to dominate life in this country: television, traditionally for entertainment; and the computer now for information. That said, the text facilities available through television (accessed by more than 18 million people in the UK every week) already show an existing willingness for viewers to access information electronically. In due course, along with the much vaunted convergence of information and entertainment will come a convergence of the technologies which deliver these media—the television and the personal computer. Thus, the user will have one window on the world and not two.

In short, the next generation of televisions will offer immediate access to the Internet and to the World Wide Web, so that the overwhelming majority of people in the UK, for example, will be on-line within, I would guess, about three to five years. What with the greatly enhanced telecommunications infrastructure, the systems will be far quicker than today, bringing multi-media information onto wall screens in many homes and transforming their lives.

Perhaps the most significant aspect of this convergence is a cultural dimension: it can comfortably be predicted, as I stress shortly, that users will come quite naturally to turn to their TV/PCs as their first port of call in any quest for information and guidance; just as naturally as they might turn to their televisions for a variety of forms of entertainment. At the same time, the interactivity which characterises personal computer use today is likely to diminish the purely passive nature of television watching and the latter will develop as a more participative pastime.

(6) Smarter technologies

It is a central theme of this book that our current capability to use IT to capture, store, retrieve, and reproduce data, easily surpasses our ability to use technology to help extract *all but only* the information we might need at any one time. Across industry, commerce and government, managers and workers bemoan the quantity of information they are expected to digest. So far, IT is often said to have given rise to less rather than more control over information—we suffer from technologies which allow more documentation to be produced and disseminated but with no commensurate facilities to help sift through and identify relevant information. IT has given us 'information overload' but precious few tools as yet to help us cope with this surfeit.

Gradually, however, a variety of emerging techniques (such as intelligent agents, expert systems and artificial intelligence) are actually helping users to analyse and manage the vast bodies of information out there. Smarter systems are emerging which themselves bring to users *all but only* the material relevant for their particular purposes. These smarter technologies represent a shift in IT towards systems that can provide help, offer guidance, solve problems, undertake research, eliminate irrelevant information and pinpoint pertinent material. In due course, these technologies will, invariably and as a matter of course, deliver useful, timely and focused information to all human beings who are on-line, doing so on the basis of an understanding of the interests and concerns of these individuals.

(7) Multi-media

The traditional way of conveying information during the past few centuries has been through script or by print on paper. In the print-based society, there have been at least two assumptions. First, it is generally assumed that printed materials (for example, books and articles) will be tackled by their readers in more or less linear fashion. Although readers may skim or speed read, there is usually a sense of progression from one end (the beginning) to the other (the finish). Although indexes and other techniques may support the reading process and enable readers to initiate their reading in the middle of a publication, once entry has been made the procedure is usually linear thereafter. The second assumption is that the body of printed material being consulted is usually dominated by text, self-contained, with clear boundaries and with a strong indication, from the face of it, of the extent of the publication.

Print-based publication, however, is quite quickly being replaced by electronic multi-media publication. In the world of multi-media, text is but one means of conveying information because it is invariably supplemented by other media such as sound, animation, video and image. Electronic publications frequently contain all these media together so that multi-media encyclopaedias of today, for example, provide text on screen with associated sound (perhaps music) or video (maybe a clip from a film) or images (for example, photographs), each instantaneously accessible at the click of a mouse.

Electronic multi-media publication challenges the two assumptions about printed materials as identified above. On the one hand, the principal means of progressing through these new media is rarely linear. Instead, the dominant technique is to 'browse', jumping within and between the media as the user prefers (this is the essence of 'hypertext' and 'hypermedia'). Users can thus take major detours from text into the world of video and then perhaps to sound, all in an exploratory spirit. On the other hand, multi-media challenges the second assumption about isolated, clearly bounded publications. Those which in the past were stand-alone come now, in the world of multi-media and most strikingly on the World Wide Web, to form one massive, seemingly infinite, single body of information. Where the conventional consultation of an encyclopaedia, for example, used to involve reading text-based entries from what was a clear beginning to an obvious end, electronic consultation today is not solely text-based and, for practical purposes, the amount of information to hand seems to be limitless.

(8) Usability

The user friendliness of systems is also set to change radically; and it is here, for instance, that the IT giant Microsoft is directing enormous research investment. On the one hand, there will be continual progress in the field of voice recognition, such that speaker independent, large vocabulary, continuous speech systems will be widely used within five years and probably less. In practice, this means that to enter text and instruct their computers, users will be able to talk to their machines in the same way as they would do to one another or as they would when using a dictating machine—with few practical limitations on the scope and richness of the vocabulary, no pauses between words and independently of the accents or idiosyncrasies of the speech patterns of particular speakers. Systems will gradually also be able not only to recognise the spoken word of individuals but also to cope with conversations in which several people are engaged.

On the other hand, on usability, the user interfaces of systems will become ever more adaptable, such that, in operation, systems will be geared to the needs, habits, quirks and preferences of particular users. No doubt through complex psychological tests, optimum interfaces will be identified for each and every user, extending from the colours of screen display through to the balance between graphical and textual information, for example.

Personalised and customisable systems to which human beings will be able to talk or which they will wear (on arm bands or weaved into clothing) will gradually remove fear of computer use and all generations within entire communities will come to be comfortable with IT as part of their daily lives. (Looking beyond ten years, and as advanced screen technology moves beyond the head mounted displays characteristic of today's virtual reality games towards active contact lenses which will fill our fields of vision entirely with computer output, we will become attached, both figuratively and actually, to our information technology.)

(9) Interpersonal and interorganisational computing

With improved telecommunications linking most computers to one another, it is becoming increasingly natural and worthwhile for individuals and organisations to take advantage of this interconnectivity and the ability to share information, so that they can work more closely together than was ever possible in the past.

When I wrote the hardback version of this book, the dominant enabling technique in this context was 'groupware'—a category of system and software specifically designed to encourage and enable collaborative, interpersonal and interorganisational activity. Groupware stood out then as the best way to allow existing and newly created information to become a shared resource which all authorised users could contribute to and draw from. Today, however, the Internet and internal wide area networks now provide competing methods of supporting and encouraging team working.

Whatever technique is preferred, however, IT generally can now be said genuinely to enable co-operative team working when the team members are not located together; as well as common access to the work product. And this can happen today in an uninhibiting and non-threatening manner.

On-line 'virtual meetings' are destined to dominate our lives, some conducted through the relatively flat medium of text; while others will be considerably enlivened by video conferencing.[7]

(10) The Web as the 'first port of call'

My tenth and final development derives from the impact of the previous nine. With all the advances to which I have drawn attention, usage of information technology is rapidly pervading society—for example, in homes, in education, in Government, in finance and commerce, in health and in entertainment. As has been said, over one third of households in England already have home computers. And the great majority of businesses today, of all sizes, deploy some form of IT, at least for their own internal purposes. As prices fall, and more uses are made available, IT will become as commonplace as the telephone and the television.

Before long, as was also suggested earlier, the natural first port of call for information, guidance and for innumerable services as well, in both a social and business context, will be the World Wide Web. Human beings will come to expect to have information technology (and, in turn, information and information services) at their fingertips and, equally, will expect all others around them similarly to be using IT.

Think then of a society, one that is carpeted in fibre, where everyone is connected to everyone, and each has immediate access from the home to guidance on most topics and this guidance is presented in wonderfully graphic and easy-to-use form. Indeed, most users will, essentially, be speaking to their televisions when they want some information. Consider that this resource might indeed become the natural first port of call for the

[7] Looking a little further ahead, by exploiting still more advanced techniques such as 'shared spaces' (being pioneered in the UK by British Telecom), users will be able to take on some electronic personae and actually venture into cyberspace and interact with others through these digital personae known as 'atavars'. Fantastic though this may sound, the 'virtual world wide web' of today shows that it will not be too long before we can 'meet' and work with one another in a distant virtual land.

majority of people. In that context, can we honestly expect that legal service will continue to be delivered in the time honoured fashion—through one-to-one, face-to-face, consultative, advisory service for which people are charged by the hour? I think not, but before I offer some rather specific predictions and recommendations, I believe it is helpful to take a step back and consider what, in theory and principle, is possible in law in the coming decade in the light of the advances in IT just outlined.

2 What will be possible in law

In the previous section, a variety of *likely* developments and trends in IT were laid out. One of the most pressing challenges for anyone interested in the justice system, or particular branches of it, is to identify the possibilities and opportunities that these developments might bring for the practice of law and for the administration of justice. Accordingly, the purpose of this section, in an exercise of what I call 'possibility analysis', is to suggest what, in turn, is *possible* in the justice system in the next decade.

When seeking to identify possibilities for the future, it is vital to bear in mind—and this is an absolutely vital theme of the book—that IT can have impact in two quite different ways:

- IT can be used to *automate*, streamline and improve existing practices, activities and organisations; or
- IT can be used to *innovate*, and so to bring about change and introduce new ways of working and carrying out tasks.

Beyond law, as I often say, the distinction is seen clearly when one thinks of IT-based cash dispensers. That technology did not automate pre-existing domestic banking practices. Instead it provided the basis for an entirely new way of conducting banking business. In the justice system too, it should be expected that IT may be used not only to streamline current practices and institutions and render them more efficient but also to change many aspects of the way in which the law is practised and justice is administered.

This section of my preface presents at least thirty possibilities for four categories of user:

- justice workers generally;
- non-lawyers;
- lawyers and judges specifically; and
- the court system specifically.

This categorisation is a pragmatic one. There can be no doubt that the categories overlap and that some possibilities could be put under two or more headings. Nonetheless, the general thrust should be clear.

Justice workers generally

For those who work in the justice system generally, a wide range of far-reaching changes are possible.

A national legal network

With many hundreds of thousands of users, a secure, confidential, reliable, private legal network (virtual) may be developed, linking together everyone who works in the English justice system. This would be a telecommunications infrastructure not just for conveying conventional messages and documents but also to carry video conferencing, databases, bundles of document images, video recordings and voice messaging as well. The network would link all users to one another, whether in court, chambers, law offices, at home or on the move. Much of the business of the courts and of legal practitioners would be carried out on this network and it would be accessible both by physical connections and by wireless technology too.

Virtual hearings and meetings

Video conferencing and telecommunications might enable the conduct of certain court hearings and other legally oriented meetings without all the parties needing to assemble in the one physical location. (A virtual meeting or hearing is one where people do not actually meet face to face but IT reproduces many of the features of such physical meetings.) As legal standards and procedures emerge, virtual hearings and meetings could come to play a major role in the justice system, not only displacing some forums of today but also enabling more frequent and greatly improved communication where, hitherto, face-to-face meetings have not been feasible. In turn, this may enable a reduction in the number of court buildings across the country.

Multi-media and hypertext-based legal bundles

In due course, the preferred and perhaps required format for the lodging of documents in the courts or the exchange of documents amongst parties to a dispute or agreement could be in electronic form in accordance with some pre-specified formats or standards. Electronic document bundles would thus be created and supplemented as they pass through each stage in a commercial or judicial process. Whereas document bundles of today come in the form of discrete and invariably printed documents, with occasional internal cross-references which readers themselves have to pursue while reading, document bundles in the future will be electronically linked to one another (using technology such as hypertext), so that users will navigate around electronic bundles as though they were single sets of information. And the information itself will no longer simply be text-based but will be presented using other media as well, including video, images, sound and animation. Thus, an electronic bundle of legal documents will be more usable and more expressive than their paper counterparts of today.

Legislation on the Internet

The electronic publication of all primary and subordinate legislation could easily be required to coincide with the conventional publication of these materials in print and paper. Whether and how these materials are consolidated, cross-referenced to one another (in the manner of hypertext), linked to commentaries and indeed charged for will clearly be a matter for further debate.

Searching for legal sources

Advanced searching techniques and 'intelligent agents' will help overcome the problems arising now from an ever burgeoning body of legal source material. Where today those who are looking for legal information or guidance must actively search through materials, technologies of the future (the 'smarter' systems discussed earlier) will greatly assist in this process, guiding users to *all but only* information that is relevant for their purposes. And in due course, new legal developments which bear on an individual's or an organisation's activities will automatically be brought to their attention, even in advance of the users being aware of the need for such input.

Multi-media transcripts

With technologies available to capture and later provide information in multi-media format, multi-media transcripts—of meetings and hearings—could be available, thus providing a record not just in textual form, but with accompanying sound and video as well, for example.

Ongoing research and development

Just as has always been the case in many hi-tech industries, research and development initiatives will become far more important in the legal world, not just for commercial organisations seeking to achieve competitive advantage and good practice in their sectors but also in Government and in the court system, where it will be increasingly important for IT to be (and be seen to be) used efficiently, productively, and competitively too (in international terms).

Non-lawyers

More radically still, existing and emerging technologies could transform the ways in which non-lawyers are guided by the law and interact with the legal system.

Legal guidance systems

Alongside all sorts of other types of information, legal guidance, legal knowledge, legal expertise and legal experience may gradually be available on the Internet, offering non-lawyers (individuals and organisations, for social and business purposes) access to structured, practical guidance on legal affairs. These systems would vary in complexity, from electronic check-lists through automated document assembly systems to diagnostic expert systems (see later). While they may not replace conventional legal services, such systems would provide affordable, easy access to legal guidance where this may have been unaffordable or impractical in the past.

A more participative legislative process

Possibilities for far wider participation in the legislative process may also be enabled through general access to the electronic information infrastructure. Actual or exploratory voting will be possible as will improved opportunities for citizens to participate (perhaps through bulletin boards or on-line discussions) in discussions about issues before Parliament or even on draft bills. Today's form of representative parliamentary democracy is a function of a print-based society dominated by face-to-face interaction. In an information society, dominated by on-line interpersonal communication, expression of opinion and the exercise of voting rights may come to be mediated through IT.

Promulgation

It is entirely foreseeable that emerging technologies could enable the majority of citizens to be notified of relevant new laws (and changes in old law too). In non-technical terms, this would involve users articulating profiles of their social and business interests. At the same time, legal information service providers would ensure that developments in the law would also be profiled and categorised and there would be mechanisms for automatic notification to these users where there were matches or partial matches between their profiles and the categorisations of the new legal developments. For businesses, such an information service would be invaluable and the revenue which could be secured from such a business service could perhaps give a low or no cost service of a similar sort for individual citizens.

Case tracking

Where case tracking and case management systems in the past have been the exclusive province of court administrators, and more recent proposals for reform suggest their extension to judges and lawyers as well, access to information about the status of particular cases (both civil and criminal) may be extended still further, beyond the court system and legal profession, to private individuals and organisations who have legitimate interests in the progress of their own cases. This could even be achieved across the Internet directly from the homes of users.

Enhanced voluntary legal services

With a full-scale national legal network in place, voluntary legal organisations may have easier and more extensive access to the experience and skills of legal practitioners across the country. Where in the past the input of lawyers on a *pro bono* basis has often depended on their physical presence at some location beyond their offices, some guidance may, in the future, be deliverable—directly or indirectly—through technology (for example, video conferencing, legal guidance systems, electronic mail and bulletin boards). At the same time, the voluntary services will be able to identify potential advisers in a more structured and coherent way, using the directories that will be available on the restricted, national legal network. An IT-based community legal service (as discussed later) is thus entirely conceivable.

Public administration systems

Routine public administration and related form filling may also be enabled and undertaken electronically. The submission of tax returns and the granting of licences, for example, will be possible on-line, as will the payment of social security and benefit claims and the provision of grants. With all such services, there could be focused guidance available for users with immediate assessment, explanation and payment, where appropriate. Such public administration systems will extend to areas as diverse as obtaining passports, driving and television licences (all probably in the form of smart cards) as well as numerous business-oriented pieces of administration, including the many formal requirements of disclosure and management imposed on those running companies.

The much vaunted 'one-stop shop' for the delivery of electronic government services will in due course extend to legal services and the justice system generally, although most thinking so far about one-stop shops has been focused rather restrictively on physical locations. Within a few years, with near universal access to the Internet, it will be more appropriate to think of 'single points of access', most of which could be electronic and in the home.

Multi-disciplinary systems and services

For non-lawyers, the availability of legal guidance and information in isolation will come to be seen as rather anomalous. The domestic user, while on-line, will gradually expect legal information to be bundled with other relevant information (integrated, say, with consumer or leisure or health information), while business users will expect and require the guidance they receive to be oriented towards the problems or projects with which they are involved rather than the underlying, individual, legal disciplines. Thus, legal guidance systems will either operate alongside or be fully integrated, as multi-disciplinary systems, with other guidance systems, extending into areas such as accountancy, banking, and business and management consultancy. Already, initiatives such as The PORT, which is seeking to provide a new City Information Infrastructure for London, are ensuring that this integration will be technically possible.

The law embedded in systems generally

Using expert systems techniques, it may be possible to develop diagnostic systems which will function alongside project management, document management and even with process control systems such that these expert systems will be able constantly to monitor the activities to which these other systems refer and will in turn be able to recognise combinations of circumstances which raise legal questions or which require legal precautions. Thus computer systems will in due course themselves be able to identify the legal implications of the tasks they themselves are performing and even to recommend or take remedial action.

Lawyers and judges specifically

Turning now to lawyers and judges more specifically, once more a vast array of possible developments can be anticipated.

Widespread institutional memories

Within organisations and bodies across the justice system, a number of enabling techniques (for example, groupware and intranet technologies) might encourage and enable the establishment of substantial internal know-how systems, which could capture the internal experience of those who work within organisations and make that information more widely available internally and more easily accessible too. Thus, the know-how that is often locked in the heads of specialists or hidden in filing cabinets will become a widely used internal information resource. For users (who may be judges or legal practitioners), this resource would also be integrated with other external information services, so that, in searching for information, systems will help users simultaneously to look within and beyond their organisations for relevant material. Users may thus come to search a combination of their institutional memories and external virtual legal libraries (see later).

A new international dimension

With a global information infrastructure in place, it will be far easier than ever before for lawyers to collaborate and maintain contact on a genuinely international basis. Judges, legal practitioners and academics will be able to establish and maintain regular dialogue with counterparts around the world as easily as communicating with colleagues in the same building. International collaboration will also be possible, through groupware, intranet technologies and video conferencing.

At the same time, the international 'law of cyberspace', it is widely expected, will gradually bring a common (but not exhaustive) body of legal scholarship and legal practice to all jurisdictions. There are already strong (but not overwhelming) arguments for treating the law of cyberspace as a jurisdiction in its own right. From this might follow far greater collaboration and overlap between and amongst lawyers across the globe.

Virtual legal teams

With the availability of groupware, intranet techniques, video conferencing and telecommunications generally, it will no longer be necessary for lawyers and judges to be physically co-located at all times in order for them to work together on the same case. Instead, these technologies may bring practitioners (and judges too, especially in relation to case management) under the one virtual roof, enabling effective, practical collaboration amongst individuals who may even be thousands of miles apart.

Large law firms, in turn, may find they have new competition in the shape of virtual law firms—these might be collaborative entities, established on a project basis, where smaller firms will be able to work together effectively, combining their talents and attaining a size of workforce which was simply not possible in the past. (Again the use of 'virtual' is intended to convey the idea that IT is bringing people together to work as though they were on one team in one physical location.)

Automated document assembly

A great deal of legal work is devoted to the drafting of legal documents. To some extent, and certainly for routine documents, this task can now be supported or even undertaken by what are known as automated document assembly or document generation systems. In operation, such systems ask their users questions, the responses to which insert or delete templates or parts of templates which have previously been set up by legal specialists. The templates are fixed portions of text together with precise instructions as to when given extracts should be used. In reliance on the users' input, the system will automatically generate a customised and polished document based on its knowledge of how its standard text should be used. Document assembly systems could be used not only to help lawyers and judges create their own documentation but also directly by consumers in supporting the drafting of far more legally reliable material than was possible in the past.

Legal diagnostic systems

This type of system, often based on rule-based expert systems technology, can provide specific answers to given problems. After an interactive consultation which helps clarify and classify the facts of a particular case, these systems may be able to analyse the details and then draw conclusions or make recommendations. In many ways, these systems are analogous to the medical diagnostic systems which offer diagnoses on the strength of symptoms presented to them. Legal diagnostic systems have already been developed which can make recommendations on sentencing, bail decisions, quantum, and many other areas of common law, legislation and regulation. While they are often thought to be of greatest use to non-lawyers, in fact they may be invaluable for legally qualified individuals when faced with problems beyond their areas of expertise. In such circumstances, they can prompt the lawyers to focus on the key issues and help ensure uniformity of approach.

Virtual legal libraries

For use across the legal profession (and even beyond), it will be possible to bring together massive amounts of primary and secondary legal source materials (in conventional and multi-media format) into widely accessible virtual legal libraries. These collections would not only be vast in scope but would have sophisticated front-ends, filters, search facilities and other tools to guide users quickly and easily to *all but only* the materials they would need at any point in time. These facilities could be available to the academic and practising branches of the profession as well as to judges.

Judicial decisions on the Internet

As judges increasingly prepare their own judgments using word-processing (perhaps through voice recognition technology) and so in machine readable form, it should be but a short final step to make these decisions widely available on the Internet. Indeed, all House of Lords' judgments in the UK and decisions from various other courts now appear on the Internet very soon after the judge has disposed of the case. This process of down-loading judicial decisions could easily be automated, thereby making case reports immediately available across the legal profession and far more effectively within the judiciary as well. The judges themselves may choose in due course to supplement judgments down-loaded in this way with their own commentary, indicating the significance of their cases and perhaps with keywords which characterise each and every decision. This additional information and ever more sophisticated searching techniques will meet the concern that this automated down-loading might lead to an unmanageable number of reported decisions.

Preface to Paperback Edition

New roles for lawyers

As legal guidance and other forms of legal information come to be widely available and easily accessible on the Internet and the World Wide Web, at least two new roles emerge for lawyers. On the one hand, there will be the new discipline of what I call throughout the book 'legal information engineering': this is the job of reorganising and presenting legal information in a form that can be of direct, practical use to non-lawyers; and this is a job which requires a blend of substantive legal knowledge together with an ability to break down complex legal topics and concepts into lay terms.

At the same time, and secondly, there will be a need for some kind of system of certification of the information and services which become available—non-lawyers will want some comfort and assurance that the systems upon which they are relying (and clearly there are profound liability issues here) have indeed been developed by appropriately qualified lawyers and some process of certification will probably be desirable. Once standards for the evaluation of services have been developed, there will be considerable work involved in reviewing new offerings as they are brought onto the information highway. It may be that the professional bodies will have a major role to play here as well.

Other providers of legal services

As legal information and guidance become available on the global information infrastructure, many individuals and organisations beyond the legal profession are likely to want to compete in this marketplace and provide legal and quasi-legal services themselves. Accountancy firms, telecommunications providers, legal publishers and electronic publishers are likely to be the main competitors, either working in isolation or perhaps in conjunction with lawyers.

Distance legal learning

Legal education will be transformed through the availability of on-line, interactive, multi-media systems, which will enable judges, lawyers and students to learn and be trained remotely, and at times that suit their diaries. Today's techniques of electronic law tutorials, computer-based law 'courseware', computer-assisted learning and computer-assisted instruction will combine with telecommunications technology to provide distance legal learning. Already, Strathclyde University offers an LL M in legal informatics to students all over the world, who are given remote access to about thirty megabytes of teaching material and are invited to participate in on-line, group, virtual tutorials. While this is text-based today, future systems will be multi-media, so that, for instance, video recordings of trials or the sound of oral advocacy will be available on-line.

On-line discussions

With all participants in the justice system able to communicate with one another electronically, this may support not just the formal conduct of business but could also greatly improve informal discussion and interaction. With bulletin board facilities, and the availability of on-line discussion services, interest groups and small communities may be established, attracting and bringing together, nationally and internationally, lawyers with shared interests in particular topics. Problems, new developments, interesting and even obscure points of law and procedure will become the focus of IT-mediated discussion, offering users a far wider community within which to communicate; and there might well be a welcome immediacy and greater stimulation and enjoyment through this communication medium as well.

The court system specifically

As for the court system, the range of possible developments are similarly wide and radical.

Unified case management

With the introduction of an agreed standard specification for case management systems, the individual systems in operation across the country could interface and operate alongside one another and function as though they were one, single system. Judges, legal advisers, administrators, and parties themselves would be able to track the progress of any case (with appropriate security precautions) through one single system and one point of access. The documentation relating to each case would also be attached to the electronic record, and so also be accessible for appropriate users. And as cases progress from one court to another, they would be transferred instantaneously and effortlessly as electronic case records.

Electronic transcription

With the advent of speaker-independent, continuous speech, large vocabulary, voice recognition systems, today's techniques for recording and transcribing—including shorthand writing, tape-recording and even computer-assisted real time transcription—may no longer be needed. Thus, proceedings in court may instantaneously, and in real time, be captured in electronic form, thereby revolutionising court reporting. So too with meetings and, for example, the taking of witness statements. Voice recognition technology could immediately deliver polished transcripts, in printed or electronic form.

Standards for litigation support systems

As ever more powerful document management systems and electronic communication systems operate together, the document loads for litigation will increasingly be stored, managed and distributed around the justice system in electronic form. Whereas there are currently many different approaches and formats used in litigation support, it would be possible to establish and even require that these systems correspond to a set of standards and formats, which could be articulated in a number of protocols appropriate for different classes of case or court (following the example of the ORSA Protocol, the standards set by the Official Referees' Solicitors' Association in England).

Various applications of IT in the court room

On those occasions in the future where dedicated court rooms are used for the hearing of cases, as distinct from virtual courts as discussed elsewhere, IT will come to play an ever more dominant role. With voice recognition technology capturing the proceedings, judges will no longer need to handwrite notes or type on their own machines but instead may annotate and comment upon the text as it appears before them (in the manner of real time transcription of today).

There could be immediate access from the court room to all primary and secondary source material, entire document sets may be made easily accessible in the court with individual pages capable of presentation on all participants' screens, some evidence may be taken remotely by video-linking, and computer and video simulations could be deployed in the presentation of evidence. Oral evidence might be supplemented by multi-media techniques which could take the court graphically through the evidence and legal arguments, while case management systems may be immediately to hand enabling decisions or directions to be implemented on the spot, with relevant documentation directed electronically to all relevant parties and bodies across the justice system.

3 The future of justice systems and the role of government

How does one meet the challenges of the future, given such a formidable array of options? This is an increasingly important question for governments around the world, because it is almost inconceivable that the possibilities and opportunities just outlined could *all* be implemented in the course of, say, the coming ten years.

The need for a strategic approach

The answer is that any justice system that is taking IT seriously must develop its own IT strategy. In the absence of a strategic approach, some of the possibilities outlined here would no doubt be realised but this would probably happen in a rather haphazard and random way. Rather than leave the evolution of much of the justice system to chance, I believe strongly that some systematic strategic planning should take place so that possibilities and opportunities of the kind laid out in this preface are prioritised in an informed, structured and controlled way; and, further, that the choices between the various possible options are made on sound policy grounds.

If a strategic approach is preferred, one vexed question that follows is whether it is desirable that the approach should, in so far as is possible, be an overarching one, applying to numerous bodies, agencies and individuals across the civil and criminal justice system, as opposed to leaving all parts to develop their own independent strategies.

It is worth reflecting here on the wide range of systems that I introduced earlier as possible in the law. It should be clear that many of the changes I outlined share two significant features. On the one hand, the possibilities tend to be generic, in that they apply to, or are relevant for, most (if not all) individual parts of the justice system. On the other hand, many of them are instances of innovation rather than automation such that their realisation would result not just in the streamlining of specific organisations. Instead these applications would often bring fundamental change well beyond the component of the justice system to which they most obviously apply and would impact heavily on neighbouring bodies, agencies or organisations.

Computerisation across the life cycle of a criminal case which goes to trial, for example, would impinge on the technology of a wide variety of bodies. The partial introduction of IT across that life cycle, which would come about if new systems were implemented in one agency but not in several others would be unlikely to deliver benefits. Future uses of IT are likely to apply across the entire justice system and establish new relationships between parts of the justice system. Major IT initiatives will challenge and perhaps even eliminate traditional boundaries. Accordingly, it would be sensible for at least some IT strategy and planning work to operate at the macro level.

IT strategy is dealt with at some length in the book but I have refined my own position over the last year or so in one important respect—I now believe that we have some considerably greater control over the future than is often supposed. This is crisply captured by those who say that the best way to predict the future is to invent it. The future is not out there like some foggy day, pre-existing and waiting to be revealed once the mist lifts. Instead, I now like to think of it more as a lump of clay—it has the potential of being fashioned into a fine sculpture but, equally, it could end up an unstructured mess. Within the confines of what is technically possible, it is up to human beings to create the future just as though it were malleable clay.

There is a difficulty here, however: although IT is now attracting far more attention across the justice systems of the globe than ever before, it is still doubtful whether most top opinion formers and decision-makers, in either the public or private sectors, have grasped just how fundamentally and rapidly the administration of justice might be transformed through technology in the next five to ten years. Thus, the world over, those who are best placed to create the future of law are often not yet fully engaged when it comes to IT.

Yet empirical evidence of the benefits of IT for justice is mounting and the impact is becoming hard to ignore on any level. Recent work on the potential of IT for the Crown and County Courts in England, for example, confirmed what had never been in doubt for proponents of IT—that the introduction even of modest technologies could bring enormous efficiency gains and costs savings to the court system. The justice system in England is a vast, document intensive and labour intensive operation, most of whose administrative and management systems were developed at a time when the throughput and workload of the courts and lawyers were far smaller. Many of the systems are crude and paper-based, orientated towards the process of administration and not the public, and few are able to cope with the increasing demands placed upon them. This currently brings high staffing costs, inefficiencies, error, delay, poor reputation and dissatisfaction. The time for computerisation is long overdue.

And yet, rendering the current system more efficient through automation is only to begin work on bringing the administration of justice into the information age. More radically still, given the inevitably pervasive impact of the Internet, and as the nation's education, health, welfare, taxation and employment services, for example, come to be administered electronically, it is reasonable to assume that there will also be pressure for the legal system to be available on-line and for legal services to be delivered electronically. This will bring not just efficiency gains but fundamental changes to entire justice systems.

A model to form the basis of strategic thinking

I would like now to propose a simple model for thinking about the place for IT in any justice system of the future. Diagrammatically represented in Figure One, the model assumes there will be three vital roles for IT in any justice system. These will be in providing and enabling:

- an internal communications infrastructure for justice workers;
- the provision of electronic legal information and services within the justice system; and
- public access to the law and legal guidance.

Each of these is addressed below, with special reference to the justice system in England.

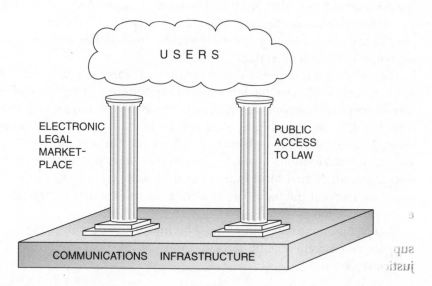

Figure One *Tomorrow's justice system*

An internal communications infrastructure for justice workers

At the core of tomorrow's justice system should be the whole set of justice workers (including judges, solicitors, public officials, voluntary workers and support staff). Following from my earlier analysis of what is possible and likely, I would anticipate that, within five years, the overwhelming majority of these justice workers (more than half a million in England, excluding the police who should be included in a fuller analysis) will be able to communicate electronically with one another and with the outside world.

While in one sense the infrastructure can be thought of as one big network, it is better imagined as a collection of innumerable 'virtual private networks' (as discussed earlier). Thus, each justice worker will have her own portfolio of affiliations, all accessible through one mail box. A typical solicitor, for example, might be affiliated to a general court system network, to the intranets of a series of professional bodies, to networks set up for particular cases, to her own firm's systems, and so forth. Each virtual network would, in effect, be discrete and separate. The key point, however, is that each would function in accordance with common and appropriate standards and the user herself would have a sole point of entry to her entire portfolio. There will be no need to log in and out of separate systems and no complex file conversion processes.

Advances in telecommunications technologies (including optical fibre and satellite) and the introduction of widely accepted standards will enable the transfer of files and of funds and provide common areas to visit to hold public and private, on-line and off-line, discussions and forums, all under conditions which will be sufficiently secure, confidential, private, reliable and capable of authentication.

This telecommunications infrastructure will carry not only electronic mail and conventional data, but will also support the transmission of bundles of documents, which are connected to one another through 'hypertext' links, so that, on arrival, recipients will immediately be able to navigate through them following explicit cross-references. These bundles will come to be delivered in multi-media format, so that users will not just read the documents in textual form but will also be able, on screen, to view, for example, relevant photographic evidence, listen to sound recordings and even watch video as well.

Finally, that same telecommunications infrastructure will, in due course, support video conferencing directly from the personal computers of all justice workers.

The provision of electronic legal information and services within the justice system

That same internal telecommunications infrastructure for justice workers will also serve as the basis for the provision of innumerable electronic systems and services for lawyers, judges and others. Across this infrastructure, for example, users will be able to gain access to edited legal source materials made available by legal publishers and other providers; and they will have direct access to services such as land registration and to agencies such as the legal aid bodies. Crucially, a good deal of court business (for example, the lodging of documents, the tracking of the status of cases and video conferencing with judges) will also be mediated through the new systems. And high speed broadband access to the World Wide Web will also be available for the legal profession across this infrastructure.

One pillar of the justice system, as shown in Figure One, will therefore be the new *electronic legal marketplace*—conventional legal services and new forms of legal service (as discussed later in this preface) will be available here on a commercial basis. As the business of both the courts and of lawyers becomes increasingly dominated by IT in the many ways suggested in this book, this electronic legal marketplace will in due course become the focal point of justice workers. But, on this model, justice workers will only be part of the user community. The rest will be the many clients of today and those users who fall within my 'latent legal market', as discussed later in the preface and throughout the book, who will dispose of their legal business electronically.

What all these users have in common is that they will need to pay for legal services delivered from this first pillar.

Public access to the law and to legal guidance

In contrast, the second pillar of the justice system, as depicted in Figure One, will be accessible by everyone in society; and at no direct cost to these non-legal users. Alongside all manner of other bodies of freely available public information, legal guidance and legal services will inevitably, I believe, be accessible on the World Wide Web, providing *public access to the law*.

In England, this is entirely consistent with central government's general movement towards the delivery of direct access, on-line government services. More particularly, the model could support the government's commitment to the establishment of a 'community legal service'. IT could help here in at least four ways, by enabling the provision of:

- legal guidance systems—systems which offer practical legal help to non-legal users (these are discussed in this preface and throughout the book);
- bulletin boards—a facility that invites users to 'post' (privately or publicly) their legal problems on on-line notice-boards, to which designated lawyers will go and respond;
- video conferencing—whereby non-lawyers can have virtual, on-line meetings with appropriate legal advisers; and
- a network of lawyers to support the voluntary sector—through electronic mail, using the common communications infrastructure, many lawyers could offer a form of secondary help, which would be support not directly to the community but by way of guidance to the many voluntary workers who inevitably need legal opinions from time to time.

All four facilities could offer legal help to individuals and organisations that would otherwise have to go without. In so doing, IT would genuinely enable greater 'access to justice'. But technology has caused me to look more carefully at that much used and oft-abused phrase.

The thrust of Lord Woolf's seminal reports, which bore this phrase as their title,[8] was on access to improved, cheaper and fairer means of resolving disputes and tackling legal problems which have already arisen. For Lord Woolf, and for most lawyers who speak about access to justice, they could equally be said to be referring to access to much improved dispute resolution. In the information society, however, access to justice may well also come to have two further dimensions.

First, if I am right and the latent legal market of today will come to have legal guidance at its fingertips on the Internet to an extent that has not been possible in the past, then this readier, cheaper and more widespread access to legal counsel will give rise, as I suggest in the book, *not* to improved dispute resolution but to *dispute pre-emption* instead. And my experience is that non-lawyers would generally prefer the prevention or avoidance of legal problems to the dispute resolution process no matter how much it is overhauled. In law, as elsewhere, prevention is better than cure; and access to legal guidance will give rise to a more just society in the same way that immunisation leads to a healthier community.

The medical analogy helps identify another sense of access to justice. I have in mind the relatively recent work on health promotion—we are advised nowadays to exercise aerobically for at least twenty minutes, three times a week, not just because this will reduce our chances of, for example, coronary heart disease but because it will make us feel a whole lot better. The idea is not only to prevent ill-health but to promote our physical and

---

[8] See n. 4 above.

mental well-being. The law also surely provides us with the means by which we can improve our general well-being; and not only by helping to resolve or avoid problems. Instead, there are many benefits, improvements and advantages that the law can confer, even when there is no perceived problem or difficulty. And yet, many people are hopelessly unaware of the full range of facilities available today (from welfare benefits through to tax planning schemes; from making a will to undertaking corporate restructuring), such that there is little chance of legal health promotion. Access to justice, in this last sense, means access to the opportunities that the law creates. This underlies my theme of the book that in legal systems of tomorrow the law will come to be seen as empowering and not restrictive.

Looking ahead, then, governments that are committed to community legal services, akin perhaps to community medicine programmes, should be aiming to improve access to justice in three senses and not just one.

The benefits of a justice system supported by IT

If realised, I believe this model of tomorrow's justice system, with a sound communications infrastructure and the two pillars of electronic legal marketplace and public access to the law, would bring a variety of benefits, including:

- *a more efficient justice system*, by making what is a highly information-intensive system more productive and less costly (in terms of the unit costs of transactions within the system if not the overall cost);
- *provision of greater access to the law*, legal guidance and so to justice, through publicly available legal information services (available, for example, in kiosks in courts; or public access terminals in shopping malls; or—vitally and soon—in the home through the Internet) which may come to be at the core of a community legal service;
- *reduction in the delays, costs and time* associated with resolving disputes, by equipping the courts and judges with systems which will manage resources and documents more effectively, enhance productivity and reduce the length of hearings;
- *greater empowerment of the voluntary sector*, by providing legal information facilities which will extend the capability and areas of competence, for example, of citizens advice bureaux and legal advice centres, and community legal services generally; and
- *stimulation of greater confidence in the justice system*: in individuals, for whom the law is too often regarded as antiquated; and for the business community whose dissatisfaction with delays is compounded by

exposure to court practices that are primitive in comparison to those found in most modern offices.

Who should develop and finance the new IT?

Who might develop and fund the implementation of the vision just outlined, given that the infrastructure and the two pillars envisaged would undoubtedly be costly and complex to put in place?

There are compelling reasons, in the UK at least, for proposing that the new technology should *not* be financed and developed from within the public sector. In the first place, in the current climate of strict control of public expenditure, it is simply unrealistic to expect that funds would be allocated to such a costly and long term investment. Moreover, the infrastructure, systems and services that are anticipated constitute a formidable technical challenge for which the public sector of today's justice system is not technically resourced or sufficiently experienced to undertake.

The alternative is to procure appropriate systems and services from private sector suppliers. This is the approach being adopted in the UK, where it is intended that a series of major IT programmes for the courts and justice system be introduced through the government's Private Finance Initiative. Just as private sector construction companies obtain government permission to build bridges (at their own risk) and charge tolls (under regulated conditions), then the plan is to do similarly with IT.

Thinking about this approach in general terms, however, it seems to me, from a public sector point of view, that the main challenge of privately financing IT in the justice system is to identify a range of IT projects which, when outsourced (for this is what it amounts to), would lead not only to increased productivity and to improved access to legal and court services but to keeping a good deal of IT off the government's balance sheet. At the same time, from a commercial angle, the projects must also offer sufficient return for the private investors and result in net cost to the state and the citizen which is less than is currently possible.

I am optimistic that this can be achieved. The reason I am upbeat is that I am convinced that the current system is woefully inefficient and there is scope for a vast array of projects that can give rise to gains in efficiency, productivity, quality and range of service. Beyond being optimistic, I also find myself excited by the possibility of first rate private sector suppliers introducing and maintaining a state-of-the-art IT infrastructure for the justice system. But my model and its funding assumes three further requirements.

First of all, unless there is commitment by the government in question to a clear, *five to ten year vision* of an IT-based justice system, then the projects in question simply will not attract private sector investment. If investors (banks and IT suppliers, for example) do not see where the justice system might be going with IT they will not fund the ventures. I have spoken to numerous potential investors and suppliers and know this to be true.

Second, and leaving aside the less concrete latent legal market, the real attraction for hard-nosed private investors in the justice system is surely not just in the courts but in their hinterland as well—in the wider electronic legal marketplace of lawyers (many hundreds of thousands of potential users, including the support staff as well as the practitioners). These investors will want to feel confident that they can capture this wider market's need for IT. And so, for example, they will find the entire internal communications infrastructure for justice workers, as outlined here, to be a more attractive target than, say, a mere intranet for judges. But if indeed these private sector suppliers will engage only if they can capture a big slice of the courts' hinterland, then the collaboration and support of various professional bodies will, in turn, need to be sought.

In the past, sadly, the many legal organs and bodies that constitute the justice system have tended not to collaborate and instead have developed incompatible systems or at least systems which were not designed to operate easily with one another. The justice system has generally been treated as a collection of quite separate information systems. IT may have brought benefits to individual parts of the system but the lack of co-ordination has inhibited the realisation of benefits for the whole. Yet, to achieve the vision outlined above, collaboration as well as funding will be vital. Is it realistic to expect it? Here again, there is cause for optimism but not for the noblest of reasons. The stark reality today is that most government agencies and professional bodies of the justice system tend to struggle with IT and would welcome some clear direction, the establishment of standards and the use of common systems. If a standard solution (with shared infrastructure, service providers and even applications) could be identified and made available to their constituencies, for most top managers this would be one major headache removed at a stroke and so they would warmly welcome such an initiative. Again I know this to be the case, having taken various soundings.

But thirdly, and the final requirement for my model to work, decision-makers across the justice system and the public in general would all no doubt agree that with such vital functions in the hands of private sector suppliers, it would be necessary to have some methods in place for managing the risks of outsourcing the technology of the justice system. Judges, lawyers and consumer groups, for example, have been understandably nervous about the IT of the English courts being managed by a powerful private supplier. They have rightly recognised that control over the court infrastructure in the future could mean having a huge impact on the administration of justice.

There are strong arguments here, then, for the setting up of some kind of regulatory body or at least structure—to control the potentially excessive zeal or even the expansionist tendencies of the kinds of major suppliers who are likely to be involved, to determine and control pricing and service levels, to set strategy and monitor performance and generally to manage the whole process rigorously.

The individuals or bodies involved could also assume, or encourage others to assume, a further regulatory function: that of setting standards for the provision of legal information systems or services, whether as part of the electronic legal marketplace or by way of public access. The issue here, as mentioned earlier, is that users of such systems (especially non-lawyers) must be given confidence from the face of any system itself that the legal knowledge and experience embodied in it was indeed engineered by duly qualified lawyers. I worry about non-lawyers relying on legal guidance systems which have been put together by individuals with no legal training. We need, therefore, some process of certification of systems, together with regulation that sets out and requires good practice in the discipline of legal information engineering.

My recommendations

Bringing my various threads together now, the widespread use of information technology in the justice system, as envisaged here, can be seen to support two fundamental commitments:

- to a society in which computers and telecommunications greatly enhance all aspects of life; and
- to a justice system under which access to the law and the legal process is widely available and affordable.

Promotion of sensible investment in IT for the justice system has the further attraction of projecting an image of a forward-looking, innovative and modern legal system able to compete effectively with other jurisdictions across the world.

Despite the likely benefits, as I speak to judges and lawyers across the world, concerns are invariably expressed about the absence of overall co-ordination of the wide range of legal bodies and individuals involved in justice systems. In particular, I hear it frequently said that, although numerous applications and solutions have been proposed, there is no agreed overall direction for IT across their justice systems in the medium and long terms. At the same time, they worry that there is considerable duplication of effort across their justice systems, in research, development, requirements analysis and development activity. Worse, they confirm that the many legal organs and bodies which make up their justice systems have developed incompatible systems or systems which have not been designed to be interoperable.

In summary, it is apparent to many that there is therefore a need the world over not just for a strategic approach but also for greater vision, direction, leadership, collaboration, co-ordination and consultation in relation to the use of IT in justice. This is certainly the case, in my view, in the UK; although I am more confident than in the past that this is now recognised by relevant decision-makers across the profession.

It must be recognised, however, that the introduction of IT in most walks of life is both technically challenging and emotionally forbidding. Success in other industries and jurisdictions suggests there is a range of well accepted non-technical factors (keys to success, it might be said) which are likely to be critical for those seeking to overhaul the justice system using IT. There is, in sum, a need for:

- a clearly articulated *vision* of a justice system under which access to the law and the legal process is made far more widely available and affordable through IT;
- a centrally co-ordinated IT strategy for the entire justice system, developed in conjunction with all relevant interest groups, indicating what investment is necessary, identifying the anticipated benefits and embracing the vision of how the legal system will function with the new technologies in place;
- unambiguous and explicitly articulated support for an IT-based justice system, from relevant, senior political figures and civil servants;
- recognition that substantial financial investment is vital if the vision is to be realised and yet acknowledgement that this funding may not be sourced directly by central government;
- commitment to ongoing, well targeted research and development programmes, aimed at generating results which will ensure that the available IT is being exploited to the full and that technical innovations are being recognised and deployed as early as possible;
- acceptance that many of the most substantial and beneficial influences of IT will come from *innovation* rather than *automation*; and
- realisation that the Internet and the World Wide Web especially (the global information infrastructure) are fundamentally changing the

nature of communications and information dissemination in society and so are likely to exert a massive influence on the development of the law.

These keys to success could provide the basis for a systematic and publicised programme for reform which in turn would help immeasurably in easing the justice system's transition into the information age.

4 The future of lawyers and the role of the World Wide Web

In the first part of this preface, I predicted that, within ten years, almost everyone will have access to what will be a much enhanced Internet and World Wide Web which will become our natural first port of call for all sorts of entertainment, information, guidance and services. In that embryonic information society, we will conduct our supermarket shopping and personal banking on-line; we will choose and book holidays, take out insurance cover and go house-hunting using electronic services which will for most purposes replace ('disintermediate') the agents and brokers of today; we will chat, face-to-face, through first rate video conferencing, to friends and colleagues around the world as though they were sitting next to us; we will be able to participate more actively in the schooling of our children and have direct access to most government services and information from our homes; we will have guidance on any conceivable topic at our fingertips, presented in wonderfully illustrative multi-media form; and information and services that are of interest to us will be brought to our attention directly without our needing to go out and search for them. In our working lives too, communication, trading, advice, funds transfer, negotiation, collaboration, management and marketing, to name but a few, will come to be dominated by ever more focused and usable technologies. Some of the systems to which we will turn will not be publicly available to everyone on the Internet but will instead be reserved for restricted classes of user. Even then, of course, these will be on-line facilities.

Will legal practice in its current form survive in this wired world? When clients are invariably using on-line resources to run their businesses and all other professions are transforming and dovetailing their services accordingly (as we can already see happening), can we honestly believe—to return to the question I posed earlier—that those who want legal assistance will be content to carry on with traditional one-to-one, across-the-desk, advisory legal service delivered in the time-honoured, consultative fashion on an hourly-billing basis? I am sure not.

Instead, alongside all sorts of other types of information, there will be legal guidance available on-line, offering non-lawyers access to practical help on legal matters. In fact, this is already happening today.[9] Across the World Wide Web, on internal intranets and on 'extranets' (to be explained), legal guidance of the sort I was predicting two years ago is available now, providing help to clients and often a new source of revenue for providers. This is not speculation about what might be tomorrow. It is part of today's landscape and what is particularly ominous for lawyers is that the providers of these services are not all lawyers. As I had forewarned in the book, legal publishers, accountants, consultants and entrepreneurs generally have already recognised the potential and snapped into action while most lawyers concoct complex rationalisations, explaining why none of this is desirable. There is little point in such denial. The genie, as they say, is out of the bottle; it is time now for lawyers to plan their future on the assumption that IT is here to stay and most will not be able to avoid its impact.

Today's and tomorrow's systems do and will, of course, vary in complexity and sophistication, from electronic check-lists through automated document assembly systems to diagnostic expert systems. But the theme in law, as elsewhere, will be that the natural first port of call will be on-line facilities and services.

All of that said, I am categorically not suggesting that all of today's lawyers will be replaced by computers. My prediction instead is that the legal work of today will divide into two quite distinct types of service, one enhanced and the other transformed by IT; and, at the same time, a whole new legal market will emerge, one which is only possible in the information age. And it is to these three categories of legal service that I now turn.

Three types of legal service

Looking ahead to the medium and long term, I anticipate that legal service will be of three quite distinct kinds: traditional, commoditised, and devoted to what I call the latent legal market. The first two will replace today's legal market, but the third dimension is new.

---

[9] Two good starting points for exploring law and legal services on the Web are Holmes, N., and Venables, D., *Researching the Legal Web* (Butterworths, London, 1997) and McGuiness, K., and Short, T., *Using the Net for Research in Business and Law* (Old Bailey Press, Horsmonden, 1997). On the Web itself, while there are innumerable places to go, the following are very useful points of departure: http://venables.co.uk/legal/ and http://www.lawsoc.org.uk

Traditional legal service

I have no doubt, for reasons that are laid out in the final chapter of this book, that complex, high value and socially significant work (which can be called, for convenience if not elegance or indeed accuracy, 'high-end work') will continue to require the judgement, experience and knowledge of skilled legal practitioners operating in the traditional, one-to-one, consultative manner. However, this conventional service will come to be streamlined and optimised through IT using, for example, ever more powerful communications and legal information systems. Pressure to introduce these systems will come in part from clients (who themselves are continually advancing in their own use of technology); partly from law reform (Lord Woolf's recommendations, for instance, assume far greater uptake of IT amongst lawyers); and in large part also from the new legal marketplace in which competitors (including accounting firms) will be using IT extensively and where legal aid work will be viable only if conducted with the considerable efficiency that IT can bring.

I anticipate that the high-end work will also be affected by another significant trend, which will probably (but not necessarily) come to be implemented through technology. I have in mind here the development of legal methodologies, for want of a better term, analogous to the so-called methodologies used by auditors and management consultants in support of large scale projects.

Like cradle-to-grave recipe books, these methodologies are highly detailed and documented procedure manuals which embody best practice and impose a standard approach on substantial audit or consulting assignments. With each phase, stage, task, and activity mapped out in advance, stipulating what should be done when, and glued together by strong project management, the idea is that the wheel need not be re-invented with every new client, duplication of effort is avoided, the service process is rendered far more efficient and huge chunks of work can far more reliably be delegated to more junior staff than would otherwise be possible.

Many seasoned legal practitioners deny that legal work can be handled in this way. In support of this scepticism, they frequently argue that each matter they handle is unique and so ill-suited to pre-articulated procedures. I have found this claim to be an exaggeration—of course all matters have features peculiar to them but there is nonetheless much in all legal work that would benefit from greater consistency of approach and improved project management at the very least. In any event, whether or not law firms are prepared to explore this angle, I am sure the accounting and consultancy giants will work in this direction.

In all, then, I expect that traditional legal service will continue to play a major role in society but it will come to be delivered more quickly, at lower cost, with greater consistency of approach and to a higher quality. IT will play its part but in automating rather than innovating.

Commoditised legal service

While high value, socially significant and complex legal work will not, as I have just said, be fundamentally changed through IT, the same cannot be said of numerous other categories of legal practice of today. I have in mind much of the standard and repetitive work of our current lawyers. Non-lawyers have for long bemoaned the cost of apparently routine legal work and many have clamoured for precisely the proceduralisation that IT can and will bring. Just as debt collection systems in operation today enable large volumes of cases to be processed efficiently and cost-effectively by para-legal staff with relatively little supervision and intervention by lawyers, then so too with countless other areas of legal work (many of which are discussed in this book), especially where the case loads are large, the problem types are recurrent and the tasks involved are highly procedural in nature.

Here, then, is what so many lawyers understandably dread: the disin-termediation of legal advisers, whether internally when firms recognise they need less legal staff for the delivery of service that can be systema-tised or, worse still, when entire legal tasks are pre-packaged, productised and available on the World Wide Web without the direct involvement of any lawyer or firm. In this connection, it will be the business of general legal practitioners that will be squeezed the most, if clients and consumers come to the view that the traditional advisory service is failing to add value.

There are only a limited number of responses open to lawyers in the face of this fundamental change. Those in denial might try to hang on to the old ways in the hope that the whole business of IT is a bad dream. I fear for their survival. Some may, rather drastically, choose to leave the law altogether, believing perhaps that the trends of which I speak are anathema to profes-sional service and simply not for them. Still others may try to diversify and take on the high-end work which I suggest will be affected far less. A few may seek to 're-intermediate' themselves by contributing their knowledge and experience, on a revenue generating basis, to the very systems and ser-vices which threaten their livelihoods.

The really entrepreneurial lawyers will take this last option a step further and seek to exploit the latent legal market.

Preface to Paperback Edition

The latent legal market

Perhaps the most important theme of this book is that there are innumerable situations, in the domestic and working lives of all non-lawyers, in which they need and would benefit from legal guidance (or earlier and more timely help), but obtaining that legal input today seems to be too costly, excessively time consuming, too cumbersome and convoluted, or just plain forbidding. This is the latent legal market, which I believe will be liberated by the availability of straightforward, no-nonsense, on-line legal guidance systems. They will not replace conventional legal services, but they will provide affordable, easy access to legal guidance where this may have been unaffordable or impractical in the past.

I have been asked on many occasions if my latent legal market is just a fancy term for the rather more earthy concept of 'unmet legal need'. In a sense it is, in that they are two sides of the same coin. The core phenomenon is that legal guidance is needed today far more extensively that it can be offered and taken. From the point of view of society generally, this is well characterised as unmet legal need; whereas from the lawyers' perspective, I regard this as a huge untapped market, happily not an opportunity for exploitation or monopoly but the chance to contribute, at a fair rate of return, to the grave problem of inaccess to justice.

Let me try to give a flavour of the kind of help that will be out there on the Web and elsewhere on-line. Several years ago, my wife was involved in a car accident. Fortunately, no one was injured but I was concerned that the circumstances could give rise to legal difficulties. It is my good fortune to have a brother, a solicitor in Scotland, who is familiar with road traffic law. I telephoned him and outlined the facts of the case. His response was instructive. He did not point me to a relevant piece of legislation; nor did he direct me to any case law; nor indeed did he say that he would write me a long letter by way of response. Instead, he told me that there were only four issues about which I should be concerned—the first concerned my insurance and insurers and he rattled off some thoughts on these and the remaining three matters.

In short—and I should immediately warn that some lawyers squirm when I say this—he gave me the kind of guidance (I call them 'golden legal nuggets' or 'desert island legal points') that a lawyer will give his friends and his family but not his clients. I accept there are often perfectly proper professional reasons for not packaging legal guidance informally but I do feel strongly that legal guidance systems on the World Wide Web in the future will be far more useful and usable if they hold punchy, jargon-free, practical pointers rather than detailed legal analysis.

It is imperative that I am not interpreted as suggesting that informal legal guidance systems will deliver a better service than conventional advisers acting in traditional, one-to-one advisory fashion. Rather, my claim about the utility of legal guidance systems must be assessed in the context of the latent legal market, where the choice is not between human advisers and IT-based guidance systems. The choice there is between the system and nothing at all—and I for one would prefer to have at my fingertips the guidance that lawyers give to their friends and family than have nothing at all.

Lawyers who have read the book often say to me that they support my ideas about the future and can see how IT could indeed transform the work of many lawyers. However, they then go on to explain why their own area of practice will in some sense be immune from the changes. Matrimonial lawyers put a particularly powerful case, arguing that their clients rely on them not only for legal advice but as a shoulder to cry on, as a sympathetic counsellor who is removed from the trauma but always willing to listen. No computer can ever replace this human dimension, the argument concludes. And I agree.

However, I still maintain that there is a latent legal market even here, one that does not replace but supplements the counselling function. Consider the innumerable, tragic instances of women seeking divorce after long sustained periods of physical violence. Lawyers often ask these clients why they have waited so long to consult them, why they have tolerated this inhuman behaviour for so long. The response so frequently, it transpires, is that they were afraid as non-earners that they would have no entitlement to house or money and may indeed thereby have no chance of obtaining custody of the children.

How much better it would be, surely, if clear, broad guidelines on basic legal issues were available, through the next generation of televisions, at low cost and in non-forbidding style, accessible from the home. If such systems encouraged users to take conventional advice earlier, as in my divorce example, then that of itself would be desirable: there is a latent legal market not just for the provision of legal guidance where none would otherwise be available; there is also as significant a need for legal input earlier in the life cycle of clients' affairs. This is the essence of the proactive legal service that I claim in the book is so lacking today. And in a world where most people's first port of call when they require information or guidance or service of any sort will be the World Wide Web, we can see immediately just how extensively usable legal guidance may eventually be consulted.

It is also important to note that these legal guidance systems are not conceived only as an informal source of legal input in people's domestic affairs. On the contrary, I have found my ideas on this matter to have been best

received in fact by general counsel in the very largest of international corporations. These skilled commercial lawyers perceive an inevitable build-
up in their legal work-load and yet a freeze on legal resources in the future
which can only be overcome by imaginative ways of packaging and distributing informal, practical legal experience for direct application by non-
lawyers across their organisations. They too have a vast latent market for
legal input and they are attracted to IT solutions more than ever before
because so many of them find that an appropriate IT infrastructure (corporate intranets) has recently been put in place and may serve as an ideal
delivery mechanism for legal guidance.

   In all, as these systems come to dominate access to the law, in business
and in domestic and social life too, as I argue in the book, the conventional
lawyer/client arrangement will be replaced by a new set of relationships,
under which those who receive guidance are more users than clients; the
lawyers who organise and analyse the material become 'legal information
engineers'; and the organisations who develop and market the legal information products and services become the providers. Looking ahead, I predict that legal information engineering is destined to be a major new job for
lawyers.

   Lastly on the latent legal market, unlike for the high value and complex
work, I expect that legal guidance systems will evolve quite rapidly to
become multi-disciplinary systems and services. For non-lawyers, as I said
earlier, on-line legal guidance in isolation will come to be seen as rather
peculiar. The social user will come to expect legal information to be integrated with other relevant guidance (for instance, with consumer or health
information), while business users will prefer the guidance they receive to
be oriented towards the realities and the flow of the ventures with which
they are involved rather than with the underpinning legal disciplines. Thus,
legal guidance systems will work alongside, or be fully embedded in, multi-
disciplinary systems, covering areas such as accounting, finance, and business and management consulting. Already, initiatives such as The PORT,
which is seeking to provide a new City Information Infrastructure for
London, are ensuring that this integration will be technically possible.[10]

Can lawyers survive on high-end work alone?

In audiences to which I give presentations, I often see a visible and collective physical relaxation in the shoulders of the lawyers present when I

[10] See Jenkins, B., and Susskind, R., 'A New IT Infrastructure for London', in Fessey, W. (ed),
The Square Mile 1997 (The Winchester Group, London, 1997), 95. Also at http://elj.warwick.
ac.uk/jilt/Itpract/97_2jenk/ (*The Journal of Information, Law and Technology* (1997)).

suggest that high value, complex and socially significant work will not be radically changed by IT. It is clear that a great many legal practitioners regard this as what they do. It is as though their first thought is that this means they may just be able to hold out until retirement before this IT business engulfs them. The big question for those lawyers who genuinely do such work is whether they can live by high-end work alone.

My current view is that it would be foolhardy for any lawyers, no matter how pre-eminent in their fields or impressive in their client base, to feel confident that their business is immune from the impact of the latent legal market. Quite apart from the massive commercial opportunities which they may be overlooking (and there is some irony in the fact that the high-end specialists and their organisations are probably the best equipped to develop legal guidance systems) there is a competitive issue here as well. I am convinced that the relatively small number of dominant high-end law firms will find growing competition not for their most highly specialised services but for other legal requirements of the very clients who do indeed pass them the high-end assignments. I have in mind general everyday legal guidance or, looking ahead, legal risk assessment and management services and indeed the development for clients of internal legal information systems and services. If firms are content to concentrate only at the tip of the iceberg, then this may be a profitable strategy for the short to medium term. But I would have thought they should be nervous about other firms, especially accounting firms, touting inter-disciplinary services beneath the surface, so to speak. As confidence in these other firms grows and the relationships strengthen then those at the tip will be ever more precariously perched, always in danger of being knocked off by competitors who have managed to establish deeper relationships with their clients.

The role of the World Wide Web

I am often asked where the World Wide Web fits into my vision of on-line legal guidance systems. The short answer is that the Web is likely to play a crucial role. Before I give the longer answer it is important to have a common understanding of the basic terminology, or at least to know what I mean by three basic terms: World Wide Web, Intranet and Extranet (it is interesting to note that these last two terms came of age in 1996—they were barely part of our vocabulary when I finished the original manuscript in late 1995).

Basic terminology and imminent developments

The World Wide Web is the publicly accessible, global information system to which Internet users around the world have access. An organisation's web site (that is, its home on the Web) can be viewed, using a tool known as a 'browser', by anyone in the world who is on the Internet. Today, as I explain shortly, the Web is regarded by many lawyers as a vehicle for marketing, as a form of global electronic publishing; and many practitioners are coming to recognise that it will in large part (but not entirely) replace print on paper as the principal way of delivering promotional material. But the Web is also the mechanism that governments tend to favour in providing direct access to public information. The Web is the natural home, therefore, for the second pillar of the justice system introduced earlier—public access to the law.

The idea of Intranet is to use browser technology specifically and Internet technology generally as the access and delivery mechanism for the management of internal information within organisations, so that users can roam around this information as easily as they can the external Web. As such, Intranet is one enabling technology that helps lawyers capture and store their know-how and then make it available across their firms. In other commercial organisations, corporate Intranets are now commonly found. These are general repositories of information that are of wide internal interest. It is here, accordingly, that in-house lawyers are now putting useful legal guidance and information; but they are doing so for internal consumption only. Intranets also have two further, related dimensions: they can be set up as a shared resource to bring individuals from different organisations under the one virtual roof; and in so doing they are often regarded as a medium to support private electronic mail amongst a given user group (for example, a Judicial Intranet would provide a common email system as well as a central repository of useful information).

My third and final basic term is Extranet. Here, access to a private body of information is provided, on a restricted basis, to a limited number of external organisations. Once again, this access is based on browser and Internet technology. Law firms are thus developing Extranets for access by their clients and favoured contacts only, sometimes as part of the value they wish to be seen to be adding to conventional services, while on other occasions on a charging basis. Indeed, Extranet is currently perceived as the principal means by which lawyers' on-line services might be delivered on a revenue generating basis. Much of the electronic legal marketplace, the first pillar of the justice system introduced earlier, is already conducted using Extranet techniques.

As just described, these three approaches—the Web, Intranet, and Extranet—seem to be relatively distinct in emphasis even though they deploy common enabling technologies. However, they are each developing rapidly and frenetically; and this is going to blur the boundaries.

Let me give a flavour of the confusion which will arise from the imminent changes. Solicitors in law firms will not be content just to have access to their own Intranets—they will also want access both to their own firms' Web sites and to the particular Extranets offered to their clients (different Extranets will be provided to different clients). And they will want to search across all three simultaneously. From the lawyers' point of view, they will want their Intranet, Web site and various Extranets to appear as one seamless system. At the same time, as law firms make ever more extravagant claims for the sophistication of their in-house know-how systems, clients will quite naturally ask for direct access to these Intranets. This will doubtless lead to the provision of more Extranet services. And, in due course, clients will unquestionably want to access the (competing) Extranets of many of their professional service providers. But they too will prefer to do so through one single point of access—this in turn is likely to be the World Wide Web itself. And, to cap it all, many clients will want their advisers' Extranets to appear to sit on their own Intranets!

If this all sounds rather complicated, I am afraid it is irreducibly so during what is a rather unstructured transitional period. Looking ahead, however, it seems to me that when the whole field has bedded down, lawyers and non-lawyers alike will want to be able to consult a wide variety of on-line sources. Some will be publicly available; others will be external but restricted; while still others will be internal. No matter what the source, however, no sane user will want to jump in and out of different systems in deference to the nature of the material. Instead, they will want the systems to appear integrated (as one 'virtual information source') and be confident that appropriate housekeeping issues (for example, security) have been handled. In my view, the common point of access will be the World Wide Web. This does not mean that all the information will be stored on the Web itself. Much will not but will instead be held on secure machines whose only connection to the outside world will be the Web-based entrance. Security at this point will be vital as the World Wide Web becomes the one-stop shop both for public access to law and for the electronic legal marketplace.

Generations of web sites

Current users will be forgiven for complaining that the set-up just outlined is a far cry from today's World Wide Web. But bearing in mind how quickly the Web has progressed over the past few years, it is not fanciful to suppose that there will be innumerable further advances even in the short to medium term.

I believe the Web for lawyers will move through four generations, each adding to the developments of its predecessors. The first generation is the most popular today—the Web being used by lawyers as a new medium for marketing activity. It is now commonplace for law firms to place their brochures and other such promotional materials on the Web; and many are finding this is a powerful and cost effective way of setting out their proverbial stalls.

The second generation can be likened to conventional legal libraries. Visitors to second generation sites, of which there are many already, browse and navigate around collections of publications, held substantially in their conventional form (for example, as articles, promotional brochures, and books). The materials are held according to the type of publication, rather than organised according to subject matter. In many legal sites, therefore, legal updates, brochures and articles are held together, so that users can see the full range of topics covered in each type of publication.

Legal disciplines are the focus of the third generation. In this mode, materials are organised according to their subject matter (for example, by legal specialities in law firms and by the subjects of courses in universities). The emphasis here is on allowing users to be exposed to all materials that relate to particular areas of law (no matter what the form of their publication).

The fourth and final generation is for me the most significant and useful. These I call 'real life' sites and they will dominate the Web, Intranet and Extranet in the future. Users will be exposed to on-line guidance which relates to problems, activities, tasks and processes which arise in daily life as opposed to information that has been stored under some library or legal classification. Non-lawyers do not care much about the nature and form of legal publications. Nor are they fussy about the particular branches of law which apply to their circumstances. Instead they generally want guidance on how the law bears on their actual 'real life' position. And so if a user needs guidance on floating a company, trading in a particular country, or claiming under a car insurance policy, he will be presented, in fourth generation systems, only with legal materials which are relevant to his particular situation. The materials themselves may be linked to formal legal sources (such as legislation and case law) or to articles or other secondary sources but the service is more likely to be packaged as practical guidance—in the form of guidance that a lawyer gives to his friends and his family but not to his clients (to borrow my phrase from earlier in the preface).

Of course, second, third, and fourth generation techniques will underlie not just the Web but Intranets and Extranets as well. But the Web and Extranets will be further supplemented by facilities whereby users will be able to make contact and instruct lawyers directly from the sites themselves. It is also entirely conceivable that when more formal one-to-one legal advice is needed, then video links may immediately be established, putting users in immediate contact with conventional advisers.

At the same time, even the first generation is requiring lawyers to rethink aspects of their businesses. I often point out to senior managers within law firms that while their individual publications on their own have tended not to be of great commercial value, when many of these are brought together, the whole becomes far greater than the sum of its parts. The upshot is that some firms are revisiting their approach to free publications, recognising that their proper place may well be as a chargeable Extranet service rather than being freely available on the Web.

The facilities on offer

I should say a little, finally, about the various facilities that will be on offer in due course. I believe at least four facilities will come to dominate legal Web Sites. The first will be search and retrieval systems which can operate across Web sites, Intranet and Extranets. Initially, these will provide basic text searching but they will gradually involve more advanced identification of materials based on concepts and meaning as well.

The second facility will be legal guidance systems, about which I have said a good deal in this preface and indeed they constitute a running theme of the book. These will present practical, step-by-step assistance on legal matters, helping visitors not by presenting extensive narrative but by delivering 'golden legal nuggets' or 'desert island points' to help them in all sorts of live situations. The technique of 'intelligent check listing' will be deployed here, whereby complex areas of guidance will be distilled into key points, beneath each of which will be succeeding layers of greater detail and guidance, together with standard form documents.

A third and more advanced facility will be diagnostic applications—using knowledge-based system technologies, users will engage in on-line interactive dialogues. These systems will elicit the details of visitors' circumstances and will draw conclusions, make recommendations and offer advice. The same technology will also be used in automatically assembling and drafting documents for users, based on their responses to a variety of questions asked of them.

Fourthly, there will be genuinely proactive services and facilities, whereby relevant legal information and guidance will automatically be sent out to interested parties who have not made express requests for these but will nonetheless come to expect and welcome such updates. 'Intelligent agents' and similar technologies will be used here, so that the information held on Web sites, Intranets, Extranets, and on linked resources, will automatically be distributed in accordance with pre-articulated profiles of the interests of the recipients.

Bringing a number of strands of thought together, it may seem rather science fictional to speak of 'real life' on-line services that can offer legal guidance, solve problems of law and even send on useful and timely information to delighted recipients without having been asked to do so. It is categorically not fictional because we do already have the technologies in place today which can make this a reality. But it does represent a fundamental change in the administration of law in society. That is why I speak in the following pages of the impending shift of paradigm in legal service and in legal process. And I try to show the many influences (commercial, technical, sociological, and ethical) that are inclining us towards this new world.

I do appreciate that it is a world that is threatening to lawyers, although some are already embracing and taking advantage of the opportunities that the radical change will bring. More fundamentally, however, it will be a world in which non-lawyers will have immeasurably greater access to legal guidance and, in turn, to justice.

That is why I remain optimistic about the future of law.

Richard Susskind[11]
Radlett, England
9 December 1997

[11] richardsusskind@msn.com

Acknowledgements

Since early 1981, when I stumbled into the field as a legal undergraduate, I have been fascinated by the possibilities of using information technology in the law. From the outset, I was convinced that technology would bring about unbelievable change to modern legal systems, even within my lifetime. Today, I am more certain than ever that a revolution in legal life is upon us. The future of law is digital, I have no doubt.

As we lurk so uncertainly in the 1990s at the doorstep of the much vaunted information society, I hope this book can offer a glimpse of what might lie just beyond. Any foresight that I might have, however, has been magnified enormously during the course of my career by a whole host of specialists along the way. And here is the place to express my thanks.

While the basic ideas underlying the book have been evolved over 15 years, it has been at Masons, where IT has been embraced so profoundly, that I have come to understand how things might unpack in practice. At the firm, I have been helped by a core group of friends and colleagues. Since 1989, John Bishop and I have developed and shared much of the vision that is presented here. Martin Telfer also played a major role in the book—I have complete faith in his technical expertise and much that is said here results from the experience I have gained through working with him. With characteristic acuity, Chris Dering directed me to a number of serious defects in the first complete draft of the book and, crucially, he encouraged me to be braver in articulating my vision of the future. Two outstanding technical specialists, Gail Swaffield and Tom Waite, also offered comments and suggestions on that first draft and these gave me confidence that many of the more technical aspects of the text were sustainable. Iain Monaghan helped in two ways: first, as my main collaborator in developing ideas and techniques in the field of legal risk management; and, second, in purging the final draft of the kind of linguistic idiosyncrasies over which we often have a laugh. And Jane Hill, who worked with me for five productive years, kept me well organised, even during particularly frenetic periods. To all of these individuals, I extend warm and hearty thanks.

Acknowledgements

Beyond Masons, I was helped by several others. Alan Paterson and Ian Lloyd, of the Centre for Law, Computers and Technology at Strathclyde University, have enabled and encouraged me to keep my hand in academically; while Christopher Millard, Amanda Finlay and David Maister, each in different ways, commented on the first draft such as to influence my final approach.

I am also immensely grateful to Brian Neill, who has for long been the most influential figure in the field in the UK, not only for spending considerable time on that same initial draft but for his wise counsel and solid support in relation to a variety of initiatives over the years.

I strongly suspect I am a publisher's worst nightmare—content not just with producing a manuscript but insistent also in having a hand in matters of graphic design, font size, layout, marketing, and production as well. Notwithstanding these gratuitous interventions by me, Richard Hart, Marianne Lightowler, Margaret Shade and Nancy Higginbotham, at Oxford University Press, all showed remarkable tolerance and forbearance and I am very appreciative of their ongoing support and hard work generally. I owe a particular debt of gratitude to Richard, whose conviction about the book continually urged me to complete the project.

It was a particular pleasure for me that my father was able to help me with the project. Although my subject matter is a far cry from his home ground of dermatology, he scrutinised an early draft with a fly's eye for detail, and was able to caution me when my words presumed too much technical knowledge on the part of the reader. Thanks, Dad.

It is a harsh reality that writing a book impinges most on an author's home life. How lucky I am, therefore, that my wife Michelle not only tolerated my nightly sessions hunched over my machine but encouraged and motivated me as well, especially in times of apathy or despondency. No husband could ever ask for greater support and understanding while pursuing his principal indulgence. So loving thanks to you, Miche.

As for my three little children, to whom I have dedicated this book, thank you for being such great kids and helping make our home such a happy place in which to have written this book.

R.S.
Bushey, England
New Year's Day, 1996.

Contents

Contents

Contents

Contents

PART THREE—THE PRACTICALITIES

List of Figures

Introduction

It is said that one of the world's leading manufacturers of electric power tools invites its new executives to attend an induction course, at the opening session of which they are urged to consider a slide projected onto a large wall screen. The image put before them is of a gleaming electric drill and the executives are asked if this is what the company sells.

The executives look uncertainly around one another and tend as a group to concede that, yes, this is indeed what the company sells. It seems like a safe bet. They are immediately challenged by the next slide, however, that of a photograph of a hole, neatly drilled in a wall.

'That is what we sell', the trainers suggest with some considerable satisfaction. 'Very few of our customers are passionately committed to the deployment of electric power tools in their homes. They want holes. And it is your jobs as executives in this corporation to find ever more competitive, efficient, and imaginative ways of giving our customers what they want, of putting holes in their walls'.

The suitably humbled executives are urged in this way to think about commercial ends not means; to focus on the needs of their customers and not to succumb to tunnel visioned, corporate enthusiasm for a particular (and perhaps quite transient) product range.

The message

There is a crucial message here for lawyers and indeed for every individual involved with the administration of law. For it is surely doubtful that clients and other citizens who become entangled in the machinations of the legal system are irreversibly tied to the way in which the law is currently administered—to solicitors in offices; to barristers and judges in the courts; to legal textbooks, journals, and law libraries; and to the existing legislative and administrative processes.

In fact, when most lay people encounter the law, they do so with a fairly clear end purpose in mind and are not so concerned with the nature of the justice system generally. They might, for example, want to make a will, seek a divorce, recover a bad debt, rent out a room, settle a boundary dispute, claim compensation, set up a business, buy or sell a home, or pursue any number of courses of action that they suspect have a legal dimension. Commercial bodies may have more complex requirements. They might want to know if there are legal obstacles, such as regulations, standing in the way of some proposed transaction or project. Or they perhaps need their position in a deal secured through some contractual arrangement. Or, again, a dispute may have arisen, on which advice is sought.

In any of these or similar events, involving individual citizens or business concerns, there is a demand for the input of legal knowledge and experience. Traditionally, lawyers have provided this input by offering an advisory service on a consultative basis. But what if similar legal input could be achieved in some other fashion? Would these potential clients jump to reject this different form of legal service, simply because it involved a change from the past? Generally, they would surely not be too concerned about any departure from tradition, so long as the service to be delivered were cheaper, quicker or better. If clients could choose to have legal knowledge and expertise conveyed to them in some improved way, they would probably welcome such an opportunity.

The challenge

This sets a major challenge for today's lawyers, in the ever more competitive market for legal services. The challenge is to investigate and devise innovative techniques for the provision of legal information, guidance, knowledge, and expertise; to develop new ways of meeting clients' needs and in so doing to think in terms of holes not drills.

And one main theme of this book is that modern information technologies can and should provide the basis of, and even the catalyst for, the emergence of a quite different kind of legal service. Beyond automating and streamlining traditional ways of providing legal advice, it is argued that information technology (IT) will eventually help re-engineer the entire legal process and result in a major change in the predominant ways that legal services are delivered and justice is administered.

I envisage that legal work will shift from being an advisory service to becoming, in large part, a form of information service, a kind of legal service which might meet most of the needs of individual citizens and businesses and yet differ markedly from the traditional means by which legal counsel has been imparted. A vast, latent, legal market will emerge on the so-called information superhighway, giving everyone (and not just lawyers) ready and inexpensive access to legal products and information services. The focus of these services will be dispute pre-emption based on readily available legal guidance rather than dispute resolution in the courts; and on legal risk management instead of legal problem solving. In the global information society, I claim, IT will help integrate the law with business and domestic life.

For members of the legal profession, I have an even more formidable message than the mere foresight of radical change in the practice of law and the administration of justice. I claim throughout the book that lawyers' failure to embrace the techniques and applications of IT discussed here will result, in due course, in their providing a substantial disservice to the community. And for lawyers' businesses, it may eventually mean commercial suicide.

For whom is this book?

But the messages of the book are intended for a wider audience than its likely readership of lawyers and members of the legal profession. While it is tempting to say that this book is also for clients of lawyers, to use this terminology would itself beg one of the central questions confronted here. For the very word, 'client', suggests an arrangement whereby a legal adviser is retained to provide an advisory service to a client on some fairly particular matter on a more or less agreed financial basis.

In the world anticipated here, in contrast, this basic set-up is replaced by the provision of legal information services, delivered through advanced computer and telecommunications technologies. On this model, the client becomes a user; the lawyer becomes a source of legal information (a legal information engineer); and the service is developed and marketed by a provider (who may or may not be a lawyer). The information itself will be presented in a way which is intended to be of more general applicability than traditional advice. And the cost of this reusable information will hardly be related to the number of hours spent by the lawyers in its compilation.

Accordingly, the book is intended to stimulate the interests of the likely users of legal information services of tomorrow and to discuss why fundamental change is afoot in the legal profession and the world of IT. It suggests how these changes might manifest themselves in the context of the administration of law, and what the consequences, opportunities, and challenges might be for all concerned.

Little knowledge of the law or information technology is assumed beyond that expected today of any competent business executive, civil servant or professional adviser. This is neither a legal textbook nor a computer manual. Legal and technology jargon has been kept to a minimum, so that business readers who read of legal and technical developments in the national press, and are at home with that level of debate, should be comfortable with the language and concepts discussed here.

I have set out to follow the arguments wherever they lead, even if they may be unsettling or damaging for lawyers tied to traditions of the past. Radical change for lawyers is foreseen here, as indeed is the demise of many of those routine legal functions that today remain their province.

To be frank, I do not believe the law is there to support the livelihoods of those who administer it. Productive employment should be a by-product—an effect and not the cause—of the legal infrastructure in place in society. If the demands and interests of society, and those of commerce and individuals, bring about a beneficial shift in legal infrastructure, lawyers must call upon or develop their entrepreneurial talents in aligning their skills with the new order if they wish to continue to make a living.

The basis of the arguments

No matter who might choose to read the book, it is important to be clear about the nature and the basis of the claims and arguments that are developed here. The foundations of the spread of allegations and predictions that I make are a fairly wide range of research and experience, based on a variety of theories.

In its theoretical parts, the book tries to *describe* our current position and predicaments and seeks then to *explain* these in a systematic manner. In that context, I identify a number of very serious problems with contemporary legal systems and the way in which the law is administered. It transpires that IT can go some considerable way to remedying these shortcomings.

A vision of legal service in the future is therefore evolved and so the book in this respect seeks to go beyond description and explanation and *predict* what is likely to befall us.

Where the book takes on a more practical orientation, the emphasis then shifts again, from explanation and prediction towards *recommendation*, in areas such as strategy, culture, finance, and education. And it is important to add that most of the changes which I regard here as likely are ones that I also welcome, from a social, moral, and political point of view. Although I have tried to disentangle my predictions from my preferences, I fear the reader may have some extra work to do here.

While my preferences rely on what I like to think is a fairly rich theoretical foundation (political, legal, management, and information theory), the more arcane and esoteric materials on which they are based are confined to the bibliographical references at the end, if only to put the work in its broader setting and to keep the scholarly critics at bay. In any event, the book is better regarded and read as a broad-brush polemic than a value-free piece of high scholarship.

For those who are sceptical about, or simply not interested in, arid theory and enjoy apparently harder facts and figures, the book may be seen to be at its most rigorous where I have relied on the findings of a variety of more or less robust, empirical research projects conducted and published by others. Through questionnaires, interviews, and investigative work, these seek to lay out what is actually happening in the world of IT and law. From these, we can discern some indicative trends in computer use within the legal profession, subject, however, to the qualifications that we must attach to any such studies which seek to report on the realities of the commercial world (I have concerns, for example, about the vested interests of those who respond, the commercial pressures that result in exaggerated statements of achievement, the validity of the statistical samples selected, and the tendentious nature of the particular inquiries made).

More anecdotally perhaps, but with greater conviction, much that is said here is advanced on the strength of my own practical experience, as an in-house adviser and management board member of an international law firm which has committed itself wholeheartedly to its investment in IT and as an external adviser to a wide range of lawyers, including solicitors, barristers, judges, and legal advisers working in-house within companies and government departments. I have seen all manner of lawyers address the challenges of their future and grapple with IT—some with spectacular success, others to staggeringly poor effect—and have learned much from this exposure.

I have to add, in all honesty, that much of what is also said here is unashamedly speculative. I have studied IT generally and its application in a number of industries and professions, I have pondered over the challenges facing lawyers and the law, and have generated a framework that seems to explain much of what is going on and goes further by offering the basis for an improved legal infrastructure for society.

In all, then, the book is best regarded as no more than a tentative hypothesis about the future of law and the impact of IT, which may serve, if nothing else, as a provocative starting-point for more informed debate on developments which go to the core of society.

The scope of the book

The hypothesis itself, however, is limited in scope. To the extent that much of what is said is oriented towards the legal systems of the United Kingdom, the arguments bear directly on all Anglo-American common law systems. I would hope that readers from the continental tradition (most European countries, for example) will also find some of the central themes to be relevant to their work—in some ways, I argue in the end, their current methods and practices will in part be embraced by common law jurisdictions in the future because of the influence of IT.

Another point of clarification may also help to establish the scope of the book—although intimately connected with computers and technology, this book is not about the issues of substantive law which IT has generated, for instance those of privacy and data protection, computer misuse, copyright, and software protection. Nor does it address the more general question of the changes in substantive law which will need to be introduced to meet the demands of the digital world. Rather, this book is about the manner of the administration of law and justice, the working practices of those involved, and the ways in which these may change in the future as a result of current and emerging technologies.

A word about timing is also in order. If I have learned anything over the years about IT in the law it is that new developments take far longer to move from the research laboratory to the market-place than might be expected. In optimism or perhaps naivety, I thought in the mid-1980s, for example, that the widespread use of expert systems in law was just around the corner. It has turned out to be a rather larger corner than I had conjectured. For a variety of reasons (technical, commercial, cultural), that particular technology has not yet been embraced with the fervour I had anticipated. And so it will be, I have little doubt, with many of the other applications and enabling techniques discussed here.

The world of law discussed here will probably emerge in the next century not this one; but just precisely when, it would be silly to guess. I am certain there will be radical change. When and how, I leave to the reader's imagination and motivation, hoping that the ideas here provoke informed debate and then action. That said, I suspect the technology will take longer in coming than the IT evangelists anticipate or prefer although it will doubtless loom large far too soon for the IT atheists. My general feel is that the major shift in a paradigm which I project will come about over the next twenty years or so; with innumerable advances and changes along the way.

The title and subtitle of the book, suggesting as they do that the future of law will be determined by information technology, may seem to be going rather too far. I am not suggesting, however, that IT is the only factor which will determine the future of law. Instead, I am claiming that the practice of law and the administration of justice will be more radically affected in the coming fifty years by IT than by any other single factor of which we can be aware today.

In sum, this book is not simply about IT and the way in which lawyers have invested in and exploited computers and telecommunications. For there is a challenge here to the way in which lawyers contribute to society, to the manner in which they provide their services, to their working practices, their adaptability and the culture of the professions generally. Ultimately it is a moral, social, and political challenge to the way in which the law, as administered today, meets the needs of those in whose name it ought to be promulgated.

How to use the book

Finally, by way of introduction, it is important that I offer some guidance on how to use the book.

Although my hope and preference is that it should be read sequentially from beginning to end (the arguments flow and develop more coherently if followed in this way), I accept that the book is something of a mixed bag and readers may prefer to dip only into those parts which appear to interest them most. For those who choose to adopt this latter approach I have included numerous cross-references which should help clarify some central terms and arguments that have been introduced in portions of the book to which such readers may not have been exposed.

As to the structure and content of the book, it is divided into four major parts.

Part One—The Theory

In Part One, I take a step back from legal practice and operational technology and focus instead on *theory*, in an effort to explain past, present, and future trends. In Chapter One, I consider various aspects of the law and legal systems and I point to a series of fundamental social and moral problems which later analysis will show can be overcome through IT. In Chapter Two, I introduce IT itself, largely without reference to the law at that stage, but principally to present a non-technical appraisal of its impact on commerce and society. And in Chapter Three, I bring the law and IT together in a series of discussions which begin to explain the emergence of legal service as an information service.

Part One therefore is concerned with the big picture—an information society which will bring a much improved legal infrastructure.

Part Two—The Technologies

In the second part, my principal concern is with the details of the technologies which enable the fundamental changes discussed throughout the book. I try here, in strictly non-technical terms, to explain IT and all the jargon which is so freely bandied around nowadays. In Chapter Four my aim is to introduce the variety of enabling techniques which are likely to lie at the heart of legal systems of the future, while Chapter Five shows how these various techniques will support what will become, in due course, the most significant applications of IT both for lawyers and non-lawyers.

Part Two is provided, then, with the slightly perplexed reader in mind—to help the lawyer or the business manager, for example, to come to grips with the basic technical issues.

Part Three—The Practicalities

The third part of the book is intensely practical. In Chapter Six, I lay out a number of case-studies, based largely on personal experience of operational systems. These support and clarify the earlier arguments of the book. Then, in Chapter Seven, I offer some guidance on the issues which are vital for any organization intent on introducing new technology—strategy, planning, management, and training.

So Part Three is recommended reading for the action-oriented reader or for those whose livelihood in some way depends on the law.

Part Four—The Vision

In the fourth and final part, I sketch out, in Chapter Eight, my overall vision of the future of law and suggest the implications of this for all who are affected by it—lawyers, judges, businesses and citizens.

Part Four is for readers who enjoy speculating about how our world and our lawyers might be in many years to come.

PART ONE—THE THEORY

1

A Law Unto Itself

The law is at the heart of our personal and social lives, it is the lifeblood of the commercial world and it is central also to our national security. Without law, life in modern Western countries would be unimaginable. It is the most important and pervasive social and political institution in all democracies of today and is the linchpin for all political movements, whether supporting the social engineering of the left or enabling the invisible economic hand of the right. It establishes in all aspects of our lives what we are required to do, what we are prohibited from doing and what we are permitted to do. It guides our conduct and also sets a moral and societal standard against which we can judge the behaviour and activities of others.

Despite all of this, on a day-to-day basis, most non-lawyers do not give too much thought to how the law is developed and administered, and to the extent to which there is room for improvement. The law and especially its central institutions—such as the courts, the legislature, the bar, and solicitors—are rather taken for granted.

Lay disquiet tends to focus on the substance of particular rules or on those apparent defects which attract great media attention. And, to be sure, the law and lawyers have always seemed to be a target for adverse comment, in shapes ranging from humour to virulent abuse. In the UK, for example, there is a level of dissatisfaction today (1995) with the court system. This stems in large part from wrongful convictions in high profile criminal cases and also from recent, substantial financial support from the state for accused individuals who are widely perceived to be a long way from deserving economic assistance.

Such aberrations are, of course, disturbing and important; but they fall short in significance of the much more fundamental issues discussed in this

11

book. The popular, high profile concerns can be addressed and overcome within the context of our current methods of legal administration. The more far-reaching difficulties call for more radical change.

So what are these fundamental problems? Let me summarize them briefly.

We find ourselves today with apparently well developed and sophisticated legal regimes which, although by and large effective, are, I believe, defective in a number of serious respects. While some of the defects themselves may be partly due to IT itself, all of them, I shall argue, can be tackled, to a greater or lesser extent, by the judicious application of technology.

In the first place, we are governed by a body of law whose scope is so great that no-one can pretend to have mastery over anything other than small subsets of a legal system. At the same time, we are every one of us, under the law, expected to have knowledge of all legal provisions that affect us, even though the means by which the law is announced and published is haphazard. Not only that, it is conventional that non-lawyers have the responsibility of deciding when to seek professional guidance on the law, even though this itself requires legal insight and understanding. Once advice is sought, clients today become exposed to a legal market-place very much in flux, one in which lawyers fight fiercely with their learned friends to win legal work and where the judges and administrators of the courts find themselves as much constrained by the need to establish financial justifications for all manner of facilities as by the requirements of justice.

Here we have mature legal systems that have in senses I will discuss become alienated from citizens, from business, from lawyers, and from society itself. Such are the pressures, however, that I argue we are on the brink of a fundamental shift in the way in which legal service is offered and justice is administered.

These problems and issues are very important and affect everyone. They are the subject of analysis and discussion in this first chapter and are referred to throughout the book.

If the law is to remain the principal means of social control, it must be manageable, available, realistic, workable, and interwoven easily with all aspects of social life. If we look reality straight in the eye, currently the law is none of these.

1.1. The Hyperregulated Society

Let me begin my analysis of the defects of contemporary legal systems by reflecting on the quantity and complexity of our law. We live today in what

I believe it is apt to describe as hyperregulated times. By coining the term hyperregulated I have in mind that we are all subject, in our social and working lives, to a body of legal rules and principles that is so vast, diverse, and complicated that no one can understand their full applicability and impact. And appreciation of but small subsets of the law is given only to small groups—generally, lawyers themselves. Being hyperregulated means there is too much law for us to manage.

To say that we are hyperregulated is not to say, therefore, that there is, as an absolute matter, too much law or that the law is simply poorly drafted or articulated (although this may sometimes be the case). It is to suggest instead that our *current* methods for managing legal materials (dominated by paper and print) are not capable of coping with the quantity and complexity of the law which now governs us.

Under the general heading of hyperregulation, I include the effect of legal rules derived both from legislation and from case-law, for these two sources of law combine to make up the great bulk of legal systems of today. For the purposes of this discussion, however, it is helpful to explore each source separately as the problems of the manageability of each are quite different.

Legislation

I use the term 'legislation' in a fairly general sense, covering any authoritative regulation expressed in some fixed, written form. In England, this category therefore includes what is known as superior (or primary) legislation (statutes passed directly by Parliament), as well as subordinate (or delegated or secondary) legislation, those rules created not by Parliament itself, but by other bodies under the authority of Parliament. Many of these are what are called statutory instruments.

In civil law jurisdictions—for example, in continental European systems—legislation in the form of code has, at least since Roman times, been the primary formal source of law. In contrast, in Anglo-American common law countries, legislation has steadily increased in significance since the early nineteenth century, not just as a way of comprehensively stating preexisting common law, but far more commonly now as a principal means of changing old law and introducing new legal provisions. Legislation is now therefore central to all legal systems of today.

Legislation is normally couched in general terms, and legal reasoning and legal problem solving involves, in part, bringing (some say 'subsuming') the facts of particular cases under these more general terms. So, legislation provides general rules which apply to particular cases.

The Theory

In the UK, legislation is proliferating, not just because of ever more ambitious Parliamentary programmes, but also because of the introduction of great swathes of secondary regulation. The financial services sector, for example, experienced an avalanche of regulation in the 1980s as a new regime was introduced and here, as with other areas in which regulation has been introduced, various explanations for this phenomenon are advanced. Some commentators regard regulation as an indispensable tool in seeking to improve social and economic welfare generally, while others regard it as a means by which the demands of more particular, private interests are satisfied.

Less controversial, in the sense that it is easier to explain (if not to justify), is the massive upsurge of regulation brought by the UK's increasing involvement in the EU. The quantity of regulation as well as the level of detail has astounded many British citizens (for example, in relation to the prescribed curvature of bananas or the entitlement of all computer users to footstools). In a frightening catalogue of the negative impact of such regulations, in their book *The Mad Officials*, Christopher Booker and Richard North recount innumerable horror stories which suggest that the implementation of many European Directives in the English regulations often gives rise to more draconian requirements or demanding consequences than the original instruments; and suggest, equally disturbingly, that overzealous and wrong-headed interpretation and application of the regulations (relating, for instance, to health and safety and to the environment) further prejudices the credibility of our regulatory infrastructure. A key issue here is the approach to legislative drafting and interpretation in England where a more literal style is adopted than in countries of continental Europe.

In combination, our national legislation and growing bodies of regulation (together with any supranational legislation such as treaties to which we are signatories), render the task of keeping apace well nigh impossible for lawyer and lay person alike. UNICE have recently gone further and suggested that excessive regulation can inhibit nations from competing effectively in the international market-place. Their report cites alarming OECD statistics, which suggest vastly different rates of 'regulatory inflation': for Finland (1980–93) 200 per cent; for France (1976–90) 100 per cent; and for the UK (1980–91) a staggering 600 per cent.

This problem of quantity is compounded by the dilemma of complexity, in that legislation is rarely an easy or light read. Drafted not with simplicity or elegance in mind, but with an eye rather to being comprehensive in coverage, devoid of ambiguity, exhaustive in detail and allowing of no unacceptable consequences or loopholes, the end result is often a complex web

14

of intertwining and apparently cumbersome and convoluted legal rules which may appear to employ regular use of jargon for its own sake (although this last perception is usually misplaced). In all, legislation can demand both patience and expertise if it is to be unravelled successfully.

For many professions and businesses, these problems associated with legislation are still further exacerbated by the lurking presence of bulky codes of conduct, statements of good practice and industry standards, many of which seem to favour a legislative style of drafting, often in the manner of minor constitutions. Although these may lack the direct binding force of legislation, they nevertheless do require scrutiny and understanding, if not full compliance, for failure to acknowledge and follow these instruments can, in certain circumstances, be taken as evidence of substandard performance.

And as if this mass of legislative and quasi-legislative materials were not enough, the position worsens when one adds to these the formidable body of case-law which also contributes to our hyperregulated society.

Case-law

It is worth taking a step back to make sure we grasp the full significance of case-law, for lawyers often rather unreflectively take it for granted, while non-lawyers tend to be somewhat surprised by its scope and impact.

When a judicial decision is made, in the first place this settles a dispute between two or more particular parties. Thereafter, the specific rule that was applied to the particular facts of the case in question can be extended (induced, it is said) and used in other cases. This may result, then, in what often seems to be a definitive legal rule of wider application, often expressed by lawyers at a level of generality similar to that of legislation.

Take an example which is perhaps the most renowned of all judicial decisions in the Anglo-American common law tradition—*Donoghue* v. *Stevenson*. Decided in the House of Lords in 1932, this case concerned a decomposed snail, a manufacturer and distributor of ginger beer in opaque bottles and a Scottish woman. After finishing her drink, it is generally thought that the lady noticed a snail in the residue and questions arose as to who should bear liability for her subsequent illness. The manufacturer was held to be liable. At the time of the decision, the ruling was thought to extend perhaps only to manufacturers of food and drink, impenetrable containers containing fluids and any consumers of such. Today, however, on the basis of the leading judgment in the case (by Lord Atkin), the case is taken as justification for attaching liability (approximately) to manufacturers of all those products which do not allow reasonable opportunity of intermediate examination between distribution and reception by ultimate consumers. So, a highly particular decision in that case served as the basis for the generation and application of more extensive rules. To be precise, a series of judicial decisions evolved, during this century, a body of successively more extensive rules.

Most non-lawyers are familiar with the notion of precedent. In broad terms but with various qualifications, courts must abide by previous decisions of other courts when faced with circumstances and issues substantially similar to those of decided cases in the past. (This is often expressed by lawyers in the Latin phrase, *stare decisis*, which means to stand by things decided.)

A precedent therefore is a court decision, sometimes recorded in a law report, which is used as the authoritative basis for reaching similar decisions in later cases. There are some complexities here, of course, not the least of which is the perennial disagreement amongst lawyers and legal theorists over the way in which one can identify the rule for which any given case purports to be the authoritative source. This rule is known as the *ratio decidendi*. Clearly, not every word of a thirty page judgment of the English High Court, for example, can be taken to be the expression of authoritative legal material (unlike the words of legislation), for many other observations are made in passing and these *obiter dicta*, as they are known, are not binding on later judges. Nor do the decisions of all judges bind all others. Crucial here is the hierarchy of courts which exists so that in English law, for instance, decisions of the House of Lords are binding upon the Court of Appeal and other lower courts, whereas the reverse is not the case. Yet even if not binding, courts lower in the hierarchy are often required to consider the decisions of other courts—and sometimes other legal systems—as persuasive.

The process by which judges decide cases and develop the law is far from uncontroversial. Indeed it is the subject of major debate in the field of legal theory. Much of this debate focuses on whether or not judges can be said to make new laws (for example, in filling apparent gaps in legislation) or whether they have less discretion and are substantially constrained in deriving decisions by existing legal principles.

It should also be added that some of the most lively arguments in court focus on the extent to which circumstances under consideration can be distinguished from those of some past case which would potentially constitute a binding precedent.

Although the non-lawyer may find case-law conceptually less tidy than legislation, it is a vital and pervasive source of law in Anglo-American common law systems. Much of the law of contract and the law of negligence in England, for example, and the law of theft in Scotland, is governed by case-law. In fact, great slabs of our lives are governed by the law as established through decisions of judges over the years and this fact adds to the phenomenon of hyperregulation.

Managing hyperregulation

How, as lawyers and citizens, can we hope to manage this hyperregulatory mass? It is a running theme of this book that IT can be of considerable help. I shall also show, ironically, that IT has itself been a contributing factor to hyperregulation. But I shall defer discussion of technology until a little later, once we have explored the conventional options and have also given some more detailed attention to the subject of IT itself (in Chapters Two and Three).

In any event, it might well be asked if it matters whether individuals have hyperregulation under control, for surely no one can be expected to cope in the face of information so voluminous and complex. The Latin phrase *ignorantia iuris neminem excusat* rears its ugly head here, however, for this maxim stipulates that ignorance of the law excuses no man. In practice, this means that all citizens are presumed to know the law, or at least cannot use ignorance as a defence or excuse. Criminal and civil liabilities can therefore flow for citizens, even if they have no knowledge of rules which they may be contravening.

If we assume that managing hyperregulation is therefore an appropriate objective, what steps can be taken?

Taking legal advice might be thought to be one option but, as I shall discuss shortly, this is often prohibitively expensive or impractical (see my discussion of the paradox of traditional legal service in Section 1.3).

Significantly, lawyers themselves also complain about hyperregulation and they too need help and guidance with this problem. In practical terms, one technique, adopted by most legal advisers, is to compartmentalize the law into more manageable chunks and so to devote available research time and background reading to preselected aspects of the legal system. However, no area of the law—no matter how specialized, obscure or arcane—is completely self-contained and there are dangers in this compartmentalization, especially those of disregarding potentially applicable, neighbouring areas of law.

Another option, currently favoured by the British Government, is to seek to deregulate (in the sense of reducing the number of regulations) and eradicate red tape. Yet this is rather like responding to a downpour of rain by seeking to reconfigure the clouds instead of putting up an umbrella. Rather than trying to confront a seemingly unalterable cause, it may be better to seek to minimize the negative effects of the phenomenon. Unquestionably, many unnecessary, redundant, and trivial regulations could valuably be eliminated but a vast body of regulation (important regulation) will remain and needs to be managed. Deregulation is just tinkering at the edges of the problem.

One further possibility is to look to the ways in which the law is made available to us, as citizens and lawyers, and to wonder whether supplementary guidance could also be provided. Pursuing this line of enquiry leads to a rather disconcerting set of observations relating to the question of promulgation.

1.2. In Search of Promulgation

So what is the formal mechanism for letting the general public know when a new law is enacted? The technical name for imparting such news is *promulgation*, a term which has an old-fashioned ring about it. In fact, it refers to a concept which is largely ignored today. Gone are the days in Scotland, for example, when Acts of the Scottish Parliament were promulgated in every country town or published at the market cross of Edinburgh; or in England, where sheriffs were once required to proclaim all new statutes throughout their bailiwicks. Instead, valid rules of law spring into life daily, very often attaching new significance to our working and social lives without most of us having any systematic means of learning of their impact.

In the middle of the nineteenth century, Jeremy Bentham, one of the most influential legal and social thinkers of all time, in his highly influential book, *Of Laws In General*, wrote about promulgation that 'The notoriety of every law ought to be as extensive as its binding force. It ought indeed to be much more extensive . . . No axiom could be more self-evident: none more important: none more universally disregarded' (page 71).

Things are no better today. As if the vast quantity and complexity of the law were not sufficient to bamboozle the public and frustrate the legal profession, our problem of hyperregulation is wildly aggravated by a disregard for the need to promulgate both legislation and case-law. And each suffers from significant, yet unrelated, difficulties.

Promulgation of legislation

Non-lawyers are usually surprised to hear that modern legislation in the United Kingdom does not need to be formally promulgated for it to come into force. Bentham, once again, put it bluntly, in *Of Laws In General,* in referring to promulation as 'that essential and much neglected branch of administration by the abandonment of which the greater part of the legislative matter that subsists is continually rendering itself worse than useless' (page 239).

It is not that legislation is not made available in publishable form. On the contrary, most UK primary and delegated legislation (rules and regulations made under the authority of powers delegated by Parliament) is published by Her Majesty's Stationery Office (HMSO) as Acts of Parliament and Statutory Instruments, respectively. These are sold at prices consistent with textbooks of similar sizes. As a practical matter, however, knowledge that legislation is available in printed form and that the rules and regulations being churned out are being reduced to print, makes these materials available in rather a vacuous way. Surely one vital social aim of promulation is to notify citizens that *new laws or changes to old laws are now in force,* raising awareness that some area of life is regulated for the first time or regulated in a different way, rather than imposing a deluge of sections and subsections on a potential readership which is unlikely to be delving into details.

Legislation appears in its most useful form not in its native form but in other conventional, legal publications, such as legal textbooks, which often have appendices containing reproductions of relevant legislative material; or texts that present the statutory material together with section by section commentary and annotations.

Major controversy has raged recently in relation to the possibility of electronic reproduction of legislative material especially when packaged together with the other information services being offered by electronic legal publishers. The nub of the heated debate has been the suggestion that HMSO is inclined to profit (and some commercial legal publishers would say profit rather too considerably) from licensing this material to electronic publishers and to others. HMSO is now a government entity known as an 'Executive Agency'—a relatively autonomous business unit managed in accordance with business principles and the commercial ethos of the private sector. To meet its financial objectives (measurable objectives are central to this new approach to government), it has been argued that HMSO seeks to generate income from what is clearly a highly marketable commodity. There are complex questions here of constitutional principle, competition law, crown copyright and public policy. The legal arguments will no doubt continue to flourish, against the backdrop of a marked contrast with the approach adopted in the US, where it seems to be policy to make legislative materials available in electronic form at production cost and in other countries whose legislation is put up on the Internet (see Section 4.5 and 5.1) as a matter of course.

There are clearly wider social, moral and political issues at stake here as well. If it is accepted that genuine promulgation is a salutary objective and that IT may provide the means by which the objective can be met, to have this promising initiative hindered by the very organ of government which, if any, should be seeking to promulgate more widely, might seem to be rather unpalatable commercial opportunism by the state. It is lamentable enough that legislation is published but not promulgated; but to fetter unnecessarily the existing publication process and potential promulgation mechanism is surely to fail to legislate meaningfully.[1]

Promulgation of case-law

If the non-lawyer is somewhat taken aback over the informality or lack of promulgation on the legislative front, the position with case-law may be even more disconcerting. And if it is disturbing for the lay person to learn that legislation is at once over-abundant in supply and yet difficult to analyse and increasingly costly to obtain, then the situation relating to other major sources of law—case-law—is surely even more bizarre.

I often wonder here if lawyers suffer from some kind of false consciousness in relation to the promulgation of case-law. As a law student, I well remember facing a monstrous reading list of reported cases and having little opportunity (or courage or confidence) to question or challenge the process. The reality is that although the English common law system relies heavily on precedent and judicial decisions are a vital source of law, our system of case-law reporting is casual and haphazard and predominantly in the hands of the private sector.

Once more, in his day, Bentham hit the nail on the head in *Of Laws In General*: 'These reports are published by anybody that pleases, and by as many people as please; and where nobody publishes, nobody cares. If a lawyer who can get no practice happens to think of this method of making

---

[1] As this book went to press, however, the government announced (on 9th February 1996) what appears to be a sensible change in policy in relation to the electronic reproduction of legislation, although it is too early to know what the practical effects might be.

money: if the executor of a lawyer happens to find a manuscript among his papers; if either of these or any other such accident happens to throw a copy into the hands of a bookseller: the bookseller without being aware of it and without caring about it, becomes a legislator' (page 187).

Only a small fraction of decided cases find their way into any form of law report. The law reporting business belongs to private industry, with legal publishers, barristers, legal academics, and law firms all contributing in various ways and in various degrees of sophistication and accuracy. Even *The Law Reports*, as produced, since 1865, by the Incorporated Council of Law Reporting for England and Wales, are not an official publication (although they are generally regarded as the most authoritative).

The judges themselves have little role to play in encouraging decisions to be reported. In Bentham's words in *Of Laws In General*: 'Caligula published his laws in small characters: but still he published them: he hung them up high, but still he hung them up. English judges neither hang up their laws, nor publish them.' (page 193.) Worse than this, other than in the highest court of the land (the House of Lords) there are no formal means of judges notifying one another of their decisions and yet these are decisions which may well be binding. A Court of Appeal judge, for example, has no official mechanism for learning of the finding in a neighbouring courtroom. That judge may hear informally; or may read a report some months later (and it takes many months for most cases to be reported); or a case may not be reported at all. Nor is there a procedure, for example, by which District Court judges are notified when their own decisions have been overruled in a higher appeal court.

The decision whether or not to report a case is often commercially inspired rather than through any passion for a coherent development of the common law. Commercial law publishers, like information retailers, will look to the marketability of the subject matter. So, cases are often reported on the strength of the novelty of the circumstances involved rather than in virtue of their establishing or clarifying important principles or rules of law.

Unreported cases can also be cited and considered binding and the tendency to do so has increased since court transcripts have been more widely available and legal database providers have loaded these on their systems. That judges have expressed concern about this is understandable—they too suffer from the pressures of hyperregulation—but the idea that only reported cases should be accorded authoritative status is absurd. If it is accepted that a minor proportion of decisions are reported, that the selection process is in part haphazard and in part commercially motivated, it would be to make a mockery of our precedent system to rest it on the shaky foundations of this small fraction.

The problem of hyperregulation in case-law should not be settled in such an arbitrary way. In all of this, as Bentham so forcefully says, there is simply no question of case-law being promulgated.

That the common law system has survived may surprise the lay reader. No doubt it has done so, but through less formal means than the publication of case reports or thoroughgoing promulgation. Rather, in the relatively small legal community, by word of mouth, through legal trade journals, and through professional networks, much more information flows than may be thought from my account. But none of these mechanisms are of direct help to the lay person whose hands should surely rise in horror at the apparently random system.

Does promulgation have a future?

The obstacles to effective promulgation may seem virtually insurmountable. The vast quantities of legislation, the controversy over the licensing of legislative material, the arbitrary nature and informality of case reporting, all seem to suggest a rather bleak future.

But there is rather a lot at stake. Recall again the presumption that citizens know the law and cannot use ignorance as some defence or excuse. While we may readily see that if this were not the case the defence of ignorance would be the most popularly invoked legal escape hatch of all, it is difficult nevertheless to reconcile this massive burden placed on all of us in the absence of any corresponding duty on the state to strive to keep us up to date on new legal developments.

Lon Fuller, the eminent American legal theorist, took a particularly strong line on the question of promulgation, in his highly influential book, *The Morality of Law*. There, he argued that one of the 'eight ways to fail to make a law' was a failure to publicize and make available the rules citizens are expected to observe. Not promulgating, for Fuller, did not simply result in a bad system of law; it resulted in something that he felt could not properly be called a legal system at all.

Whether or not one feels justified or sufficiently outraged to withhold the label 'law' from non-promulgated rules, we are surely defying common sense to suggest that we are under some obligation to comply with laws of which we could not reasonably have been aware. More than this, basic principles of moral responsibility are ignored in binding citizens to laws which are not made known to them—in Western systems of morality, we ordinarily only held one another responsible for our intentional acts or omissions or those caused by our carelessness. While we would all think it ridiculous to smack a child for contravening a rule which had been formulated two minutes previously in the parent's head but not conveyed to that child, legal responsibility in absence of promulgation has strong analogies with this scenario.

I accept, however, that there is a question of practicality here. If it were simply not possible to promulgate legislation and case-law more effectively, there would be little point in whinging. And, in Bentham's era, still firmly in the age of print on paper, but without word processors and photocopiers, it may have been that more widespread distribution and notification of newly enacted laws was just not feasible.

With the technologies discussed in this book, however, the position is quite different. In the coming years, far more materials will be made readily available and easily accessible. For this availability of IT to support the promulgation process, the relevant political and legal systems must also embrace and support a policy of free distribution of public information (such as legislation) and a willingness by legal officials to accept so-called unreported cases as authoritative and as relevant as those which appear in the traditional law reports.

1.3. The Paradox of Reactive Legal Service

Even if we could sort out hyperregulation and promulgation, there is a further difficulty in practice for the non-lawyer. The problem stems from the way in which the advice of lawyers is generally sought.

Traditionally, clients come to their lawyers once they, the clients, have perceived they have a legal problem. It is only then that the legal adviser is called upon to react. In this sense, I say that legal service is reactive. Solicitors in private practice, for example, rarely have much control over when their clients decide to seek help. If the client needs assistance in resolving a dispute or in completing a transaction, the timing of the lawyers' involvement tends to be in the hands of that client. The same is often also true of in-house lawyers (in industry or government) who regularly characterise themselves as 'fire-fighters', struggling always to respond to the demands of their colleagues in management.

Problems with reactivity

There are two major problems here. First, it is unlikely that clients who are not themselves lawyers will be able to recognize all their potential legal problems and even those that they do perceive may in any event be noticed too late to allow the most effective precautionary steps to be taken. Second, clients may not themselves be able to prioritize amongst legal assignments and may direct work to be done in an order which does not reflect the relative legal risks involved.

The paradox of traditional, reactive legal service is that the very decision as to whether and when to instruct lawyers itself requires legal insight and understanding. Thus you need to know quite a bit about the law if you want to be able to instruct lawyers at the optimum time and to balance, according to importance, competing claims for scarce legal resources. The paradox seems to suggest you need to be a lawyer to know when best to seek legal guidance.

Many corporate clients are increasingly suspecting that reactive service (a service which they themselves instigate and encourage) is unsatisfactory and are now speaking to their lawyers about adopting a more proactive approach. It might be said, to force the point home, that they are coming to prefer a fence at the top of the cliff to an ambulance at the bottom.

In dispute-oriented matters, I believe it is helpful to say that the theme of proactivity is that of *dispute pre-emption* rather than dispute resolution; while in transaction and project related work, lawyers are being retained not just to crystallize in legalese a deal which has already been agreed upon by the parties, but as advisers both on the management of likely future legal risks and on the use of the law as a tool to manage other risks (for example, commercial or organizational risks).

The problems illustrated

The question of reactive and proactive service is well illustrated in the context of the management of projects. Many project managers are suspicious of lawyers and regard the law as cumbersome, full of jargon and divorced from the realities of day-to-day project management. In the past, this has sometimes led project managers to work in isolation from the intricacies of the legal system, leaving the law to lawyers without attempting to integrate good legal practice with sound project management discipline. Yet there has been a danger here—that of failing to manage legal risk effectively.

That the law is relevant for projects can hardly be doubted. All significant projects are governed by the law—by obligations either created voluntarily by the parties (by contract) or imposed by the law of the land, for example, by the law of negligence. Of course, it is sensible in any project that key business and technical issues are expressly and formally addressed in a written agreement and so most project managers tend to want contractual coverage of matters such as price, timing and delay, variations, specifications at various levels, and allocation of basic responsibilities. Sadly, the relevance of such issues is perhaps brought most sharply into focus when disputes arise, as so often happens in the construction industry and increasingly in the computer and telecommunications industries as well.

If projects are delayed or there are cost overruns or the end product fails to meet expectations or (as is the case with safety critical projects) some personal injury or death results, an acute awareness of the law inevitably develops and highly complex legal debate can result. But by that time, lawyers frequently suggest it is too late to use the full facilities of the law. 'If only you had come to me three weeks ago', it is often (unhelpfully) intoned.

The law, then, tends to rear its head most noticeably for many project managers at cradle (contract negotiations) and then at grave (in the resolution of disputes) but often not in the intervening period, at times when those crucial preventative measures that can be taken are regarded as the esoteric province of lawyers. Invoking legal help is at the discretion of the project managers and rarely within the control of lawyers.

Yet project managers often lack the legal insight to know when consultation would be beneficial. And they often lack the budgetary authority to instruct lawyers in the absence of some patently legal event such as the delivery of a writ.

Surely, in years to come, the law should be made more widely accessible and integrated with project management discipline so that the managers can benefit from legal input throughout the course of their projects without needing to call upon legal advice in the traditional, reactive fashion. This would require a general shift towards a structured approach to legal risk management.

Towards legal risk management

It is helpful, in passing, to clarify what legal risk management is *not*. It is not intimidating clients into instructing lawyers by listing a daunting body of applicable regulations or obligations of which the clients were hitherto blissfully unaware. Nor is it a fancy term for the apparently less glamorous service of contract drafting which (through the judicious deployment, for example, of bonds, guarantees, and warranties) does of course in some sense involve the management of legal risk. Nor again is it simply a good title or subtitle for legal articles or conference presentations.

Rather, what is anticipated by the term legal risk management—as a distinct discipline and approach—is the provision of legal services proactively, using techniques and adopting a perspective that would perhaps normally be regarded as the province of strategy and management consultants.

Many lawyers will claim that they are already proactive. Most are not. Nor can they be until they change their working practices fairly radically. Genuine proactivity goes beyond the *ad hoc* foresights of bright lawyers. It requires the deployment of techniques (often based on IT, as I show in Section 6.3) similar to the more structured and formalized processes and procedures developed for other tasks by the first rate strategic consulting organizations. Not until these techniques are established and injected by lawyers into the hearts of organizations and at key points in the life cycles of all relevant projects can lawyering sensibly claim to be proactive.

These techniques include comprehensive (often automated) legal audits, reviews, and health checks which assist in surveying the general effectiveness and efficiency of clients' legal affairs, looking at matters such as exposure to liability, preparedness for litigation, soundness of document management practice, quality of standard form contracts, and the mechanisms in place for the identification of legal problems. Additionally, these audits involve assessment of clients' compliance with relevant legislation and regulations.

Legal risk management methodologies should also become the order of the day, akin to those already used by consultants in risk assessment generally. These methodologies can stipulate, in advance, what legal precautions and measures should be adopted by clients in the context of their ongoing operations and activities and—crucially—*when* they should be so adopted. The idea is to inject legal check-lists and guidelines into appropriate places in the life cycles of projects and deals and so to help clients identify, manage and control potential legal risks at the most effective times. In this way, legal risk management can become integrated both with project management and with wider corporate practice.

Clearly, a shift towards proactive legal service of this sort would require lawyers to reorientate themselves, using a more familiar analogy, from practitioners who cure diseases to those who administer a more preventative medicine. This would demand that lawyers release themselves from the confines of considering the particular consequences of highly specific facts to functioning (as academic lawyers have always done) at a higher level of generality by considering the implications of a wide panoply of potential scenarios, risks, and opportunities.

The emergence of legal risk management as a distinctive approach clearly has implications for lawyers in private practice whose work is likely to move in this direction in response to the needs of clients. But there is also much of importance here for in-house lawyers, some of whom have recently found that the allocation of their own internal legal resources can be made very effectively in light of a legal risk review of their organizations. Such an analysis can pinpoint those parts of the business that are most exposed from a legal, and so commercial, point of view. Further, it can then encourage a reorientation of legal attention towards the high risk areas and often away from the traditional focus of legal concern which may have been driven by clients and not by risk analysis.

The latent legal market

In embracing techniques of proactivity, lawyers will discover what I call throughout this book *the latent legal market*—the kind of circumstances in which non-lawyers today are generally unable to benefit from the legal input they require because conventional legal service is too expensive or impractical in the circumstances. The exploitation of *the latent legal market* is one of the great challenges and opportunities for lawyers. To give a taste of arguments to come, I claim in this book that IT will be the prime facilitator for the development of this market, by offering the means to provide easier and less costly access to legal guidance.

In conventional, reactive legal service, when a legal risk has been perceived and a lawyer instructed, there is an expectation that some *optimum* disposal of the matter will be achieved. In contrast, legal risk management techniques are often brought to bear in respect of legal risks that would otherwise not be managed at all or would be addressed too late. And in this context, in *the latent legal market*, it may be entirely tolerable (commercially and as a matter of practicality) that any solution reached may be well short of the optimum position. The point is that the legal risk *is* being managed. Without such techniques, such risks would not have been managed at all or may not have been manageable. Thus there can be improvement if not perfection.

1.4. The Pressurized Legal Market-place

What of the market-place in which the challenges of hyperregulation, promulgation, and reactivity are to be tackled? Is it amenable to upheaval on the grand scale? I believe it is a rapidly changing market-place where change is not just possible but necessary. Indeed it has become what I call a 'pressurised legal market-place'. Figure 1.1 summarizes the pressures and the discussion that follows shows they are being imposed from various quarters, from within and beyond the profession.

Figure 1.1 The Pressurized Legal Market-place

Greater competition for lawyers
The greater demands of clients
Internationalization of the business world
Changes in the legal profession
The need for more sophisticated practice management
A strained Justice System
The prevailing economic conditions

Greater competition for lawyers

In the first instance, there is far greater competition, within the legal profession, amongst practising lawyers. Here law firms can be said to compete in two market-places, in that they compete for client work and they are in competition for staff. And in both dimensions, the rivalry has become intense.

One of the major changes in the UK has been lawyers' approaches to marketing and public relations. With the relaxation of regulations governing advertising and marketing has come a far more aggressive approach to the promotion of legal services. Advertisements in the press, brochures, conference presentations, direct mailings, and all manner of related techniques are now common, such that clients are exposed to a far wider range of legal service providers than in the past.

At the same time, compulsory competitive tendering in the public sector and analogous approaches in the private sector, require many law firms seeking new work to devote considerable energy and time to the preparation of proposals and to presentations at 'beauty parades'. And, in England at least, firms find themselves crossing swords with competitors from around the country: this puts particular pressure on City-based (London) lawyers whose rates and overheads tend to be higher than regional practices.

In-house lawyers, in the public and private sectors, face similar pressures. Board level demands on in-house legal departments to add value and decrease expenditure have led to programmes of market testing, whereby the cost, range, and quality of services in private law firms are formally compared with that of the internal legal team. This has led to some in-house legal departments being outsourced (transferred into private law firms) or even eliminated altogether.

As pressure mounts within the profession, there is, simultaneously, an avalanche of competition from suppliers of other professional services. In the UK, lawyers and accountants have for long competed in fields such as tax, trusts, and insolvency; and more recently in regulatory matters such as financial services, data protection, and European regulation. In continental Europe, the major accounting practices have large teams of lawyers on their payroll while Arthur Andersen's recent strategy of acquisition may set a similar trend in the UK.

The competition now extends well beyond the accountants and their related management consulting practices. For example, licensed conveyancers now compete with property lawyers, while claims consultants, project managers, and litigation support specialists are making ever more powerful pleas to be more heavily involved in litigation, although perhaps not in advocacy.

Overall, the traditional boundaries between professional services organizations are breaking down. External competitors do not deny that there are some legal tasks which trained lawyers are uniquely positioned to discharge. But they are suggesting that there is a market for legal services which extends well beyond this unique province for lawyers.

The greater demands of clients

The client community is in flux as well. There was a time not so long ago when clients invariably took legal advice at the premises of their lawyers. Today, it is equally common for legal advisers to visit their clients or indeed to turn up wherever they are directed. This shift in location for legal meetings is symbolic of a wider change in the relationship between lawyers and their clients. The market for legal services has become a buyer's market and looks set to stay that way for the foreseeable future.

Today's clients seem far more discerning and demanding than in the past. Clients want higher quality work and quicker service. They are requiring greater value for money which usually translates into paying lower fees. Some are also in need of a wider range of services and ask at the same time for lawyers with high degrees of specialization. To meet this set of requirements, clients now seem far more inclined to shop around, a phenomenon some lawyers rather disingenuously refer to as 'diminishing loyalty within the client base'. There is also an inclination to be far more rigorous about the management of legal service providers—gone are the days of the blank cheque and the blank sheet on which lawyers write their own instructions.

Internationalization of the business world

A further dimension of challenge and change for lawyers is the globalization of the commercial and industrial worlds. Increasingly, business transactions and relationships have an international flavour. No longer can competent commercial lawyers confine their attention and expertise to single legal systems or jurisdictions. Now, they must have far greater insight into a variety of jurisdictions and a full understanding of the way in which different legal systems interact with one another—this is the field of international private law and is now central to commercial legal practice where once it was peripheral.

The internationalization of business has led some firms to establish offices around the world; others to set up formal alliances with local firms in selected jurisdictions; while still others maintain less structured arrangements whereby contacts are maintained and referrals are made. In any event, lawyers in the UK now regularly find themselves in direct competition with their counterparts from other jurisdictions.

International competition in this market-place is not confined to law firms, but can also be said to extend to the jurisdictions themselves. The City of London, for example, takes some pride in being a leading centre for the resolution of international disputes (for example, by arbitration), but is clearly in direct competition with other business centres for which this kind of legal work is seen as desirable, perhaps for the business it brings for the lawyers involved, but equally for the status it may lend to a city. And various cities are jockeying for position in striving to capture market share in various other aspects of the law (for example, The Hague is now said to be the forum of choice for patent litigation).

Changes in the legal profession

Within the legal profession itself, certainly in the United Kingdom and also in many other jurisdictions, major changes are also afoot. In England, for example, the civil justice system has been under continuing review during the last decade and most recently by Lord Woolf in his valiant attempt to increase access to justice across society. The focus here, as with many proposed reforms, is increasingly on the consumer; the client; the user of legal services. State funding of legal services for those who are unable personally to bear costs of recourse to the law has also been reviewed and assessed on a rolling basis.

These reviews, in seeking to increase the social utility of the legal system, have brought additional challenges for lawyers practising in England—in seeking to streamline the civil justice system, Lord Woolf, for example, encourages judges to take greater control of cases and so reduce the extent to which lawyers are able to dictate the pace and scope of legal work; while the recent legal aid reforms impose a considerable burden on lawyers to systematize and proceduralize their routine legal work (indeed, failure to do so may render legal aid work commercially not viable).

While such changes affect solicitors and barristers, other innovations shift the balance between the two branches of the profession. Solicitor advocates, in England, for instance, now have rights of audience—are permitted to appear—in the higher courts of the land which were previously the sole province of barristers. There is therefore a new entrant to the market for legal advocacy services and these solicitor advocates are likely to capture an increasing share of the available work. At the same time, however, it is for the first time possible for clients to instruct barristers directly, where in the past they had to feed their requirements through an instructing solicitor.

English legislation and regulation have also enabled a further change of significance—multi-national legal firms are now permitted so that the partners in one firm can come from a variety of jurisdictions. It is generally thought that multi-disciplinary partnerships will eventually be permitted and these will offer 'one-stop shopping' for professional services (legal, accounting, surveying, actuarial, for example).

The need for more sophisticated practice management

Such changes in the legal profession have led both solicitors and barristers to take management more seriously. Many medium and large law firms have introduced quasi-corporate management structures and in so doing take significant steps away from the original notion of a partnership (although relatively few partners are comfortable with a complete division between ownership and control).

In practical terms, taking management seriously has involved nurturing and maintaining a law firm's major assets—its people, its clients, its expertise, and its premises. This has been achieved by introducing administrative infrastructures, increasing investment in training, building up marketing and public relations capability, exploring and introducing quality programmes, far greater attention to human resource management, and, for some, expenditure in research and development as well. IT is also now recognized as an indispensable tool—many lawyers in management have come to appreciate that the quicker, cheaper, better, and more varied service that clients are demanding requires greater productivity and efficiency in the management of their information (legal and non-legal), and they suspect that IT has its role to play here.

In the 1980s, specialist non-lawyers were often recruited to take responsibility for all of these management functions, but lawyers' general intolerance of, and inability to manage, non-legal professionals has combined with cutbacks to reverse this trend.

The buoyant financial and commercial markets of the 1980s of course helped to fuel investment in improved management and enabled many larger practices also to move to more lavish premises. Only the largest practices, however, enjoyed genuine economies of scale and when the buoyancy deflated somewhat in the early 1990s, many firms found the demand for rigorous practice management more urgent than ever. In this context, legal managers have given considerable thought to their gearing and leverage (the number of fee earners per partner) but the inclination to build up teams of junior lawyers has been thwarted somewhat by clients who, in the 1990s, are often more inclined to pay a little extra for the experience of partners, rather than the relatively costly rates of less experienced lawyers.

Most lawyers remain fairly uncomfortable managers, however, and many will confess to regarding management as an obstacle to commercial success rather than an enabler. Whether such sceptics have not had the benefit of exposure to impressive managers, or whether the partnership structure itself is inherently unmanageable once a certain size is achieved, remains a little unclear.

In any event, the pressures which give rise to a perceived need for management are further compounded by a more recent phenomenon, that of greater mobility of partners. Where 'partnership for life' was the ruling ethos in the 1970s and 1980s, there is now considerable movement of partners between practices, which itself causes uncertainty and unrest.

A strained Justice System

Looking beyond the practice of law to the administration of justice more generally, the legislature and court system are also under pressure. Each year, Parliament in the UK seems to be faced with an increasingly daunting programme of legislation, much of which is vital to the welfare of society but, because of the limited time available, can receive restricted Parliamentary attention by way of open debate. It is one crucial aspect of hyperregulation that vast amounts of legislative responsibility is now, of practical necessity, being delegated to government departments, local authorities, and other authorized bodies and implemented in the form of a burgeoning body of statutory instruments and other regulations.

The legislature is therefore presiding over the generation of ever-increasing amounts of primary and secondary sources, material which is becoming more extensive and complex in nature.

While the legislative process remains somewhat obscured from public scrutiny, the court system tends to fall more naturally under the gaze and microscope of the lay person. Here, the non-lawyer is generally heard to bemoan the dispute resolution process, noting it to be too time-consuming, confrontational, stressful, complex, and also disproportionate in cost to the value of most issues in dispute.

Even if practising lawyers do perpetuate these difficulties (sometimes in the interests of their clients; at other times not), the state-provided court system itself is at the root of some of these problems. Not the least of these are delays and bottlenecks in securing appropriate courts (physical locations and judges).

In law, as elsewhere in the public domain (most notably, in the provision of health services), large numbers of worthy cases compete for resources (courts, judges, legal advisers) which are necessarily finite. Because the reality is that access to the court system in the UK is greatest for those either of considerable wealth (as Lord Justice Mathew put it, 'In England, Justice is open to all, like the Ritz hotel') or of such insufficient means as to be entitled to financial assistance by the state. However, the majority of people simply cannot afford to enforce their entitlements in full scale litigation, as is so clearly demonstrated in the field of medical negligence.

The implementation of recommendations such as those of Lord Woolf will no doubt go some considerable way to relieving these pressures and resources—by reducing the elapsed time of the dispute resolution process, by lessening unnecessarily combative behaviour by parties, by simplifying the court procedures, and by generally encouraging the cost of dispute resolution to be proportionate to the value of any claim at issue. However, in what appears to be an increasingly litigious society in the UK, these steps cannot eliminate the pressures which are building up in the public administration of justice. A more acceptable future must surely be premised not just on the streamlining of the court system but also on dispute pre-emption. In both respects, as I shall show, IT can be of considerable help.

The prevailing economic conditions

The pressures on legal practitioners and the justice system more generally, are also related, no doubt, to the wider economic conditions prevailing in society. These conditions affect both individuals in their social affairs as well as commercial bodies in their business dealings.

During the business boom of the mid to late 1980s, lawyers reaped the rewards of being key enablers, by oiling the machine of rapid and effective trading. And, in the commercial world, clients often seemed pleased to instruct their lawyers liberally in support of their wide-ranging programmes of commercial activity. The prosperity of lawyers was an unambiguous reflection of the wider success and frenetic activity in the business community. Cash was also available to support aggressive litigation, even in circumstances which betrayed only minor prospects of success.

As the recession hit and business belts were tightened, then lawyers saw a downturn in demand for their services. Fewer transactions meant fewer calls for legal input, while litigation budgets were slashed. Legal practices which had been geared up to satisfy a burgeoning economy were, as was said euphemistically, 'downsized' or 'rightsized' to match reality.

While the modest economic recovery allows the more optimistic to speak of being in post-recessionary times, most lawyers today still speak of a shrinking market for legal services and one in which there is greater competition than ever before. Again, to jump ahead a little and anticipate my later arguments, to take this view is to ignore or fail to recognize the potential of *the latent legal market* which IT will help realize.

The challenge of change

With lawyers under such commercial pressure, with disillusionment with the justice system, and an apparently shrinking market-place in which legal advice is dispensed less where common sense suggests it is needed more, change seems inevitable. Lawyers want to regain prosperity, governments want to be seen to be delivering justice, and society should expect a legal infrastructure which can support rather than hinder in times of increasing legal complexity. Anathema though it may be to many of the lawyers at the helm, change and upheaval is now endemic in our society and those who cope with the change most effectively are those who seek to understand the agents of change thoroughly and manage the change process head-on.

Traditionally, lawyers have not been thought to be good at dealing with changes in the market-places and environments in which they operate. Lawyers have been regarded as reluctant managers, conservative in approach, and resistant to change.

While there is some force in such generalizations, it is ironic that another species of change is fundamental to the work of lawyers and judges and is generally handled very well indeed. I am referring to changes in the law itself. From law school onwards, lawyers are trained to expect that legislation will be repealed and amended and that judicial decisions will be distinguished and overruled. Anticipating and dealing with that kind of legal change is second nature to all competent practitioners.

The challenge of change for lawyers is to extend their facility for coping with legal change to the management of change in the market-place in which they work.

1.5. The Alienation of Law

The pressures in the legal market-place combine with hyperregulation, lack of promulgation and the paradox of traditional legal service to result in a rather isolated legal system. The law assumes a rather unhealthy life of its own, an expanding and self-sustaining system increasingly alienated from those in whose interests its very existence can be justified. It is not just that the law has become alienated from the citizen (although this would be worrying enough), but there is ample evidence to suggest that it is also alienated from the business world, from lawyers themselves, and so from society generally.

Alienation from citizens

In a vague and rather general way, it cannot be denied that citizens are guided by the law and operate within the framework of conduct which it establishes. General knowledge of the law of the land is picked up from the media and trade publications, from conversation with friends and colleagues, and, but far less frequently, from government sponsored awareness raising campaigns. By serendipitous osmosis, it would appear, a broad sense of the law's requirements enters into the citizen's consciousness but few lay people can say with any confidence that they have a firm grasp of their legal entitlements and obligations.

Citizens interact with the law in four broad scenarios. In one set of circumstances, they recognize that their situation and prudence combine to call for legal counsel and so they may seek advice on matters such as moving house, preparing a will, renting out a room or seeking a divorce. Although all are common and regular occurrences in our society, these activities nonetheless are generally now perceived as needing the direct support and advice of lawyers. There is a strong sense in most citizens' minds that pitfalls await the unsuspecting citizen who lacks a legal adviser. A legal intermediary, a middle man, is thus needed to progress and, in turn, charge fees for prosecuting everyday tasks.

On other occasions, secondly, citizens have a strong sense there is a legal flavour to the situation in which they find themselves, but instructing a lawyer would seem rather absurd. When shops display signs which indicate that their policy on returning goods 'does not affect your statutory rights', most people suspect that the law affords them some kind of protection, but few will have any working understanding of the legislative regime which does indeed afford all manner of protection, if only consumers were knowledgeable enough to enforce their rights. Equally, when people buy goods on credit, take out insurance policies, rent household appliances or open bank accounts, the detailed standard form documentation to which they append their names clearly has legal significance but most non-lawyers would be hard pushed to know the nature of that impact and generally sign on faith and draw some comfort from their strong suspicions that many other citizens have similarly committed themselves.

The third type of interaction between the law and the citizen occurs on a daily basis—citizens acquire rights and assume duties by the hour, although many may be oblivious to this. In buying train tickets, purchasing lunch, visiting the doctor, going to the cinema, the legal regime—including, for example, the law of contract—is at play, although rarely invoked expressly.

Only in a fourth set of circumstances—when things seem to have gone badly wrong or remarkably well—do lawyers seem to come into their own in guiding clients who find themselves in situations well beyond everyday eventualities (although the paradox of reactive service often results in this guidance coming too late).

Generally, however, the law remains a rather passive resource, in principle protecting the citizen and empowering the laity with rights, although the quantity and complexity of the law is so forbidding that few, if any, can take advantage of it.

Alienation from business

Similarly, in the business world, there is a gulf between the law in books and the law in action. When executives refer to their in-house lawyers as their 'business obstruction unit' this is not intended as a compliment. Lawyers are seen as obstructive rather than facilitative and are often regarded as erecting obstacles to otherwise impeccable commercial arrangements. Further, it is often thought that the law itself has failed to develop sufficiently to accommodate the rapid changes of the business environment of the 1990s (in the information technology industries, for instance).

For their part, lawyers will generally bemoan the manner in which they are instructed—so often too late in the life cycle of clients' activities. Late on a Friday afternoon the large pile of draft contractual material may be dropped on the lawyer's desk accompanied by the disconcerting confirmation that this deal is to be concluded 'first thing on Monday morning unless you see a major problem'. Lawyers who are instructed for the first time in a deal at this late stage will quite properly almost always find some difficulty. The mutual dissatisfaction of lawyer and client here derives in large part, of course, from the shortcomings of reactive legal service. Nonetheless, such a situation is common and leads business people to regard the law as detached from commercial reality.

This suggestion that the law has come adrift from the commercial world it supports and regulates is further fortified by the comment I have heard expressed by many senior businessmen to the effect that 'the best contract is one that stays locked in a desk drawer'. Here, the pragmatic business person regards the drafting and negotiating of contracts as a formality, almost a ritual, which, once completed, clears the way for the real business activity. While it is tempting to reject this view as absurd—the contract is surely the means by which an entire commercial relationship is established and sustained and should be the guidebook and touchstone throughout the course of a commercial arrangement—perhaps a more important point is that this is how senior business figures, as a matter of fact, regard the law. These individuals hanker after clarity in their relationships and a workable apportionment of risk and responsibility, but they do not generally see the law as the instrument which achieves this in a pragmatic way. They rely, rather, on their 'understanding' or the 'spirit' which arises from their deal-making and it is clear that they do not feel this is reflected in a workable and practical way in legal contracts. As one senior executive put it to me: 'legal advice is ten a penny—trouble is none of us can understand it'.

This scepticism and lack of confidence is enhanced still further in the event of some disagreement arising from drawer-closeted contracts. On receiving legal advice, clients come to realize that they did not fully understand the implications of the documents they signed and, if full-scale litigation ensues, they become entirely disillusioned with the system, which, as said, seems to be time-consuming, expensive, confrontational, debilitating, and often conducive to the end of an ongoing commercial relationship.

On top of this dissatisfaction with contract and dispute resolution, business people often also claim to suffer from the impact of hyperregulation. Despite valiant attempts by hordes of professional advisers to guide the business world, for example, through the mass of European regulation descending upon us, most business people have no confidence that they are complying, they have little faith in the relevance of the regulations in any event, and compliance is a matter of good or bad fortune rather than strategic planning.

Tax law, company law, and financial services regulations, are perhaps better mastered (again with professional help) but none of this comes naturally if the law is regarded as a parallel world; and not a fully integrated component of the business environment.

Hyperregulation can result in projects or ventures being rejected or neglected due to perceived legal obstacles and further lack of confidence in the legal system results.

The paradox of reactive legal service also has direct impact for business. When lawyers shake their heads and regret that the client should have sought advice earlier or when, unbeknown to the non-lawyer, some scenario is escalating perilously from a legal point of view, the lay person may quite naturally feel frustrated that they lack the legal insight to know when best to put their matter before a lawyer.

Equally, the average business purse cannot withstand instructing lawyers in anticipation of all new deals or potential disputes. In one further respect, therefore, the law remains remote from the businessman—looming ever present and potentially applicable, but requiring investment to inject it into business affairs.

Alienation from lawyers

Every lawyer lives in fear of missing some new legal development. Hyperregulation and non-promulgation result in no lawyer having mastery of the entire legal system and even the most proficient of legal advisers, in seeking to keep up-to-date, as I have said, tend artificially to compartmentalize the law and devote their attention to those areas closest to their practices. But no area of law is completely self-sufficient. And all lawyers are aware that the law might change at a crucial time—even in the middle of a negotiation or in the course of a trial—and they may well be oblivious to this. Ignorance is certainly no defence for the lawyer and the prospect of a negligence action looms large in most solicitors' minds as they go about their daily business. And this apprehension of accountability is not just restricted to solicitors. It is shared also by barristers and judges.

Lawyers are frustrated also by the pressurized legal market-place. While non-lawyers may have little sympathy for advisers who reminisce nostalgically about the boom legal times of the late 1980s, nonetheless many lawyers have suffered a considerable reduction in income and find themselves competing far more intensely. This more competitive market-place couples with relaxation of the regulation of marketing to open up for lawyers the world of glossy brochures, beauty parades, competitive tendering, media handling, and conference presentations, an environment which makes many practitioners rather uncomfortable. The market-place in which they now operate is a far cry from the rarefied profession they thought they were joining. For those who wish to be clinical professional advisers, following the highest disciplines of professionalism and probity, the whole legal service infrastructure seems to have come off the rails somewhat.

The dominant reactive tradition is also a source of frustration and alienation for lawyers. Most would welcome an opportunity to be involved earlier in handling their clients' affairs, in risk management and dispute pre-emption rather than last minute problem solving and crisis control. Selling this notion to a client is another matter. Most will retort that 'it is expensive enough instructing lawyers when we are already in difficulties—do not dare try to sell your services *before* we have problems'. Although this is ultimately misconceived because the overall cost of legal work can be reduced by the more proactive participation of lawyers, one has to have sympathy with clients who are nervous about shelling out cash in respect of risks into which they have precious little insight. The legal market-place as currently constituted and clients themselves simply do not enable and encourage proactive lawyering and this is frustrating for lawyers.

Lawyers also view defects in the justice system generally with an embarrassed ambivalence. The hourly billing system, which can reward inefficient legal practice and penalize the well run firm, nonetheless serves as a foundation for profitable work. And in respect of litigation, while lawyers generally join the bandwagon of criticism over the time wasting and cost escalation, the lip-service paid to alternative methods of dispute resolution (such as mediation and conciliation) remains half-hearted not least because of its potential, negative impact on the bottom line.

The Theory

Until alternative sources of income are clearly available to lawyers, it is unrealistic to expect thoroughgoing support for rejection of the system which provides their livelihood. So lawyers waver between biting the hand that feeds them and criticizing a system from which they are increasingly detached.

Alienation from society

When the law has become detached from the individual, adrift from the business world and creative of frustration and ambivalence within the legal profession itself, we are surely moving rapidly towards a legal system which is alienated from society itself.

The quantity and complexity of law combine with its lack of intelligibility and inaccessibility to constitute a societal infrastructure which is—quite literally—disintegrating from the community and state it is meant to sustain.

Lawyers themselves have for many years been criticized for perpetuating legal complexity in their own interests, for promoting rather than helping to resolve disputes, and for using legal language to prevent access to the law by non-lawyers. Whether or not these perceptions are accurate, the lack of confidence in the law and scepticism about the legal system cannot be helpful in relation to the institution that, after all, provides a framework within which the business and commercial worlds operate.

If it could be said all the same that the law is the cornerstone of societal values and popular morality, then the problem may not be so grave. But few beyond the profession would characterize the law in this way. The media's portrayal of the general level of dissatisfaction, the consequent low regard in which lawyers and legal institutions are held, together with a perceived conservatism and inflexibility, collaborate as factors which cause even the most enlightened citizens to have misgivings about the relevance and effectiveness of the legal process, as currently constituted.

Although this may be said to lend undue credence to perception as against reality, this view sits alongside the alienation of citizens, of business and of lawyers and suggests a mismatch between advanced western legal systems and the societies in which they should have their dominion.

1.6. Today's Legal Paradigm

The trends, observations and analysis of this chapter help us piece together what I call the 'legal paradigm' of today. I borrow the term 'paradigm' from the philosophy of science where it is used to refer, approximately, to the currently accepted view of the world and to the prevailing mind-set and accepted background assumptions in a particular field. When there is a fundamental change in these assumptions and a discipline is then regarded in an entirely new light, there is said to be a 'shift in paradigm'. One of the clearest illustrations of such a shift in science was when Einsteinian theory superseded the Newtonian model in physics.

At the heart of this book is the suggestion that we are on the brink of a shift in legal paradigm, a revolution in law, after which many of the current features of contemporary legal systems which we now take for granted will be displaced by a new set of underlying premises and presuppositions. Much of the law will be radically different.

I defer my projection of the details of this new legal paradigm until the end of the study in the final chapter. For now, the priority is to identify and articulate twelve central features of today's legal paradigm and I do so under two broad categories—legal service and legal process, as illustrated in Figure 1.2 and discussed in the remainder of this chapter.

Figure 1.2 Today's Legal Paradigm

Legal Service

advisory service
one-to-one
reactive service
time-based billing
restrictive
defensive
legal focus

Legal Process

legal problem solving
dispute resolution
publication of law
a dedicated legal profession
print-based

Legal service

The delivery of legal service today can be characterized in many ways. For current purposes, I find it helpful to focus on the following seven, each of which has been explicitly referred to already or follows naturally from the discussion so far.

Advisory service

Legal service of today is predominantly advisory and consultative in nature. Generally, the lawyer is asked to provide advice in relation to the specific details of a client's case, problem or circumstances. The relationship is advisory in that the lawyer's response takes the form of recommendations for action (or inaction), focusing only on these particular details; and so too with any implementation of the advice (for example, by drafting a contract or commencing a court action). It is relatively rare for the lawyer to be invited to impart knowledge at a more generic level, in the form of reusable legal guidance or information; rather, the advice tends to be more disposable in nature, geared to specific circumstances, and to be relied upon only in the context of these specifics.

One-to-one

It follows that legal advice today is offered, in two senses, on a one-to-one basis. On the one hand, the advice is focused, as just mentioned, on the unique circumstances of one particular case; on the other hand, the basis of the lawyer/client contractual relationship is such that the advice should only be relied upon by that one individual client for whom it has been specifically tailored. Legal advice is generally not delivered with a view to its being recycled by the clients for their own future use in other circumstances, nor for distribution or usage by others.

Reactive

Traditional legal service is reactive, in that the instigation of legal work is in the hands of the clients themselves and it is to their instructions that the lawyer reacts by initiating the advisory process. Rarely do lawyers have the opportunity to dictate their own point of entry in the life cycle of a transaction or dispute (although in-house lawyers are—in theory—better placed to do so than legal practitioners in private practice).

Time-based billing

In commercial practice, most lawyers of today bill by the hour. Hourly billing rates vary according to many factors, including the geographical location of the office from which the adviser works and the nature and complexity of the advice on offer. The amount due from the client is generally calculated by multiplying the number of hours spent on a matter by the hourly rate. Critics of this system argue that it can and often does reward the inefficient lawyer who takes longer than necessary to complete tasks; and, conversely may penalize the efficient practitioner who is able to complete assignments in shorter times than competitors.

High hourly rates (partners in law firms in the City of London, for example, regularly charge in excess of £250 per hour) have a remarkable duality. In the context of the overheads (especially property) facing many City practices and profitability targets hanging over many lawyers, such a rate may seem barely adequate. Yet if these self-same lawyers are called upon to pay other professionals at a commensurate rate, the figure is often then regarded as absurdly high.

The best lawyers can often do when clients challenge the value of their services is to adapt the response of the nineteenth Century artist, James Whistler, who when asked the question 'for 2 days' labour, you ask 200 guineas?', retorted 'no, I ask it for the knowledge of a lifetime'.

The problem with hourly billing lies not in the value which lawyers can add through an hour's work. Rather, it is that there is insufficient incentive for lawyers to maximize value and, further, the system does not encourage lawyers and clients to think of the value of the service rendered as opposed to the costs incurred.

Restrictive

For most non-lawyers, the law seems to erects obstacles; it restricts courses of action, it obligates or inhibits; and to that extent is often a barrier to the achievement of domestic, social or commercial goals.

In 1961, in his seminal book of legal theory, *The Concept of Law*, Herbert Hart made much of this theme. For Hart, most people regarded the law as 'duty imposing' and in so doing, he said, they disregarded or failed to take advantage of the law's 'power conferring' capabilities. These perceptions persist today. Few businessmen, for example, would describe the law as facilitative or empowering.

The Theory

Defensive

Most legal advisers are defensive in the sense that they engage not in one but in two distinct tasks when providing legal advice. On the one hand, they are in advisory mode, conveying their conclusions to assist clients in their wider social or commercial decision making. On the other hand, lawyers tend to be trained to protect their own position and that of their firm in parallel—it is a rare lawyer, for instance, who writes an important letter of advice to a client without also reflecting on her own liability implications in doing so. Have reasonable steps been taken to ensure the currency of the advice? If loss, damage or injury followed directly from reliance on this advice, could there be an action in negligence? These are the kinds of questions that spring quite naturally to lawyers' minds. It is arguable, however, that this leads to a rather defensive species of lawyering, where the interests of the client are sometimes prejudiced by the risk aversion induced by the prospect of a professional negligence action.

Legal focus

Coming hand in hand with reactive legal service is the tendency for lawyers to have little or no influence on the wider strategic or commercial context of a deal or dispute on which they are called upon to advise. Gone are the days, it seems, of the lawyer who is the 'man of affairs', the all-round business adviser who combined pragmatism and nous with legal insight. Today, although lawyers either deny or bemoan this, it is all too common for their activities to be restricted to legal analysis (or, at least, the client's perception of this) without inviting their wider involvement in broader commercial and business issues.

In part, this is perpetuated by the legal profession itself, however, with many lawyers still spending their working lives operating in departmental structures which reflect the subject matters of textbooks or law lectures (property law or tax, for example) rather than the industries or markets which they serve. The way lawyers, especially in law firms, package their services is rather too introspective, focusing on legal disciplines rather than facing the market. Similarly, across the services markets, the providers, quite naturally, cluster in organizations which match their initial specialist training (in law or accountancy or banking, for example) rather than the realities of commerce. In the real world, commercial problems do not come neatly packaged as, say, legal or accounting matters any more than legal problems arrive subdivided into textbook branches of the law. And yet the focus and point of departure of so many legal advisers remains legal rather than commercial.

Legal process

Moving beyond legal practice to the administration of justice more generally, I would point to five factors which typify the legal process of today's legal paradigm.

Legal problem solving

Given lawyers' essential reactivity, it is inevitable that their focus is on the solving of legal problems, once they have arisen or been perceived to subsist. This contrasts with the more strategic management of legal risk which might come about through their earlier participation in the affairs of clients. Although some lawyers may argue that their advisory work extends well beyond that of solving legal problems, it is nonetheless the view of most clients that lawyers are generally there to remove problematic legal obstacles rather than, say, to facilitate and enable broader commercial objectives through a business-like grasp of the underlying legal framework.

Dispute resolution

In the context of disputes, the legal advisers' main role, therefore, has evolved as one of assisting in their resolution. The principal presumptions here, of course, are that a dispute has actually arisen and only then do lawyers become relevant (as a necessary evil). There seems to be little appreciation of lawyers' potential role in advising on ways in which disputes can be pre-empted in the first place by their prescribing a more preventative legal medicine.

In common law jurisdictions, the dominant mode of dispute resolution remains that of adversarial adjudication, whereby a judge, as an impartial arbiter, has to choose between two competing sets of argument (legal and factual) which generally are in diametric opposition to one another. Not only has the adversarial ethos extended also into the (often excessively and unjustifiably) combative ways in which parties treat one another but the presentation of evidence to the court itself invariably involves advancing competing document loads. Here we have bodies of information in conflict, which is exacerbated by current methods of communication—parties to a contract keep entirely separate records, held and retrievable in different ways.

Publication of law

In contemporary jurisdictions, the so-called promulgation of the law is largely restricted to a publishing exercise with little state involvement, commitment or control. Legislation and regulation may well be printed and marketed by some government agency devoted to publishing but increasingly these materials are sold on a commercial basis and at margins akin to the private sector. In relation to case-law, not only is the publication process operated by private sector companies, but the materials selected for publication are themselves often chosen according to commercial criteria rather than through any constitutional commitment to the widespread dissemination of new, binding, legal developments.

A dedicated legal profession

The quantity and complexity of the law alone conspire to underline the need for a large body of professional legal advisers to guide their clients and plan for the future. The lawyers remain the custodians of the formal legal sources and it is only they who have the confidence and insight to be able to convey their impact to non-lawyers.

Lawyers, in other words, hold the key to the vault containing the law, a stronghold which cynics argue the legal profession guards a little too jealously. Slightly more pejoratively, it is sometimes suggested that the legal profession has a state-granted monopoly for the release of legal information. Certainly, the legal profession does today hold a key position in a democratic society, as a vital interface between individuals and the state.

Print-based

Finally, the legal process and the justice system of today continue to be dominated by print on paper, in legislating, in resolving disputes, and in advising clients and handling their affairs. Although IT has been playing a greater role in recent years, especially in photocopying, fax, and word processing, these uses remain supportive of the generation and dissemination of print and paper rather than the electronic creation and transmission of digitally stored information which this book claims will be at the heart of the future of law.

2

The Advance of IT

If the law, lawyers, and justice are having something of a rough time, IT (by which I mean, broadly, computers and telecommunications) may be thought to be on a veritable roll. The commercial world, public service, and the lives of individual citizens are being transformed by technology. Even allowing for the hype—and exaggeration is rife—the information revolution does look set to exert as much if not more fundamental upheaval than its industrial counterpart of 200 years ago. For this reason, when I pause to reflect upon it, I consider myself immensely fortunate to be living in a time of such rapid technological progress: in but a few decades, we will see technical and social change of a magnitude barely paralleled in history. We will come to belong to an information society where, for example, on-line, interactive, multi-media systems will play a major role in all of our lives.

Even the 1980s were remarkable from a technological point of view. One thinks immediately of the advent of personal computers, the acceptance and usage of fax machines and the widespread deployment of portable telephones. This last technology is a fascinating case study in change. When I was a schoolboy in the 1970s, the idea of wireless communication using nifty little handsets like the ones we saw on *Star Trek* belonged unambiguously to science fiction. It was quite simply inconceivable that such devices could become widely available. In this one example, we can see how difficult it is to predict what might happen in technology; how amazing progress can be made in such short order; and how quickly and easily we are able to accept some innovations.

As for the 1990s, this decade looks set to bring even more radical advances than ever before, not just in converging the applications of the previous decade (for example, the three technologies just mentioned will all be in one, hand-held, single unit), but also in introducing new developments and uses.

In light of the previous chapter's criticisms of legal service and the legal process, it might be thought that IT can immediately be introduced as the panacea to overcome all the perceived deficiencies. However, it would be premature to do so, because although it is a central argument of this book that IT can indeed help overcome current difficulties facing the law and lawyers, it is also an important theme that IT has itself given rise to some of the very problems identified in the opening chapter of this study.

It would be to oversimplify the position to portray IT as the modern solution from one of the newest professions to the problems facing one of the oldest. That said, it is, of course, important not to underestimate the power and potential of IT. And so, before directly tackling the use of IT in law, it is appropriate to undertake a preliminary assessment of the nature of IT and of current and future trends.

In so doing, one can immediately be confronted by a wide variety of ways in which IT can be introduced and classified. Much does depend on one's perspective, so that at one level, for example, the computer scientist might want to highlight progress in IT in terms of the evolution of *hardware* components (say, from valves to transistors to integrated circuits and onto the so-called fifth generation computers). But this would mean precious little to the lawyer.

There are three other levels of explanation which might be thought to be of relevance to the lawyer and the business manager. There is what I call the *architectural* level of explanation, which seeks to clarify IT, or particular applications, in terms of its underlying engineering and its component parts. An architectural definition will speak not only of the nature and power of the hardware involved, but also of any underlying telecommunications infrastructure and software, and, further, will include reference to application software as well as system software.

In contrast, another form of explanation is *functional* in nature, pointing to the way in which IT is actually used and to its effects on existing tasks, processes, and practices. Technology is clarified in this way by showing whether it automates existing processes, or changes practices and organizational structures or even gives rise to some body of information which is a valuable but unanticipated by-product.

My final category of explanation is *purposive* and those who seek to clarify under this heading will be doing so in order to answer some such questions as: Why is IT being used at all? What is the point of IT in some particular context? This sort of explanation digs deeper than the functional one which describes the effects of IT, in that purposive explanation strives for some more basic motive for engaging IT, in terms perhaps of commercial goals or social objectives.

Generally, lawyers and business managers are far less concerned with hardware and architectural issues than with the final two levels. Accordingly, in this chapter, I devote the first two sections to these functional and purposive explanations, respectively (I do not attempt anywhere in this book to explain how computers and telecommunications work). After that, I discuss the benefits brought by IT and then outline various ways in which the power of IT is burgeoning. But I do temper these observations by showing that some techniques and technologies are advancing at greater haste than others, leaving some anomalies in their wake. I also felt it fitting to conclude the chapter by highlighting some (current) limitations of IT.

2.1. Automating, Innovating, and Informating

Imagine some thirty years ago that you needed money in the middle of the night. Did you go down to your local bank, approach a hole in the wall, peer through, and ask a bank teller for £20? Did a hand gripping bank notes then emerge and release the money to you, thus concluding your business? Was it this manual process that was automated offering us today the facility of cash dispensers?

Automation or innovation?

While we would all be quick to say that this was not how domestic banking developed, the illustration does challenge our tendency to regard IT simply as a tool for automating existing practices and activities. Another and far more exciting view is to look upon IT as a resource which also facilitates innovation, something which can give rise to quite different ways of accomplishing commercial goals and social objectives.

Cash dispenser technology did not, of course, automate or motorize (as some would have it) a pre-existing banking practice. Rather, this new technology created an opportunity to provide an entirely new way of conducting banking affairs, one that now dominates and benefits customers and banks alike.

The lesson here—and this is one widely accepted across industry and commerce—is that the greatest business benefits of IT come from harnessing its power in *changing* business processes (and not simply automating what already goes on). In popular management terms, this is often referred to as business process re-engineering and extends to changing people's working practices, the structure of organizations, and the ways in which businesses collaborate and compete with one another.

The strongest advocates of innovation through IT go further. For example, in *The Corporation of the 1990s—Information Technology and Organisational Transformation*, which reports on a massive investigation of IT usage across major US corporations, it is said that: 'As MIT's Management in the 1990s Research Program has shown, just to automate what is today being done is to grossly misuse the potential of the new technologies' (page vii). The MIT study goes on to examine numerous illustrations of the way in which IT has transformed many US companies.

Informating

At the same time, they and others acknowledge another dimension to IT—*informating*, a concept which refers to a by-product of automation, namely, the streams of information that are generated incidentally during the automation process. This notion was first introduced and analysed by Shoshana Zuboff, in 1988, in her important book, *In the Age of the Smart Machine.*

A fine illustration of informating is found in relation to IT support for the retail industry. When retail businesses sought many years ago to automate their stock control systems, the primary business objective was to ensure that a system was in place to ensure the availability and supply of goods could meet the demand. Thus, a purchase once logged might trigger a message to some central warehouse to replace the sold item. Through automation, paperwork was avoided, instructions were sent immediately, delivery schedules were tightened, and the life cycle of purchase through to replacement was shortened considerably. Yet, beyond this automation another benefit was noted. In monitoring purchase information to improve stock control methods, it was found that valuable information was being gathered—quite unintentionally at first—about all sorts of trends in the market, for instance, about different demands in different locations and different demands at different times of day or periods within the year. The automation process yielded information which continues to be used as a crucial management resource and as the basis for action and often change as well.

So, although IT may popularly be thought to speed up or reduce the cost of what already goes on, this is too restrictive a view because, through innovating and informating, IT is also fast becoming a vital agent of change.

2.2. Commercial Benefits and Social Advantages

Turning away from what I term functional to purposive explanations of IT, an ongoing challenge, both for the IT industry and for its users, is to identify the broad classes of benefits which accrue from the successful use of technology. I find it helpful to consider the question of benefits under two headings—commercial and social. Although the pursuit and realization of commercial benefits is of particular interest to the world of business, some of the commercial benefits laid out below are of far wider application and can impact directly on any individual or organization in their financial affairs (domestic included). Social benefits are those which accrue to individuals and to society generally, where technology offers facilities and options which seem to enhance the quality of our lives and cohesion within society.

Although the benefits laid out below are expressed in fairly generic terms, many have been identified with a particular eye towards the use of IT within a legal context.

Commercial benefits

Underlying most commercial investments in IT is a desire to bring about one or more of the six commercial benefits discussed below.

Cost control and cost reduction

Many organizations introduce IT with a view to saving money. On this view, IT is seen as a tool for reducing or containing overheads, as a means of trimming or holding down expenditure. Much of the investment in IT in the 1960s, 1970s, and 1980s was inspired by a desire to control if not reduce costs and there is some considerable correspondence between this class of benefit and the use of IT as a means of automating existing tasks and processes. Typically, IT might be brought to bear to routinize or speed up repetitive manual tasks and so to reduce head count or enable greater productivity without increasing the size of a workforce.

Office automation and accounting systems have often delivered these benefits. Yet the cost can be high in what can appear to be a black hole of investment. The chief executive who said 'we cannot afford any more business benefits' rightly noticed that it can cost a lot to try to save through IT. And many managers report that IT does not reduce the numbers of workers within an organization anyway. Rather, teams of manual clerks are replaced by teams of systems analysts. Of course, cost control and reduction is not achieved only through cuts in salary expenditure. For example, electronic communications can reduce expenditure on stationery and conventional postal service and it can obviate the need for some (but not all) travel expenditure. In any event, the nature of the desired benefit is clear. The use of IT is intended to save money, an advantage which organizations profit from themselves or perhaps pass on to their clients or customers.

Enhanced performance

Another much sought after benefit is that of doing a better job through the use of IT. In service organizations, the emphasis here is on enhancing the performance of the workforce and there are various dimensions to this. Some hanker after increased productivity; others strive for improved effectiveness; while still others set their sights on greater quality and consistency of work (and perhaps less stressful and more enjoyable work as well). More usually, IT brings a subtle mix of these advantages although often in combinations and with consequences not always originally anticipated.

Using technology to enhance performance is in part an issue of quality and in part a question of providing greater value for money. And these are the watchwords of most of today's professional services organizations, such that this benefit usually appears higher in the IT agenda in the 1990s than cost control. Although much performance enhancing technology takes the form of automation, these benefits tend to appear at the market edge, at the business end, of organizations' activities; in other words, in the front rather than the back office.

A new source of profit

Many businesses look beyond cutting costs and enhancing performance with a view to exploiting IT as a novel source of revenue, profit or increased return on equity. It is here we often find innovative uses of technology and IT forming the basis of new ways of delivering a conventional service or perhaps a new service altogether. Those whose mission is to use IT as a new source of profit themselves become part of the IT or information supply industry, whether in setting up systems or services or using IT as a new vehicle of delivery.

Differentiation

On a quite different tack, some investors in IT seek to differentiate themselves from their competitors by their imaginative deployment of the new technology and in so doing gain competitive advantage from being perceived as different in ways which are relevant in the market they serve. In the pressurized legal market-place, for example, a number of firms around the world can be seen to be placing heavy emphasis on this category of benefit, although they must be clear in their own minds if what they want is new technology or simply a glitzy marketing initiative.

Seeking differentiation can be a high risk strategy, in that the maintenance of this posture of differentiation requires continual pioneering (at the 'bleeding' and not just 'leading' edge, some would say) with exposure to the dangers and expense which this so often entails. Continual innovation rather than automation is what is needed. The payback, however, can be considerable (hence the dictum, 'no pain, no gain', as others would have it), particularly in environments like the legal market-place where competitive tendering is becoming commonplace and having distinct or unique features helps both in being short-listed for invitations to tender for work as well as in the tendering process itself.

Support for broader aims

Some investments in IT are made principally, or exclusively, to support some broader, overarching, strategic goal or policy objective. When a company has a general commitment to enhancing internal communication, for example, it may be that its introduction of IT is justified on the ground alone that the technology supports this more general aspiration. Similarly, when a body in the public sector pledges to make its documentation more widely available, its use of IT to achieve this aim can, on its own, be justifiable in business terms.

Risk management

In a sense, a catch-all category of commercial benefit, my final category of risk management has three aspects. First, a very large number of organizations, in competitive markets, invest in technology simply to avoid being left behind. I like to refer to this form of risk management, euphemistically, as seeking to pre-empt competitive disadvantage. It is remarkable how many legal practices are driven towards technology by the fear (usually groundless) that all their competitors are embracing technology (communicating electronically twenty-four hours a day and dipping into databases round the clock) with great success.

A second form of risk management has some affinity with the first variant but is better thought out and reflects sounder business thinking. This is the risk of losing opportunities which IT could afford and, in particular, not making the most of an existing IT investment. Many users and managers have the strong sense that their existing, usually expensive, technology could do much more for them given some further investment.

The third form of risk management may shortly be upon us. This is when IT is introduced in the fear that not doing so could constitute a failure to meet appropriate professional or industry standards or, worse still, actionable negligence.

Whichever of the three varieties of risk management is inspiring some IT investment, the resultant technology tends to fall into the automation rather than innovation category.

Social advantages

Beyond the use of IT in a commercial context, there are other significant benefits which technology can bring, for our leisure, social, political, and cultural activities (and some of these bear directly on the legal system).

Educational benefits

IT is set to exert phenomenal influence on our educational systems and the way we learn. As can be seen from domestic multi-media applications, technology can enrich and animate knowledge and information, such that delving into complex matters which might otherwise be rather tedious if conveyed through bare text, can become fascinating and compelling when delivered through a mix of text, graphics, video, and sound. These new media, together with ever more polished computer-assisted learning and computer-based training systems, combined also with telecommunications technology and the distance learning possibilities which this brings, will surely transform our educational system so that far more people will have greater access to far larger stores of information, all presented in a more pleasing fashion.

The pursuit of knowledge for its own sake

The study and use of IT and information systems can also be regarded as an activity worthwhile pursuing for its own sake. Just as some people find intellectual stimulation in disciplines such as philosophy and pure mathematics, IT (and particularly its development) can similarly become an object of fascination and a source of pleasure in its own right.

I should say, however, that this is not to support the quite different (and invariably damaging) phenomenon of business investment in IT being technology-led, driven by enthusiasts, and dictated by enabling techniques rather than benefits, functions, and purpose.

Democratization of information

Another vital social benefit of IT is its potential to make important information more widely available and easily accessible to the general public. Vast bodies of information in our society are, in theory and principle, 'public'. In practice, however, such collections of information are too vast to be manageable, too complex to be intelligible to the average person, and available in too few places. In law, this is the nub of the problem of hyperregulation, exacerbated in part by non-promulgation.

We can see a new divide appearing in society between those who have ready access to, and understanding of, technologies which can deliver information and those who are being left behind. Potentially more profound than the division between those who have land and capital and those who do not, this new social schism may turn out to be a temporary setback if I am right, as suggested later, that we are in a transitional period between data processing and knowledge processing (see my discussion of *The Technology Lag* in Section 2.3).

Communications

A final category of social benefit arising from IT (final in this context at least) derives from the vast societal changes which the telecommunications revolution is bound to bring. Both in enabling human beings to communicate more conveniently, regularly, and reliably with one another (see Section 4.5) and in virtue of the vast range of information (including entertainment, media, and knowledge sources) which will shortly be piped into our homes as pervasively as other utilities (gas, water, and electricity), our society will emerge as one with enormous freedom of choice. And the working and leisure hours of many of us are set to be transformed through telecommuting and teleworking, which in turn may reduce pressures on overcrowded urban conurbations.

Politically, telecommunications will provide the means to support more informed political choices by individuals, to enable expressions of their views, and for them to contribute to and participate more actively in societal decision making. At the same time, we must also recognize the dangers of such radically improved communications, in that all manner of criminal activities (pornography and fraud, to name but two) can be perpetuated on the very same communications infrastructure which should bring so many social improvements.

2.3. The Technology Lag

To the casual onlooker, it may appear that all aspects and applications of IT are developing at a roughly similar pace. This is not so. In fact, the differences in rapidity of progress are at the heart of a fundamental issue in IT which I call *The Technology Lag.*

From number crunching to data processing

In the beginning, computers were in the business of number crunching. Able to perform massive and complex arithmetical and mathematical calculations which otherwise would often have been too complex and detailed to undertake manually, computer technology dramatically proved its worth during the Second World War in code breaking and in support of the development of advanced weaponry. The same technology was also put to service in complex numerical analysis for industrial and commercial purposes.

The functions and operations of computers in these days (1940s and 1950s) had been anticipated long before (by visionary mathematicians as early as the seventeenth century) but no one in previous centuries was to foresee the wider potential of IT once harnessed in support of what can be termed 'data processing' and 'knowledge processing'.

Leaving aside the details of the underlying hardware and software, the early computers can be regarded as having been devoted to the manipulation of numbers. It was soon recognized that the processing power of computers could also be applied to non-numerical data which could be represented in the computer in digital form. In the era of data processing (DP) that followed, computer systems went beyond code breaking and calculation to performing tasks which required the capture, storage, retrieval, and manipulation of both numerical and non-numerical data. DP also gradually enabled interactive computing whereby users themselves can interact with systems and are able to instruct and receive feedback through ever-improving user interfaces.

Powerful data processing systems proliferated in areas as diverse as airline booking, banking, stock control, payroll, space exploration, and all manner of military and government applications.

Characteristic of the era of data processing was the development of LEXIS, the world's largest legal information service. Said also to be the largest single database in the world (save for a number of intelligence and security agencies), LEXIS effectively stores the full text of a massive amount of primary legal source material (legislation and case-law) as well as huge quantities of secondary writings (journals and periodicals, for example). Manually entered by thousands of data entry clerks in the Far East in the early days, this text was made available for users who could then search within it for the occurrence of key words, in isolation or combination. This was—and remains—data processing on a massive scale.

From data processing to artificial intelligence

In the mid 1950s, a hybrid group of scholars and scientists around the world sought to push back the frontiers of computer technology still further by developing systems which could process not just numbers and data but knowledge as well. In 1956, the term 'artificial intelligence' was coined and this referred, broadly, to those systems which were designed to perform tasks and solve problems which had hitherto been thought to require human intelligence. Various sub-fields of artificial intelligence evolved, including robotics, game playing, natural language processing (allowing computers to understand the ordinary languages of human beings), and speech recognition (computers that recognize and can process human speech). One further aspect of this field was devoted to computers which could solve problems, draw conclusions, and in some sense reason—these were to become the central tasks of systems which have variously been called knowledge-based systems, intelligent knowledge-based systems, expert systems, and knowledge processors. The central idea is clear—as well as capturing and representing numbers and data in computer systems, the goal was to transfer knowledge into computers so that systems could apply this knowledge in discharging tasks well beyond the scope of data processing.

Theorists and practitioners agonized—as they still do—over what knowledge is and confusions and uncertainties in terminology are highlighted, if not perpetuated, by the emergence of 'information' and 'information processing' as the fashionable terms. Precise analysis and clarification of these concepts properly belongs to the branch of philosophy known as 'epistemology' and is well beyond the scope of this study. In functional terms, however, the shift from data processing, through information processing on to knowledge processing is all about increasing the performance, range, and scope of computers, moving the technology from mere number crunching and data storage and retrieval to tasks which would depend on knowledge and intelligence.

In all of this, there is a phenomenon which is absolutely crucial for the future of law.

The basis of The Technology Lag

Although data processing is firmly established and successful and the terminological shift to information processing rightly implies that what is held in the computer and the processing involved is more refined (some say information is data with some value added), it must be recognized that knowledge processing, even as conceived and anticipated in the mid-1950s, has yet to assume the dominant position heralded by the pioneers.

In summary, our ability to use computer technology to capture, store, retrieve, and reproduce data, wildly surpasses our ability to use technology to help analyse, refine, and render more manageable the mass of data which data processing has spawned. We are great at getting information in, but not so good at extracting the information that we want. I would like to characterize this disparity as *The Technology Lag*. It is the all-important lag between data processing and knowledge processing.

The key point about *The Technology Lag* is not just that we are more successful in programming computers to process data than knowledge. Rather, there is a far more significant phenomenon here which is that data processing, through technologies such as photocopiers and scanning machines, has actually created problems and these are problems which knowledge-based systems are not yet sophisticated enough to overcome.

In law, for example, senior barristers and judges regularly reminisce about trials in the past when complete document sets could be held under the arm or in a briefcase. They curse the photocopier and attribute today's escalating costs and delays in the courtroom to the document analysis and management tasks which that technology seems to require of us. Current litigation support systems, based on data processing, only go some small way to conquering the document mountains and it will be some years yet before advanced enabling techniques such as conceptual retrieval, expert systems, and hypertext are refined and applied successfully to help manage the difficulties which earlier technology has left as its legacy (all of this is explained in detail in Chapters Four and Five).

So, too, with massive legal information systems such as LEXIS which may indeed hold vast quantities of data—the problem is that the searching techniques are not yet sufficiently knowledge-based to help users secure *all but only* the relevant documents for their particular purposes.

The Technology Lag is not exclusive to legal information processing. It is said that during the Gulf War, satellite technology, which enabled the capture of millions of digitized images of enemy camps and movements in troops and armoury, was not matched by computer-based tools for analysing such images and so much potentially vital data went unanalysed.

Generally, across industry, commerce, and government, managers and workers bemoan the quantities of information they are expected to digest. So far, IT is said to have given rise to less rather than more control over information—a product of *The Technology Lag*, in that we suffer from the technologies which allow more documentation to be produced and disseminated with relative ease but with no commensurate facilities to help sift through and identify relevant information.

The Technology Lag is crucial for present purposes because it affords us one model of explanation for some of the dilemmas laid out in the first chapter. The problem of hyperregulation, for example, can be traced directly to the availability of technologies which enables the creation of more regulation and the increased dissemination of that information. But there is an absence of any appropriate, accompanying technologies for grappling with and mastering the ever increasing, resultant legal information load.

More generally, I believe that we will not have progressed to a thoroughgoing information society (see Section 3.4), until *The Technology Lag* is overcome and knowledge processing is equal to the task of extricating us from the information management dilemmas left by its ancestor, data processing.

2.4. Burgeoning Performance and the User

Despite the sobering implications of *The Technology Lag*, we read and hear regularly of Moore's Law, attributed to the co-founder of Intel, that the performance of microchips doubles every 18 months and yet the technology gets 30 per cent cheaper each year. The statistics are impressive and are undeniable. Yet they can be a little misleading because they focus on easily quantifiable factors such as the power of microprocessors, the capacity of discs, the clarity and resolution of visual displays, the physical dimensions of the computers themselves, the numbers of users, and the speed of transmission of information.

But they ignore the fact that these rapid developments in IT outstrip our capacity to exploit it effectively and to adapt culturally in adopting it. The claims tend to focus on hardware, the physical machines and their performance, and on telecommunications, whereas the struggle in developing knowledge-based systems, for example, is rooted in our comparatively modest progress in many aspects of software development and end-user applications. So while it is hard not to be trite about progress in IT, there is equally a danger of being excessively cavalier.

Subject, therefore, to the challenges which arise out of *The Technology Lag* and also to the various limitations of IT, as discussed in the following section, it is instructive, from the end user's perspective, to reflect, in functional terms, on the palpable improvements we can continue to expect.

Greater power and capacity

Again, the figures are daunting. The performance of chips (microprocessors) is said to have improved about 25,000 times since they were invented but 25 years ago. And within the next 25, it is predicted that one personal computer will be as powerful as the sum total of all of today's machines in California's Silicon Valley.

While for most lawyers and non-lawyers alike, the type and speed of chips is a rather arcane matter, clouded by the apparent use of codes (for example, '486DX') rather than everyday descriptions, ever-improving chip technology does have the direct effect for end users that their machines seem to respond and function more quickly (although the cynic might say the result is minimum degradation in performance whenever more demanding and powerful upgrades of software are loaded).

Similarly, in relation to capacity, users do not need to have a direct grasp of memory technology and disc storage concepts to appreciate that machines available today can hold more data and software and run larger and more applications than was possible in the past.

A major manifestation of advances in capacity is CD-ROM technology, which stands for Compact Disc Read Only Memory. This technology dates to the mid-1980s, using the same kind of discs as those for audio CD players. Measuring 10cms. in diameter, these discs can store huge amounts of information (a single CD can store over 650 megabytes, equivalent to over 450 high density 3.5in. 'floppy' discs). To give some sense of the storage capacity, Oxford University Press publish their entire, 20 volume, second edition of the English Oxford Dictionary on one CD.

Because of this impressive storage capability, CDs are the preferred medium today for holding the large files which make up multi-media applications (text, sound, video, image and animations rolled into one) and for the delivery of large-scale electronic publications.

I believe, however, that CD will turn out to be something of a temporary and transitional storage medium and will, early in the next millennium, largely be superseded by other technology—to be more precise, I suspect most of the information on CDs today will be delivered as cheaply and quickly via on-line systems and high volume, broadband telecommunications (carrying video and audio signals) based on fibre optics. However, CD remains an exceptionally powerful, low cost, widely available—albeit interim—phenomenon with its modest physical dimensions belying its impressive storage capacity.

In any event, other memory technologies are succeeding in the laboratories and are also likely to supersede CD. Holographic memory, for instance, holds the promise of storing the entire contents of the British Library in a unit the size of the average paperback book.

In summary, for users, greater power and capacity means that their machines respond and execute programs faster and they can store more information in increasingly richer formats (not just text, but sound and video as well, for example).

Increasingly portable

The physical chunk of kit that is the computer is also subject to regular change. Most noticeably, machines seem to be shrinking.

Whereas the so-called 'portable' machines of the mid-1980s were no such thing (even the term 'luggable' machine assumed some considerable strength on the part of the lugger), portables of today are remarkably compact and light, becoming more so as one progresses down in size through the categories of laptop, palm top, to personal digital assistants (PDAs as they are known in the trade).

In mid-1986, I was the proud possessor of a then state-of-the-art portable, yet mains electricity dependent, personal computer which boasted a disc capacity of 10 megabytes which was remarkable at the time. Just ten years later, for a variety of purposes, I use a hand-held machine (operating off two pen-light batteries) which now can have the self-same storage capacity as my 1986 kit, but at one-tenth of the price (not even allowing for inflation), at one-twenty-fifth of the weight and one-fiftieth of the size (volume).

The quality of visual display in portable machines has also increased dramatically. The resolution of screens (the number of dots per inch (dpi)) improves readily (on average about 100 dpi) and should eventually become as sharp in everyday computers as print on paper (laser printing of today being about 300–600 dpi, and high quality published materials around 1400 dpi and above). Colour screens are now commonplace and are far easier on the eyes than the bright greens and oranges of the past.

Gradual (but generally less dramatic) progress made in battery technology also allows users of portables to carry huge quantities of information in their briefcases without unwieldy lengths of cable. And advances in telecommunications are now able to provide the option of access to yet further materials, on both a wired and wireless basis.

Before too long, there will be no practical limits on the amount of information—as text, image, video, animation, and sound—users will be able to have at their fingertips wherever they are. Nicholas Negroponte goes further, in *Being Digital*: 'Multimedia will become more book-like, something with which you can curl up in bed and either have a conversation or be told a story. Multimedia will someday be as subtle and rich as the feel of paper and smell of leather.' (page 71)

Greater versatility

The 1990s seem to be the era of personal 'multi-computing'. Local area network technology, for example, provides a sophistication of *multi-user* and information sharing facilities which vastly improves on systems of the past. Computer users can now work together in teams within their own organizations rather than in the solitary confinement which characterized the early days of personal computing.

New and emerging operating systems (such as Microsoft's Windows 95 and IBM's Warp) also allow PC users to *multi-task*. This means users can run more than one program at one time: for example, they can work on a spreadsheet while concurrently printing from a word processor and at the same time be sorting and searching through lists of documents held in a database. No longer do users have to do one thing at a time.

Both domestically and commercially, *multi-media* technology moves the computer from the era of storage and retrieval of text to one in which sound, video, graphics, and animations, enabled largely through CD technology, also become standard fare on the computer menu. Information can thus be packaged and presented in more palatable forms than in the past.

Less isolated

What is more, in ways that are described later in this book (using systems such as the Internet and the World Wide Web—see Section 4.5), computer users now find it relatively straightforward to connect not just to their colleagues within their organizations but also to contacts in other organizations as well. Through techniques such as electronic mail, conferencing, and bulletin boards, it is now widely held that an entirely new form of human interaction has come about, the collective user base becoming a global 'virtual community' enabled by 'computer mediated communications'.

Two sets of technologies have converged here—the billions of pounds of investment in personal computer technology sits alongside decades of effort in global telecommunications to allow even schoolchildren (if not yet their parents) to transfer messages and documents to one another and engage in computer-mediated, on-line, free form discussion.

More usable

The power and capacity, the shrinking in dimensions, the multi-computing, and the interpersonal and inter-organizational computing would all be mere puff, however, were it not for the great strides which have simultaneously been made in improving the usability of computers and telecommunications.

Whereas computing for two or three decades was for computer scientists, the IT industry has gradually put layer after layer of software in place, so that the average end user is kept well out of the way of ones and zeros, system software, and programming languages. Now the end user generally harnesses the potential of IT through user interfaces designed for the average mortal rather than the computer scientist. (The interface is the part of the system—the front end—with which the user interacts directly.)

Far more intuitive in operation than the so-called character-based systems of the past, these graphical user interfaces (see Section 4.7) themselves are evolving rapidly and combine with other emerging technologies such as voice recognition (see Section 4.8) to make the whole process of end user computing more natural and far less daunting than in the past. Within a few years, it will be common for us to speak to our computers and for them to talk back and the keyboard is likely to diminish in importance.

In his fascinating, recent book, *The Road Ahead*, Bill Gates says 'If personal computing still seems too hard or confusing, it doesn't mean you aren't smart enough. It means we still have work to do to make them easier' (pages 257–8). This is what increasing usability is surely all about—bringing IT to the users, rather than requiring the reverse.

2.5. The Limitations of IT

Although the progress in computing over the last fifty years represents one of the most remarkable achievements in the history of mankind, it is important to pause before delving further into its impact on legal practice and the administration of justice to reflect on some of the (current) limitations of IT.

For present purposes, I distinguish between two kinds of limitations: technical on the one hand, and moral on the other. The first category relates to what computers cannot currently be programmed to do or to help with (note that I do not delve here into difficult questions of mathematical computability); while the second pertains to those areas of social life which it may be considered ought not, from a moral point of view, to be subjected to, or replaced by, some variant of IT.

These are very different types of limitation: one technical, empirical, and variable across time; the other moral, prescriptive, and perhaps immutable.

Technical limitations

In the 1960s, bolstered by inter-disciplinary fervour, a number of the leading scientists in the field of artificial intelligence (AI) genuinely seemed to believe that computers were set, in fairly short order, to become as intelligent as human beings. They seemed to conceive of few technical limitations. Herbert Simon, later a Nobel prize winner, is said to have predicted in 1965 that within twenty years, machines would be capable of doing any work that a man can do. A fellow founding father of AI, Marvin Minsky of MIT, we are told, rather more dramatically suggested that we would be lucky if the next generation of computer systems are willing to keep us (human beings) around the house as household pets. While some savage critics have rejected these prognostications and aspirations as silly, it is perhaps safer to say that their timescales were overenthusiastic. In any event, it is more instructive for current purposes to consider the ways in which AI has so far failed to fulfil its promise.

Natural language processing

Current computer technology constrains the user so that when she requires something of her machine this cannot be expressed fully in natural language (such as English or French) but rather is achieved by using some formal language (for example, structured, English-like statements or programming languages) or by selecting from some predefined set of instructions.

In short, computers cannot currently process natural language. They may accept natural language as input, but what they then do with it, using today's technologies, is still rather hit and miss. Computers cannot understand what human beings are meaning when they speak or write. Although much progress has been made in this field, this same limitation currently prevails in relation to computer systems translating from one language to another.

Although modern systems are now more sophisticated, the traditional tale of a computer system translating 'hydraulic ram' in one language into 'water sheep' in another, teaches us an important lesson; as does the translation of 'out of sight, out of mind' into 'invisible insanity'. So too does the tale of the intelligent robot wandering around the London underground system for the rest of time—it had seen a sign saying 'dogs must be carried' and was searching in vain for a dog to carry before proceeding. The lesson in all of these tales is that human beings' ability to understand natural language derives not only from our insight into particular words, but also from our appreciation of the wider context in which words are used. Ambiguities and absurdities are exposed as such only by agents who have this wider grasp of the meanings of words and their contexts.

In so far as natural language translation involves the mapping of individual words in one language to an apparently parallel word in another language (by reference to its most common usage), this is bound to give rise to errors of translation in absence of some wider understanding.

The Theory

The challenge of natural language processing is that of endowing a computer with sufficient information and knowledge to provide it with precisely this wider appreciation. In practice, this means that users of some legal information system who have hopes of switching their machines on and simply chatting through the problem will be disappointed.

The problem of understanding context is but one of the challenges facing the natural language processing community but it bears on a related issue, that of 'commonsense reasoning'. For many years, AI workers have strived to inculcate common sense into computer systems, by which they mean general knowledge of the world (and not just an attempt to encourage computers to behave sensibly). The difficulty with common sense and general knowledge, if I may grossly oversimplify, is that there is an awful lot of it and most of it remains unarticulated.

So many of our decisions and actions in everyday life are based on our general knowledge, including our more or less crude ideas of physics and psychology (we have a rough understanding of the behaviour of things in the physical world and people in the social world to be able to predict what will happen in given situations—if I throw this ball up it will come down; if I throw this ball up into your face, you will not be pleased). It is this understanding of the world which in part helps human beings to process natural language.

Perhaps the most impressive work in this context has been conducted over the last ten years at the CYC project in Austin, in the United States, where the research group has articulated about 100,000 discrete concepts and about one million pieces of common sense knowledge about them. Yet, despite these valiant, ongoing attempts to represent truly vast quantities of common sense and general knowledge in computer systems, those who have short and medium term interest in the future of the legal profession need not worry about the short-term impact of this work on their plans.

This limitation does, however, pose serious problems for those involved in computer-based legal reasoning, because many legal concepts—such as 'fair', 'reasonable', and 'probable'—are applied in practice not only on the basis of application of legal rules but also in dependence on non-legal, everyday understanding of these ideas.

Knowing what they do not know

A further limitation is that current computer systems are not impressive at knowing what they do not know. In contrast, human beings are good at knowing what they do not know; although perhaps reluctant to acknowledge this in particular circumstances.

This can be illustrated by a short experiment. If you are asked when your birthday is, you will immediately know that you know the answer to this question. If you are asked, say, your brother's birthday, you may hesitate for a second or two in pinpointing the date but you may have the feeling that you always knew that you knew it (that it was 'in there' somewhere). In contrast, when most of us are asked if we know the date of birth of Albert Einstein, not only do we not know the answer, but we also—and immediately—know that we do not know.

This capacity of human beings instantly to know what we do not know has not yet been simulated in computer systems. On introspection, one of the difficulties here, of course, is that we do not know how we know so quickly when we do not know something! It does not feel as though we look down a list of birth dates and after exhaustive examination of such a list infer from the absence of Albert Einstein's name that we do not know his birth date. (It may be that this is what goes on, but that is not the impression I have.) In contrast, computers which have been programmed in the traditional way do not have this self-awareness and self-knowledge of their limitations.

In practice, system developers introduce closure rules of the sort that 'anything that is not explicitly represented as known is defined as unknown'. While this works on some occasions, in the development of many advanced information systems (such as expert systems—see Section 4.3), a rather laborious further step has to be taken—that of actually articulating those facts and rules which systems do not know.

An additional level of knowledge is therefore expressly included which then allows computers some greater insight into their own limitations (but even this is not foolproof, not least because one can force the need for an infinite regress of self-knowledge—knowledge about limitations and then about the limitations of these limitations and so on). In development terms, this also imposes an enormous overhead—about one-quarter of the knowledge and information held, for instance, in the Latent Damage System (see Section 6.1) is express knowledge about the areas of law which are beyond the scope of that system.

Reading from a screen

It is remarkable how little we know, even today, about the psychological aspects of presenting text through visual display units as compared to the presentation of text on paper. Indeed, it has only been in the last twenty years or so that specialists in human / computer interaction have put their minds to making the best of this alternative medium. Cognitive psychologists, in particular, have contributed to the field. Several fascinating studies have examined human beings' ability to proofread and understand the contents of word processed documents as compared with text displayed on computer monitors. Results of these enquiries suggest our accuracy in proofreading and comprehending hard copy is slightly—yet reliably—higher than reading from monitors. It has also been found that we suffer substantial reduction in reading rates in reading from screen as opposed to paper. This can have considerable practical impact in law. For example, even if evidential material can be stored and retrieved more easily by using computers, it is crucial that maximum comprehension is maintained.

Screen technology does not yield the level of resolution (dots per inch) in most personal computers even of laser printed text and until it can we must expect that less information will be conveyed from screen to user as opposed to print to reader.

The dimension of tactility also seems to be important. Human beings like to handle books and journals, for example. The look, feel, and even smell of print and paper are often important to us. Until we are as comfortable with screen mediated information, we have here an important psychological limitation of IT.

Moral limitations

Moving away from technical limitations, there is a very different category of limitation which concerns the ethical limits of applications of IT.

One of the pervasive dilemmas in the applied sciences, particularly acute in areas of medical science such as genetic engineering, is that of prohibiting the exploitation of some advance on moral grounds. In computing and in medicine, there are some scientists who argue that once some discovery has been made or some invention created or innovation fashioned, then it is inevitable that someone, somewhere, will exploit it for gain. While this may be a robust prediction supported by formidable empirical evidence, it does not follow that all advances should be uncritically exploited and applied in practice.

It is both trite and true to observe that technical advances of themselves are morally neutral and that it is human beings' applications of them that are morally charged (our current systems of morality tend only to make sense in relation to the intentional behaviour of conscious human beings, although some visionaries claim that autonomous intelligent robotic systems of the future will require moral systems of their own).

I believe it is desirable that we, as a world community, afford ourselves the opportunity to reflect publicly on uses of IT which may be technically possible but morally unacceptable. I know of no more passionate and convincing contribution to this issue than that of Joseph Weizenbaum in his influential (although now slightly dated) book, *Computer Power and Human Reason*, first published in 1976. A computer scientist, Weizenbaum was inspired to demarcate some moral limits for artificial intelligence in part by responses to the intelligent systems he developed himself in the 1970s. While he retains a healthy scepticism in that book about the potential of artificial intelligence, he nevertheless identifies uses of computer systems that he knows or suspects to be technically possible but is emphatic should be regarded as morally unsustainable. No matter what may be possible, he argues, there are some applications of IT which we should be able to identify as morally unacceptable. Into this category, Weizenbaum puts computer applications that are 'obscene' (page 268) including those that 'propose to substitute a computer system for a human function that involves interpersonal respect, understanding, and love' (page 269) as well as those 'which can easily be seen to have irreversible and not entirely foreseeable side effects' (page 270).

In a legal context, it is possible that many readers may have similarly passionate misgivings about extending information technology into the administration of justice. It is my purpose here to encourage that ethical debate but not to engage in it directly. Let me give just one example. This relates to the possibility of computerization of judges (see Section 8.2). Even if it becomes possible in centuries to come for machines to replace aspects or all of the judicial function, would this be morally and socially desirable? Some would say there is little point in dwelling upon such a remote possibility and we would do better to focus on more likely, shorter term applications. I have some sympathy with this but I do have grave concerns about how little serious social thought and ethical analysis is devoted to IT today as we lay the foundations of our IT society of tomorrow. Although we are on the brink of an entirely new era of humankind, very few philosophers or social commentators have explored the ramifications in the depth that it surely merits.

In the early 1980s in the UK, in response to public and scientific concern over techniques such as *in vitro* fertilization, a major national programme of inquiry and consultation was launched, leading to the report by the philosopher, Mary (now Baroness) Warnock. The topic received massive attention from the media, the public, the academic world, and scientific community. The inquiry greatly heightened general understanding of the central issues and the main problems were clarified if not resolved. It seems

The Theory

to me there is urgent need for a similar scale of debate on the social and ethical implications of IT. And the outcome of that would greatly assist more particular thinking about the moral limits we might seek to demarcate in our use of IT in the law.

3

Law as Information

In Chapter One, I considered a number of thorny problems with contemporary legal systems. While I concentrated largely on the effects of these problems on social and business life, it is easily seen that the same difficulties can also be assessed in terms of *information*. For example, hyperregulation refers to legal information being of unmanageable quantity and complexity. Lack of promulgation means that certain legal information is not disseminated adequately and then made available to those who need it. The paradox of reactive legal service suggests that legal information is too costly to invoke and neither reusable nor integrated with business and social activities. And the pressurized legal market-place indicates that the sale and delivery of legal information is perhaps becoming too costly and cumbersome a process for both lawyers and clients.

In Chapter Two, I went on to discuss IT (broadly, computers and telecommunications) in terms of its functions and purposes, the leaps in its progress but with reference also to its limitations. Bizarre though it may seem at first blush, it is worth adding to that analysis by reflecting for a moment on the term 'IT' itself. It stands, of course, for information technology, but it is easy and commonplace to overlook the significance of the 'information' part. When most of us talk about IT, we tend to think about computers, in isolation and linked together, and we may reflect also on the chips embedded in all manner of other devices (dishwashers, motor cars, and microwave ovens, for example). The management and manipulation of information do not spring naturally to mind. We acknowledge that what the technology achieves is remarkable but we seldom articulate this in terms of information.

The same is true on the corporate scene. Typically, management boards recruit Directors of IT but once they have the machines and cabling in place, they often come to realize they do not really understand the information they do use and could use in their businesses. To avoid the tail continuing to wag the dog, they then appoint a Chief Information Officer or the like, who takes a step back and considers the information requirements of the organization. The CIO (as that person may be known) is driven by information needs and not by technology. IT often becomes a vital vehicle for the delivery of information but it does not, on this model, dictate the content of the information itself.

Too often, the 'T' of 'IT' has taken precedence over the 'I'. Lawyers should try to avoid this. If the profession and its clients face significant problems which relate directly to information, then some considerable time should be spent in analysis and clarification of the information dimension rather than by simply throwing technology at the problems.

With this in mind, the purpose of this chapter is to take a preliminary look at the interrelationships between the law and information and to suggest some tentative models and ways of looking at the key issues which should help us in our broader quest of predicting the likely future of law and lawyers.

First of all, to set the scene, I present a potted summary of IT in the law in the UK. Then, I explore the various types of legal information on which lawyers currently rely and I link this analysis to technology. The two sections which then follow introduce new concepts: a continuum of legal information which helps us understand the similarities and differences between advice offered by lawyers and the information presented by systems; and an analysis of how the law changes during phases of civilization dominated in turn by orality, script, print, and then IT. Finally, I draw together the findings and arguments of the book so far and suggest that legal service is emerging as an information service and in so doing is offering potential solutions to the problems laid out in the first chapter.

3.1. A Brief History of IT in The Law

Widespread investment in IT for the legal profession in the UK began in the early 1970s. And in the period that followed, the emphasis was overwhelmingly on automating the law office rather than automating the lawyer.

From back office to front office into client office

The 1970s and 1980s were characterized by 'back office' applications of IT, especially word processing and accounting systems. Similarly, in the court system, the leading applications were administrative in nature and very rarely extended into the courtroom for use by judges.

This, then, was *back-office automation*, the computerization of existing functions and processes, with a view to greater efficiency and the control or reduction of costs by replacing administrative staff with machines and by executing back-office tasks more quickly.

Until the late 1980s, a terminal or personal computer on a lawyer's desk was a rarity in the UK. The main applications of IT for lawyers themselves, for legal research purposes, were legal information retrieval systems and, most notably, LEXIS. Again, however, this system remained metaphorically and literally in the back office, requiring purpose-built, dedicated terminals which were generally located in legal libraries—although a tool for legal research, this physical placement of LEXIS terminals was symbolic of the back-office role most lawyers allocated to IT.

From 1990 onwards, however, all branches of the legal profession seemed to awake from their slumber and, with the advent of ever more powerful and networked personal computers, began to take the technology from the back office to the front office, from the IT cupboard in the basement, and from secretaries' desks, into the rooms of lawyers themselves. While some such machines were no more than expensive paperweights, many lawyers—solicitors, barristers, and judges—began to use IT themselves. At first, this was again dominated by automation (as opposed to innovation) and especially word processing; and many legal practitioners and judges became adept at drafting directly on their own machines. In the early 1990s, considerable interest was also shown in litigation support technology through which document loads could be handled more effectively in the context of resolving disputes. At the same time, legal publishers began to explore electronic publishing and gradually sought to make useful legal sources available electronically, most commonly on CD. But the emphasis still was on automation, albeit in the front office.

Portability of machines was fast recognized in the early 1990s as holding great potential and this, together with internal local area networks and external electronic communications, led a small phalanx of more inspired enthusiasts to recognize that it was possible to innovate through IT and to bring about radical change in working practices.

Electronic communication between lawyers and their clients emerged as a key illustration of the way in which there could be substantial change in relationships between lawyers and those they advised. In the UK, 1995 was the year in which electronic communications for lawyers began to take off, bolstered largely by the general hype about information superhighways and the Internet; as well as by the introduction of the legal electronic network known as Link.

Thus, the technology within twenty-five years had moved from the back office through the front office and reached into the client office itself.

At conferences and exhibitions, as well as in relevant trade magazines, there was growing conviction in 1995 that IT would indeed exert considerable influence on lawyers' working lives. Back-office applications, of course, became ever more sophisticated, especially practice management systems, complete with marketing and personnel databases. However, in forums such as the Society for Computers and Law and ITAC (Information Technology and Courts Committee set up by the Lord Chancellor in 1985) there had been this quite definite movement towards applications of IT for lawyers themselves. Market studies showed an upsurge in investment in front-office and client office systems, while a pilot project on IT for judges (JUDITH—Judicial IT Help) was held to have been a success and led to commitment by the Lord Chancellor's Department to providing portable computers and a suite of applications to 300 judges by the end of 1995.

Comprehensive support and endorsement for IT was also expressed by Lord Woolf in 1995, in his Interim Report (*Access to Justice*) to the Lord Chancellor concerning the streamlining of the civil justice system generally. IT was argued there to be a vital enabler for the more general changes being advocated—for instance, in areas such as judicial case management and providing guidance to citizens on legal matters.

Pressures

Over and above the dramatic developments in IT which clearly encouraged and enabled greater investment, lawyers' gradual uptake of IT, especially in private law firms, was stimulated by two sets of pressures.

The legal market-place

On the one hand, the pressurized legal market-place drove lawyers to run their practices in a more business-like manner, using IT for management purposes to support, for example, time recording, billing, collecting, the management of work-in-progress, and control over bad debts. Advanced practice management systems helped considerably here but some of the more enlightened managers in law firms went further in recognizing that crucial competitive edge for lawyers is gained by making the most of their two vital assets—the lawyers themselves and their know-how.

Their response to the pressurized legal market-place was to strive continuously to improve the performance of their fee earners and to do so, in part, by trying, through the machines on their desks, to put at lawyers' fingertips all the information which they needed for their daily practice. This was not just legal information but all manner of non-legal materials as well (information, for instance, about client companies, the financial markets, media reports, and market research).

To maximize the other vital asset, the know-how, law firms invested in major programmes to capture and store their 'institutional memory', their collective, corporate wisdom. Once again, the idea was that this would be delivered onto the desks of all lawyers through IT.

The use of IT by others

The second set of pressures which led to greater uptake of IT related more closely to IT itself. These were external pressures, such as increasing enthusiasm for IT amongst judges and barristers. When judges invited solicitors to arrange for pleadings to be submitted in machine readable form, for example, even the most Luddite of lawyers sat up, took notice, and adopted appropriate technologies. Equally, I saw senior barristers with positive past experience of litigation support systems requiring that systems be put in place as a condition of their participation in new cases—once more, this left even the technophobic solicitor with little room for manoeuvre.

New, high profile ventures in the legal market-place were also a significant driver. The publicity surrounding the vast distribution (over 100,000 free copies) of the Link software for electronic communications amongst lawyers, for instance, changed expectations and helped shape a perception of e-mail (electronic mail) for lawyers as a natural, evolutionary step for the profession. Indeed, most solicitors found it difficult not to respond in some way.

The activities of lawyers in other jurisdictions also had some impact, either as perceived through published research, such as the Chicago Kent College of Law Large Firms Surveys, or as observed in practice while collaborating or competing with foreign law firms. I know of one firm which lost a significant client when, in the context of a major, international transaction, their lack of effective word processing, electronic communications, and high speed printing capabilities compared so unfavourably with the facilities of the American lawyers on the job. The client took this to be a manifestation of sloppy management and lack of commitment to quality.

Initiatives within the profession also influenced lawyers' inclination to use IT. The development of The ORSA Protocol was a case in point. The Official Referees Solicitors' Association set up an IT subcommittee to establish some standards for the use of litigation support systems in the courts of the Official Referees (judges in England who specialize in technical disputes, largely in the construction, engineering, and IT industries). While these courts had frequently been facing huge document loads which were crying out for litigation support, law firms had been tending to bicker with one another over the selection of systems, with each boasting unrivalled merit for their own preferred packages. The subcommittee, with representatives from a number of major litigation practices, sought to cut through these debates and we wrote The ORSA Protocol which laid out standard formats for various aspects of litigation support. Although it was in no sense binding, a number of the judges strongly encouraged its usage, most solicitors accepted its recommendations, and it motivated those who were previously unaware of litigation support to take it far more seriously.

Harking back to my discussion of the business benefits of IT, in which I referred to the motivation of risk management (see Section 2.2), a further pressure on many lawyers was precisely this fear that their competitors were forging ahead with IT, leaving them scrambling about aimlessly in their wake. The pressure to pre-empt competitive disadvantage seemed to overpower many lawyers, even though their worries about competitors operating in high-tech, paperless offices linked electronically and effortlessly to the rest of the world, were usually without much foundation.

The final pressure I should mention has surely been the most compelling. This is the pressure from clients. As clients themselves began to deploy IT across their organizations and grew to appreciate its impact and benefits, they viewed with increasing incredulity those lawyers who, for example, handled millions of documents in a dispute with index cards and teams of paralegals. Clients gradually expected and sometimes required a minimum level of usage of IT and in the US a certain level of technical capacity began to become a prerequisite for eligibility for short lists when work was being tendered competitively.

In 1992, a friend from one of the City's most prestigious legal practices telephoned me and said that their most important client had asked that they start communicating electronically with one another. My friend confessed that no one in his firm knew what that meant. It turned out to mean a major programme of investment in IT in the three years that followed.

A snapshot

Traditionally, then, most lawyers in investing in IT chose to automate rather than innovate; and this automation was in two dimensions. First, lawyers sought to introduce law office automation (for example, for billing and accounting) to improve the way legal practices were managed. The second, more ambitious type of automation involved attempts to automate some *lawyering* activities through applications such as litigation databases, and know-how systems that sought to capture and make available lawyers' collective experience and expertise. This second category of automation certainly brought costs savings and enhanced performance but, by and large, these applications still fell within the model of automating past practices rather than using IT to change and radically improve legal service and, in turn, offer significant competitive advantage for both clients and their lawyers.

Perhaps the greatest management challenge that has faced lawyers grappling with IT has been this move beyond successful automation to strategic innovation, so that IT could change legal practice and the delivery of legal services, both cost effectively and qualitatively.

Other than through electronic communication, another example of innovation has been law firms providing computerized document drafting systems to corporate clients in order to support clients' in-house generation of specific classes of agreements rather than these firms being instructed to undertake the preparation of every individual contract (see Section 6.3). A further illustration has been external lawyers developing and licensing computer-based legal information systems to clients rather than providing one-to-one advisory services whenever legal assistance is required (see Section 6.3).

Many more illustrations of innovation are peppered across this book. These, and similar examples have, of course, raised fundamental questions about what legal service is, how it should be delivered, how lawyers should charge for their work, and how responsibility can be shared when legal information falling short of advice is relied upon by clients. However, these are questions which have gradually been faced squarely, especially by those lawyers keen to innovate using IT and, more importantly, in response to clients who have increasingly been expecting this kind of innovation.

To some extent, lawyers have also experienced the informating effect; and quite some time ago, in relation to legal accounting systems. The original motive in introducing these systems was to automate the accounting function. But this automation also gave rise to valuable, internal management information, in that the systems could be queried to identify, for instance, profitable practice areas and fee earners, and to identify all manner of other trends in law firms (see Section 6.2).

More recently, this informating effect has moved from the back office to the cutting edge of legal practice, most significantly from the combination of word processing technology on the one hand and document management systems on the other (see Section 6.2).

IT for lawyers, then, has already meant much more than automating and streamlining existing legal working methods. Progressive lawyers have been innovating and informating and the early signs are that business benefits from this will accrue to both lawyer and client.

It is often thought by lawyers that they have been far slower than all other industries and professions in embracing IT. I was recently involved in a comparative analysis of ten quite different sectors in the City of London which suggests, however, that lawyers are rather too self-deprecating in this connection. Entitled *Focus on IT in the City*, and commissioned by the Worshipful Company of Information Technologists (London's 100th and newest Livery Company), the report does show that IT is pervasive in, and indeed is the foundation now of, some City sectors, such as international banking, securities trading, and derivatives. Yet various other sectors—for example, insurance, fund management, and the media—are, by and large, no more committed to IT than lawyers have been, and remain focused on back and front office automation. This is not to praise the legal profession's deployment of IT but it is to challenge those who would reject lawyers as the lowest of the low tech.

Where lawyers do rank fairly low, however, is in their treatment of suppliers, many of the larger of whom (household names) have perhaps now lost interest in the field. At the outset, in the mid-1980s, major players expressed considerable interest in the profession's networking requirements, for example, but they seem to have been browbeaten by solicitors' incomparable behaviour while procuring IT, vacillating (as they inevitably seem to) between high-handed disinterest on the one hand through to treating the system selection process, on the other, as though it were a piece of upper court litigation. Needless to say, there is little question of lawyers embracing the talk of partnering with suppliers which is so fashionable across other industries and professions.

3.2. Legal Information, Legal Tasks, and the Role of IT

Lurking behind any contemporary analysis of IT for lawyers must be the unassailable premise that lawyers are in the information business. They are main exponents of information management and information processing. Lawyers acquire information through education and training, capture and retain information as part of their stock-in-trade, and sell information to clients who ask for it to be applied to their circumstances. Lawyering is, arguably, more information intensive than any other industry or profession.

In the current legal paradigm, lawyers are a vital interface (the cynics would say a bottleneck) between citizens and businesses on the one hand and the formal legal sources (legislation and case-law) on the other. Lawyers are the laity's window on the law and legal information.

In a world now embracing the (allegedly novel) contention that information and knowledge are commodities of prime value in any first world economy, this has surely always been true in the law. Anything of value in the law has always been conveyed as some form of information, although it is only in the last few years that we have begun to look upon legal service explicitly in this way and explore its implications for the future.

In business terms, as I suggested in my analysis of the pressures which have led to lawyers' gradual uptake of IT, improved financial performance and competitive positioning can be achieved by putting useful information (legal and non-legal) at the fingertips of fee earners as well as through readier access to easily manipulable financial information.

A variety of questions arise. What types of information are relevant here? In what ways do lawyers use this information? What role can IT play in improving legal information management? I deal with each of these questions in turn in this section.

Types of information

Lawyers work constantly with information. In advising clients, they rely on a variety of legal oriented information sources, including legislative materials, case reports, textbooks, journals, opinions, advices, practice directions, codes of practices, precedent documents, formal and informal procedures, personal experience (some of which is documented), and in-house know-how held in a variety of forms. All of these information sources are constantly monitored and updated in light of change. (If readers would like a far more detailed analysis of this kind of information and knowledge, this is attempted in my book, *Expert Systems in Law*.)

Beyond legal information, lawyers also rely on general economic, political, and commercial information, relating, for instance, to particular industries, markets, geographical areas, companies, and projects. They also need access to information about people—for example, expert witnesses, clients, contacts, competitors, foreign lawyers, barristers, judges, arbitrators, and fellow fee earners. All of this information is also subject to frequent change.

Lawyers also have to cope with case-related information—the facts and circumstances of cases upon which they are called to advise. Some of this is presented orally by their clients and captured in file notes from meetings with them. Invariably this information is also captured by wading through seemingly endless piles of lever arch files containing correspondence and records. Further, this case-related information is also gleaned from witness statements and other investigations.

At the same time, managers running law firms also depend heavily on financial information. Accounting information is vital, relating, amongst other issues, to fee income, profitability, overheads, internal resources, billings, collections, work-in-progress, bad debts, the value of time billed, supplemented by management information which delves further into details and trends by assessing performance, for example, by fee earner, department, supervising partner, work type by industry, and so on.

Many lawyers would say, quite understandably, that they are inundated with too much information. At the same time, most would also tend to express concern about keeping up to date with all manner of relevant developments. Equally, it is often said that there is insufficient communication of information within firms and across the profession.

Too much information? Not enough information? Information which is spread unevenly? All of this adds up to one paradox of the information age which we find ourselves moving towards—while recent developments in IT should surely mean we can gain access to all but only the information we need, the reality seems to be that we are less informed and focused than in the past. The paradox has its roots, of course, in *The Technology Lag*—in short, IT is a lot better at creating, gathering, storing, and reproducing information than it is at sorting, searching and retrieving. Photocopiers, word processors, fax machines, scanners, and communication links are all superb mechanisms for generating and copying but they have left lawyers with the formidable challenge of managing and controlling their produce. And because IT is not yet equal to this challenge, there is more work than ever for human information managers.

This paradox affects all industries and professions. However, in its current form, as I have argued, the problem is a temporary one, in that new techniques and technologies in the field of knowledge processing are emerging and their focus is far more on the analysis and use of information rather than its reproduction and storage.

Legal information processing tasks

Turning now to the ways in which lawyers use information, I confine my attention here principally to legally oriented information (the legislation, case-law, publications, know-how, and so forth) and, to a lesser extent, to case-related information (which is the basis of the facts of any case). These two categories are at the heart of legal advisory service of today. More than this, the management of them will underlie legal information services of the future.

At the risk of what may seem to the information scientist to be gross over-simplification, it seems to me that lawyers engage in the following six broad categories of legal information processing task (hereafter, shortened to *legal tasks*) as laid out in Figure 3.1.

Figure 3.1 Legal Information Processing Tasks

---

document drafting
sending and receiving information
document management
information consultation
following procedures
analysis and problem solving

Although there are variations in emphasis, I believe these are (in no particular order) the basic building blocks of legal information processing, no matter what kind of legal work is involved, be it dispute resolution, advisory, transaction-based, judicial or legislative.

Document drafting

The drafting of documents, in conventional or electronic form, is a central function of all lawyers, from legislative and contract draftsmen through to litigators preparing writs and judges writing their decisions. Sometimes, documents will be drafted afresh on a genuinely blank sheet of paper. On other occasions, a document being created will contains extracts from pre-existing material (whether explicitly as quotations or embedded without sign of its ancestry).

Sending and receiving information

Lawyers do not work in isolation. They are constantly in communication with others, in meetings and conferences, by telephone, by courier and traditional postal systems, and more recently through electronic communication. They send and receive information to those who instruct them and to those whom they advise. There is a constant flow of information to and from the lawyer's desk.

Document management

Electronic or print-based documents, whether created by lawyers or received by them, require management. In litigation, lawyers are often faced with mountains of documentary evidence, while in advising on transactions, succeeding drafts and background materials quickly build up. Ideally, lawyers should be rigorous and systematic in their document control, to support both the initial task to which they pertain and to make it possible to have ready access to this work product at some later stage.

Information consultation

All lawyers have the ongoing need to consult information sources. I use the term 'consult' in a broad sense here and intend it to embrace the perusal, browsing, dipping into, glancing through, exploration, digestion, marking up, and annotating which lawyers must do in order to gain mastery either of potentially relevant legal sources or of a document load which constitutes the background to some matter. The chief characteristic here is that the lawyer does not know, word for word, the contents of the information being consulted and considered. To a great extent, information consultation is a voyage of discovery with a view to establishing legal or factual premises for later, more formal, legal reasoning and legal problem solving.

Following procedures

Whether laid down by the law itself, by custom within a firm, or by personal habit, lawyers frequently conduct their affairs by following procedures.

These are a highly structured form of information. The doctrine of precedent combines with common sense to make it natural for lawyers to handle like cases in a similar fashion and so lawyers tend to set up and comply with step-by-step procedures for handling all manner of tasks. Lawyers, or at least good ones, seldom behave randomly. Rather, their decisions and actions are often pre-orchestrated by procedures required by the law or proven to be successful in past practice. One of the key skills of lawyers is to set up procedures for dealing most efficiently and effectively with new developments in the law.

Analysis and problem solving

My final category of legal task is that of analysis and problem solving. This refers to the activity of lawyers when drawing conclusions and coming to decisions on the strength of the information before them. To opt for exclusion of some clause, to join a third party in an action, to counsel against some course of action—all of these are situations which presuppose there has been some analysis and problem solving, which, in turn, has been dependent on information gathered and accepted for current purposes. Analysis and problem solving in this context involves the application of legal information to case-related information.

The role of IT

Once we can analyse many aspects of legal work as a series of *legal tasks*, it might seem but a short step for a systems analyst to show the ways in which IT can help to automate, streamline, and improve the way lawyers go about their business—for example, word processing for document creation, telecommunications for sending and receiving documents, document image processing for document management, advanced text retrieval for information consultation, hypertext for following procedures, and expert systems for analysis and problem solving. (Chapter Four explains each of these technologies.)

However, the growing literature and experience in what is generally known as business process re-engineering warns against too great a fixation both with computerizing existing tasks and with the organizational structures which have developed to discharge such tasks. Instead, it is recommended that there should be greater focus on *processes*, which are sets of tasks and activities which *together* give rise to an end result, a product or service which is of direct value to a customer, client or user.

The Theory

Recalling the anecdote at the start of this book, the manufacturer of power tools encourages their executives to focus on processes which could lead to what their customers wanted (holes in walls) rather than on the traditional tasks (drill production) which underpinned their business. Thinking in terms of processes, the argument runs, is more likely to lead to more imaginative business solutions.

Similarly, in law, although it is illuminating to match technologies to tasks and it does serve to highlight how relevant IT might be for lawyers, planning and investing in IT should not stop there. If lawyers confine their attention to picking out tasks which look amenable to computerization, they are likely to miss greater opportunities for more radical and beneficial change.

I find it helpful, in seeking to understand current and future roles of IT in the law, to consider the topic under four headings. Although there are many other dimensions—such as strategy, planning, management, training, and technical infrastructure—the four I have in mind can be understood for current purposes in relative isolation.

The first of the four headings is what I have already called legal information processing tasks (*legal tasks*). These are the things that lawyers do, whatever their fields of expertise. I refer to the second as that of the *enabling techniques*. These are the techniques, such as hypertext and telecommunications which, as I have just hinted, can be used to undertake the tasks. More significantly, these techniques not only enable tasks, they also enable *applications,* which constitute my third category.

Applications, as I characterize them, are the major uses to which lawyers put IT. Litigation support systems, for example, are best regarded as those uses of IT which help lawyers conduct litigation. Too often, and rather confusingly, litigation support is instead portrayed as one technique (for example, full text retrieval) or as a way of discharging just one task (for instance, document management). Given that the process of litigation involves all six categories of information task and can benefit from many conceivable enabling techniques, it is wrong-headed and limiting to confine it to particular tasks or techniques. It is better to regard it as an application of IT which supports some central legal process, although I admit it is early days yet in our identification of legal processes as distinct from tasks.

In other words, applications are enabled by those technologies which match the tasks that, in turn, underlie the processes in question. This analysis is the basis for the following two chapters of the book, which deal with enabling techniques and leading applications, respectively.

The fourth heading is that of *packages.* One of the major challenges for any consultant advising lawyers is to lead discussion away from dwelling with too much intensity on the relative merits and benefits of particular off-the-shelf packages (for example, the old chestnut in the world of legal word processing—the alleged contest between Microsoft Word versus WordPerfect). Such debates, if I am frank, tend to be the province of hobbyists rather than those who strive to achieve business benefits and competitive advantage from the strategic use of IT. The selection of packages should begin once users are clear about the nature of the applications they want. Packages should support applications. But too often, they are selected (and indeed developed) on the strength of tasks and techniques rather than processes and applications. In any strategic discussion of IT for lawyers, packages can be left to one side without any great loss.

3.3. The Legal Information Continuum

Consider a spectrum of legal information, with the printed, formal sources of the law (legislation and case-law) at one extremity (the left-hand side) and human legal experts dispensing legal advice at the other (the right-hand side).

At each end, we have the two extreme categories of sources from which legal guidance can be drawn. The formal legal sources are the raw data of all legal processes; whereas the expertise brought to bear by lawyers in specific cases is the product of extensive analysis, manipulation, and application of that data.

I call this spectrum *The Legal Information Continuum.* On it, as shown in Figure 3.2, we can also place a variety of enabling techniques which can serve as vehicles for the delivery of IT-based legal guidance. In my version of the continuum, I have imposed some of those techniques identified in the next chapter as crucial for the future of law. Leaving the technical details aside for now, these are software techniques which allow us to package and present legal information in a variety of ways.

I have placed the techniques along the continuum, in positions which indicate their proximity either to the conventional publication of information on the one hand or to human legal advisory service on the other. Generally, the nearer a technology is to the right-hand side, the more sophisticated and useful its guidance will be. An expert system, as a legal problem solving system, will hover quite close to the human end of the continuum. Where, in contrast, a technology is closer to the left-hand side it is therefore thought to have greater affinity with the presentation of legal information in its conventional published form. Basic text retrieval systems, which store searchable text in a form much like that found in books, is at home nearer the formal sources.

Figure 3.2 The Legal Information Continuum

Enabling techniques

basic text retrieval systems	enhanced text retrieval systems	hypertext systems	intelligent checklists	diagnostic expert systems

printed legislation and case law	printed textbooks and commentaries	information services		human general legal practitioners	human legal specialists

Sources of legal guidance

Also on the continuum are general legal practitioners, who are, of course, providers of legal information, but not advice as focused or polished as the specialists. Not very far from the other end sit published secondary sources, such as textbooks or articles, which are not the embodiment of the law but descriptions of the law.

The Legal Information Continuum serves as a useful model for analysis of a wide range of phenomena.

The nature of the guidance

As one moves along the continuum, from left to right, one no doubt passes across the blurred and much debated boundaries between legal data, legal information, legal knowledge, and legal expertise. Consistent with this, it follows that the reliable disposal of a legal problem can be achieved either by a human being in isolation; or through the application of various techniques of IT with the guidance of systems often supplemented by human advice. And as we traverse the continuum from left to right, these techniques that are deployed will need to be accompanied by progressively less human involvement, intervention, and supplementary advice.

For example, legal textbooks on their own will rarely yield a legal solution for a non-lawyer, but will require substantial additional analysis by a human legal adviser. Moving further along, a hypertext system may offer a non-lawyer some considerable guidance and provide a useful frame of reference which will often (but not always) require supplementary human legal input.

Much will depend, of course, on the complexity of the legal matter at issue, but for any given single issue, it is clear that the further to the right one moves amongst the technologies on the continuum, the more focused the guidance should be and, in turn, there should be relatively less need for additional human assistance.

It follows also that as one moves towards the right of *The Legal Information Continuum* that the guidance offered becomes more directly usable. By this I do not mean that legal experts should be more user-friendly than, say, legal hypertext systems (although this may be so). Rather, given that the guidance as one moves in a rightward direction is of a higher degree of specificity, then the more focused it should be on the particular requirements of the user (or client, as the case may be). The end product, in other words, becomes more usable for most purposes.

Legal liability

The continuum also serves as a useful model for analysing the legal liability implications of computer systems which offer legal guidance. At one end, as any practising solicitor will be quick to agree, most legal advisers can most certainly be held liable for losses resulting from advice which was negligently provided. At the other end of the continuum, however, the English courts have always been reluctant to attach liability to authors whose negligent misstatements have allegedly caused loss to readers who have relied upon them. Scholars and students of computer law have for long agonized over the place along the continuum where the courts might choose to draw a line between systems which give rise to actionable loss and those that do not.

This book does not seek to address this fraught issue (although the question is lurking throughout), but I think it unlikely that the courts would simply draw a line in some one-dimensional fashion. Rather, they will surely look also to the broader circumstances of any case and the extent to which it was reasonable for a given user to rely on the guidance offered; to the relationship, if any, between the system provider and the user; to the commercial context of the operation of the system; to the level of expertise (legal and technical) of the user; and to the nature of any supplementary human guidance which might have been sought. *The Legal Information Continuum*, therefore, brings the issue sharply into focus but does not provide any short cuts to the likely judicial view on the matter.

Market trends

In my analysis of the pressurized legal market-place in Section 1.4, I did not identify legal publishers amongst the current competitors of legal advisers. Nor would many lawyers.

Yet, the traditional legal publishers around the world and the smaller, entrepreneurial outfits as well, are investing heavily in IT and firmly recognize it is important for the delivery of their conventional products. As publishers produce text retrieval systems on CD-ROM and using hypertext, for example, if we look at *The Legal Information Continuum* as representing a market-place, we can see the legal publishing world is striding forcefully from left to right.

To be sure, they have made greater progress than practising lawyers moving in the other direction. It is true that some more innovative legal practices are charging clients for remote access to their in-house know-how systems; or delivering large contracts in hypertext form, together with additional commentary on the impact of clauses; or developing electronic check-lists and prompts to help clients manage their legal risks. But these initiatives remain exceptional amongst legal practices.

The time is also ripe for new entrants to the market—electronic publishers (not specifically legal) are information service providers, who will also find in law a fruitful area for diversification. And so too might other professional services organizations such as the international accounting and consulting practices (see Section 8.1).

As a simplified model of the legal market-place, therefore, *The Legal Information Continuum* can show quite starkly why fierce competition might be on its way. The packaging and delivery of legal information services using IT may become attractive to other information service providers. So far, in moving from right to left along the continuum, in using IT in the provision of legal service, the legal profession's response has been minimal.

The economics of the Continuum

What are the economics of *The Legal Information Continuum*? What is the impact on the legal market-place of legal guidance being received from some information service in the middle of the continuum? What will become of conventional legal practice?

The cost of legal service along the continuum can be considered from two perspectives; that of the user and that of the provider.

From the user's point of view, the cost of legal service generally increases as it moves from left to right along the continuum. This is to be expected, in that, as we have seen, the information received becomes more focused, more highly structured, and more usable as one moves from raw legal data through information service to advisory service.

User costs

User costs, however, must be further subdivided into base costs and supplementary charges. The base cost is the cost of the guidance received directly from the service without any further supplementary guidance (human or otherwise). But, as we have also seen, it is unlikely that information gleaned from some service towards the left of the continuum will, of itself, be of sufficient guidance to the non-lawyer. The supplementary cost is the cost of any additional service which combines with the base service to provide sufficient guidance, that is, a solution for the user.

The vital point here is that routine legal problems, well modelled in advance in more sophisticated information systems (towards the right hand of the continuum), are unlikely to require much, if any, supplementary service. Routine legal matters thus become pre-packaged, productized, and, it would seem to follow, less costly (and sometimes far less costly) than the expense of conventional legal advisory service in respect of identical legal problems.

In contrast, the non-routine legal problem—the complex or difficult case—will not be settled by reference only to some information system; rather, the full facilities and talents of legal advisory service will need to be brought to bear, either in isolation or in combination with some information service (see Section 8.2).

The net result is a legal market-place in which routine legal matters may be disposed of for modest sums through consultation with some legal information product or service, while the challenging and complex legal conundrums, well deserving of the experts' talents, will remain the province of traditional legal advisory service, and delivered in the time-honoured fashion.

Early signs of this over the last few years can be seen in computer-based debt collection, computer-assisted conveyancing, and personal tax calculation systems. Formerly, each of these applications required the application, on a one-to-one basis, and each time afresh, of lawyers' advisory skills, with the cost structures which that entailed.

All of this, therefore, is good news for the consumer of legal services for whom legal costs may soon be appreciably less as these information systems are developed.

The Theory

Supplier costs

From the supplier's point of view, we can distinguish between establishment costs, development costs, and application costs.

The establishment costs are those incurred in setting up the base of knowledge on which the information or advisory services rely. Other than for the formal legal sources (the raw data) for which the establishment costs might be regarded as those of the legislature itself, establishment costs are generally those incurred in educating the lawyers whose expertise is either embodied in some system or employed in an advisory function. Although the quality of education and its impact on the student and practitioner may vary, this is something of a fixed cost, and its value is reflected socio-economically in terms of the overall contribution of legal understanding to social and commercial life.

The development costs are those overheads attributable to the information or advisory service rendered. For the information system, it will be systems analysis and legal information engineering costs (see Section 8.1), together with the value of the time devoted by lawyers in the development of the systems; whereas with lawyers offering advisory services, there are far fewer preparatory costs but the overheads of running an advisory service are reflected here.

Finally, there are the application costs, which for the information system will be the cost of the system itself (whether sold as a product or service) together with any supplementary costs required in the event of the need for further human guidance. Application costs for legal advisers today are generally based on hourly rates but may move towards some value billing model in the future.

Legal advisory work may well continue to be profitable for lawyers in so far as it is required, but if the central thesis of this book is correct, and routine legal matters will be dealt with through legal information systems, then the market for advisory work may well shrink.

The alternative for the lawyer, in this event, is perhaps clear—the lawyer reorientates her expertise and knowledge and seeks to package and sell it through some information service on a one-to-many basis rather than in the traditional one-to-one advisory manner.

The major commercial challenge here for lawyers in doing so is to retain their foothold as those who are the legal information engineers and suppliers of information because it is likely that new entrants to the market (for example, conventional legal publishers, electronic publishers, and system development companies) may be keen to exploit this market.

For the market itself will be very different from today's. This will be the far larger *latent legal market*. If legal information is more manageable, accessible, and less costly to consult and apply, then it may be that it will be consulted more frequently and the overall value of the market may not diminish (a higher turnover of low margin, legal information consultations may be as financially rewarding for lawyers as the conventional market where there are fewer consultations but higher margins are achieved).

3.4 The Law and the Information Substructure

Turning now to a different relationship between the law and information, there is considerable scope for further thinking and research on the significance for the law of what I call the 'information substructure' in society.

The information substructure is the dominant mechanism by which information is transmitted and conveyed in a society. The academic literature suggests a model for this substructure useful for our analysis—the model proposes four phases of information substructure, where societies are dependent, respectively, on orality, script, print, and then IT. (In part, this follows the analysis of Walter Ong, in his splendid study, *Orality and Literacy*.)

The subject which deserves great scrutiny (an ideal subject for a doctoral research project) is how the substance of the law and the way it is administered differs across these four phases.

Some valuable work has been done here by Ethan Katsh in his book, *The Electronic Media and the Transformation of Law*. I have sought to take this approach further, however, by concentrating on the delivery of legal services to clients and also by taking account of *The Technology Lag* which I believe requires us to consider the impact of being today *between* the phases of print and IT.

It is intuitively obvious that the nature of law and the way it is administered is conditioned by the information systems which are available for its storage and its dissemination. Thus, the information substructure, no doubt in complex and subtle ways, to some extent determines and constrains the quantity of law, the complexity of law, the regularity with which the law changes, and the people who are able to advise on the law. It is clear from research and writings on the history and development of communication as well as from legal anthropology and sociology, that the information substructure of society impacts considerably on each of these factors.

The Theory

And I believe when we look at this impact across four fundamental stages of development and communications—through the stages dominated in turn by orality, script, print and then IT—then we can project, with some confidence, future developments in the administration of justice and the practice of law.

The age of orality

It is hard today to imagine what a society stripped of script, print, and IT might have been like. As Ong puts it: 'Fully literate persons can only with great difficulty imagine what a primary oral culture is like, that is, a culture with no knowledge whatsoever of writing or even of the possibility of writing. Try to imagine a culture where no-one has ever "looked up" anything. In a primary oral culture, the expression "to look up something" is an empty phrase: it would have no conceivable meaning. Without writing, words as such have no visual presence, even when the objects they represent are visual. They are sounds' (page 31).

Nonetheless, we can infer, from what might be regarded as the natural constraints inherent in a community only capable of oral communication, some likely features of the law during the phase of orality.

Although it is probable that the memories of human beings were better exercised and more retentive, it was surely not possible for there to have been huge quantities of detailed regulation covering all aspects of human life. No one could have remembered the equivalent even of tiny fractions of the quantity of law in force today. In the words of Herbert Hart, in *The Concept of Law*, in primitive society there were 'primary rules' of conduct, laying out what was obligatory and prohibited. The law itself was not fixed in canonical, verbal expression, and was not subject to a highly literal interpretation. Rather, the general thrust of the rules of conduct was expressed in fairly general terms, as broad principles of which most people were generally aware.

The content of the law then would have been far less complex and detailed than today's. From our twentieth century armchairs, we might feel it more apposite to characterize this type of law as custom (this kind of retrospective analysis is fraught because it is potentially superficial to assess societies of the past in terms of concepts and models of today).

In any event, change in the law (for want of a more neutral term) would have been fairly infrequent, in large part because there were no mechanisms for formally recording and promulgating such change.

Mastery of the law would have been given to only a few, senior elders of the community, of almost mystical status, who could recite the obligations and prohibitions in force and were called upon to apply them in situations of doubt. They were also responsible for passing down the law from generation to generation.

The era of script

When we turn to reflect on the era of script as the information substructure, Ong is sobering in his findings: 'Writing . . . was a very late development in human history. *Homo sapiens* has been on earth perhaps some 50,000 years . . . The first script, or true writing, that we know, was developed among the Sumerians in Mesopotamia only around the year 3500 BC' (pages 83–4). And again: 'Indeed, language is so overwhelmingly oral that of all the many thousands of languages—possibly tens of thousands—spoken in the course of human history, only around 106 have ever been committed to writing to a degree sufficient to have produced literature, and most of them have never been written at all' (page 7).

With the advent of script, in agrarian society, it became possible in writing (and other pictorial representations) to augment the capacity of human memories and so the quantity of law could and did increase. As it became articulated in a fixed form which was open to scrutiny (admittedly only by the relative few who could read), the law itself came to be expressed with greater precision and rigour. Legal jargon and shorthand evolved as mechanisms for expressing concepts which were frequently deployed and so a new level of complexity was introduced.

Although the recording of change in the law was facilitated by script, the inability to reproduce material and disseminate it widely other than by manual transcription (which was, in any event, error prone) became a natural constraint on the frequency of change.

Again, however, it was necessary to have access to specialists—those who had a grasp of the evolving body of legal concepts and jargon (where the average citizen did not have). These individuals were both sources of advice on conduct and also called upon to settle disputes when the law, as articulated, was in doubt or disagreed upon. These individuals were lawyers. As Katsh puts it: 'it is the development of writing that provided the environment lawyers needed for their development. Lawyers are not found in oral cultures or in minimally literate societies. Where the rules were widely known or disputes were settled nonlegally, a separate group of persons with specialised knowledge about rules would be unnecessary' (page 203).

Print-based society

With the advent of the printing press, in the middle of the fifteenth century, came a revolution in legal as well as social life. As Katsh says: 'Law as we know it would not be possible without the special properties of print . . . print structured the capabilities and functioning of law in various ways. It is not "fine print", as much of the public believes, that characterises the law, but print itself. Print affected the organisation, growth, and distribution of legal information' (page 12).

With print, not only did it become easier to produce text, but, crucially, the capability to reproduce and disseminate printed material, exerted a radical influence. The quantity of legal materials was able to expand rapidly, extending into many more areas of social and commercial life. In a literate society, where the dominant means of expression became print on paper, exhaustive detail and so complexity seemed to evolve as objectives in themselves.

More significantly, with printing's capacity to reproduce and disseminate massive amounts of information came the facility for change in the law. Indeed, the mechanisms for change became more formalized, both in legislating and in the development of case-law through the doctrine of precedent.

More than ever, then, there was, in what became a print-based industrial society, a pressing need for specialist help to handle the increase in quality, complexity as well as the volatility of the law. Advisory and judicial roles became more clearly distinguished and a dedicated legal *profession* and judiciary evolved. Gradually, only suitably trained individuals were permitted, by law, to offer legal advice in certain circumstances, while the dispute resolution process became increasingly formal.

IT—in a transitional phase

Our move into the age of IT has brought the capability for everyone to become printers in their own right. With powerful word processors available, legislators and draftsmen are barely constrained in their capacity to generate the printed word. The reproduction of printed material has also entered a new era: first with photocopying technology; later with transferable word processing files and high capacity laser printers; and, more recently, with telecommunications technology, text can be transmitted and disseminated electronically and at minimal cost.

IT cannot be blamed entirely for the huge quantity of legislation and case-law which is now available (both in print and in electronic form in massive databases), but it has certainly not helped to check the verbosity of legislators around the world. In part, IT has a case to answer in helping to engender hyperregulation.

Similarly, in the age of IT we have legal provisions that are more complex than ever before. The specificity and detail of so much legal material today so often renders the law impenetrable and too complex. It is as if the relentless detail and mathematical imperative of computer programming has, by trans-disciplinary osmosis perhaps, been inculcated into legal draftsmen of today. In a world increasingly dominated by IT, its methods and ethos now permeate our law.

What is more, IT facilitates change in the law. In contrast with the eras of orality and script when change was a rarity, with IT available, the prevailing attitude towards documentation is that it is dynamic *by nature*, and subject to regular alteration, rather than static. At all stages in the life cycle in the generation and application of the law, IT supports rather than inhibits change.

With more legal source material than ever before and with the added challenge of some of this being available in legal databases that are themselves impenetrable, are specialist lawyers more or less in demand in the era of IT? In fact, it appears to have led to an increasingly lawyered society, with vast and growing quantities of law of unparalleled complexity, which, to cap it all, is subject to this unprecedented frequency of change.

On this view, should we not conclude that IT is having a tragic effect on the law? I think not, for to do so would be to make the mistaken assumption that we have completed the move from our industrial print-based society into what can be called the IT-based information society. I believe instead that we are still in a transitional phase between these two eras and what you have just read are some of the rather unfortunate consequences or features of being in this transition. During this transitional phase, the main role of IT will largely be in streamlining and optimizing current legal practices—in automation rather than innovation.

I anticipate that once we are *fully* ensconced in the IT-based information society we will look back on this profile of the law, together with the problems of Chapter One, as but a transitional blip.

The IT-based information society

At the heart of this prediction is *The Technology Lag*. Indeed, the shortcomings of the transitional phase are fine illustrations of the way in which our data processing capabilities have, so far, surpassed our knowledge processing capacity. Word-processing, database, and electronic transmission technologies are all classic applications of the world of data processing, in which the creation, reproduction, and dissemination of printed text have become an art form. Data processing supports quantity, complexity, and change in the law. But we are now refining our techniques in the field of knowledge processing and gradually developing systems which will help us analyse and manage the vast bodies of information we have created for ourselves. And these systems will themselves help us pinpoint *all but only* the material relevant to our particular purposes as users.

Once these technologies are in place, quantity becomes a non-issue because users will be assisted with accuracy in the retrieval of manageable quantities of legal materials; complexity will largely be hidden from them, as systems will effortlessly guide hitherto perplexed users through the labyrinths of the law; and change will either be hidden from the user with updating a continuous phenomenon or, more proactively, be brought to the attention of users by systems which themselves have the ability to monitor all relevant developments for individuals.

Perhaps even more radically, knowledge processing will spawn a multitude of legal information products and services for direct consultation by non-lawyers and so, in the information society, there will be less rather than more reliance on specialist legal advice.

I must stress that this vision of a transformed legal service on the strength of knowledge processing is not one which is likely to be realized in the next few years. Researchers have battled for a quarter of a century in trying to develop knowledge-based systems for lawyers and the results so far have been modest. Elsewhere, however, the investment in using IT to harness the power of information is enormous. I have some considerable confidence (some might say faith) that advances in knowledge processing will be stunning in the coming twenty five years, thus easing us from this transitional period into the fully fledged, IT-based information society. (In passing, on a matter of terminology, I use the term 'information society' in this book where others might refer to the 'knowledge society'. No particular significance should be attached to my preference—the terms can be considered to be interchangeable for current purposes.)

3.5. Legal Service Emerging as an Information Service

It is time now to pull together the many themes that I have introduced in the first three chapters of this book.

My fundamental claim is that IT will enable and help bring about a shift in paradigm of legal service, a fundamental change from a service that is substantially advisory in nature today to one which will become one of many information services in the IT-based information society of the future. In turn, basic aspects of the legal process and the administration of justice will also alter radically.

In the transitional phase between the print-based industrial society and the IT-based information society, where the principal role of IT is in stream-lining and automating, we have also seen that the law is in a disconcerting state of flux, in part due to the impact of IT. We can further see some significant changes which hint strongly at the shape of things to come.

My purpose in this section is to sketch out some likely features of law in the IT-based information society, in which it will emerge, I claim, as a form of information service. Despite the burgeoning performance of IT, the shift in paradigm cannot be complete until *The Technology Lag* is no more. Much of what is said here, therefore, is premised on great advances in knowledge processing as a counterbalance to the great strides already made in data pro-cessing. Once developed and refined, the principal role of knowledge pro-cessing will be in innovating and re-engineering legal service and legal processes rather than automating and streamlining legal practice of today. In this way, the delivery of legal service and the administration of justice will move gradually from right to left along *The Legal Information Continuum*, away in most cases (especially in *the latent legal market*) from the legal advi-sory services of experts towards the IT-based packaging of legal guidance.

My plan of action in highlighting the likely shape of legal information ser-vice in the information society is to assess, in turn, the likely impact on the problems and challenges laid out in Chapter One (although I leave details of technical implementation and thoughts on broader implications until later in the book).

Hyperregulation under control

As I suggested earlier, hyperregulation is a worrying phenomenon which itself has been enabled by IT. Were it not for the staggering ability of technology to capture, create, reproduce, and disseminate information, we would not be nearly as hyperregulated as we find ourselves today. There is some irony, therefore, in the likelihood of IT being hailed as the saviour when in fact it is taking several decades to overcome problems partly of its own creation.

The central point on the control of hyperregulation is that the techniques and applications discussed in the following chapters will, in time, dissolve the problems of quantity and complexity of legal information. It is not that there will be less legal material or that it will necessarily be any clearer in its composition. Rather, the material itself will be organized and made available in a way that will result in both quantity and complexity being hidden from the user. Technology itself will help strip away irrelevant material, presenting to the user *all but only* the relevant information which bears on his immediate concerns. An initial interactive consultation in order to establish the user's area of interest and enquiry will enable the system to pinpoint relevant sources and cut away the mountains of material which have no bearing on the current circumstances. The extent of this mountain should not and will not be of any interest to the user, who will only ever be exposed to manageable quantities of legal information and legal guidance.

Once identified, it will not then be a question of dumping extracts from legislation or case reports onto the user because the materials themselves will be structured and annotated so that he may be led in a controlled way through the material with, for example, check-lists or prompts being provided where appropriate, and with relevant documents being generated along the way.

These techniques will apply equally to the management of legislation and case-law, with these sources intertwining, cross-referring, and synthesizing where appropriate. From the perspective of the non-legal user, the focus will, in any event, be on practical guidance without necessarily exposing the underlying formal sources. The layer of practical notes, check-lists, and commentary may seldom be peeled back by the non-lawyer to expose the underlying, authoritative material.

As it becomes commonplace for judges to draft their judgments in electronic form, these will gradually be transmitted automatically to some repository and later subjected to analysis and synthesis by those lawyers whom I will later describe as legal information engineers (see Section 8.1).

To avoid any misapprehension, it is vital to understand that, in absence of highly developed natural language processing, much of this engineering (the organization, structuring, cross-referencing, and addition of commentary, check-lists, and so forth) has to be done manually by this new breed of lawyer. It is an awesome project to add value in this way to huge amounts of primary source materials. No doubt, it will not prove practical or commercially viable to subject many arcane areas of law to this treatment. But, gradually, in most areas of social and business life, legal information services of this sort will be available.

Reinstating promulgation

When it comes to promulgation, the challenge of its reinstatement (or perhaps its introduction in the first place) is rather different from that of controlling hyperregulation. For hyperregulation, the question was whether or not IT could help overcome the quantity and complexity of legal information. To a large extent there was an assumption that the problem relates to individuals who are already deeply engaged in the activity of searching and sifting through large bodies of information.

With promulgation, in contrast, the challenge is greater because it is that of making lawyers and non-lawyers alike aware, in the first place, of new law or changes in old. While, in principle, our entire statute-book and body of case-law could, for example, be made available on the Internet (and will be, I believe, despite the current controversy over HMSO in the UK), this of itself does not enable everyone to be informed of new and changed laws which apply to them. There is a vast chasm between putting legal sources on the Internet and users learning of the existence of laws which directly impact on them.

Promulgation, meaningfully so called, must extend beyond availability of legal information to the creation of awareness of new and changed laws.

It is entirely foreseeable that emerging technologies will soon enable everyone to be notified of such new and changed laws. In non-technical terms, this would involve users articulating profiles of their social and business lives. At the same time, developments in the law would also be profiled and categorized and there would be mechanisms for automatic notification of these users where there were matches or partial matches between users' profiles and the categorizations of the new legal developments. For businesses, such an information service would be invaluable and the revenue secured from this service could perhaps fuel a low or no cost service of a similar sort for individual citizens.

Overcoming reactivity

The shortcomings of reactive lawyering cannot be overcome by lawyers acting in their advisory capacity. If their clients are to manage their legal risks effectively, by conducting legal risk audits, and introducing legal input earlier in the life cycle of transactions, projects, and disputes, then new techniques will be required to provide this legal input in a more cost effective and assimilable way than through direct involvement of lawyers.

In information terms, the challenge here is to make the necessary legal knowledge and expertise available at the ideal time but without the need for direct consultation with lawyers on each and every occasion. What about a computer-based check-list or set of prompts which takes the owner of a small business through key areas of legal risk, including, for example, likely liabilities, defects in document management, and basic questions of employment law? Or for salesmen out in the field who are anxious to clinch a deal and might otherwise expose their organizations to unnecessary legal risk, a similar check-list or an automated document generation system could reduce exposure for their companies.

Here we would have management of legal risks which would otherwise go uncontrolled. These are illustrations of the realization of *the latent legal market* in which legal information products and services are helping to provide timely guidance.

More generally, IT will be a key enabler in the development of proactive legal services. Proactivity requires earlier legal input into projects, transactions, and disputes and this may only be possible through consultation with legal information systems rather than with legal advisers which is so often neither practicable nor viable today.

Relieving the pressure on the legal market-place

Many lawyers believe that IT is set to increase rather than decrease the pressures on the legal market-place. They fear that an already shrinking market will be streamlined to an extent that some or many lawyers will not survive. For those who confine themselves to competing in the traditional legal market, it could well be that only the fittest and leanest will endure. The rest have the option of engaging or developing entrepreneurial talents which can help them flourish in *the latent legal market*. As ever, suicide is an option not a necessity.

It is therefore only the conventional legal market-place in today's legal paradigm which I believe is a pressurized one. *The latent legal market* of tomorrow's legal paradigm is a land of opportunity, where lawyers make a business of legal information systems and users benefit from legal input where this would not have been possible or viable in the past.

Signs of change

Even in the current legal paradigm, there are indications of the emergence of this legal information services market (see also Section 6.3).

Imaginatively produced legal information packs are now being sold in bookshops, offering guidance, for example, on landlord and tenant agreements, debt recovery, the pursuit of small claims, as well as will drafting, taxation, and conveyancing. Standard form documentation is provided alongside step-by-step help, which takes the user patiently through each phase of the process in question. These would sit on the right-most edge of the part of *The Legal Information Continuum* which we allocated to conventional publications, because they go well beyond declaration or recasting of the law and distil the sources into directly usable form.

IT has already taken these packs a further step, mainly for lawyers at this stage, but paving the way for legal products for the consumer. I have already mentioned the computer-based debt collection systems, computer-assisted conveyancing and tax calculation applications that are now readily available. These operate on processes which, in the past, required the one-to-one attention of lawyers' advisory skills, each time afresh. They have now been routinized and systematized.

With the great leaps in IT which it is reasonable to expect, such systems and many others will be upgraded and become available for direct use by non-lawyers.

And when legal information products and services become widespread, the problems of hyperregulation, promulgation, and reactive service will dissolve. Citizens will have less justification for disillusionment. Businesses will benefit from more readily available legal guidance and lawyers will have a fresh set of challenges in a world where legal sources will become more manageable. This will be a society integrated with, rather than alienated from, the law and will constitute, in the end, a fundamental shift in legal paradigm. Before we can look harder at that world, it is appropriate to spend some time understanding the enabling techniques, the leading applications, and then the practicalities which will make the new legal paradigm a reality.

PART TWO—
THE TECHNOLOGIES

4

Enabling Techniques

I must confess to having been hesitant about including this chapter in the book. It is about the various techniques of IT which I believe will enable lawyers and others to benefit from the applications discussed in Chapter Five.

The techniques which I introduce now (summarized in Figure 4.1) will, in my view, be at the heart of the IT which will improve and change the practice of law and the administration of justice. The question of how these techniques will be used in practice is deferred until later (in Chapters Five and Six).

Figure 4.1 Enabling Techniques

enhanced text retrieval
hypertext
expert systems
document image processing
telecommunications
groupware and workflow
graphical user interface
voice recognition

One main difficulty here is that the technicalities are always in danger of distracting the enthusiast from the key issues of strategy and policy which should underlie most uses of IT. I believe passionately that the enabling techniques, as I call them, are of no particular significance in themselves. What is crucial is how they are used.

The Technologies

Yet it amazes me how often I am asked to advise lawyers on their strategic use of IT and arrive at their premises to be confronted with a newly purchased scanner. The person who has been responsible for the procurement then launches into a Messianic justification for the new toy, exhibiting one of the primary pitfalls in IT, that of being led and driven by the technology itself and constrained by no underlying business purpose.

My objective in introducing the crucial enabling techniques is not, therefore, to encourage their immediate purchase but to provide sufficient background detail to help clarify how the applications work and deliver benefits.

That said, the world of lawyers can be divided into those who are inherently interested in IT and those who are most certainly not; those who enjoy taking the back off a computer to see how it operates and those who have no interest in doing so; indeed, those who keep a screwdriver in their desk drawers in anticipation of some repair or enhancement and those who are content to leave such tasks to others. Both categories of lawyers may be interested in this chapter but those of the more technically inclined camp may be disappointed that I do not delve into too much technical detail. For the other camp (which is far more heavily populated), this will probably be a relief.

The techniques discussed are not confined to those that will underlie future systems for lawyers. Rather, the analysis extends also to those, such as expert systems and hypertext, which will support the delivery of legal information and guidance directly to non-lawyers.

Although dealt with separately for the introductory purposes of this chapter, the techniques should not be regarded as distinct and self-contained. In practice, as Chapter Five shows, some of the most potent applications in the law combine and employ various techniques at once—there is therefore no simple one-to-one mapping between enabling techniques and applications.

The first three techniques discussed in this chapter—enhanced text retrieval, hypertext, expert systems—have already been mentioned in the context of *The Legal Information Continuum*. These are of particular relevance to the packaging and presentation of legal information. The other techniques—document image processing, telecommunications, groupware and workflow, the graphical user interface, and voice recognition—are something of a mixed bag, in that they do not all support legal service and the legal process in the same way. Nonetheless, they are, in my view, all very significant for law and lawyers.

Finally, by way of preamble to these crucial enabling techniques, I have not dealt with those that are already mainstream, such as word processing and simple databases, or back office, for example, practice management systems. The emphasis instead is on those emerging and vital techniques which will build upon those that are already influentially and successfully deployed.

4.1. Enhanced Text Retrieval

Since the era of script, the bulk of lawyers' work has been with text—in digesting, creating, storing, and communicating text. Whether in script or print, text has been absolutely fundamental to legal practice and to the administration of justice. With the advent of IT, an additional text processing function has now become a reality—that of searching within text which is stored in what is known as machine readable form. When stored in this format, it is possible to search for specific words without having to read through the entire document set in which they occur.

At least, that is the theory. And it suggests that text retrieval techniques should be able to support two of our six basic *legal tasks*—document management and information consultation. As I shall show, however, that theory is defective, largely because it does not accord with reality. In the real world, basic text retrieval is too often fettered by crucial shortcomings. But these may gradually be overcome by a variety of promising enhancements.

A potted history of text retrieval in law

It is said that the legal profession stumbled upon legal research by text retrieval through the work of John Horty in the late 1950s. Horty had been given the unenviable job of changing each and every occurrence of the term 'retarded child' in Pennsylvanian state legislation with the less pejorative 'exceptional child'. But so full of errors did he find this task when done manually that he decided to try to harness early text processing technology to undertake what we would now call a global find and replace routine. Once the relevant text had been translated into machine readable form with a view to conducting this exercise, Horty quickly saw that he could use the system in another way. He could select words and the system could jump immediately and painlessly to all their occurrences throughout the regulations. Thus was born legal research using computers.

The doubters were quick to claim that this technique was surely only suited to legislative and regulatory material where the terminology was relatively constrained and formal. In England, during the 1960s, Colin Tapper showed otherwise and his early research suggested that text retrieval could be equally useful when applied to case-law. And in the mid and late 1960s, the same enabling technique was also brought to bear in helping to search through huge document loads in litigation.

Basic text retrieval

Turning to details of the technology itself, the general idea, as the name suggests, is to store documents in such a way that they can be retrieved by instructing the computer to search through the text for the occurrence of words. These words are often referred to as 'keywords' and can be searched for in isolation or in combination. For example, the user of a system that holds large quantities of regulatory and background information on environmental matters, could require the system to search for all occurrences of the word 'waste' and the system would then identify all those documents in which that term appears. Alternatively, or additionally, the user may wish to search for those documents in which the word waste occurs within a specified number of words of another term such as 'toxic'. Through a number of techniques, the searches can be refined and achieve considerable sophistication, allowing for conjunction ('ands'), disjunction ('ors') and other combinations of words. Ideally, users are able to formulate their searches to yield a manageable number of 'hits'; and some systems even seek to provide some kind of relevancy ranking which suggests which of the hits are most likely to be of use (in practice, this is often rather crudely done).

Perhaps the best known commercial system in the legal profession is LEXIS, one of the largest databases in the world. This system spans many jurisdictions and holds huge quantities of primary and secondary legislation, case reports, and secondary writings as well. The LEXIS system, perhaps more than any other, has confirmed the potential of managing large amounts of regulatory information using text retrieval techniques. And there are a growing number of rival databases which operate under similar principles. Like LEXIS, some of these systems are 'on-line' which means the user has to dial up and access a host machine in another location while, more recently, entire text retrieval systems are available for standalone machines on CD-ROM.

Whatever particular techniques are used, however, the underlying motivation is the same—to make textual information available in searchable format so that users are able to identify documents on the basis of words which occur within them. While this has proven to be a powerful technique, it must be conceded that this method of accessing documents by keyword search requests is not without difficulty. In particular, sloppy, naive or inexperienced users can produce searches that are formulated too widely, in which case the system retrieves an excess of documents, many of which are irrelevant. Alternatively, too restrictive selection of keywords can result in failure to identify all relevant documents.

We are a long way from the ideal, that of these systems having total and precise recall, being able, that is to say, to retrieve *all but only* the relevant documents for a user's particular purposes.

So although this basic text retrieval may seem superficially attractive, unless users are skilled in the formulation of keywords, results of the use of these systems are often disappointing. There is, of course, far more to legal research and problem solving than searching for the occurrence of words within documents. The immediate attraction of having huge volumes of text at users' disposal is somewhat dampened by experience of trying to retrieve all but only what is relevant in the circumstances. Here we can see *The Technology Lag* in action very clearly—IT offers a fine and seemingly bottomless storage medium but it is far from spectacular in helping users get at what they want.

It is also fair to say that the utility of these systems does vary according to the type of text being searched. Generally, the more formal and structured the document type, the more useful these systems tend to be. For example, when users search within statutory materials and they are familiar with legislative drafting, they can make educated guesses about the likely language of the draftsmen. However, where the information stored is letters of advice to clients or file notes, the range of terms and expressions is far wider and less technical; and accurate searching is far more difficult. What is more, in searching using systems such as LEXIS you will often not know in advance if there is in fact any document which will satisfy your search request. In contrast, with litigation support systems, the user has frequently read the entire document set beforehand and is searching for a document he has already seen (he may remember that the document mentioned the name 'Monty' and so search, no doubt with considerable success, for all documents containing that name).

Generally, however, it is widely agreed both by lawyers and by information scientists that there is room for substantial improvement in basic text retrieval technology; and that the improvements should tackle shortcomings which we can attribute both to human users and to the technology itself.

Some improvements involve the integration of basic retrieval with other, quite different techniques, such as hypertext and document image processing, both of which are also discussed in this chapter. At this stage, in reviewing what I term enhanced text retrieval systems, I prefer to concentrate on three other techniques which are better regarded as natural extensions to the basic technology. Together, these three enhancements are likely to improve the utility of text retrieval systems greatly and so move the technology significantly from left to right on *The Legal Information Continuum*.

Intelligent agents

One of the latest and most intriguing techniques for overcoming the problems of basic text retrieval is that of 'intelligent agents'. Although still the subject of more experimentation and speculation than actual live usage, the fundamental idea is eminently plausible and strikes me as being of great potential. Intelligent agents (of one type) are programs which can be instructed to roam around specified bodies of new information in search of materials which are likely to be of interest to those who instruct them. Like tireless and ever-willing paralegals, these agents monitor the content of documents as they are loaded and draw attention to those that seem relevant.

While it might be thought that intelligent agents would need to work on the basis of natural language processing and are therefore beyond the scope of current technology (see Section 2.5), they need not be that sophisticated. On one model, intelligent agents could work like this. A user would build up a detailed profile of her social and business interests selecting these from a rich set of categories which have been articulated in advance. At the same time, the information services community would commit not just to loading the entire text of documents but also to providing further information which classifies all searchable materials, using the same category set as that employed for users' profiles. The intelligent agents can be instructed for a specified or indefinite period to monitor all new materials and to identify all matches, in effect, between the interests of the user and the subject matter of the new information. Thus, a user passionate about nineteenth century French painting and concerned about European environmental regulations relating to waste might log on to her machine in the morning to learn of an auction in her locality and a high powered meeting of ministers in Brussels.

Alternatively, such information would be ready and waiting on the breakfast table, embodied in that same user's *Daily Me*. This is the fascinating notion, as described by Nicholas Negroponte in *Being Digital*, of a personalized newspaper which is generated each day but is filled only with items which have been specified in advance as being of interest to the particular reader. (The prospect of never receiving a newspaper stuffed with reports of cricket or football is, for me, joyous beyond words. Instead, my *Daily Me* would have huge coverage of track athletics.)

For intelligent agents to work, user profiles and document classifications must be detailed, accurate, and precise. Even then, given the amount of information being generated in our world, users will be well-advised to state further requirements. For example, a user might add refinements such as his preference for no academic articles, for pieces only in the English language, and for no items more than 2,000 words in length. Additionally, most users might want, in the first instance, to be provided only with an index of relevant items (perhaps ordered according to superficial relevancy) indicating matters such as the title, author, length, level of technical detail, and the source of each piece of information.

In any event, there is more than a glimmer here of a useful tool to help diminish the effects of *The Technology Lag*, with technology itself being used to seek to overcome information overload.

In relation to the law, intelligent agents are a promising technique to help encourage promulgation, in that new legal developments could be brought automatically to the attention of lawyers and non-lawyers. There is the basis here also for an innovative information service for clients—as lawyers add materials to their own in-house know-how systems (see Section 5.4), these could also be classified so that relevant materials could immediately be routed to clients with matching profiles. With clients operating on the same groupware system (see Section 4.6), notification of the arrival of this information could pop up on their screens and the details could be accessed there and then. There would be no need to dial up periodically to see if anything new had arrived.

Intelligent agents should offer an especially proactive enhancement to basic text retrieval systems in that they might deliver information even when it has not been explicitly requested for a particular purpose. It is, then, the basis of a novel form of information service rather than a way of improving an existing advisory service.

For those users who do not aspire to such proactivity, there are other enhancements which support the more traditional explicit searching on particular occasions for specific purposes. Most notably there is conceptual retrieval and augmented search formulation.

Conceptual retrieval

Those who argue that there is more to legal problem solving than searching for the occurrence of keywords within documents will often suggest that legal reasoning and research involves familiarity with, and manipulation of, legal *concepts*. Legal work is not about words, the argument will run; the key issue is surely that of meaning. Users want to identify documents that concern their problems. Whether or not they contain particular words is rarely a concern in itself.

Accordingly, groups of researchers have developed methods of augmenting the basic approach to text retrieval with what are referred to as conceptual retrieval techniques. The objective here is to allow users to search through massive bodies of legal data, not just on the basis of the occurrence of keywords but in terms also of the fundamental concepts relating to any problem at hand. This could mean, for example, that systems will search not only for the precise words—the strings of characters—articulated by the users but also for words that, as some might say, are 'semantically implicit in' or 'conceptually analogous to' these original requests.

The first generation of such systems offered thesaurus facilities, so that a search for 'contract' would also identify documents in which there appeared synonymous terms such as 'agreement' (rather than users needing to search explicitly for 'contract' *or* 'agreement' and to rack their brains for all other synonyms).

Later generations of systems have been far more ambitious and continue to be the subject of scholarly research (although there are few available today on a commercial basis). These systems go well beyond the location of words and their synonyms into the world of artificial intelligence and one of its sub-disciplines, that of natural language processing. One approach, for example, is to seek to build models of central legal concepts, models which can be embodied in search requests and even retained for use again at a later stage.

When searching for 'contract' using this approach, a user might build a new conceptual model of contract, or use an existing model. Such a model might include some kind of representation (often depicted as a network with quite abstract relations between people, actions, events, and things) of the fundamental components of a valid contract, such as offer and acceptance, consideration, the intention of the parties to create a binding legal relationship, and so forth. The system would then seek to analyse bodies of text in an attempt to find documents whose words and phrases corresponded to the elements of the model. Thus, in this example, a document might be retrieved and declared by the system to be relevant not because it contains the word 'contract' or any of its synonyms, but in virtue, as it were, of its general drift and language, which matches and satisfies the underlying model of contract.

This more advanced approach does require very rich natural language processing capabilities which are not yet easy to use. Nor indeed, as I have said, are they widely available. Indeed, given my earlier observations about the obstacles facing the field of natural language processing (see Section 2.5), it may be that the AI approach is destined to disappoint for many years. I have wondered for some time, however, if there may be a useful analogy here with voice recognition. Just as the AI research in that field failed to deliver commercially usable systems and it was a statistical approach that brought that technology to the market-place (see Section 4.8), then so too with text retrieval systems—I would welcome more work on statistical modelling techniques for legal text retrieval to determine if that might yield more positive, practical applications.

Augmented search formulation

My third and final category of enhancement for basic text retrieval systems comprises tools which help users in actually formulating the search requests themselves. The principle here is that guidance on the use of a system is offered to users before the actual searching within the database begins. Search formulation is a formidable speciality in its own right and users should welcome any help they can obtain. Every observation made in this connection can apply equally to the development of intelligent agents.

One tack is to develop a 'front end' to a system. This operates as an interactive module which takes the hands of less experienced users and patiently walks them through the process of articulating and refining searches, offering prompts and guidance throughout the consultation. It will ask the user questions, help to pinpoint relevant terms and concepts, and assist in ensuring that the request leads to that overriding objective of retrieving *all but only* the relevant documents. Using a powerful front-end should be like having a first-rate 'power user' at your side, a coach and trainer whose expertise is passed along to you as you work. These systems can be built using classical 'knowledge engineering' techniques of artificial intelligence—and in the spirit of expert systems (see Section 4.3) they can embody the knowledge of expert users of text retrieval systems and make that expertise available to others. This type of enhancement works best, however, if confined to relatively small and manageable aspects of search formulation.

Another approach to offering support in search formulation is having access to what might be regarded as off-the-shelf search requests. Rather than re-inventing the wheel and agonizing over some request which others may already have articulated before, users will gradually have access to pre-articulated searches. Some of these might be particularly complex or useful search requests which colleagues within the user's own organization have spent time developing and have been saved as a piece of know-how for future use. For example, if a skilled user of a text retrieval system spent some time articulating a search request that would help identify most documents relevant to the topic of 'collateral warranties', it would be helpful for later users with similar requirements to draw that request from a library of past search requests and so avoid repetition of the formulation process.

Looking further ahead, it can be expected that a law firm will enjoy competitive advantage over others if it has a range of these pre-articulated search requests which enables the delivery of a better or quicker or cheaper service to clients. These search requests (heuristics of a sort) could serve as key in-house stock-in-trade for lawyers. Or they could become a tradable commodity in their own right: libraries of search requests may be marketed to clients and even competitors (if the price is right). These would be particularly valuable if rich, conceptual models were involved.

4.2. Hypertext

Of all the enabling techniques with which I have been involved during the past five years, none in my experience has captured the imagination and stimulated more interest amongst lawyers than hypertext, a technology which dates back to the mid-1960s. Indeed, it is often said that hypertext will be to the lawyer what the spreadsheet has become for the accountant; that it is an enabling technique which corresponds perfectly to the natural working habits of those who deal with legal materials. Having seen several powerful hypertext systems operating in practice and delivering benefits in a commercial context, I think these observations are not wildly off the mark. Certainly, we can expect many of our crucial legal documents of the future to be enhanced and delivered through the use of this technique.

In relation to the six categories of *legal tasks* of Section 3.2, hypertext most obviously impacts on document drafting by adding further layers of information to documents which are created; on document management especially in the control of lawyer's work product; on information consultation in that hypertext presents users with a highly intuitive means of browsing through legal documents and materials; and on following procedures by offering the means of packaging legal guidance in the form of check-lists or intelligent on-screen prompts.

Sadly for current purposes, the concept of hypertext is far easier to demonstrate than to describe. Ten seconds into a live demonstration invariably engenders the response 'ah ha', in contrast with even the most articulate explanations which tend to leave audiences confused.

The potential recognised

My favourite route into revealing the power and potential of hypertext is through an anecdote relating to a project with which I was involved in the late 1980s. This was the development of the Latent Damage System (discussed in greater detail in Section 6.1), which I believe was the world's first commercially available expert system in law. The heart of the system is a complex, rule-based representation of this arcane area of law, a model of England's leading authority on the topic at that time, Phillip Capper. This is a legal diagnostic expert system (see Section 4.3) with over two million alternative paths through it. It works on the basis of an interactive consultation with the user, whose answers to questions determine the particular path taken by the system. At the end of the consultation the system offers a number of conclusions, the central one being the date after which the legal action in question can no longer be raised.

Almost as an afterthought in designing the system, we decided to add a body of 'help screens', chunks of text which users could browse through if they wanted further explanations of the questions, or an indication of the thinking underlying the queries, or references to relevant legislation and case-law. The question and answer session is suspended while users read these help screens. In preparing each screen, we chose about six to eight interesting concepts from each page of text, and created small menus at the bottom of each screen, from which the user could select and then have the opportunity to explore the selected item in more detail. For example, one screen alludes to the overlap between contract and tort and that overlap is itself picked out as a menu item. If the user wants to know more about this issue, he simply selects that item (entitled, 'contract and tort') and is taken immediately to further clarification of this overlap. In this way, the user can navigate around hundreds of help screens, clarifying difficult concepts and dipping into source materials as well.

When the system was completed, we demonstrated it widely. Despite the power of the rule-based expert system component, there was (rather frustratingly for the designers) greater and universal acclaim for the help system. Lawyers liked the idea of being able to browse and navigate across pages of text and in so doing having greater control over the direction of a research enquiry than the more rigid expert system structure allowed.

This help system was, unbeknown to us, an early version of a hypertext system in law.

The nature of hypertext

Today, users of modern hypertext systems are now presented with text on screen which, at first sight, looks like an excerpt from a word processor (WP) file or from a conventional publication. Hypertext adds value to conventional, two dimensional text, however, by allowing its users to jump, in a variety of ways, from the document they are viewing (in the manner of the 'help' facilities which come with most Microsoft Windows-based software). By pointing a mouse at 'live' parts of the text, or on 'buttons' as they are often called, and then clicking, a user can, for example, follow up a cross-reference and be transported to another part of the same document or perhaps to another document altogether. The user can stay at the new portion of text or backtrack to the original. At other places, the user can point and click at different words and a definition of the selected word will pop up on the screen. More advanced systems also allow users to launch other applications, such as spreadsheet or multi-media presentations, again by clicking on an appropriate button.

Although hypertext has been likened to an 'electronic book', this belies its navigational flexibility and its capability to integrate with other techniques. It also neglects the task of the author which is considerably more onerous when a hypertext system is being developed than when a manuscript is being prepared for conventional publication.

In a traditional printed book, the words, sentences, pages, and chapters are presented in the order constructed by the author. It is generally assumed that a book will be read sequentially and the task of conventional authoring takes this for granted. This is supported by the very physical nature of books, which, although amenable to browsing through indexes and contents pages, are nonetheless discrete and self-contained bodies of information contained between two covers.

The author of a hypertext system, in contrast, creates an information space around which readers will roam, often in directions and along pathways not directly conceived by their originator. Linking also to other bodies of information and applications of IT, the author in the information age does not have the luxury of operating with text which will be read linearly within a finite number of pages. The production of the various linkages is of itself a major additional task.

For legal material, the essence of hypertext is its ability to link documents together electronically so that users, with no technical knowledge at all, are able to browse through a body of information, jumping, at the click of a mouse, from one document to another. It is an ideal mechanism for enabling users to follow up cross-references (where in the past fingers would be kept inserted in many places in a book), for providing context sensitive help, and generally for offering a navigational tool through which users can browse around legal and related information.

Further, hypertext applications can be delivered in a form which allows the users themselves to embed links or add comments while browsing through the text.

So full implementation of hypertext is not simply the display of pieces of text on screen, but is a mechanism which can enable users to contribute to, as well as navigate freely and undaunted around, vast and highly complex information spaces. Hypertext hides the quantity and complexity of documents from its users. It is, as might be expected from its name, one natural antidote for hyperregulation.

An illustration of hypertext

An illustration of the application of hypertext technology is the FIDIC system developed at Masons. The system holds the full text of Parts I and II of FIDIC, the standard form, international construction and engineering contract. Users, who need have no technical expertise, are confronted initially with what looks like the contents sheet of the contract. By pointing and clicking at elements in the contents list, the system will take users to selected clauses and thence to sub-clauses.

It offers users a number of additional facilities. For example, if a term is contractually defined within the agreement, then the definition of the term can be called up onto the screen simply by placing a cursor over the relevant word in the text and clicking on a button of the mouse. Similarly, whenever there is a cross-reference to another clause, then the user can jump to this part of the contract, again just by pointing and clicking. Other information is also held in readily accessible form, so that a user wanting explanation of the clauses of the contract can, once more, at the touch of a button, call up context sensitive expert commentary, prepared by a specialist construction lawyer, which clarifies each clause and sub-clause, as required by the user.

The system also combines full text retrieval systems with hypertext, so that users might search in the first instance for documents on the basis of keyword occurrence. Then, having identified some relevant documents, they are able thereafter to jump easily into other relevant documents that have been linked, to the retrieved materials, in anticipation of users' needs.

This system demonstrates a very powerful way in which technology can animate text, and help users manage what would otherwise be very complicated cross-referencing between documents.

Hypertext in law

Using analogous techniques, various legal publishers have now recognized the power of hypertext; and hyper-linking, as it is known, is becoming common in electronic legal publications. Instead of reading footnotes to legislation on paper, for instance, users can instead point, click, and then jump on screen from regulatory material to relevant commentary and notes and from there onto, say, the text of pertinent case reports and analysis. Here is an exciting way to animate legal texts which hitherto have been published conventionally using print on paper. Exciting though it is, however, most contemporary attempts to use hypertext still fall firmly into the category of automation. They tend to involve presenting conventional books on computer screens, with some text searching thrown in; but they do not yet offer any fundamentally new way of undertaking legal research. The full power of hypertext is not yet being harnessed in the law, which is probably a temporary phenomenon characteristic of the transitional phase between the print-based and IT-based societies (see Section 3.4).

I have a related concern about hypertext and that is that it may become typecast as many commentators extol its virtues only as an advanced publishing tool. The danger here again is that of overlooking all manner of other innovative applications to which this enabling technique is well suited. For example, law firms can also use hypertext as a medium for the delivery of contracts they have drafted, so that clients may receive a final agreement'in electronic form packaged perhaps with commentary on a clause by clause basis enabling users not just to read the actual terms and conditions themselves but also to dip into some expert gloss and clarification and to navigate around the documents through the cross-references. Here the client would receive a traditional legal service (contract drafting) as well as a proactive legal product—an information service offering ongoing guidance on the impact of the contract. While some lawyers would reject this out of hand as reducing their future market for advisory work arising out of the contract, others may see this form of service as a source of added value, differentiation, and competitive advantage. In the latter group, some may seek to charge clients for providing such an information service while the remainder might choose to absorb the development costs and bundle the information service with the advisory service.

Other applications of hypertext abound. When combined with groupware (see Section 4.6), for example, this technique can be deployed as a fine work product management tool, enabling a team of lawyers to collaborate effectively and share the fruits of their labour in a usable way—this is illustrated in the context of a case-study relating to a piece of litigation in Section 6.1.

Hypertext is also ideally suited as the basis of what can be called on-screen prompts, sets of steps which guide users through complex procedures, especially where there are detailed and specific requirements with which compliance is expected (see Section 5.4). Masons has developed such prompts for the process of preparing bundles for trial in the High Court and for taking out injunctions. Equally, this can be used as a vehicle for the delivery of legal know-how directly to non-lawyers. I have prepared such check-lists for activities such as attending a business meeting and handling telephone calls, which put sound legal practice at the fingertips of non-lawyers in situations where they would otherwise be unlikely to seek legal advice. Domestic applications are also conceivable. Prompts and check-lists could easily be compiled, for instance, to guide lay people on what steps to take after a motor accident or in the event of dissatisfaction with goods that have been purchased.

Most significantly perhaps, in a far wider context than that of law, hypertext is rapidly becoming the favoured technology to support the delivery of information services generally. This is most immediately apparent in the World Wide Web (often known simply as the Web—see Sections 4.5 and 5.1), the facility that has been in large part responsible for the burgeoning interest in the Internet. The Web offers users of the Internet a much needed navigational facility so that they are able to browse more easily around the massive bodies of information. Leaving the details aside, the key point for now is that the underlying technique for this navigation and browsing is hypertext and the intuitive pointing, clicking, and jumping to which I referred earlier is ever-present for users of the Web. The impact of this is likely to be considerable because the publicity, exposure, and prevalence of the Web is such that its mode of operation itself will set *de facto* standards for information services. In turn, for the law to be packaged in this way will

119

seem natural to Web users and so less forbidding than the specialized publications or legal information systems of the past.

As a means of structuring and organizing legal material, of providing commentary on such documentation, and of pulling related material into one easily accessible information source, hypertext stands out, therefore, as the most likely candidate for the most far-reaching exploitation in the 1990s and well beyond.

Here, as in so many other dimensions, however, standards must also be developed. While our presentation and publication of legal materials in conventional forms has evolved and become relatively standardized over centuries, it is, of course, still early days for hypertext. In practical terms, legal hypertext systems of today tend to look, feel, and handle very differently. There are no conventions amongst publishers, for example, regarding the appearance of buttons (should words be in particular colours, fonts, or sizes?) and there are substantial variations in style and approach even between systems produced by the same supplier. For the user, this can be very confusing. A reader knows what to expect from a book but it will take time for that same level of confidence and comfort to be engendered by hypertext systems.

4.3. Expert Systems

Artificial Intelligence (AI), as I have mentioned, is concerned with the development of computer systems that can perform tasks and solve problems of a sort for which human intelligence is normally thought to be required. For example, AI programs have been written to understand the spoken and written word, to translate from one language into another, and to recognize images and objects in the physical world. Many techniques of AI have been applied in law, including neural networks, case-based reasoning (which does not mean reasoning with case-law), logic programming, and natural language processing.

Expert systems and knowledge-based systems

Further categories of AI system, which I have always felt held the greatest promise for legal practice, are referred to as 'knowledge-based systems' and 'expert systems'. These are closely related and are computer applications that contain representations of knowledge and expertise, respectively, which they can apply—much as human beings do—in solving problems, offering advice, and undertaking a variety of other tasks.

In law, the idea is that these systems will apply their legally oriented knowledge in guiding users through complex legal issues; in identifying solutions to problems; in planning tasks, compiling documents, and managing the flow of cases; and even in offering advice and making specific recommendations.

The broadly agreed goal of workers in the fields of expert systems and knowledge-based systems is to use computer technology to make scarce expertise and knowledge more widely available and easily accessible. For the lawyer, having this access to scarce, valuable expertise at the touch of a button can, in principle, give rise to greater quality and productivity and quicker, more efficient service; this as well as a patent competitive advantage over firms not using the technology. The client too would benefit: from a higher quality of service and, in principle, a speedier and cheaper one at that. And looking ahead, this distillation and encapsulation of expertise will gradually be available to the non-lawyer as a very advanced form of information service.

If there is any distinction at all between expert systems and knowledge-based systems, it is that the former are more powerful than the latter in that the former hold expertise and not just knowledge. For present purposes, I use the term expert systems fairly widely to encompass knowledge-based systems as well.

Expert systems are likely to have greatest impact on three of the *legal tasks* introduced in Section 3.2—document drafting, following procedures, and analysis and problem solving. This is apparent from four identifiable classes of expert systems as applied in law.

Diagnostic systems

These systems offer specific solutions to problems presented to them. From the facts of any particular case, as elicited by such a system, it will analyse the details and draw conclusions, usually after some kind of interactive consultation. These systems are analogous to the medical diagnostic systems which make diagnoses on the basis of symptoms presented to them. An example of a diagnostic system in law would be a taxation system that could pinpoint the extent to which and why a person is liable to pay tax, doing so on the basis of a mass of details provided to it. The first commercially available diagnostic system was The Latent Damage System, developed by Phillip Capper and me. That system identifies, in cases involving latent damage, the date after which a legal action is time barred, and is described in greater detail in Section 6.1.

A diagnostic system can be likened to a law book that rewrites itself, each time it is consulted, so as to address and solve the particular problem of each reader; or to a book that will point automatically to all but only those of its sentences, paragraphs, and pages which are relevant for any given legal question.

Planning systems

In a sense, planning systems reason in reverse. For these systems are told about a desired solution or outcome and their purpose is to identify scenarios, involving both factual and legal premises, that justify the preferred conclusion. In tax law, a planning system could recommend how a taxpayer should best arrange his affairs so as to minimize his exposure to liability. The knowledge held within planning systems can be very similar to that within diagnostic systems. What is quite different is the way that that knowledge is applied. The best known planning systems operate in the tax field and have been developed by the large accountancy and consulting firms.

A fine example of a planning system is THUMPER, an expert system that advises on Stamp Duty. The user of THUMPER indicates what specific commercial transaction is under consideration, such as the acquisition of a business. In turn, the user is invited to indicate only those matters that bear on the transaction under consideration and which may have impact on any liability to stamp duty. The system analyses the facts presented to it and generates a report on the stamp duty payable, referring also to any relevant exemptions; and as trends emerge, the system is then able to provide planning advice.

The intelligent check-list

This third category of system assists in auditing or reviewing compliance with legal regulations. Compliance reviews must be undertaken with relentless attention to detail and extensive reference to large bodies of regulations. Intelligent check-lists provide a technique for performing such reviews. They formalize the process. In taxation, an intelligent check-list approach could be used to assist in the review of a company's compliance with value added tax (see Section 6.1 for a description of the VATIA system). More generally, many law firms have now developed fairly structured paper-based check-lists and these could themselves be expanded and developed into intelligent systems (perhaps in conjunction with hypertext as well).

Intelligent check-lists can also assist with complex tasks which require extensive expertise and knowledge that is in fact procedural in kind. Intelligent check-lists can act as procedural guides, taking their users through such complex and extended procedures, ensuring that all matters are attended to and done so within any prescribed time periods. An example of such a system would be one that managed the flow of a complex tax evasion case, providing detailed guidance and support from inception through to final disposal. Some of the so-called decision support systems (for example, for debt collection or conveyancing) could well form the basis of more sophisticated knowledge-based procedural guides. There is also an overlap here with workflow systems (see Section 4.6).

Document assembly systems

Finally, there is document assembly, an approach to computer-assisted drafting rapidly gaining popularity in North America. It is the first application of expert systems to gain acceptance amongst UK lawyers. These automated document generation systems—also referred to as document modelling systems—store templates set up by legal experts. These templates contain fixed portions of text together with precise indications as to the conditions under which given extracts should be used. In operation, such a system will elicit from its user all the details relevant to a proposed document. This is done by the user answering questions, responding to prompts, and providing information. On the basis of the user's input, the system will automatically generate a customized and polished document relying on its knowledge of how its text should be used. In the short term, this sub-field of expert systems is likely to yield the most promising commercial applications for lawyers. Indeed in the US there are over twenty software packages available for the development of document assembly systems; while some firms actually sell finished applications that other practices then purchase and use. For an extended case-study of document assembly, see Section 6.3.

Questions of feasibility

Can legal expertise really be extracted from human experts, then transferred into computer systems and thus made available to less knowledgeable users? It would be to oversimplify a little to say 'yes', it has already been done (see the discussion of The Latent Damage System, in Section 6.1). For in that one crucial question, there are really five queries tucked away. These five ask whether building expert systems is technically possible, jurisprudentially sound, commercially viable, organisationally suitable and strategically appropriate.

Significantly, since around 1987 the first two questions—about technical and jurisprudential feasibility—have been asked less frequently. Operational systems have themselves responded positively and more convincingly than learned articles could ever have done. The focus now is on the third and fourth questions—whether these systems can fit easily into organizations considering their introduction and offer sufficient payback as well. The honest answer to both is that it is still too early to know. But experience from other jurisdictions and other professions does suggest that cost effective expert systems could indeed be built and introduced successfully to law firms.

What we can say with some confidence, however, from a commercial point of view, is that building expert systems is more challenging—technically and from a legal perspective—than developing enhanced text retrieval systems or hypertext systems. Indeed, as we move along *The Legal Information Continuum*, from left to right, more effort (and so cost) needs to be expended in setting up the systems in the first place. Basic text retrieval systems require some design work but no fundamental restructuring of the legal information. Enhancements to these systems require some considerable additional effort in adding further layers to the information. Moving further along the continuum, hypertext demands some internal structural work in establishing cross-references and links and even the addition of further bodies of information. But, when it comes to expert systems, a fundamentally new representation of the domain is undertaken, which is inevitably a major exercise. As my case-study shows in the context of document assembly (see Section 6.3), I believe the development of expert systems can still be extremely cost effective, both for clients and lawyers. The question for me, therefore, is not so much one of whether expert systems can pay for themselves but whether the same benefits can be achieved by using more modest enabling techniques from further to the left on *The Legal Information Continuum*.

Regarding the organizational and cultural issues arising from the introduction and use of expert systems, these are similar to those that relate to the use of IT generally within the law and I address these in Section 7.4.

It is revealing that the legal profession has largely ignored expert systems technology (unlike the accountancy giants), although many lawyers do acknowledge there is considerable potential here. But they often see its application as suited for all firms other than their own. Things are done a little differently in their firms, it is claimed, and there is not much done there that would be done better were technology at play. This last claim, at once wrong-headed and myopic, encapsulates in microcosm the poverty of lawyer's uptake of IT. It is looking at expert systems only as a way of automating whereas the strategic use of IT, as I have been at pains to point out, involves capitalizing on the power of the technology to effect change; to innovate. Herein lies the response to the fifth question asked earlier, the one that challenges the strategic relevance of systems: the entrepreneurial and visionary law firms of tomorrow are those that today are recognizing the place for technology such as expert systems as an agent of change and a central source of inspiration in their strategic plans.

4.4. Document Image Processing

One of the drawbacks of text search and retrieval systems, according to many users, is that the words as they appear on screen do not faithfully reproduce all the features of the print and paper which they represent. This has been one of several motivations for the development and use of document image processing (DIP) technology, which, in terms of the *legal tasks* introduced in Section 3.2, directly supports two vital jobs for lawyers, those of document management and following procedures.

Motivations for DIP

In the days of character-based systems, the green lettering on black background on most computer screens bore no relation at all to the physical document which would be printed. With the advent of the graphical user interface (see Section 4.7), and its WYSIWYG capability (what you see is what you get), when a search is conducted across the original WP documents, the layout, font, and appearance will be similar to the hard copy. This formatting and layout is often (but not necessarily) lost, however, when the text is moved over into some text search and retrieval system.

In any event, even the graphical user interface cannot help when it comes to all the other information held in a document. In relation to a letter, for example, there may be a signature, annotations in the margin, a date stamp, and even a coffee stain, all of which, in different ways, have information content and may be relevant or at least a prompt to the human memory. The manner in which a document is laid out also conveys information about the document—often, we remember nothing more of a document other than, for instance, that the key part was in, say, the top paragraph of the second page, which we might remember was short and right justified.

The point is that we remember documents not just on the basis of the words held within them but also on the strength of other pieces of information, some vital and others extraneous.

This has been one of a number of reasons why the commercial world has invested in the development of DIP systems. In these systems, it is not the text from a document which is held in searchable form, but images of entire documents, complete with date stamps, coffee stains, and so forth. This can be likened to storing a set of photographs of the documents which can be pulled up onto the screen in their entirety and are completely faithful, therefore, to the original. In many ways, DIP systems are like computerized microfiche. They store images and they do so in remarkably little physical space. But because DIP systems store the information digitally, they can combine effectively (unlike microfiche) with other applications of IT.

The basics of DIP

Full DIP systems have various components. There will be a scanner which is a device, much like a conventional photocopier, for capturing the images of documents and representing these images in a form which be can stored, in a computer system, usually in an optical disc storage system which is WORM-based (write once read many). As the images are loaded, they are indexed, automatically or manually, and it is against this index that users are later able to search and retrieve their documents. If, for example, an index holds the details of the date, author, and recipient of a document, then typically a user, on her workstation, will specify the details of the document she needs (for instance, a document dated 1 February 1994 from Smith to Jones) and, once recognized in the index, the scanned document image could then be transmitted from the optical disc device, across a network perhaps, to the user's machine. There the image can be viewed and, in some cases, annotated or printed out.

The scale of DIP systems varies enormously from those holding a few thousand documents and costing as many pounds to those storing millions of images at a commensurate price. Beyond the law, there have been a variety of applications. Some business users aspire to the paperless office by using DIP systems to capture the images of all incoming and outgoing correspondence and documentation. In the insurance industry, the same technology has been used (in conjunction with workflow systems—see Section 4.6) to streamline the processing of claims and to enable far speedier movement of standard documentation amongst the many individuals through whose hands (but now across whose screens) the documents must pass. Others use DIP to overcome problems of physical space shortage: once images of documents are scanned into the systems, the originals may be archived well away from the office (some go a step further and destroy the originals but this may raise difficult evidential problems if the documents were ever to be relied upon in the courts). Still others store images as a compact, and even portable, information resource. In this way, individual papers from large document loads are readily accessible without leafing through books or files.

DIP technology is powerful but still developing rapidly. Several challenges remain, not the least of which is that the rendition of documents on screen is at a lower quality (in terms of dots per inch) than that of print on paper (typically, 100 dots per inch on screen, as compared with 300–600 by laser printer and over 1400 in printed books). The result is that comprehension rate is lower and error rate higher when viewing images on screen as compared with reading the original document. This is a complex area of study for cognitive psychologists, however, and error rate may be attributable to many other factors beyond screen resolution.

On a more practical level, the current, industry standard monitor of a PC is not as long as that of, say, an A4 sheet of paper and so the entirety of individual images often cannot be viewed on one screen if they are to be viewed at their original size.

Character recognition

Perhaps a more fundamental frustration with DIP systems, however, is that users cannot search for words held within the document whose images are stored. This is a vital point. From the point of view of storage, images are held as collections of black dots and not as searchable text.

If users are wanting the facility to identify and retrieve words in documents, the information on the image has to be converted into machine searchable form.

This conversion can be done manually, by rekeying the text, or by a variety of IT-based techniques, especially OCR and ICR (optical character recognition and intelligent character recognition, respectively). These recognition systems, broadly, assess the shape of individual characters and

The Technologies

the image and, by pattern matching analysis based on models of the shapes of letters, are designed to identify each character accurately. Often this character recognition process is conducted at the same time as the process of scanning the images into the system in the first place. This seems to have led to an unfortunate sloppiness in the use of the word 'scanning'. Strictly, it should refer only to the process of loading the images; but the term is also used (incorrectly) to refer to the combined loading and character recognition processes.

In any event, after character recognition, the documents are meant to be available both as searchable text and retrievable images.

There is often heated debate about the accuracy of OCR and ICR. Suppliers of scanning installations and bureaux which provide scanning and character recognition facilities will often claim a level of accuracy well above 90 per cent. When dealing with original documents in pristine condition and clear typeface, this is a fair indication and the technology can be a boon. But bitter experience of having to cope with third generation photocopies, complete with coffee stains and date stamps, suggests a far lower success rate in the real world and the need for extensive review and revision of the resultant text.

Some users (especially lawyers) seem to be uncomfortable with any recognition process with a hit rate of less than 100 per cent. Others recognize that a lesser level of accuracy can nonetheless still provide a facility far more powerful than conventional, manual methods of the past. The most ingenious argument in this context that I know of is that considerable inaccuracy character recognition (even only 50 per cent of words) can be overcome by the formulation of more sophisticated search requests. This argument would suggest that a lawyer looking for documents in which the case of *Donoghue* v. *Stevenson* is mentioned, may indeed fail to retrieve 50 per cent of the relevant documents in these circumstances if the search request was confined to the string of characters 'Donoghue'. However, if the user request was for 'Donoghue *or* Stevenson' then, we are led to believe, it would be statistically very unlikely, even with a 50 per cent character recognition success rate, that both words would be spelt incorrectly. It would only take one of the words to have been identified correctly for the search request to retrieve the relevant documents. Ingenious though that argument may sound, I have yet to meet anyone who would take complete comfort in it in practice.

Often users of DIP systems do not, in any event, want all the images to be converted to text. Most image management systems allow users to select areas of text within images of particular relevance and the OCR or ICR process can be confined only to these blocks of text. This technique is often combined with the use of annotation facilities whereby users can attach notes referring to individual images and the selected portions of text themselves become searchable. Some imaging systems also support the facility to put highlight marks on images just as one would do normally with paper and marker pen.

A major attraction of DIP

Beyond the lure of the paperless office and the natural deployment of DIP in workflow scenarios such as in the world of insurance claims processing, a major attraction of this enabling technique, especially for lawyers and judges, is the ability to load entire case loads of documentation into some portable format. Whether in support of litigation or transaction work, it is enormously attractive for the more peripatetic lawyers to be able to drop the equivalent of wall-fulls of files into a small grip. While images of documents take up far more disc space than machine readable versions (by a factor of about 15) and so cost more to store, the benefits of portability frequently outweigh the bills for disc storage (and, in any event, this continues to fall in price).

As more external published materials are published electronically and internal know-how is made available (either by dialling in or through applications which have already been downloaded), a lawyer or judge can now have a case preparation room and a library in his dining room at home, at the client's office or in a hotel bedroom in some far flung location.

4.5. Telecommunications

Of all current aspects of IT today, telecommunications seems to be attracting the greatest investment, the most outrageous media coverage, and the most frenetic political attention. Broadly speaking, telecommunications is all about the electronic transmission of information in digital form. This is not only textual information but also sound, video, graphics, and animations as well.

For the law and lawyers, telecommunications penetrates to the very heart of two of our broad categories of *legal task* (see Section 3.2): sending and receiving information; and information consultation.

Many lawyers will be familiar with some basic aspects of telecommunications. They will have some sense that the telephone lines which support oral phone calls (still the dominant means of communication across large distances) are now also being used for the transmission of computer data as well as voice between organizations. This generally requires the use of a modem (shorthand for modulator/demodulator) which converts the digital signals emitted by computers into the analogue form which conventional telephone systems transmit and then back into digital form at the other end so that the receiving computer can understand it.

They will also be aware of another way for computers to communicate, where a collection of computers (often on one site) are linked to one another by cable or wiring known as a 'local area network' (LAN). LANs have a number of key components. They usually have a powerful, personal computer known as a 'file server' which stores the information and software shared by users on the network. Computers connected to the network are often referred to as workstations; while the network operating system is software which controls the transmission of information and software across the network. LANs may also share printers and other output devices. By use of further telecommunications links (usually leased lines), two or more LANs can be connected into larger groups called 'wide area networks' (WANs).

This appreciation does not, however, offer sufficient insight into the likely potential of telecommunications. There are several further dimensions to the revolution in telecommunications and I have something to say about each by way of expansion on the received wisdom. First of all, there are the leaps being made in the underlying technology. Then, of course, there is the Internet and the World Wide Web. And there is also the emergence of the global telecommunications and information services industry.

Telecommunications technology

In the first instance, there have been staggering technical advances in the capacity and flexibility of transmission media, able to carry ever higher volumes of information. Developments and refinements in copper cable, radio transmission, and in satellite technology, for instance, continue at an impressive rate. The most remarkable progress, however, has been made in fibre optic cable, which has become the standard bulk transmission medium throughout the world. Today, fibre optic systems can transmit the equivalent of 80,000 concurrent, high quality telephone conversations over one single optical fibre and will shortly be able to carry 300,000 on a fibre pair.

Nicholas Negroponte, in *Being Digital*, is forceful on the question of fibre (page 23). 'Think of the capacity of fibre as if it were infinite', he says. 'We literally do not know how many bits per second we can send down a fibre. Recent research results indicate that we are close to being able to deliver one thousand billion bits per second. This means that a fibre the size of a human hair can deliver every issue ever made of the Wall Street Journal in less than one second. Transmitting data at that speed, a fibre can deliver a million channels of television concurrently—roughly 200,000 times faster than twisted pair' (traditional cabling).

In the UK alone, there are over two million kilometres of fibre and the core of the country's telecommunications network is entirely fibre-based. Fibre also runs between many countries, with the world's first commercial under sea fibre laid from the UK to Europe in 1986. In the words of Negroponte, 'from the perspective of bits, the entire wired planet will eventually be fibre' (page 26).

At the same time, advances in digital compression have greatly enhanced the capabilities of existing networks and allow larger volumes of data, video, and other media to be transmitted. The newly developed digital wireless systems and projected clusters of telecommunication satellites will, in due course, also provide the potential for the transmission of digital signals (sound, data, and other media) to and from any point on earth.

These technological advances are enabling a vital convergence of the previously distinct industries of telephony, entertainment, information, and data transmission. No longer need the services of each sector be delivered across distinct networks. They can now be combined. Text, video, graphics, animation, and sound can be delivered across a single transmission system and so a huge selection of telecommunications and information services can be fed directly into homes and businesses across the world. All this is technically possible although not yet permissible in all countries from a regulatory perspective.

The Internet and the World Wide Web

The reality of this technological progress is to some extent marred by the relentless media hype over the two related phenomena of the Internet and the World Wide Web. (If you aspire to being even remotely hip, do refer to these as The Net and The Web, respectively.) In combination, these two are said to be the makings of the so-called 'electronic information superhighway'.

The Technologies

The Net

The Internet traces its origins to the United States in the 1970s as a group of government networks called 'Arpanet' (Advanced Research Projects Agency Network), a project spawned from the US Defence Department's experimentation with networks. Other organizations began to link up and now the Internet is said to consist of over 30,000 networks (public and private), 5 million host computers, around 50 million users across the world, and is growing, some says at about 15 per cent each month. More than this, the number of users seems to be rising exponentially which lends some support to Negroponte's otherwise unbelievable remark: 'My guess is that one billion people will be connected [to the Internet] by the year 2000' (page 182). Note that there are about 600 million users of the telephone today.

For many users, the most significant facility of the Internet is electronic mail, the ability to send messages and other computer files to any other user anywhere in the world. Although this may suggest the Internet is one vast network, in fact it is a collection of tens of thousand of networks which are connected to one another and are able to operate together because they share a common set of communications standards and protocols.

I am a committed user of the Internet, of this network of networks, for the purpose of messaging, and can confirm that it not only streamlines and improves one's existing communications, it also enables entirely different communications patterns. I am now able to exchange messages with a range of international contacts with a rapidity and convenience that was simply not achievable in the past. The world of the Internet is not inhabited, as the sceptics would have us believe, only by 'geeks, nerds and boffins', as is so ably shown by Howard Rheingold in his eye-opening book, *The Virtual Community*.

The Web

Yet for many aficionados of the Internet, the global messaging is but a secondary feature. The rubber really meets the road, they would say, in the Internet providing access to information sources in greater quantity and diversity than civilisation has ever known.

This dimension of the Internet has been boosted beyond measure by the advent of the World Wide Web, a system which effectively adds a vital layer to the Net, rendering it both more usable and more useful. Introduced in 1990 by scientists at CERN (European Laboratory for Particle Physics in Switzerland) to enhance communications within a relatively small international research community, Net users quickly recognised its potential and embraced it with great enthusiasm. Today, the Web is the fastest growing part of the emerging global information infrastructure.

At first glance, a 'page' on the Web appears as a page from a glossy magazine, complete with text, images, and graphics. On closer scrutiny, users see that some words and parts of the screen are highlighted or 'live'—by pointing and clicking at these, in the manner of hypertext linking, users can then be conveyed to another page, which may be more text or another image of the same document; or it may be a link to another page in a document sitting on a Web site halfway around the world. In this way, huge amounts of information are being loaded onto machines, these materials are being linked to one another across the globe, and the whole lot is being made available to users who are able to roam freely around an unimaginably large body of information. This means that users can browse around documents on a particular topic which may be held in a university department's machine in, say, New Zealand, and with one click can jump to further information on that matter, as made available in California perhaps, by some multinational conglomerate. When users are transported in this way, they are sometimes said to be 'surfing the Net'.

Many lawyers are jumping on the bandwagon, setting up their own sites, loading materials (brochures and articles, for example) which they think might be helpful for potential clients. And they are also setting up flashy 'home pages', at the front end—the modern equivalent of yesteryear's (often garish) neon signage. Few seem absolutely sure of what they are actually doing in all of this, but in the spirit of early settlers convinced of a golden future, there is optimism, excitement, and conviction that a key to prosperity has been found. The main justification for enthusiasm, in my view, is that the Web of today is an embryonic global information infrastructure. It gives us some insight into the way in which information services (and so, I claim, legal services) might be delivered in years to come. Lawyers are enjoying setting out their stalls in the new electronic marketplace, even if they are devoid just now of saleable merchandise. Their time will come.

It is, of course, early days yet for the Web generally. Indeed much of the available information across all sorts of disciplines falls short, in quality terms, of what we would ordinarily expect of publishable material in the conventional sense. At the same time, some of the information is plain defective, well illustrated for me by one version of the periodic table which is said to be accessible, but with seven elements missing, demonstrating neatly that many involved with putting information up on the Internet are still more infatuated with the delivery vehicles than passionate about the value and integrity of the information.

The Technologies

Generally, I find navigating around the World Wide Web is most productive when I am looking for some information which I know is likely to be there. Used alternatively, however, as a first port of call when initiating research or solving problems it can make looking for a needle in a haystack look focused and manageable. Here we see *The Technology Lag* in one of its most blatant forms. IT has been used to capture and store unparalleled amounts of information but techniques are not yet available to help us pinpoint *all but only* the information that is in there somewhere. With intelligent agents and conceptual searching, however, will come greatly improved utility.

Other solutions are also being advanced. One model suggests that the Internet is an information market in which value production can be desegregated, so that one group can make raw data available and others can provide the added value and improved means of access, intelligibility, and usability. In law, for example, governments might do no more than load primary source materials and leave it to entrepreneurial others to set up front ends which point users in appropriate directions, and to add indexes, links, and filters, all of which would render the data more valuable and accessible.

Of course, there are other major outstanding issues which remain to be resolved. Security, for example, is a big headache. Critics make much of the possibilities of criminal treatment of systems and data (forgery, pornography, destruction); of invasion of personal privacy; and of the risks of commercial or sensitive information being open to scrutiny by others. Payment over the Internet, by 'e-cash', is also a problem today in that there is not yet a generally accepted and secure means of being remunerated for information services rendered. There are also question marks over the general reliability of the Net and anecdotes abound of messages and documents not being delivered or arriving months too late. Some of the misgivings are exaggerated while others are of genuine concern. I have every confidence, however, that the problems will be solved—the political and commercial interest and investment in the Internet is so great that with this will there will certainly be a way.

In summary, the Net and the Web are of monumental significance not for the benefits and facilities which they can deliver today, but for the insight they give us to the possibilities of tomorrow, of an untold wealth of information at our fingertips and untrammelled access to all other human beings with whom we might ever want to communicate. But it is even more than putting the entire British Library into everyone's lounge and linking all citizens to one another. Once more Negroponte puts it well: 'The information superhighway may be mostly hype today, but it is an understatement about tomorrow' (page 231). What we have here is one of the vital first steps towards an IT-based global information society, a society quite different from the print-based industrial society, as exemplified in the law by the shift in legal paradigm which this book anticipates, a shift towards a world in which the law is available and accessible to all.

The global telecommunications and information services industry

This vision of the Internet and the World Wide Web combines with the technical developments mentioned earlier to herald an emerging global information society, complete with its own information market-place which will radically transform our social and business lives.

Massive effort is being expended in progressing from the embryonic global information infrastructure which exists today, and of which the Internet is a part, towards a higher capacity, more interactive, quicker, more flexible, and less costly worldwide communication service. Investment in improved technologies to enable greater bandwidth, improved processing power, and increased compression and storage capacity is being made. Work also continues on the establishment and enhancement of standards, interfaces, protocols, and transmission codes which will enable smoother interconnection between networks, fuller inter-operability amongst services and applications, and strive also to achieve higher standards of privacy, security, confidentiality, and reliability of the networks.

In parallel, in a discipline well-known for its surfeit of divergent schools of thought, there is one topic on which management theory currently seems to be speaking in a single voice. That topic is *information* and the unanimity of view is over its centrality to developed nations' prosperity in coming years. Where land, goods, and capital dominated economic thought in the past, information is the commodity now attracting greatest global interest and acclaim. How we capture, organize, store, and disseminate the stuff is perhaps less clear. But technology, there can be little doubt, will play a crucial role. And telecommunications technology is at the heart of all prognostications in this connection.

In the United States, dramatic scenes are being played out. And the players are major, on any view. President Clinton and Vice-President Gore are strong proponents of the development, across the country, of what they call 'information superhighways', their transnational fibre optic network on which practically any quantity of information—as text, sound, graphics or video—can be sent and received. Through this superhighway they hope to achieve the long-awaited convergence of computing, communications, and media, thereby putting at the fingertips of the citizens of the nation all the available information (for personal and business purposes) that might ever be wanted. Just as transport infrastructure has been fundamental to western economies in the past, Clinton and Gore argue that information infrastructures will be crucial for their future. Their plans for the information superhighway have developed into a commitment to a more sober 'national information infrastructure' (NII) initiative and, in turn, to a 'global information infrastructure' (GII). No doubt their success in the former is planned as a precursor to their dominance in the latter.

In Europe, for some years, DG XIII of the European Commission has also been investing heavily in understanding and removing the barriers to the completion of what is regarded as the internal information services market in Europe. (Interestingly, many of the barriers are legal—problems of copyright, liability, and proof, for example.) The focus here is often not so much on the techniques that may support information services. Rather, it can be gleaned from many projects and reports that information is regarded of primary importance and that we must resist being driven by technology in shaping our information society.

More recently, a European vision was encapsulated, in the report of the Bangemann Group on Europe as a global information society, in mid-1994; while the G7 ministerial conference on the information society, held in early 1995, expressed support for the global information infrastructure.

These trends in Europe clarify a number of matters which should inject some humility and realism into English lawyers' quest for some electronic legal network on the basis of telecommunications technologies (also see Section 5.1). First, lawyers are not the only human beings seeking to manage information more effectively—this same challenge is set to be central to the world's leading economies in the coming decade and there will surely be technical developments and indeed systems put in place that will make lawyers' objectives more attainable in the next few years. Second, we can see the information services market has two quite distinct elements: the information; and the technology that delivers it. Lawyers, like others, must focus on both. Third, many commentators consider that the coming of the information services market will require fundamental changes in the information processing industries and professions. Lawyers must now begin to consider the impact on their world of these major shifts and must plan, strategically, for the change management that will be required.

In practical terms, advances in telecommunications will mean that by the next millennium towards one billion people, living in a global village, will have access to 'information appliances', as they are coming to be known, each capable of immediate connection to one another, with no practical limitations on the amount and nature of information which can be transmitted. While many of these appliances will be tomorrow's personal computers, others will be enhanced television sets or telephones with screen displays or hand-held devices (even wallet sized) as well. Not only will each be able to connect to all others, but everyone will also have ready access through these appliances to an exponentially expanding body of information, relating to all aspects of our lives.

As for today, however, already we can see powerful, interactive, multi-media personal computers are becoming popular in the domestic household and soon these will be as common as televisions and videos are today. PC/TVs, combining computer and television hardware in one, are being sold widely. With appropriate software and modems, these systems are now being connected to one another, across the public telephone network, or through one of many other cabling systems; or by cellular or satellite link.

At the same time, computers in the workplace are set to become as pervasive as chairs and desks. All aspects of our domestic, social, and working lives will be affected and enhanced by these developments. In this context, even the most conservative, technologically reticent, and ostrich-like lawyer must anticipate a shift in working practice. A lawyer tomorrow without a computer and telecommunications facilities will be as inconceivable and intolerable as a lawyer of today without a telephone.

4.6. Groupware and Workflow

Built to a great extent on the back of progress in telecommunications, relative newcomers to the world of IT and very fashionable in 1995 (although by no means, in my view, a passing fad) are the closely linked enabling techniques known as groupware and workflow. Together, their main impact, in terms of the *legal task*s which I have mentioned (Section 3.2), will be in sending and receiving information within and amongst organizations; document management in the context of individuals working in groups; information consultation; and in systematizing the following of procedures. Above all else, however, these techniques should encourage and enable far more effective team working within law firms, communication across organizations, and the more structured management of legal affairs generally.

Groupware

It has been said that if the 1980s was the decade of personal computing, the 1990s is that of interpersonal computing. It is indeed true that the ten years following the advent of the personal computer were dominated by users who operated in isolation from one another, in stand-alone environments, where one machine held all the data, programs, and systems to which the single user needed access. Large quantities of information were built up on unconnected and isolated islands but generally only those who loaded the information had later access to it.

With interpersonal computing has come the reality of computers being linked to one another, most commonly today across networks within organisations and through modems and public telephone networks between organisations. I like to divide interpersonal computing into two categories—passive interpersonal computing and active interpersonal computing.

By passive interpersonal computing, I am referring to users of computers realizing greater benefits either by sharing computing resources (for example, useful data or software held centrally on a file server on a network) or by sending documents or messages to one another through whatever connection may be in place between users' computers.

Active interpersonal computing involves the further dimension of users making a concerted effort to harness the connectivity and shared access facilities so that they can collaborate in the production of their work in a way and to an extent which was simply not possible before computers were linked to one another. With active interpersonal computing, existing and newly created information becomes a shared resource which all authorized users can contribute to and draw from.

The term 'groupware' (the name given to software which supports 'work group computing') is often used, both by suppliers and users, in relation to passive interpersonal computing, such as electronic mail. Yet groupware is at its most powerful and likely to yield the greatest benefits when it is used in the active sense. Here, technology is generally said to support and encourage team working, especially when members of the team are not gathered in the same physical location. Enhanced communication, greater productivity, more successful collaboration, valuable information held once only, sensible exploitation of existing investment in networking, elimination of the need for some middle management functions—these are the benefits being claimed in the industry.

A variety of off-the-shelf software packages available today are said to belong to the groupware category. The majority, however, including many advanced electronic mail packages, are actually of the passive interpersonal computing variety. Only a very few products, and most notably Lotus *Notes*, deliver active interpersonal computing and so offer a capability well beyond file sharing. These operate in the realms of team-based information sharing amongst many different machines, with the facility for changes to files in one location to be replicated across all participating sites.

One can see immediate relevance and advantage for professional services organizations, where skilled individuals are required to pool their varied knowledge and expertise and work together towards some common goal for a client. Trained often to think and perform as individuals, traditionally there have been few tools or techniques to help diverse specialists come together, and to remove any unnecessary barriers between disciplines. Groupware does not simply automate the rather weak professional team working of the past. Instead, it innovates (especially when used in conjunction with workflow systems) by enabling common access to work product in an uninhibiting and non-threatening manner. Levels of communication can be transformed and interaction amongst the team becomes the rule rather than the exception. When several lawyers are working on a major dispute or transaction, for example, the ability to share work product and research sources can be vital. Also, on an ongoing basis, modern law firms require a mechanism for capturing and disseminating their firmwide know-how, a central receptacle of information, knowledge and expertise, into which valuable experience can be poured and from which practical guidance can be taken (see Section 5.4). Groupware is just such a mechanism.

One related and powerful illustration of active groupware comes bundled with most PC-based video conferencing systems and this is a facility which enables users connected by video link also to work together on the same computer file (perhaps a spreadsheet or WP document) although they may be many miles and even continents apart. The more powerful versions of this software allow either user to become the primary author of the file and so to make adjustments to the file on their own machines with the resultant changes appearing on the monitor of the other.

It is limiting, however, to think of groupware only as supporting 'team working'. While this should give rise to improved performance of teams within one organization, or groups drawn from a number of organizations, focusing on this might detract from the more radical possibility of groupware reaching from the front office into the client office and becoming a dominant mechanism for client service.

Where passive inter-personal or interorganizational computing has supported clients in periodically hooking up to their advisers' databases and drawing down relevant information, groupware of the active variety will comfortably support the automatic provision of useful information and guidance. In essence, the replication facilities of groupware can ensure that this kind of information seems actually to reside with the client. This application of groupware breaks down the distinction between advisers' systems and client systems and brings the two parties together as one work group. The notion of creating work product and then delivering it to a client then disappears. Automatic dissemination becomes the final stage of the task of creation and the whole process becomes less advisory in nature, replaced by ongoing feeds of up-to-date information relevant to the client. Proactive legal service can be provided more naturally from such a platform, as lawyers see it as their business to be making relevant information available—their know-how—on a continuing basis.

In this way, groupware can be regarded as an enabler both for streamlining and enhancing the traditional advisory approach to legal service and the smooth delivery of law as an information service.

Workflow

The IT industry finds a close association between groupware and 'workflow' computing. Where groupware supports the activities of teams and collective decision making, workflow computing is directed instead towards supporting clearly structured processes, with easily identifiable sequences of predetermined steps. Workflow is also at its best where there are teams operating together but here the technology goes beyond workgroup computing in that it controls the order in which tasks are conducted, alerting users to key milestones, generating documents, and allocating tasks across groups. Workflow computerizes procedural tasks.

Workflow finds its natural home for lawyers in supporting the management and running of cases, both by lawyers and judges. Workflow management is proactive in its approach to progressing a series of procedural tasks. These systems make sure that all tasks are presented to the appropriate participants in the correct order and accomplished within defined time-scales. Groupware products differ in not being as proactive and leaving more of the initiative to users.

Workflow applications have much in common with the discipline of project management, a field which I identify in several places in this book as one from which lawyers and their clients could benefit enormously.

By reducing a legal process to a rigorously timetabled model embodied in a workflow system, procedural complexity can be hidden from lawyers and non-lawyers, errors of timing and of the allocation of responsibilities can be reduced, uniform quality can be imposed (sometimes allowing formal quality standards to be more easily achieved), and it becomes easier to implement change because of central control.

4.7. Graphical User Interface

Perhaps the key component of any computer system for direct use by lawyers and non-computer specialists is the user interface. This is the part of the system that controls the way in which the lawyer can use the technology: what the system looks like on screen; and what a lawyer needs to do (for example, press a key or click on a mouse), to get the system to do what is wanted. For most people, the user interface must be simple to understand and intuitively obvious in operation. If it is cumbersome or complex then—no matter how sophisticated the rest of the set-up might be—the system will invariably fail to meet business or social objectives.

The growing importance of the interface

Traditionally, computer systems were horrendous from the user's perspective. This did not affect or worry most lawyers too much because, in the early days, IT was rarely used by lawyers themselves but instead was available for secretaries and support staff. However, as machines have appeared on fee earners' desks, user friendliness has jumped rapidly up the IT agenda in the legal community.

At the same time, there has been a shift recently across industry towards the view that computer systems are in fact mainly for use by average mortals and not just for computer specialists. In the words of an American commentator, David Liddle, it has now been acknowledged that: 'It's time to get computing out of people's way. Those who are proud of their ability to withstand pain can continue to do computing. The rest of them need to be given a user interface that lets them go ahead and do their job.'

In the past, user interfaces were character-based (in effect, only alphanumeric symbols on the screen), while, more recently, there has been a radical shift towards a graphical user interface, known often as 'GUI' (visually, lots of pretty pictures on the screen as well as text).

The Technologies

The fundamental difference between GUI-based systems and character-based systems is that the former depend only on recognition while the latter require recall. Users of GUI-based systems simply recognize symbols that intuitively represent commands or instructions they wish to implement, whereas in character-based systems users are required to recall (often counter-intuitive) words or commands to get the system to do what they want. For example, to start a word processing package using a GUI-based system the user may need only to use a mouse to 'point and click' at a little picture that denotes word processing (perhaps a hand with a pen), whereas the user of a character-based system may need to type some such command as 'c:\wp\wp', which is far from memorable and intuitive.

I believe that the appropriate interface for lawyers and for legal information systems is the graphical user interface. Some IT specialists reading this section will be thinking my point is so self-evident that it is not worth making at all; and many computer users may think I have been labouring the obvious. Yet, there remains, in 1995, an appreciable number of lawyers (in private practice, in government, at the Bar, and on the Bench) who steadfastly refuse to progress to GUI and still fervently defend their use of character-based systems. By and large, these ostriches are conservative users of long standing who have suffered character-based systems for some time. They are either reluctant to abandon the investment they have made (in training and systems) or simply unable or unwilling (a variant of flat earthism) to understand the benefits which GUI brings. Sadly, they are joined by many dyed-in-the-wool data processing managers who see no benefits (to them as opposed to their users) of adopting GUI-based systems. While I hope, therefore, that this section of the book will (and should) rapidly become out of date, it seems that the arguments in favour of GUIs are still worth rehearsing today.

In summary, the graphical user interface can support and enhance all the *legal task*s introduced in Section 3.2 as well as each of the leading applications outlined in the following chapter.

The best known GUIs, I think it is fair to say, are those developed and championed by Microsoft—*Windows* (especially in its 3rd version which dates to 1990) and *Windows 95* (which, as I write this paragraph in August 1995, is just days from release and, no doubt, from taking the world by storm). The GUI does, however, predate Microsoft's versions of it and in a chequered and controversial history can boast its commercial genesis in Xerox and later Apple and a development cycle which involved some of the most colourful figures in the history of personal computing.

For lawyers, given their working practices of the past, combined with their general lack of training in IT and often a related fear or scepticism, it is well recognized by managers as crucial that the user interface of any system in no way discourages usage of the system. My experience, which is supported by current wisdom amongst lawyers in the US and across many industries worldwide, is that lawyers are more likely to use IT, and use it productively, if their systems are GUI-based. Similarly, when we look ahead to the provision of legal information systems to non-lawyers, I believe it will be vital that the legal guidance is accessible in ways which are intuitive. More than this, they should be recognizable and the dominance of GUI interfaces on the Internet through the World Wide Web (see Section 4.5) is likely to add to its widespread appeal.

The benefits of GUI

So what are the benefits of using GUI-based systems as compared with character-based systems? Generally, GUI-based systems are easier to use, quicker to learn, they facilitate more effective combination of applications, and they can more faithfully represent (visually) original versions of documents. And these are advantages which should be recognized by lawyers responsible for IT and by technical staff as well.

Ease of use

In terms of ease of use, the GUI tends to incorporate features described by the rather remarkable acronym WIMP, which refers to the screen format being dominated by moveable (often overlapping) Windows, the use of Icons to represent commands and instructions to the system, the deployment of a pointing device known as a Mouse, and the availability of Pulldown menus displaying options to users. All of these features contribute to more intuitive operation of computer systems than was possible in the past.

Given that GUI-based systems require their users not to memorize cumbersome, convoluted, and counter-intuitive commands but rather require simple recognition of symbols and the progression through natural steps, lawyers generally find these systems are far easier to use.

Quick to learn

Many reputable studies by computer scientists and cognitive psychologists have suggested that the GUI also reduces the learning time of users who are faced with new applications, and, in turn, leads to use of more application packages per machine than when there is a character-based interface. The

The Technologies

IT industry itself has unambiguously recognized this popularity of the GUI and in response has even moved some of its most relentlessly character-based operating systems and applications onto one of a range of GUIs.

For the legal profession, once lawyers have learned one GUI-based system, experience suggests that learning other graphical systems will be a quicker and less painful process, because GUI-based applications tend to 'look and feel' the same, with basic instructions, such as saving and printing, invoked in the same way across different applications. This seems to result in legal users making use of many more applications than would be the case where the systems are character-based.

Combining applications

A further advantage in using GUI-based systems, running in an environment such as Microsoft Windows, is that data can easily be transferred from one application to another. For example, a lawyer using a litigation support system within a GUI environment, when analysing a document, can easily 'cut and paste' from the database in which she might be searching into a compatible word processing package. Indeed, in an environment dominated by Windows, the screen can be split so that the database appears on one side and the word processing package on the other.

An even more advanced feature common to some graphical packages is the ability to allow data to be dynamically exchanged and updated. For example, a table from a statute may be held in a graphical database and linked dynamically to the same table in a word processing document, such that the updating of one will automatically revise the other.

WYSIWYG

My final user interface issue is the way in which the text itself appears on the lawyer's monitor. One drawback with conventional systems is that the text on the screen often bears little or no resemblance to the original text in the typewritten source materials. In GUI-based systems, where there has been a conscious attempt to render the text on the screen identical in layout, font, and colour, to the original documents, lawyers tend to react forcefully and positively to this. They seem immediately more comfortable with a system whose contents visually resemble the materials with which they would deal manually.

Again, the use of GUI-based systems facilitates such a rendition of the text, because there is an additional benefit of the GUI in terms of what is sometimes known as WYSIWYG (what you see is what you get). The GUI's accurate font rendering and use of colour allows documents to be displayed almost exactly as they appear in hard copy. This, in turn, seems to give many lawyers exactly what they need in relation to computers—a feeling of comfort, familiarity, and confidence that they are not in an entirely alien world.

But the story does not end with the GUI. Interface specialists predict that systems of the future will appreciate the needs and preferences of their individual users and will even adapt in anticipation of their specific needs and quirks. Systems will be customizable and highly personalized. In this context, we read of MUIs (multimedia user interfaces), MUDs (multi-user dimensions), and even MOOs (MUDs, object oriented) and the massively hyped concept of VR (virtual reality).

One step in the general direction of adaptive user interfaces is voice recognition systems, my eighth category of enabling technique.

4.8. Voice Recognition

It was in 1983, in the context of artificial intelligence, that I first came across attempts to develop speech recognition systems. At that time, the task seemed well nigh impossible. How could a machine tell the difference between the sounds speakers make when uttering 'abominable' and 'a bomb in a bull'; or between 'she is at anchor' and 'she is a tanker'? Current wisdom then had it that the correct configuration of words could only be identified if the computer had a wider 'understanding' of context and meaning. Thus, computational linguists, experimental psychologists, computer scientists, and even philosophers of mind agonized over the challenge of programming computers to understand speech and the meaning of words.

Progress seemed to be slow and I ceased exploring the field, rather pessimistic about its prospects. Over a decade later, I was amazed and intrigued to learn that speech recognition for personal computers had all but been perfected, with dazzlingly high accuracy rates.

A statistical not AI approach

It transpires that the labs had cracked this one, not through artificial intelligence (AI) and not by programming computers to understand or recognize words as human beings do. Rather, using the considerable processing power of technology, it had become possible to build statistical models of language which help tackle problems such as that of homonyms (for example, 'to', 'two', and 'too') and phrases of the 'she is at anchor' variety.

On the strength of analysis of a vast numbers of documents (containing over 100 million, it is typically said), the systems are now able to predict, on a statistical basis, what words are most likely to appear alongside which others. This language model is made up of sequences of words and data about the frequency with which they occur in the written language. This has nothing to do with meaning or understanding. It is all about statistical likelihood.

Contemporary speech recognition systems, based on statistical models, come in various shapes and sizes. Speaker-dependent systems are those which recognize the sounds of particular individuals, their pronunciation, accent, intonation, and speed of expression—and this is done by studying the individual speech patterns in advance and building an acoustic analysis which can anticipate the way in which these individuals will pronounce almost any word. When combined with the language model, this acoustic analysis can predict what words are most likely to be spoken in a given context and so can deal with homonyms and ambiguities.

These are distinct from speaker-independent systems, which are designed to recognize words, no matter who may be speaking. Speaker-independent systems are limited, however, to far smaller vocabularies than speaker-dependent ones and often are used for issuing basic commands to a computer (known as voice activation) rather than for the entry of text.

A further distinction is between isolated word and continuous speech systems. In the former, the speaker is required to leave a short interval (about a tenth of a second) between words and so to make recognition significantly easier; while in the latter, users speak at their usual and comfortable pace.

Finally, there is a distinction between those systems which immediately display the words on screen as they are spoken as against those which record an entire speaking session and process that recording in a batch, returning the resultant text some time later (this period will no doubt continue to shrink as the technology is developed).

The automation of dictation?

Voice recognition is clearly a development of significance to lawyers. Traditionally, lawyers have never been major users of the keyboards, either because this is a task they deem the preserve of the secretaries; or because their finger speed and typing abilities have always fallen well short of the productivity reached by dictation machine plus secretary.

For those lawyers for whom the keyboard is the last remaining obstacle in the exploitation of IT, voice recognition may be vital. Although many uses of IT, particularly information retrieval and research, do not require much keyboard activity, others (such as document creation) presuppose an acceptable speed of text entry if the process is to be effective.

For most lawyers today, a speaker-dependent system, with large vocabulary, will be preferred. Such a system will recognise around 30,000 words and, particularly if users speak in isolated words, the recognition rate should be high.

Many lawyers want to see the text appear before their very eyes as they 'voicetype' (IBM's name for this). Although it is perhaps less of a cultural upheaval to adopt the batch approach mentioned earlier (championed most notably by Philips), this is simply to automate the existing dictating approach. In contrast, where the text appears on the screen as the user speaks, this enables and encourages a new working practice, whereby lawyers can see immediately what they have just said and thus avoid duplication of words or clumsy, cumbersome syntax. This is not possible, of course, with conventional dictation.

The impact of voice recognition

I have no doubt that we will all be talking to our machines regularly by the turn of the millennium, but not just to create letters and reports. In the morning, for example, we will probably walk into our rooms and say something like 'Machine on. E-mail. New messages' and then we will reply to our messages orally through voice recognition rather than by keyboard. (Sometimes, of course, there will no need for it to be converted into text and we will just exchange voice mails—digitally recorded messages.)

Other applications for lawyers, in due course, will be the automatic creation of minutes of meetings, witness statements, and notes from conferences with barristers, where today these are time-consuming and often inexact exercises in manual transcription.

In the courtroom, court reporting will eventually be transformed and the immediate creation of transcripts from hearings (through speaker-independent, continuous speech, large vocabulary systems) will be virtually instantaneous. Tape recording, stenography, and even computer-assisted real-time transcription may no longer be necessary.

Voice recognition and voice activation, like the graphical user interface, are well capable of supporting and enhancing each of the *legal task*s out-lined in Section 3.2 and all of the leading applications described in the next chapter.

While the impact of voice recognition promises to be profound, I should point out the danger of overstating its immediate utility for the novice user. Lawyers who hear of voice recognition often become very excited, thinking as they do that because typing skills are no longer necessary (in fact, two finger prodding has often sufficed), then IT is within their grasp within but a couple of minutes' instruction. There is, of course, far more to becoming a productive user of IT than familiarity with the keyboard. Even with the most intuitive GUIs, there is some basic and unavoidable groundwork to be done, for instance, in understanding the fundamentals of the GUI (not quite so intuitive first time round), in launching applications, printing doc-uments, and managing files, and in appreciating basic principles of secu-rity. Voice recognition is not the quick fix which many lawyers hope for.

Voice recognition may be a great productivity tool for existing users but it does not eliminate the need to train people who are new to IT.

5

Leading Applications

Let us now turn to how IT can be used in law. While so far I have mentioned applications only in passing, my purpose in this chapter is to make six leading applications of technology the primary focus of discussion. In my view, these six are, for the foreseeable future, the most significant for lawyers and users of legal information services.

Figure 5.1 Leading Applications

electronic communication
text creation and production
litigation support
internal know-how
external information retrieval
case management

While the classification into the six groups is not as tidy as some purists would want, my intention is not to identify a set of mutually exclusive groups. Instead, I want to identify categories of application which can each be the basis of self-contained, workable IT projects with a practical focus. I know from experience, for example, that law firms *can* launch litigation support and case management initiatives. These and the other four categories can be handled and implemented relatively easily, given the organizational and administrative infrastructures of legal practice today.

The six categories do overlap with one another, in that some rely on the same enabling techniques, while others perform similar *legal tasks* (see Section 3.2). More than this, some of the applications actually use one or more of the others (for example, external information retrieval relies on electronic communication).

There is an interesting comparison to be made generally here with the world of accountancy. When spreadsheet technology was developed, this immediately captured the attention of accountants and took their profession by storm. Here was an application of technology which went to the very heart of their daily work and in this single use of IT accountants found immediate value from technology. In contrast, there has never been a single winning application ('no killer app.', as some might have it) which has been capable of winning either the hearts or the minds of a critical mass of lawyers. No single package or tool has been immediately applicable to current working practices in the way accountants have been able to exploit spreadsheet technology. Instead, the introduction of technology to lawyers has been incremental and *ad hoc*; and most committed and satisfied legal users report that they came to be so because of an eventual combination of tools and applications. These collectively convinced them of the worth of IT.

There are few overnight legal converts to IT. None of the following six on its own is likely to change the world view of a technology atheist or agnostic. Together, however, they give some cause for belief.

5.1. Electronic Communication

As the international business world buzzes in anticipation of the much vaunted electronic information superhighways, how is the legal profession preparing for the telecommunications revolution? To be frank, the response thus far has been modest. Few lawyers are at the vanguard of the relevant technological advances, and here, as with so many potential applications of IT in the law, the jury seems to be out indefinitely.

For information systems specialists, this apparent reticence of lawyers is remarkable. Surely, it is argued, the daily lives of all lawyers are so dominated by the processing and transfer of information that IT holds a key to renewed prosperity in what has become, in my terminology, a highly pressurized market-place for legal services? Lawyers, the enthusiast will claim, are quintessential information processors, who work constantly with all manner of information—legislation, case-law, legal textbooks, information relating to client matters, as well as accounting and management information, marketing information, and personal and internal know-how. More than this, so much of a solicitor's job involves the sharing of this information and its transfer to others; to colleagues, barristers, other firms, the courts, and other agencies; and also its sale to clients. So why not communicate electronically?

It is undeniable that a lawyer with no more than a computer, a modem, and the inclination, can, in terms of the *legal tasks* identified earlier (in Section 3.2), send and receive information and consult information using IT. And if this is done with a modicum of technical proficiency, appropriate procedures, and sensible security precautions, the business benefits for clients can be considerable—less costly, more responsive, better focused, and more controllable legal service. For law firms there can be benefits too. Those who pioneer effectively can enjoy competitive advantage while others can at least secure a more robust set of client relationships.

Why then are many lawyers ignoring the potential of recent advances in telecommunications technology?

Leaving aside the general conservatism that hinders the profession and is widely cited as cause of lack of uptake of anything new, it is in fact with some justification that lawyers are currently cautious, even cynical. For there were a number of attempts in the UK, from the mid-1970s to the early 1990s, to deliver general purpose, electronic networks for the law and all of these foundered and eroded much of the goodwill that there once had been.

One of the genuine difficulties here is that lawyers do not find it especially illuminating or helpful to be told that they are information processors or information managers, quintessentially or otherwise (although most have not read the third chapter of this book). Rather, they prefer to be introduced to the basic uses and practical, tangible benefits of electronic communications and to understand their direct impact on their financial performance and working practices.

Basic uses of electronic communication

A useful point of departure for present purposes, therefore, is to reflect on the principal uses of electronic communication for lawyers, not from a technical or information science angle but in functional terms and in the context of lawyers' daily activities.

Six basic functions of electronic communication for lawyers can be distinguished. None of these should be beyond the reach of the average lawyer although it should be noted that the applications discussed can be implemented in a variety of ways that range, from the user's perspective, from painless through to intolerable; and from a systems administrators' point of view, from elegant to 'kludge'.

The Technologies

To transmit and receive messages

When most lawyers think of electronic communication, they have this function in mind. The generic term used here tends to be electronic mail or 'e-mail', allowing users to send messages to other computer users and to receive messages as well. This facility is fairly commonly used by lawyers across local area networks within their practices but there is increasing interest, largely driven by clients, in lawyers communicating this way with other computer users beyond their firms (using one of a number of available systems). This is the move from interpersonal computing to inter-organizational IT. Generally, e-mail is used as a substitute for telephone conversations, exchange of memoranda, and informal letters.

But e-mail has a few crucial advantages over these conventional means of communication. First of all, it is possible with e-mail to send the same message to many recipients at the one time and yet with negligibly more effort than that expended in sending the message to one single user. Electronic reproduction and distribution of messages is trivial compared to the equivalent tasks of using the telephone or paper and print. A second advantage is that effective communication by e-mail does not need to be, as they say, synchronous, that is to say, all participants in the communication exercise do not need to be available and contributing at the same time. Many telephone companies are reporting that two-thirds of all calls seem to be only one-way communication—a message is being imparted, an order placed or a query lodged. E-mail is asynchronous: you send your message and rather than it being read on the spot, it is picked up and dealt with at a time convenient for the recipient. No more 'telephone tag'. Third, e-mail can change and greatly enhance communications. In organizations with offices in many locations, for example, e-mail can bring everyone under the one 'virtual' roof. Sending a message next door involves precisely the same effort as firing it across the globe. In turn, this can make for greater team working and participation, a stronger sense of involvement, and improved working relationships.

There are dangers as well, however. One leading supplier of IT products is said to close down its e-mail system each day from 10.00a.m. to 2.00p.m. to allow their employees to get on with their work. It is also reported that the Chief Executive of one of the world's leading telecommunications companies has eight secretaries devoted to responding to his e-mails (all employees have access to him through e-mail).

To transmit and receive documents

Moving beyond the transmission and reception of messages, there is great scope for transmitting entire documents electronically—for example, succeeding drafts of contracts—and thereby removing the need for faxing and retyping. This was one of the major motivations behind the early work on the development of legal electronic networks in the UK, in that the developers saw the potential for lawyers in different locations to produce several revisions of documents in rapid succession without the need for retyping. It should be noted that what is being transmitted and received are actually computer files and so this application is not restricted to text-based documents but can also be used to transmit other information, for example, spreadsheets, databases, and images. There are a range of concerns often rightly expressed by lawyers in this connection, especially about reliability, security, authentication, and confidentiality. And these are issues which the telecommunication service providers are currently addressing with gusto.

One immediate appeal of electronic communications as the basis for sending and receiving documents is that it is readily perceived to reduce transaction costs (faxes, couriers, retyping, proofreading, for example).

To gain access to internal know-how

Another application of electronic communication that is currently attracting great interest within the legal profession is the creation of access (locally or remotely from around the world) to databases of internal know-how, to the 'institutional memory' of a firm, as it is often termed, so that lawyers can benefit from the accumulated expertise and experience of colleagues within their practice. Rather than holding information in filing cabinets or lawyers' heads, the motivation here is to allow lawyers to dip electronically into the firm's collective wisdom. I deal with this at some length in Section 5.4, but it is worth putting a marker down at this stage to remind us that the notion of know-how systems would not be viable were it not for electronic communications.

To gain access to external information

Similarly, users who wish to gain access to external information held in online databases also depend on electronic communications, usually across the public telephone network. Most lawyers are familiar with large database services such as LEXIS, holding vast quantities of primary legal source material with some secondary sources as well. There are many analogous legal databases around the world to which lawyers can gain access through a variety of information services. Other services can often be helpful for lawyers, although not offering purely legal material. For example, many practitioners find it useful to search through daily newspapers and journals for potential clients' names or for articles on particular topics. Generally, the theme here is that lawyers use electronic communications facilities to locate relevant information, browse through it, and perhaps download the documents into their own machines (where the law of copyright permits this). Again, I consider this to be a leading application of IT and so consider it in its own right in Section 5.5.

To provide access to information on particular matters

Looking ahead, and consistent with recent trends in the United States, a further application of electronic communication for lawyers is providing clients with ready access to information relating to particular matters being handled. For example, clients can be offered the opportunity to access part of their lawyers' systems and be able to identify the status of various matters in progress, which is particularly useful where a large number of cases are being dealt with simultaneously. Sometimes referred to as 'status reporting', this should enable clients to manage their advisers far more rigorously. The reports can vary in detail, from a brief indication of where the matter is currently sitting in its likely life cycle through to in-depth information about how much time is on the clock and the extent of the outstanding fees.

To engage in free-form discussion with other users

The final application of electronic communication covers facilities such as 'bulletin boards' and 'conferencing' (both fall under the more general head of 'computer-mediated communication'). These enable users to communicate with others who share a common interest in topics. They can leave their ideas, observations or questions on a metaphorical bulletin board which can be picked up and responded to by other users; while conferencing involves the establishment of a more structured format for the exchange of views amongst users on pre-specified topics. It is also possible to have real-time interchanges amongst users, so that lively debate can be conducted by participants from all corners of the world as though gathered in the same room.

The poverty of electronic legal networks

It is quite clear from the six applications of electronic communication laid out above that there are many practical and relevant uses available for lawyers today. So what progress has been made in the UK?

Progress?

I have undertaken a fuller analysis of this in *Computers and Law,* the journal of the UK-based Society for Computers and Law. In summary, my survey of advances in the UK does not reveal a profession bonded by a common recognition of the importance of electronic communication amongst lawyers. Nor does it speak of a single, coherent, pre-competitive, and collaborative movement focused on streamlining and enhancing the inefficiencies of the past. Rather, we see a piecemeal approach, made up of a number of sterling attempts by individual enthusiasts overlapping with some law firms doing their own thing.

Whether inspired by gifted enthusiasts or the conviction of various legal institutions, the legal electronic network projects of the 1970s and 1980s invariably suffered from delivering systems which were opaque to non-specialists, incapable of integration with working practices, and not sufficiently useful to merit persistence in overcoming these shortcomings.

Some firms were not entirely deterred by the disappointments of these various projects and took it upon themselves to explore less ambitious avenues, by introducing internal electronic mail, direct communication links with some clients, and even collaboration amongst international groups of firms.

Reasons for failure

But it is important to try and understand why electronic communications and networks for lawyers failed in the UK and elsewhere. I suggest there were three main reasons. First, most developers ignored the needs and culture of the legal profession; second, most developers did not make sufficient *information* available; and, third, most developers treated the field as primarily a technical challenge. I should say a little about each.

Regarding developers' failure to respond to the needs and culture of the legal profession, there has rarely been any thoroughgoing attempt, for example, to ask practising lawyers themselves what they might want and how they believe any solution might be integrated with current working practices. What of systems put together by lawyers, it might well be asked? Ironically, when lawyers-cum-developers have designed and developed systems, these may have been well suited to other enthusiasts but they have not been immediately usable for the overwhelming number of lawyers in England who have little or no personal experience of using IT.

Most lawyers will only contemplate using systems that are very simple to use: no requirement to remember long, counter-intuitive commands; just straightforward applications that demand little training and sit comfortably with other systems available in-house. With the advent of the graphical user interface for PCs, this is now a realistic prospect.

A further factor often lost in the ether is that lawyers may not tend to be thrilled about proposed innovations that clients themselves have not requested or are at least not expressly keen on. Although there is now gradually more interest amongst clients in communicating electronically with their lawyers, this has not traditionally been a focus of client concern. If the market has not been demanding, it should not have been surprising that lawyers kept the topic fairly low on their agendas and concentrated on other matters.

As a final illustration of the needs and culture of lawyers, it should have been appreciated some considerable time ago that unless and until a critical mass of users can be assembled, electronic communication will never achieve its potential for lawyers. There is here, of course, the perennial problem that lawyers may not want to be users until most others are—a 'Catch-22' conundrum if ever there was one.

Turning now to the availability of information electronically, it must be accepted that most of the emphasis and debate on communications has been on sending and receiving messages and documents, a use of IT that has been kept fairly separate (at least in many users' minds) from the *legal task* of consulting information through search and retrieval techniques. Although much of the information available on-line today is often said to be of dubious value for most practitioners, this is not the point. The issue, rather, is that the general trend in the information industry around the world is to combine messaging and document transfer with information services. The answer here again is to find out what information lawyers would really like to have at their fingertips and to make that accessible through some system that also facilitates the conveyance of messages and documents.

Finally, on building for success, it must now be time to cease thinking about this whole field in technical terms. Most of the technical challenges have surely now been met and lawyers should not need to hear about them. What with many machines now having internal modems, the flexibility of the graphical user interface, and the burgeoning telecommunications industry generally, electronic communications for lawyers should now involve no more than connecting machines to telephone sockets or plugging into networks and lawyers transferring and accessing information by responding to self-explanatory prompts.

If the legal profession is to progress towards a more generic network—its own legal information highway—experience from more prosperous information services markets suggests, in summary, that there are three critical success factors for lawyers to pursue: from the outset, a critical mass of committed users; availability of useful information; and simple technology to deliver the information.

Lexis Counsel Connect, Link, and beyond

What of the future? Putting past developments behind us, I am currently very optimistic about the way ahead, partly because of trends in information services generally and in part because of two current initiatives—Lexis Counsel Connect and Link—which I believe offer us a taste of an exciting and innovative future. For me, these are the first generation of useful and usable legal electronic networks.

Lexis Counsel Connect

Lexis Counsel Connect (LCC) was originated by American Lawyer Media, an affiliate of Time Warner Inc., said to be the largest legal journalism company in the world. UK lawyers may know of American Lawyer Media through its US national monthly, *The American Lawyer*. LCC, formally launched in early 1993, is described as an electronic network which allows law firms to put their memos, newsletters, and other work in the hands of the in-house counsel who need it. Through their own PCs, members are encouraged to communicate with each another and also to gain access to LCC's vast library of information, from notes of important cases to reports written by leading law firms. It is said there are over 30,000 legal briefs held on the system.

The idea, then, is that law firms use LCC as a means of distributing their know-how to in-house lawyers, thereby avoiding the conventional postal system and making the information available in more accessible form. In-house lawyers, for their part, will therefore have ready access through the system to expertise on most topics.

LCC is distinguished from other on-line systems by offering access to more focused analysis rather than the uninterpreted primary source material hitherto available. Clients can access the brief bank, a legal memo library, directories of law firms, lawyers, expert witnesses, and updates of recent legal news. Moreover, the system offers conventional electronic message and document transfer as well as conferencing facilities and discussion groups.

In summary, and consistent with the American information society ethos, LCC has been hailed as the new electronic highway for forward thinking members of the profession. While there may be thoughts for it to be made available in some way to lawyers in the UK, LCC seems primarily, at this stage, to be a US tool. It now has about 25,000 users.

Link

The UK's home-grown system, equivalent (in many ways) to LCC is Link—Legal Information Network. Launched in May 1994, this on-line network for lawyers is a venture of Legalease and John Pritchard, the entrepreneurial solicitor, publisher, and legal author, who is the author of *The Legal 500* and the Editor-in-chief of the magazine, *Legal Business*.

Link was advertised widely in the UK and around 100,000 free copies of the system were distributed across the profession. Currently, it has over 6,500 users and is promoted as an on-line information system for lawyers, containing case reports, legal journals, electronic mail, and other services designed for lawyers. A range of legal information is made available through Link, including current legal news (UK and European), a law library of case reports and periodicals, legal directories, legal forms, and a legal indexing service as well. Additionally, through Link, users are able to undertake company searches, trade mark searches, and credit checks. Two final touches are direct book ordering from a leading legal book shop and an option to gain continuing professional development points by sending answers to questions from other Legalease publications through the system. Perhaps its main impact, however, has been as an electronic mail system for the legal profession, in which capacity it has enjoyed some considerable success.

LCC and Link have much in common. Both are provided by significant publishers to the legal profession; not conventional legal publishers but modern, information service providers who have recognized lawyers' interest in less formal publications than traditional statutory material and legal scholarship. They have created and to a large extent dominated a market whose main purpose is to provide information about lawyers and law firms as well as the law itself. All this information, and more, is readily available through their systems, and particularly to in-house lawyers—the clients themselves.

The systems themselves, in terms of their uses, have similar scope and go beyond networks of the past which have tended to be for one or other but not both of e-mail and information service. Both systems offer e-mail, document transfer, access to external information, and bulletin boards. If lawyers' clients are also users, then the systems can also be used as a medium for reporting on the status of work being done.

Yet there are significant differences between the two services. Most generally, my impression (certainly in relation to the UK) is that LCC is more immediately attractive to lawyers who are already committed users of IT. In contrast, Link seems to be directed to the legal profession at large and could well be many lawyers' first exposure to IT. Their approaches to cost are also different. LCC has tended to charge a monthly fee (gradually reducing in amount). In contrast, the philosophy of Link is that its basic services are free for users (as opposed to information providers), with premium services, such as company searches, attracting specific charges.

More fundamentally, LCC and Link have so far taken quite different stances in the vision they are projecting, in their strategic marketing. The message of LCC is that the system is all about changing the way lawyers do business, of revolutionizing legal practice, and of challenging conventional assumptions about lawyering. On a personal note, I have to say I find this approach highly imaginative and stimulating (indeed much of this book is devoted to this very theme).

However, the promotional activities of Link are more likely to strike a chord with the average legal practitioner in the UK, in that, although they do share the vision, the actual message conveyed is that of a practical service, linking lawyers together, offering access to useful information, and making the whole thing a natural development from current practice (they also help ease lawyers through their transition to IT by advising, for example, on suitable modems). LCC majors on revolution, while Link is about evolution.

Ownership and control

A fundamental question does arise, however, and it is an issue that was hotly debated in a related context in the US with industry and government taking very different positions. The question is—who should own and control an information service if it becomes so central to society or groups within society? In the US, the debate concerned the information superhighways themselves. One strongly held government view was that this resource was too fundamental to the welfare of the economy and to US citizens to be left in the hands of private enterprise. Leading industrialists countered that if it were left to government, the highways would never be built. So far, given the flurry of activity by several corporate giants, it appears the private sector may well prevail.

On a smaller scale, it might be said that any legal information service such as LCC or Link should have been developed and be controlled by the professional bodies in the law or by relevant government agencies. But we must be honest with ourselves here and accept that an innovative information service of the type being contemplated is unlikely ever to emerge from anywhere other than some private enterprise rooted in the information sector. While this is a sweeping statement that could stand much further elaboration, the undeniable fact is that past attempts by professional bodies (across the world) to provide such services have largely failed. But this is not to say that the profession should not seek to exercise some influence on the development and use of systems such as LCC and Link.

Innovation through electronic communications

Looking ahead, for many lawyers the main motivation for using systems such as Link or LCC and so communicating electronically, will be the demands of clients who have been convinced of the benefits and begin to insist on doing business this way (hence, LCC's and Link's focus on in-house lawyers). In turn, this could result in radical change for the legal profession.

Consider the challenge for a construction lawyer in this new era. Rather than confining work on, say, collateral warranties, to drafting them and advising on their impact in given circumstances, a law firm might compile guidance notes on this subject and make them available to all users roaming the electronic legal highways.

A firm's expertise would be widely promoted in this way; potential clients could climb the learning curve on the subject without always instructing legal advisers; and those who later want more focused advice may then quite naturally turn to those lawyers whose initial overview has proven useful and impressive.

This reminds me of the international rock star who was said not to be too bothered about the pirating of his recordings. When challenged on what he would do if he learned his music was being reproduced without royalties in some far flung place, he retorted he would go there and put on a few concerts. This lateral leap of innovative thinking is a model for lawyers who will need to revise their views on attracting and winning new clients; on giving out with a view to pulling in.

A strong business imperative emerges for those firms hesitating today over whether to contribute to such networks. Failure to set up one's metaphorical stall in the emerging electronic legal market-place might well mean lost opportunity—spontaneous awareness of law firm's specialities may soon be derived from users' experiences while on-line; and invitations to tender and requests for proposals will inevitably be distributed through this medium.

A glimmer can be seen here of the new legal market-place, of tomorrow's legal paradigm, in which lawyers will package their knowledge as information products, not immediately discarded after use, as effectively happens with most current legal advice, but as commodities capable of attracting new clients and being reused on numerous occasions by different clients.

Here also is a potential legal market that begins to harness the power of IT not simply by automating what already goes on but by re-engineering various business processes; evolving from lawyering as an advisory service towards legal service as an information service. Thus may begin a trend towards what can be called legal process re-engineering (see Section 6.3).

Do legal networks have a future?

Looking ahead, I have grave doubts, however, if it will make sense in the future to have legal electronic networks which are distinct from the more general, global information systems and services—such as the Net and the Web—which are evolving so rapidly and are surely vital for the future of law. Should the legal networks and services be one lane, as it were, on the generic information superhighway or a separate network altogether?

One main issue here is that of convenience. I know an attorney in Chicago who claims he has to log on to eighteen different client e-mail systems every morning to pick up his messages. This should be avoided at all costs. Most users prefer operating through one system only, so that all messages are routed into one mailbox and all information services can be accessed from a single point of departure (a so-called universal mailbox). Most lawyers do not want to log onto a legal electronic network for some business, another system for other work, and perhaps yet another for internal communications and services.

If the goal is indeed to provide only one entry point, this can be achieved in a variety of ways. Legal networks could be taken over and subsumed by the larger, global systems. Or they could sit separately but alongside these global networks and be fully inter-operable with them so that jumping between the two would be no more involved than movement within one. Both LCC and Link now offer access to the Internet from their systems, which is a step in this direction. Or it may be that the legal networks act as the lawyer's front end to the global information infrastructure, as their initial means of access to the Net, the Web, and their offspring. A lawyer has to enter the system somewhere so why not do so in a module which is also likely to have relevant contacts, addresses, and information most readily to hand.

From the user's point of view, it may also be, therefore, that the analogy with physical road systems breaks down at this level of analysis. For practical, operational purposes, there is little difference in being a lane or a virtual lane or a metaphorical legal service station with a slip-road onto the highway.

5.2. Text Creation and Production

All lawyers create and produce text. Arguably, they do so in greater abundance than any other profession, industry or trade. But as we have moved from a script-based society, through a print-based society towards an IT-based society, our means of producing and reproducing text have changed radically. In the era of script, production was by hand and reproduction involved tedious repetition of the original task. In a print-based society, there were two levels of activity for the production of printed documents: first, the origination of the text, perhaps by handwriting, shorthand dictation or dictaphone; and, second, the representation of this original model by the printer or typist. And printing and photocopying technology enabled reproduction with comparatively little effort.

In the fully-fledged IT-based information society, we will have one layer of activity in the creation of documents, for the user will directly enter the text himself into whatever system is in use. Some users will prefer to type using keyboards as their means of text entry. But in due course, speaker independent, large vocabulary, continuous speech voice recognition systems will dominate this process (see Section 4.8). As users speak to their machines, the words will appear instantaneously on their screens, not simply automating the dictation process but enhancing and changing it by allowing immediate scrutiny of the words as created (in contrast to shorthand or electronic dictation, where there is a necessary delay between the act of speaking and the opportunity to scrutinize what has been drafted).

I use the term 'text' advisedly here because much of what is now input to machines will never see the light of day in the physical sense. Increasingly, text created by, for example, word processor, is not printed and sent in that form to recipients. Rather, the text is conveyed in electronic form, read and digested by its receiver, and filed or deleted without the creation of a physical document. It is no longer strictly accurate, therefore, to talk only of the creation and production of documents, because this ignores the electronic medium for dissemination. In terms of the *legal tasks* (see Section 3.2), then, text creation and production embraces both the drafting of documents and the sending and receiving of information.

A dominant enabling technique

When most lawyers think today of technology in support of the creation and production of text, they tend to have word processing (WP) technology in mind. And, of course, it is true that most of the contracts, writs, regulations, reports, and letters of advice that we currently see are indeed the product of some IT-based WP system. Word processing has undoubtedly had a major impact on the practice of law; for example, in law firms whose WP has, until recently, been largely a secretarial function, or in barristers' chambers where, for some time, counsel themselves have been users. WP was a leading back-office application of IT in the 1970s and 1980s.

When it comes to the business benefits of WP, contradictory views abound. Advocates claim quicker turn-round of higher quality documents and so cost savings and improved performance; while critics suggest it can result in an increased and unwieldy number of drafts as well as the uncritical generation of unfocused documents. For example, in relation to initial documentation in conveyancing, solicitors sometimes say that WP has shifted onto the recipient the onus of deleting many unnecessary provisions. Quite unjustifiably, this job seems to be part and parcel of sending printouts of so-called standard sets of documents.

Few could contest the flexibility that WP technology affords, however, in being able to move, manipulate and alter text easily, and to print material in a wide variety of fonts and formats. More recent advances add other major benefits: for example, some packages enable changes to documents to be marked clearly on later versions, together even with notes explaining these additions and deletions.

A first impression might be that word processing is a classic instance of automation—the computerization of the early typewriting process. Yet this is to assume that the technology serves the function only of streamlining or optimizing the text production process.

I find it fascinating that some successful users of WP in the legal profession also report that, far from rendering them what the cynics would call 'expensive typists', the technology can deliver major advantages as an intellectual aid for the authors of documents. The ease with which users can move text about, together with advanced features such as 'outlining', result in WP being a fine tool for the structuring and organization of materials as well as for the formulation and drafting of text itself. So those who draft contracts and legislation come to praise the virtues of WP, not just because they can easily embolden, underline, or italicize words, or because of very handy features such as revision marking (the facility whereby the actual changes made in a document are recorded on the new draft), but because it becomes an indispensable resource which assists in organizing and ordering their thoughts.

Many judges say the same and will claim they can prepare judgments more clearly and coherently using WP, using the technology as an innovative drafting aid and not just as a substitute for quill and parchment; pen and paper; or secretary, dictaphone, and typewriter.

Beyond word processing

Although WP has been the dominant enabling technique for text creation and production, it is very limiting to see it as the only relevant technique or to regard it in isolation.

Users of current WP systems, for example, also find 'copy and paste' facilities to be invaluable. These enable portions of text to be extracted not just from other word processed documents, but also from text retrieval or hypertext systems, and then inserted in working documents.

In the production of documents, desktop publishing (DTP) has had an important role to play in producing hard copies of documents of a quality previously attainable only through conventional printing processes.

And in the commercial world generally, text has increasingly been integrated with graphics and spreadsheets producing files and 'compound documents' whose words can be considerably enhanced by powerful images such as charts and pictures. It is true that lawyers have been slower than others to move beyond text but they will gradually be inclined to do so as they see the benefits in other documents to which they are exposed. In any event, WP, DTP, spreadsheet, and graphics facilities will, as a matter of course, be integrated in single packages and the rigid demarcation between different representations on screen and paper will gradually disappear. The focus instead will be on the production of these compound documents.

There are other enabling techniques which can automate the text creation and production process still further. At a fairly crude level, using what are known as the 'macro' features of most word processors, a system can automatically insert standard chunks of text. In this way, for example, 'I look forward to hearing from you, Kind regards, Yours sincerely' can be placed in a letter at one keystroke. And this can even be activated and inserted by voice recognition systems.

Innovating through text creation

Expert systems technology takes this approach one step further still, by enabling the drafting of documents to be the product of an interactive question and answer session. As described earlier (see Section 4.3), the idea of this branch of expert systems, known as document assembly, is that the creation of a document is not undertaken by cutting and pasting (literally or by machine) from previous documents but by responding to a series of questions presented to the user. Stored within a document assembly system are a series of templates and instructions as to when these standard chunks of documents should be used. Thus, the users' responses will cause various pieces of text to be inserted or deleted, sentences to be included or removed or will result in particular words being placed within the text or taken out altogether. After an interactive consultation with a document assembly system, a polished first draft can be produced.

At Masons, we developed a system to generate commercial leases and also an operational system that is integrated with electronic communications and database technology to create the documentation relating to estate conveyancing. This experience, together with the case-study in the next chapter (Section 6.3), led me to believe that the principal users of document assembly will not be lawyers at all. Rather, lawyers will embody their document drafting know-how in packages which will become a form of marketable information service. For the domestic user in *the latent legal market*, there will be standard letters of complaint or inquiry for all sorts of occasions, while for commercial organizations, all manner of legally robust, business documentation will be available at sensible cost.

Informating with text creation

Potential interrelationships with other leading applications for lawyers give rise to a further dimension to text creation and production. The connection between text creation and production and internal know-how systems, for example, can be particularly close. And when document management systems are being used (see Sections 5.4 and 6.2), the text being created is simultaneously consigned to the organization's central know-how repository and is later searchable and retrievable.

Taking this one step further, if authors take the additional modest step of embedding the text in a special mark-up language, then the file created can automatically be developed, as a by-product, into an immediately navigable hypertext system which could then be placed, for example, on the World Wide Web or on an equivalent, browsable, system internally (see Section 5.4).

There is also an intriguing option here for legislative draftsmen and publishers who could quite easily create their statutory and regulatory material with a view to using a mark-up language which, on publication, would enable these sources to be immediately rendered as usable and browsable legal information systems to which additional sources and commentary could be added (by them or by others—see Section 4.5 on the desegregation of value). With legislation could come hypertext links, for example, to parliamentary debates, with extracts from Hansard; while government departments might develop their own versions of legislation, complete with explanations of the rationale behind clauses (for instance, the underlying ministerial thinking). In due course, production of information systems will become part of the legislative process itself and may well influence and change the drafting methodology of parliamentary draftsmen.

5.3. Litigation Support

One of the first *front-office* applications for lawyers was litigation support. Primarily for direct use by legal advisers themselves, litigation support convinced many a practitioner that IT could be central to legal practice and to the actual delivery of legal service. The term 'litigation support' can be a little confusing, however, because it is used by lawyers in a variety of contexts and can refer to one or more of three applications of technology in the arena of dispute resolution.

First, and most commonly, litigation support is the use of IT to help manage and control the document load which lawyers have to master to advance and prepare their client's case. This is my main focus of attention here in this section but it may be helpful to introduce and say a few words about the others before I delve into any further detail.

The second category of litigation support, then, is the use of IT to store and make readily available the work product of lawyers as they progress through a case and generate their own sets of documents. I call this work product management and return to it both in my discussion of case management (in Section 5.6) and by way of case-study (in Section 6.2). In both contexts, I suggest hypertext is a most useful technology for linking relevant documents to one another and so enabling users to browse across crucial work product (including pleadings and witness statements) and evidentiary material (files of correspondence, for example).

The final sense of litigation support is where it refers to the use of IT in the courtroom itself. This embraces laptop computers for judges, computer assisted transcription, displaying documents on monitors across the courtroom, graphics for the presentation of evidence, and even video simulations of events at issue. In Sections 6.1 and 8.2, I say a little more about judicial and courtroom applications. As for the use of IT in presenting evidence, this has caused far greater stir in the United States, and other jurisdictions where civil juries are commonplace, than in England, where interest in this kind of technology has been confined to criminal cases. Even then, many senior advocates and judges harbour reservations about the lack of relevant court procedures to control this use of IT and are alive to the possibility of technology being misused in misleading jurors and judges. At a litigation support conference in 1991, this hesitation was captured by Lord Griffiths—in paraphrasing one of Disraeli's aphorisms—by suggesting that 'there are lies, damn lies and graphics'. What lawyers will think of virtual reality applications, which will surely come to the courtroom in due course, one can only begin to guess.

Litigation support as document management

Returning to the most common usage of the term litigation support, in this sense the focus is almost exclusively on the *legal task* (see Section 3.2) of document management. It should be added immediately, despite the extensive local literature and bravado, litigation support is very much in its relative infancy in the United Kingdom. In contrast, it was first introduced in the United States in the mid-1960s and has been embraced extensively there since then.

Litigation support is, of course, but one of a number of document management activities for the lawyer and there is an ongoing debate in law firms over whether their approach to it should be part and parcel of their more general, firmwide document management strategy or whether a more flexible approach and less well defined strategy is preferable. As a practical and commercial matter, I incline towards the latter school, because the demands of individual cases can be so diverse—for example, in the attitudes and existing systems of clients, barristers, and judges—that it is rarely appropriate for a law firm to stipulate or impose its own technical infrastructure on the various parties involved.

In practice, there are two main aspects to any litigation support project. The first is the selection and implementation of appropriate technologies for the task. The second is the exercise of entering the documents, or information about them, into the system—this can be done in a variety of ways; some manual, others computerized. For the purposes of this book, my main interest is in the first part of the process.

To put the application still further into context, the main thrust of litigation support is to *automate* various aspects of trial preparation. Rather than having teams of paralegals and junior lawyers thumbing through mountains of files and photocopying extracts well into the small hours of the morning, litigation support technologies streamline these manual processes. Searching, retrieval, cross-referencing, and annotating can all be automated using IT. Lawyers can locate relevant papers more quickly than when using manual methods. While the cynics are right in saying that litigation support is simply coping with the chaos IT created through photocopying technology, it is still an improvement that is long overdue.

Whether the facilities reduce the cost of litigation for clients is in doubt. I am of the view that this application generally enables lawyers to do far more for their clients (more thorough and comprehensive work) in the available time and so for the same (but not less) fees.

For the avoidance of doubt, litigation support does not obviate the need for an initial appraisal of each document. In the absence of natural language processing (see Section 2.5), I cannot see how any competent lawyer can avoid looking through case documents once, for it is only then that the relevance or otherwise of the documents can be assessed. The point of litigation support is that the full document load should not need to be read or searched through manually, in its entirety, *more* than once.

The potential of this technology is particularly clear in complex technical cases, such as construction or computer disputes, where the party that has mastery of the documents can enjoy a clear strategic advantage over others. But lawyers invest for other reasons as well: the overriding aim for some (contrary to my view about its impact) is to control the costs of the dispute by handling the documentation more efficiently; while others are motivated by a desire to keep apace with opposing parties who have indicated they are using IT (or it is suspected that they are). Some lawyers in the United States are even said to be committing to litigation support for fear that failure to use these systems may constitute negligence.

The three enabling techniques

Three techniques have dominated litigation support over the past decade. One approach is to compile a computerized index of all documents relating to a case. Each document can be represented in a database as a collection of 'objective' features (for example, date of document, author, recipient) as well as subjective features, requiring lawyers' classifications (such as whether a document is privileged or prejudicial to the client's case or raises a particular point of law). Once set up, such a system can sort all documents, for example, in date order or by authors' name. Additionally, the system can search and produce lists of documents sharing particular features: for instance, a list of all privileged documents written by Company X to Mr Y between two specified dates. In large cases, electronic indexing of this kind can be applied to good effect at the level of files rather than individual documents. In this way, a searchable list of files is created.

A second and complementary approach to litigation support uses document image processing technology (see Section 4.4). This is the process which can be likened to taking 'photographs' of individual documents and so this technology can cope well with materials which are neither printed nor typed, such as drawings or documents with handwriting, signatures, marginal annotations, date stamps, and so forth. Users of systems that hold images cannot search for individual words within the imaged documents (the text is not in machine readable form). Rather, they can view these images as if perusing microfiche on a computer screen. A database containing images has several uses. It can enhance an indexing system by offering users immediate access to images of the documents which their searches have identified. Where there are problems of physical space or storage difficulties, large quantities of documents can be assembled in very small working areas. For the user who is constantly on the move, this means entire case loads of documents can be taken along and displayed on a portable machine, usually using CD for storage. It will not be long, therefore, before litigators will be able to have complete documents sets and law libraries at their fingertips wherever they may be. In the short term, CD technology will enable this. Looking further ahead, global telecommunications and information services will do the honours, enabling lawyers and judges to retrieve documents from remote sites. In the courtroom too, document image processing can reduce the amount of paperwork that needs to be handled by judges, juries, and participants.

The third technique is to build a retrieval system that holds not an index but the full text of a collection of papers. This should enable lawyers to search quickly and easily within the entire text of documents for the occurrence of single words (for example, names of individuals, companies, places, or terms such as 'warranty' or 'delay') or for words in combination (for instance, the name of a company within a specified number of words of the name of an individual or a phrase such as 'defective software'). Upon first hearing about this approach, most lawyers think that this is what they want. Further insight into the shortcomings of basic text retrieval (see Section 4.1) usually disillusions them about these superficial attractions.

I believe the real benefits of litigation support come with a subtle combination of these three techniques and with hypertext-based work product management systems as well. On one particularly promising model for the future, a senior lawyer's first exposure to a subset of documents will be through a litigation workstation with a very high resolution, large, television-sized monitor. This system will contain the images of documents which have been preselected by junior lawyers and paralegals, and each will already have been objectively indexed. The senior lawyer will read through the images of the documents on screen, adding subjective commentary (in the manner of notes on yellow stickers), to the more significant papers, into the index; and selecting (by a pointing device) important portions of text to be converted from image into searchable form, using optical or intelligent character recognition techniques. The end result will be a sophisticated index, a database of searchable extracts and commentaries, as well as the images themselves. Using hypertext, this document management system will be linked directly to the letters of advice, reports, statements of claim, experts' reports and all the other work product created by the litigation team. Such a system would be invaluable, for lawyers and clients, both in preparation for trial and in the courtroom itself.

All for one or one for all?

The sophistication needed here is in selecting one or more of the three appropriate technologies for any case at hand, a decision over which lawyers often agonize. For the Scylla and Charybdis of litigation support are throwing all the techniques at the one case or selecting just one technology for all the documents. While it is commonly thought in addressing the needs of particular matters that the same selected techniques should be applied to all the documents, in reality, this is unworkable and commercially inappropriate and leads either to overkill or to missing an opportunity. The rule of thumb in selecting technologies for litigation support, therefore, is that it should be neither all for one nor one for all.

In other words, the use of litigation support and the selection process should not be driven by technical factors. So what factors should influence the use of litigation support and the selection of technologies? A common view is that litigation support is only relevant for the very largest of cases, size here referring to the value of the claim at issue or to the number of documents involved. I would contest this vigorously. Some high value claims involve very few documents and the use of IT may be unnecessary in such instances (although some litigators in the United States and Australia use basic indexing on all cases, at the very least as a tool for the listing of documents). At the same time, some disputes which do not rest on large quantities of documents nonetheless are complicated and the small number of papers may interrelate and overlap to such a degree of complexity that indexing and hypertext, for example, can provide an ideal guide through the maze.

If value and size are not determinative, it might be thought that types of case (by industry or area of law, for example) attract distinct technologies. It is true that construction disputes, for example, seem to be well suited to litigation support but this is because they are document intensive, which, as I have said, is not of itself a conclusive driver; or because they are labour intensive. This last feature calls for the use of groupware to support team working but, again, does not point to which of indexing, imaging or text retrieval is best suited to any particular case.

From involvement in numerous litigation projects, I have come to the firm view that the selection of techniques should be dictated very largely by the *relative significance* of the documents themselves. In any dispute, the documents can be categorized according to their likely impact (which, to make matters difficult, can change as a case progresses). One classification I have found helpful is into 'A+' (critical), 'A' (important), 'B' (background), and 'C' (peripheral or irrelevant). Additionally, one client has rightly added 'A/B' (those which may come to be seen as important).

If documents are categorized under these headings, the task then is to match litigation support technologies to each class. For A+ documents, which the legal team will want to have immediately to hand, all three techniques may be appropriate, so that the users can examine them in various formats, and cross-refer easily between them, using hypertext as well, to link them to one another and to their own work product. In contrast, class C documents may only justify objective document or file indexing. The fundamental point is to direct more technology at the correspondingly more significant documents—an obvious suggestion perhaps but one which is almost universally ignored.

Where's the rub?

Those who consider litigation to be too confrontational, costly, stressful, and time consuming and believe it is in any event undertaken only in the interests of lawyers, often find in litigation support the makings of a panacea. Here they think is a promising source of enhanced productivity, quality, and efficiency and in turn the means by which disputes might be pre-empted, settled earlier or resolved at lower cost and greater speed.

So where's the rub? Why are all lawyers not using litigation support technologies?

Lawyers themselves have a range of misgivings, only some of which are rooted in their incomplete picture of what can actually be achieved. Others are due to the absence so far of commercial imperative—if there is no clear payback or demand, why bother? Added to which, lawyers' preference for secretive exploitation of IT does not help (see Section 7.4); nor does the reluctance throughout the 1980s to work together in pre-competitive, collaborative spirit in establishing standards and settling on compatible systems (although the ORSA Protocol in England has been a very positive, collaborative step—see Section 3.1).

A further obstacle is the widely held belief that it can rarely be cost effective for the purposes of litigation to transfer documents from paper into machines. Historically, this has been true, but the undoubted advances in optical and intelligent character recognition technologies, together with the emergence (as in the US) of external bureau services devoted to indexing, data entry, and imaging, combine to suggest that this obstacle is gradually becoming negotiable. Moreover, as clients themselves increasingly use computer-based document management systems for their own administrative purposes, it will be a lesser task to convert from these systems to litigation support systems than the current challenge of moving from paper to system. In promoting this synergy between document management systems and litigation support systems, the more proactive lawyers in the profession should actually be advising on the potential compatibility of these systems (see Section 6.2).

One genuine problem is the unfortunate uncertainty over a crucial issue—costs. First of all, there is the quite understandable worry that litigation support is a very pricey business. When addressing lawyers, it is revealing that recounting the story (perhaps apocryphal) of the law firm which on one case 'exceeded its unlimited budget for litigation support' tends to occasion nervous laughter rather than unbridled and genuine mirth.

The difficulty here extends beyond the lack of confidence that lawyers have in cost estimates and projections for litigation support projects. More fundamentally perhaps, this application of IT substantially changes the cost profile of a piece of litigation. Many legal advisers, at their clients' behest, may minimize effort at early stages in the dispute process, perhaps pending the outcome of some settlement negotiations. In contrast, investment in litigation support requires a front loading of expense, an up-front expenditure in setting up the systems. For cases that are 'never going to settle' (of which, in my experience, 90 per cent still do), this investment may seem justifiable. For those which everyone feels sure will not reach the court, there is always a general nervousness about putting systems in place—the euphoria of a negotiated settlement can be diluted considerably by the appearance of a massive invoice for litigation support. As against this, I have heard it forcefully argued on both sides of the Atlantic that the establishment of imaginative litigation support systems of which the other side comes to be aware can itself help bring about earlier and more favourable settlement.

But a further complication is that there has been no binding decision yet, in the UK, on whether the costs of setting up and running litigation support systems can be recovered by a successful party in litigation from the unsuccessful party; or indeed whether or not litigation support systems are covered by legal aid. This is far from ideal. It is simply unacceptable for solicitors to be unsure how to respond when asked to advise their clients on the recoverability of development and staffing costs incurred in litigation support.

Another related anomaly arises from the general requirement that lawyers charge on the basis of the hours spent on a task; a phenomenon which can, in principle, and does in practice, reward the inefficient firm and penalize the well run practice. When litigation support systems are used, and if time can be saved (although I have my doubts, as I have said), total time spent becomes a less reliable indicator of the value of a service. Cynics have suggested that lawyers will be reluctant to become too efficient with technology until there is a move beyond the billable hour.

It would be sad if lawyers' uptake of litigation support technology was inhibited by inapposite billing and cost recovery practices.

Yet none of the perceived problems seems to be insurmountable, as the more progressive litigators are showing by their successful deployment of the new technologies. Indeed, ignoring litigation support is fast receding as a commercial option. As barristers with positive experience come to expect solicitors to use computers; as the courts encourage and require parties to employ the various enabling techniques; as professional bodies and independent inquiries support this use of IT; and as clients realize that a higher quality, lower cost, wider ranging service is available from hi-tech solicitors, legal Luddites will soon struggle for their day in court.

The future of litigation support

For clients, developments in litigation support raise challenging questions about the suitability of the lawyers they instruct. A further set of criteria in selecting legal advisers now emerges, relating to the extent to which lawyers have appropriate technology skills and support. If in major cases of the future, all parties have the documents held in litigation support systems (loaded perhaps by some external bureau), a key point of differentiation amongst practices will be law firms' relative proficiency in exploiting the data in these systems. Are the lawyers adequately trained in advanced searching techniques? What practical experience and track record do they have with litigation support? Do they have permanent, first-rate support staff? Are they using advanced techniques, such as conceptual searching, augmented 'front ends', and hypertext to enhance the basic systems? Are they capable of advising proactively on versatile document management systems? Do they understand the complex legal questions, regarding issues such as admissibility and authentication of evidence, that litigation support systems raise?

Certainly, a question today for all clients is whether their current lawyers are investing sufficiently in IT in preparation for the central role it is destined to play. The stage is set for major change in the world of litigation. Even by 2000, large-scale or complex litigation without IT will be virtually unimaginable.

5.4. Internal Know-How

Many law firms hold themselves out to be specialists in particular areas of law. In reality, it is often a moot point whether their clients actually benefit from the firm's collective expertise as opposed to the experience and knowledge of the particular lawyers who may be advising them at any one time.

In the past, it was possible in most firms for lawyers to pop their heads around colleagues' doors, asking 'has anyone done one of these or seen one of these before?' Although some firms do simulate this process through electronic mail (see Section 6.2), as most firms have grown larger, it has not been possible to dip into colleagues' expertise so readily. Instead, internal organizational structures—such as departments, units, and groups—have led to firms becoming clusters of rather self-contained islands, with insufficient sharing of know-how. The result has been internal inefficiency and failure to deliver value for money in the provision of services to clients.

To overcome this, and to seek to provide a higher quality, more cost-effective service, many firms have launched know-how projects. IT has been thought to have a major role here in providing a repository in which the 'institutional memory' resides, where the cumulative know-how can be held and, in principle, made available to others; but not imposed nor used uncritically such that creativity or originality might be discouraged.

A variety of approaches to in-house know-how systems have been attempted and adopted, with varying degrees of success. This remains perhaps the most challenging aspect of IT development for lawyers, offering the promise of a means of harnessing the most valuable resource of practitioners—their expertise—which is all the more powerful when combined with that of others.

I find it helpful to distinguish between five basic approaches to the development of internal know-how systems. These are discussed in this section. In each case, the common theme is that the information and knowledge itself has been generated by, and is the intellectual property of, workers within the organization in which it is gathered. As well as being *internal*, the other principal feature seems to be that the materials which are made available are very much *practical* in orientation, focusing, as the term know-how suggests, on how to get things done. (The category of know-how can also be extended a little to cover documents such as the opinions of barristers which may have been produced for a law firm but not by it.)

There is an interesting cultural theme running here as well. Whereas traditional legal service assumes that there is one principal process involved, that of passing advice to clients, when there is a passion for the creation of know-how, lawyers have to recognize that there is also now a second process, that of contributing to their firm's collective know-how. Lawyers at once advise clients and enhance their practices' intellectual resource.

As to know-how systems themselves, in our earlier terms (of Section 3.2), this application supports a wide range of *legal tasks*, including document management, information consultation, following procedures, and analysis and problem solving.

The precedent bank

In particularly well organized legal practices, standard form documents are gathered together in one place, so that they can be used again in appropriate circumstances. Such precedent documentation can be anything from short letters to lengthy contracts. The common theme here is that a cautious decision has been made to make these materials available for reuse. And a comprehensive precedent system will not only contain the document itself, but also useful commentary on it and a point of contact for further discussion.

These precedents or styles may have been based on actual letters or agreements, but have been stripped of the details and variables of particular cases. In contrast, but still within what I am calling the precedent model, is the reproduction and gathering together of documents which themselves have actually been used in respect of particular transactions or disputes. Here, even greater care is required and substantial commentary is needed. For example, if such a repository of documents includes a copy of the final contract which was negotiated on a transaction, then it would be important for someone intending to use it as the basis of a later document on a new matter to know those clauses where points were conceded to the other side (it is for this reason that many lawyers prefer to have first drafts rather than, or as well as, final drafts in their collection of precedents). In either event, the compilation and collection of precedents requires considerable human intervention and analysis. IT can be of little help in identifying appropriate documents or generating commentary. Its role in this context is mainly to provide a medium for storage and a mechanism for retrieval.

There is one, ambitious exception to this, though, and that is where document assembly techniques are used (see Section 4.3). These systems can be regarded as going one step beyond the retrieval and usage of precedents, in that a collection of precedents are embodied as templates within document assembly systems and, on the basis of interactive consultation with them, appropriate parts of the precedents are selected and compiled together to produce a final document automatically.

The legal storeroom

Typically, at the embryonic stages of a firm's know-how initiative and before any formal precedent system is in place, a junior lawyer, paralegal or information officer will be charged with the task of trawling through filing cabinets of historical documents in search of useful letters of advice, reports, contracts, pleadings, and so forth. Senior lawyers are asked to rack their brains and then raid their files in an attempt to capture the know-how locked in cupboards or secreted in their heads or apparently lost in the ether. After initial enthusiasm, this venture ordinarily runs out of steam fairly promptly with but a few hundred documents isolated.

Generally, lawyers find it easier to start gathering know-how and putting it in what I regard as their legal storeroom by committing to select only those documents which are created *after* the know-how initiative is launched. The task of going back is so daunting that of itself it can discourage and delay know-how projects for months.

Once documents have been selected for inclusion in the storeroom, the manner of their IT-based storage can vary. Indexing is important, by reference, for example, to subject matter, author, and document type. The subject matter is all-important and rich vocabularies and thesauri of legal terms and concepts are available to help compile this part of the index (which for current purposes can be likened to an electronic card file). Ideally, there should be a restricted set of terms which can be used for categorizing subject matter. This same set of terms—and it need not be a small set—should also be available to those who subsequently search on the index. The intellectual activities of categorizing on the one hand and search formulation on the other should thus be similar and so mutually supportive. It should become a way of life for lawyers.

Where the documents have been created internally on word processors, it is also a relatively straightforward task to transfer this text into a text retrieval system and thus be able to search within the documents in their entirety and not just in an index. An imaginative further step is to establish hypertext links between these documents, thus creating the equivalent of a scaled-down, internal World Wide Web for internal use (my notion of a 'Firm Wide Web').

The legal storeroom model does rely on lawyers playing the game by selecting documents for inclusion on an ongoing basis. In practice, many lawyers are reluctant to select documents and contribute very few. Sometimes this is due to laziness but more often lawyers will worry about their work withstanding the later scrutiny by colleagues or, alternatively, there can be concern about junior staff using the material uncritically. One way of tackling this problem is by assigning *all* work product to the storeroom, as the next approach suggests.

Work product retrieval

Work product retrieval is the phrase American lawyers use to refer to facilities whereby relevant work done in the past can be identified easily by colleagues and reused where appropriate on later matters. Work product retrieval systems are a type of know-how system which are created with the direct support of technology. Based usually on document management systems (see Section 6.2), the purpose of these systems is to create and offer access to the cumulative output—work product—of an organization and where the constituent documents are appropriately indexed, to offer easy access across the organization to relevant documents which have been created by others.

This technology is widespread in the United States and is closely related to word processing. The idea is that, on creation of a document, a simple form must be completed on screen. This form invites the user to pick from a pre-articulated list of keywords which describe the subject matter of the document. Additionally, there is provision for input of information regarding the author of the document, type of document, date of document, and so forth. In this way, information and know-how can be gathered at the point of creation. Later, users can search through the index of documents that will be created and—most importantly—can again do so by selecting from the same pre-articulated list of keywords.

Work product retrieval systems, therefore, capture documents as they are created and redirect them to some central repository, unless the author has indicated this is inappropriate. The emphasis of selectivity shifts away from lawyers selecting what should be included, as with the legal storeroom model, to deciding when a document should not be incorporated, which is the philosophy of work product retrieval systems. The author will also have an opportunity to add any commentary or gloss that may be needed, given that it will be widely available and easily accessible.

Work product retrieval systems offer access, on an index and text retrieval basis, to a far more comprehensive body of documents than the legal storeroom or precedent bank. But the likelihood of any of those being tailored or directly applicable to the particular circumstances of individual matters is far less than with these alternative systems, especially than with the precedent model, where conscious decisions have been made either to make the document available or to strip out the particulars and so put a skeletal style at everyone's disposal.

On-screen prompts

While much information relied upon by lawyers is held in textual form, some of the most valuable know-how is more procedural in nature, detailing and explaining how particular tasks and activities are to be conducted—what steps should be taken, in what order, and within what time-scales.

To that end, it has always been possible to compile check-lists, a common tool by which less experienced practitioners can be guided by more seasoned lawyers' wisdom as distilled into a usable set of prompts. Short paper check-lists, however, tend to get lost easily and are never to hand precisely when needed. Longer check-lists often look too cumbersome and convoluted to be of direct practical application.

Many complex tasks facing lawyers and their clients require extensive expertise and knowledge which have in the past often been encapsulated as notes and procedures in paper check-lists. On-screen prompts are computerized implementations of these paper check-lists but are easier to use, store, and maintain. They can take their users through complex and extended procedures, ensuring that all matters are attended to and done so, if relevant, within a prescribed time period.

The attraction of holding prompts in electronic form is twofold. First, they can be held securely in one place and be constantly available for easy access. Secondly, the systems can hide complexity from users, in that, at any one time, the user is presented with one screen of information containing elements of a prompt, hidden beneath each of which will be further information and perhaps other prompts. Rather than being faced with long and daunting paper check-lists, much of which is often not relevant for the particular tasks of individual readers, the on-screen prompt approach exposes users only to those issues which they select as relevant and thereby renders the review process more manageable.

The technique of on-line prompting is most easily delivered using hypertext, an enabling technique discussed in Section 4.2. In operation, therefore, such a system will present a series of items on the screen and further information on each can be obtained by pointing and clicking on the topic of most interest to the user. The prompts can also have internal cross-referencing and the ability to roam from item to item at the user's will.

Two demonstrators of this technique are operational in Masons. One deals with the various steps to be taken in preparing bundles for trial at the Queen's Bench Division of the High Court in England while the other walks users through the fundamental steps involved in taking out an injunction. The concept is straightforward. Users are presented with what appears to be a simple list of tasks and topics. Further help on each is also available by simply pointing and clicking on relevant elements, which will bring up, variously, further prompts, clarificatory text or may even, as with the injunctions check-list, transport the user into a standard word processing file which is designed as a precedent for the particular stage of the process in question.

From a technical point of view, these systems are relatively easy to design and develop. What seems to be more controversial is their legal substance over which there can be endless debate.

More advanced on-screen check-lists can also be developed using the branch of expert systems which I referred to as intelligent check-listing (see Section 4.3). On this model, the system is interactive and rather than leaving the user to browse and navigate as with hypertext, he is exposed instead to a more tightly managed question and answer session. This, in turn, can be integrated with document assembly so that after running through the intelligent check-list, an audit trail can be printed together with appropriate documentation. The VATIA system, described in Section 6.1, is a good example of this more advanced approach.

Know-who systems

In practice, having access to materials written by others or to detailed procedures is no substitute for a one-to-one chat with a specialist in the field in which you are working. If I am called upon to draft an exclusion clause, for example, it is far more useful to be able to talk briefly to a leading specialist in this area within my firm, outlining the individual circumstances of my case, and hoping that that expert will be able to put her hands on documents best suited to my purpose. Not only does this eliminate a tiresome trawl through potentially irrelevant documents, but I also have the added advantage of the human interaction which most lawyers tend to enjoy.

A different model of know-how formalizes this approach into what I call a *know-who* system. Such a system requires a detailed inventory to be compiled of all lawyers within an organization, together with their skills and areas of expertise and an indication of the areas in which they are clearly the leading available authority. Thus equipped with a comprehensive source of information about who knows most about what legal topics, each named specialist is then encouraged to develop her own, rigorous (even if idiosyncratic) information systems so that they can respond easily to enquiries.

In operation, a lawyer can quickly locate a specialist in an area of concern and that specialist, through her own preferred technologies, should be able to put her hands immediately on relevant materials. A *know-who* system is, therefore, a skills inventory combined with a user base of specialists with their own personalized information systems.

From internal know-how to external information retrieval

As law firms have built up their own internal know-how systems, their marketing machines have simultaneously rolled into action proclaiming they have unrivalled distillations of expertise and experience at the fingertips of all their lawyers. This know-how, they have continued, is rigorously organized, usable by junior lawyers, and accessible from anywhere in the world across their global telecommunications links.

It all sounds great but it was surely predictable that clients (often non-lawyers) would ask if they could have access to this selfsame rigorous distillation of know-how. And asked they have. Some firms have said 'no' claiming that this know-how is their stock-in-trade; others have said 'of course' and have bundled limited access as part of their traditional advisory service; while still others have recognized a commercial opportunity here and have said 'yes, but at a price'.

The last group are making the first, faltering steps from right to left along *The Legal Information Continuum*. They have begun to capitalize on the informating effect of internal know-how systems—in creating this in-house repository, a new revenue source has been generated as a by-product. There is innovation here as well, as access to legal information service becomes a new way of doing business. More dramatically, one of the Big 6 accountancy firms has recently projected that, by the year 2000, one-quarter of its entire US fee income will come from the provision of professional information in this manner. As electronic communications and groupware technology are refined and hypertext and expert systems are further exploited, the service which will be on offer could be most impressive. And as intelligent agents become usable, law firms will set them searching not just for materials reflecting their own areas of interest but also those of their clients.

All of that said, it is likely nonetheless that law firms will tend for some time yet to be selective in the materials to which they offer access and will withhold such internal know-how as is deemed to be a major source of competitive advantage. But I suspect lawyers will keep their crown jewels under metaphorical lock and key only until such time that the price is considered right for the sale of such know-how in the legal information services market of tomorrow.

Eventually, once internal know-how itself is made commercially available, my terminology will becomes a little confusing, if not redundant, in that users of this know-how will not regard it only as internal know-how but will treat it also as an external information service. Thus there is a blurred boundary between internal know-how and external retrieval.

There will soon be another source of confusion between these two categories. I expect and hope that law firms will soon start to bring together all their know-how sources (including precedents, their document stores, work product, prompts, and know-who) into single, internal systems, based to a large extent on hypertext technology. Users will be able to browse around these various sources, which will effectively become, as I call them, their own 'Firm Wide Webs' (others are beginning to use the term 'Intranet' in this context). A natural next step will be to establish links between an organization's Firm Wide Web and the World Wide Web itself. For example, a user may start on her Firm Wide Web, by invoking on-screen prompts; from which she might jump via a link to some standard form document; and, thereafter perhaps to some statutory source. But this last leap might take our user from her Firm Wide Web to the World Wide Web (where the statute is held) and the user may be oblivious to this, if the systems are, as they say, integrated seamlessly. Lawyers may not necessarily know, therefore, as they dip into the information at their fingertips, whether they are accessing internal or external information. At the same time, for users from beyond such a law firm, those parts of that firm's 'Intranet' or 'Firm Wide Web' which the lawyers are happy to make public, will be browsable and will seem like any other part of the Web.

5.5. External Information Retrieval

In the conduct of legal business today, lawyers do very frequently rely on source materials which have been produced beyond their own organizsations. If the name of the game from the lawyers' point of view is to make all the information which they need available through their computers, internal know-how systems must therefore be supplemented with the facility to retrieve external information in electronic form.

This information includes primary legal source materials, such as legislation, statutory instruments, and case reports and extends also to secondary sources, such as textbooks, articles, and other representations of the law. Beyond legal writings, lawyers also need access to many other sorts of information, including, for example, news coverage, market analysis, company details, and economic, political, and demographic indicators.

Traditionally, the packaging and delivery of external legal information (which is my main concern) in printed form was the sole province of the publishing industry. With the advent of electronic publishing, however, the boundaries between traditional publishers and other information providers have been blurred and it is now possible for all manner of organizations, small and large, to disseminate information in electronic form (most noticeably on the Internet through the World Wide Web). Whereas the term 'external', in traditional publishing terms, would have meant 'produced beyond the legal profession', this adjective can now only be taken to refer to information produced beyond one's own organization. As we have just seen, as law firms themselves enter the world of publishing know-how (both conventionally and in electronic form), they too become providers of external information in so far as other law firms and the external market are concerned.

Text retrieval

In the early years, from the late 1950s to the mid-1980s, IT-based delivery of external legal information was dominated, in research and then in practice, by full text retrieval technology (as discussed in Section 4.1). With such systems, users specify keywords, that is, words which they consider to be relevant for their enquiries. These prompt the system to search for the occurrence of such words within documents. Although defective in the significant ways noted, this method of document retrieval has remained dominant up to the present day.

The best example of this technology is the LEXIS system, now owned by Reed International, and synonymous for many years with computerized legal research itself. Originally a repository only of primary source materials, more recently the LEXIS database has been extended to embrace secondary documents as well. While it was in its infancy, users had to have dedicated workstations to gain access to LEXIS, but the system now runs on personal computers with a much enhanced (graphical) user interface as well.

In the United States, LEXIS seems to have been a resounding success, although I have heard cynics say that LEXIS holds every proposition of American law and its opposite as well!

In the UK, its introduction has been less successful, although it is not known if this is because English and Scots lawyers do little research or whether the system itself is not sufficiently easy or useful for the English lawyer. (The research habits of UK lawyers is a whole topic of study in its own right. Empirical evidence suggests that most practising lawyers rarely look up the law. Whether this might change if materials were at their fingertips is a question which exercises market researchers in the world of legal information provision.)

What is clear is that the early aspirations of legal technologists, who foresaw lawyers of the early 1990s having all necessary and useful legal information at their fingertips, have not been realized. But five factors are changing this position, and doing so rapidly.

The relevance of CD

First, the production of legal materials on CD-ROM has now captured the interests of all serious legal publishers in England. To the technologists, this may seem rather puzzling because CD is no more than an effective medium for the storage of large amounts of data. More than this, it is likely to be an interim technology because advances in telecommunications (technical and commercial) will, in but a few years, give inexpensive and speedy on-line access to external services, through World Wide Web, its equivalent or its successor. Why then should such an interim technology galvanize the publishers into action? The answer, I suspect, is partly practical and partly psychological. As a practical matter, CD offers the opportunity—today—of delivering huge amounts of legal material in a highly compact form. It makes electronic legal publishing commercially viable *now* rather than in a few years' time. Psychologically, lawyers can comfortably grasp the power of CD technology without being unduly daunted: they can handle the idea of a shelf full of law books on one disc but seem to find it less easy to come to grips with being connected down the telephone line to a collection of legal information which is said to be larger than any single physical library in their jurisdiction. Being connected on-line also has a further psychological twist and induces a sense of near panic in the user where the charge is based on 'time on-line'. In contrast, with CD, there is a visible and finite physical manifestation and a licence which clearly scopes the cost of usage. Being able to show a lawyer a CD which holds the rules of the Supreme Court in England or decades of the All England Reports, brings the power of IT more sharply into focus than vague chats about seemingly endless collections of documents held in some awesome computer system overseas.

Enhancements to text retrieval

The second factor relates to full text retrieval technology itself and the various ways it will be enhanced in the coming years. As outlined in Section 4.1, raw text retrieval systems are set to be supplemented by intelligent agents, augmented search formulation, and conceptual searching mechanisms.

The net result here will be systems holding text, as previously structured and organized, yet easier to operate and likely to deliver more relevant and focused information into the hands of users. It is commonly said that legal text retrieval systems simply do not work (an exaggeration) or do not give users what they want or expect. There can be little doubt that some of the alleged shortcomings of the systems themselves could be overcome by greater proficiency in search formulation by users. Yet, the average lawyer does not feel at home in putting together complex search requests and so the advent of retrieval systems supplemented by the various techniques just mentioned will surely increase confidence and success in the retrieval of external information.

Hypertext

Those who are sceptical of full text retrieval systems believe that the addition of various complementary and supplementary techniques is simply tinkering at the edges of the greater problem, which is that the text held within these systems is insufficiently structured ever to yield usable, valuable, and directly applicable information. Such protagonists often call for a radical shift in approach and hypertext is generally cited here as the key enabling technique. While there can be a tendency to overstate its potential and value, I have little doubt that hypertext is a powerful third factor in my projected upsurge of usage of systems which retrieve external legal information.

As described in Section 4.2, hypertext encourages information providers to structure and organize materials in a way which allows the users to navigate and browse quite naturally through complex bodies of often interrelating documents. In this sense, hypertext supports a different form of research because browsing in this way is quite unlike the retrieval of documents on the basis of words within them. Experience suggests that lawyers are far more comfortable with the form of interaction which belongs to hypertext, preferring to click on 'hot spots' than to formulate search requests. Legal publishers across the world have now recognized the

185

strength and potential of hypertext and it is emerging rapidly as a preferred delivery mechanism for much legal information.

The Net and the Web for lawyers

Hypertext also underlies the fourth factor which I suggest will help bring about greater usage of external legal information systems and services. This factor is that of the information revolution being brought about through the Internet and the World Wide Web, systems which were introduced in Section 4.5. Whatever the future may hold for these two phenomena, the current and projected level of usage of these systems, both domestically and in business, is such that the manner of their use will set a strong trend in information retrieval. And the so-called browsers which allow users to gain access to and retrieve information on the World Wide Web are all hypertext-based. Not least through the use of Internet and World Wide Web at home, lawyers and non-lawyers will increasingly find it quite natural to use IT-based information systems as a principal source of guidance and service in all aspects of their lives. This greater confidence and reliance on information systems beyond the professional environment will further help clear the way for lawyers to access external information, as a matter of second nature, in their daily practice, rather than using conventional library facilities.

The information society

The fifth factor which will catalyse greater uptake of IT-based legal information retrieval systems will be the more general explosion of information services across society. With home computing and the World Wide Web in place, citizens themselves will regularly enjoy access to a wide range of information services, relating to leisure and entertainment, personal financial planning, health and welfare, education and training, and government. As it becomes commonplace for users to dip into previously unfathomable depths of knowledge and information there will be continuing demand in this information society for further facilities and new sources of information.

In this way, non-lawyers will be able to benefit from legal guidance, invariably in situations in which conventional legal service would have been impractical or far too expensive—this is the essence of *the latent legal market*. Hypertext will be a central technique in delivering legal information products to non-lawyers. But this use of hypertext will extend beyond the text browsing features which are so popular today. For hypertext will also be the basis of many on-screen prompts, giving step-by-step guidance on legal matters, packaged in concise and manageable form. Workflow techniques will also be embedded in such applications, patiently taking non-lawyers through the labyrinths of the law. And expert system technology will also play a role, both in providing self-contained legal problem solvers and, in the shorter term, offering automated document generation of, for example, relatively standard contractual arrangements.

In the IT-based information society, the business of developing, providing and marketing systems which carry external legal information will change beyond recognition. Indeed, few conventional assumptions about this enterprise will survive. (This is the essence of the shift in legal paradigm to which I return in Section 8.4).

Whereas the tendency with external information retrieval has always been to talk about it as an application which supports only the *legal task* (see Section 3.2) of information consultation, the legal products and services which will be available in the future will go far further, by delivering more focused guidance, for example, on drafting particular documents, on following procedures, and even on analysis and problem solving. The retrieval of external information will, therefore, assume a place on *The Legal Information Continuum* increasingly towards the right-hand side and will come to be regarded as the retrieval of legal information services.

Gradually, these services will become available through a variety of services and systems: guidance for non-lawyers on the Net via the Web; for lawyers, and their in-house clients, through electronic legal networks such as Lexis Counsel Connect and Link, and (as today) through on-line services and CD packages. Only time will tell whether all of these services will eventually coalesce into one massive, seamless, global information service. Alternatively, it may transpire that the systems will remain relatively distinct. The legal profession might strive to evolve and maintain an information superhighway of its own and for its clients, for example (although I would not support this). Much will depend on the power and influence of the interested parties (see Section 5.1).

5.6. Case Management

Case management is a relative newcomer to any list of leading applications of IT for lawyers and is now rapidly gaining credence and even acceptance within the legal profession. In Lord Woolf's report, *Access to Justice*, for example, case management by judges is a vital component of his sweeping reforms and is portrayed as one key to streamlining the civil justice system, reducing the extent to which litigation is unnecessarily combative and yet retaining the traditional benefits and strengths of the English adversarial system. Equally, in connection with changes in the legal aid system in England, case management is also widely hailed as the indispensable tool for any competent legal practitioner who seeks to work within the challenging framework set by the state and yet still retain some acceptable level of profitability.

While commentators and practitioners alike are therefore welcoming and pursuing the introduction of case management, there remains some confusion over what this whole topic is about. Are we concerned with management of *lawyers*, and if so does this mean lawyers working in teams? Or is case management concerned specifically with *cases*, in which event does this mean individual cases, or collections of cases? Who is responsible for the managing? Is it lawyers, judges, or clients themselves?

In fact, it is not especially helpful to be too stipulative or restrictive in defining case management. Instead, one vital thread should be noted and developed: that the techniques of the discipline of project management can valuably be applied in a legal context. These techniques can help bring about the resolution of legal problems and the management of legal risks more effectively and efficiently, and to a higher standard, than the less rigorous, more haphazard methods of the past.

Case management, then, is a type of project management. IT is not absolutely necessary for the practice of case management, but it is proving immensely useful for lawyers in two broad categories of application: case flow management systems; and case-load management systems. In my jargon about *legal tasks* (see Section 3.2), case management is predominantly about the following of procedures but it supports information consultation as well.

Case flow management systems

To help progress individual cases, judges, lawyers, and clients can use case flow management systems. Designed to drive cases efficiently from the initial filing through to final disposal (in whatever form), in one simple form such case management systems may be no more than computerized diarying and scheduling applications, establishing timetables for key events and tasks in the life cycle of a legal matter. As a passive, consultative tool, this can offer users the facility to establish the status of any matter, the progress of the case so far, and projected time-scales for later phases. Armed with such an application, judges can regularly monitor progress and, for example, discern slippage or delay with the minimum of fuss.

Looking ahead, non-lawyers who are involved with some court action should themselves be able to log onto equivalent systems from home and find out their positions immediately. There are surely significant social benefits therefore to be derived from case flow management systems, in that it should eventually be possible for court centres, as a matter of course, to allow access to their systems and so to enable individuals to gain a ready understanding of the state of any actions in which they may be participating.

This level of case management can be achieved through a combination of readily available technologies such as diarying, database, and project management. Further refinement, using workflow software, for example, will deliver a system which can itself actively prompt users to action; and let them know at appropriate times which milestones or deadlines are approaching, or which tasks require completion. For the lawyer with a large portfolio of cases, therefore, upon switching on his machine in the morning, a range of tasks can be presented, representing the total work programme across the case-load.

Again, this technology can be adapted for the non-lawyer as an information package of sorts. Do-it-yourself small claims or debt recovery packages will become available, for example, taking the lay person, on a step-by-step basis, through the various tasks which must be undertaken, in the right order within appropriate time-scales.

In its most refined form, either for lawyers or non-lawyers, case flow management systems can be used in support of highly proactive legal service as a means of embodying sound legal practice into the life cycles of central business processes (see Section 6.3).

Work product management systems

Also falling under the category of case flow management systems, but deserving of separate treatment, are what I call work product management systems (as distinct from work product retrieval systems mentioned earlier in this chapter). Especially useful for cases being handled by a team of lawyers, the idea here is to collect, organize, and then make available all the documentation produced by these lawyers during the conduct of the case (see Section 6.1 for a case-study of this application in action). In large and complex cases, solicitors, barristers, expert witnesses or advisers, and in-house lawyers together frequently generate huge quantities of letters of advice, reports, plans, pleadings, witness statements, and other legal docu-ments. Rather than consigning these to conventional filing systems and so limiting the ease with which this vital information can be retrieved, with a work product management system these materials can be collected and stored in a more flexible way so that clients and the team of advisers can have the know-how of the case at their fingertips. The documents can be linked and cross-referred to one another and annotations and observations can be attached to documents and so are accessible to all team members. The lawyers should also have the added luxury of greater confidence that they are less likely to offer advice on the same matter more than once. This helps avoid the particularly embarrassing situation in which different lawyers from the same firm offer contradictory advice on the same point.

On large projects, over long periods, work product management systems can be invaluable repositories of the experience and expertise accumulated on a particular case. And as lawyers or others leave the team, their know-ledge can be preserved. Equally, professionals new to the task can have a ready-made information system which can ease them into the past work product in a focused and practical way.

Work product management systems can also play a role in the court-room—the judge can be tracked through complex arguments by being nav-igated around a collection of relevant and interrelated documents. The barrister can show how important parts of the pleadings, for example, relate to witness statements and to correspondence; and can jump effortlessly from one to the other and in so doing provide a crisp summary of the key points being advanced.

The flexibility in work product management systems can be achieved through hypertext technology, while the information sharing facilities can be attained through the judicious use of groupware techniques.

Work product and case flow management systems should invariably be made available to clients. This can be done through status reporting sys-tems, which allow clients, often by remote access, to obtain up-to-the-minute information about the status (for example, the progress made and the costs incurred so far) of particular matters on which they are being advised. Equally, many clients find it useful to be given charts, graphically depicting the proposed plan for a case, cost estimations, and the progress made against this plan. When presented in the form of bar charts (specifically by Gantt chart, where each project step is represented as a bar), clients can very quickly grasp the overall shape of an action, the key mile-stones, and the relevant, critical paths.

Case-load management

The second broad category of case management system is that of case-load management. The focus here is not on the progress of individual cases but rather on the control of a collection of cases, perhaps those of individual lawyers or judges, but equally across entire law firms or court centres. The management challenges here relate to the allocation of resources (mainly human) and involve the organizational and logistical tasks of ensuring that busy people who are in demand are in the right place at the right time and expected not to be in two places at once. Additionally, case management in this sense can help minimize the generation of impossible work loads, especially for those lawyers who tend to be over-committed. In turn, this can reduce the delay and disappointment which results from overbooking.

While commonplace in other trades and industries, it remains relatively rare for lawyers to be structured and rigorous in their allocation of work. And yet in most law firms, where few lawyers are occupied full time on any particular case, a tool which can allocate appropriate lawyers with relevant skills to the cases being handled, in accordance with the demands on their time and their projected availability, is very useful indeed.

So too with judges—although little can be done to alleviate the scarcity of their time and the pressing time-scales within which they operate, this pressurized resource can be more efficiently allocated, and balanced against other factors (such as courtrooms, lawyers, and witnesses), by deploying IT than by using conventional, manual techniques.

At a basic level, common diarying, scheduling, and database technology can provide the basis of improved case-load management, if only by making relevant information centrally available and easily accessible. But it is dedicated project management software that is really equal to the task. These systems are designed specifically to allocate resources to specified times, dates, and physical locations. And with sophisticated techniques such as critical path analysis, milestone schedules and manufacturing cycle charts, these systems ensure that the case-loads allocated are not just possible but optimum in the circumstances.

There are commercial benefits here for the client as well in that the status reporting facilities mentioned earlier in relation to case flow management can apply equally to case-load management, so that where a number of cases are being handled for a client, they can instantaneously obtain an update on progress across their entire case-load.

PART THREE— THE PRACTICALITIES

6

Case-Studies

I turn now to intensely practical matters, by devoting this chapter and the next one to exploring IT and the law in action together.

Here I return to the important distinction introduced in Section 2.1, that between automating, informating, and innovating. Throughout the book I have given examples of each of these functions. Now, I go further by presenting more detailed case-studies of the practical applications of each. All but one of the case-studies are based on firsthand, personal experience of the systems in question. I have selected those which have left the most lasting impressions on me, either because they so clearly demonstrate the power of some applications or because they clarify the central claims and arguments of this book. Automating emerges clearly as a tool for streamlining legal processes; informating is seen to create opportunities to exploit the by-products of automation; while innovating results in the re-engineering of legal service generally or of legal processes in particular.

6.1. Automating and Streamlining

The most vital function of IT during the transitional period between the print-based industrial society and the IT-based information society is that of automation. While I may be accused of having projected automation as an altogether less mission-critical and less glamorous function of technology, I should stress that in fact I believe its benefits extend well beyond the interim role I have cast it in focusing on its primacy during the transition.

Automation is about computerizing, motorizing, routinizing, and systematizing existing processes. As such, it can afford countless opportunities for streamlining and improving many aspects of our domestic, social, and working lives. Most of its potential dangers—for example, that of automating a process which is defective to begin with—have been adequately rehearsed by others and are now well understood; and can be effectively managed anyway.

A more subtle trap in automation initiatives, however, is to confine attention to back-office, administrative systems. This is often to neglect the front office where imaginative and leading edge automation can still be a very substantial source of business benefit and competitive advantage, as the case-studies in this section suggest.

Intelligent check-listing—VATIA

In 1988, when I was working with the international accounting and consultancy firm, Ernst & Whinney (now Ernst & Young), we developed an intelligent check-list which was designed to allow the firm's general auditors to tap into the knowledge and expertise of the firm's Value Added Tax (VAT) and Customs Duty Group without needing to refer every point of difficulty or doubt to these specialists.

Used in the presence of clients, the system was conceived as 'an intelligent assistant' to support those appraising the adequacy and compliance of clients' VAT systems and procedures. The general commercial knowledge of the users combined with the specific VAT expertise within the system to produce an effective and comprehensive analysis of a client's VAT position with little direct participation of the firm's VAT experts. The first version of the system ran on the firm's then standard audit portable computer and by spring 1988 was installed on over 600 machines throughout Ernst & Whinney's twenty-six UK offices. Eight years later, it continues to be an invaluable tool on major audits.

Although neither developed nor used within the legal profession (and this may well be portentous), VATIA is still a fine illustration of the way in which legal knowledge and commercial experience can be packaged and delivered for use by non-lawyers using modern techniques of information systems.

The system was developed in response to a new VAT regime which introduced a formidable scheme of civil penalties and required businesses to pay greater attention to the adequacy of their VAT systems. In anticipation of vast penalties being levied for non-compliance and mis-declaration, Ernst & Whinney had to identify an appropriate way of continuing to undertake reliable VAT reviews. On the one hand there was the possibility of recruiting many more VAT specialists who would be deployed on every audit. Alternatively, there was the option of using some form of IT to make the firm's scarce VAT expertise more widely available and easily accessible. Given the first choice appeared to be both too costly and impractical, the second, it was recognized rapidly at that time, called for the use of expert systems techniques. Tailoring an off-the-shelf expert systems package for the project, even the first version of VATIA (VAT Intelligent Assistant) was comfortably able to take its users patiently through the complexities of VAT regulation, providing them with a series of questions and details that were specific to the audit at hand. The user provided information to the system by answering 'yes', 'no' or 'don't know' by selecting from menus or by entering short pieces of text.

VATIA is akin to a large electronic check-list, reminding non-specialists of questions they ought to ask and providing context sensitive help screens to assist the user where the questions may be complex or arcane. Further navigation within the system leads the user to explanations of VAT concepts and a glossary of terms. At the end of a consultation (taking, on average, between one and two hours) the system provided a printed summary (a document assembly feature) of all the areas of concern that had arisen, dividing this analysis into sections of varying levels of urgency and significance.

The system is thus based on expert systems technology in its mode of analysis and document generation. The exploratory help material was in many ways a forerunner to hypertext (indeed this was the same technology as that used for the Latent Damage System's help text (see Section 4.2)) but, overall, the system is best perhaps regarded as an intelligent checklist. Although the term 'intelligent' raises more questions that it answers, it does highlight the fact that VATIA is packed full of highly distilled expertise and that the basic prompting of the conventional paper check-lists is augmented in a focused way by a consultation which takes the user only through those parts of the check-list which are relevant to the audit at hand.

In fact, the system superseded a previous regime of paper check-lists, which research had shown were not used sufficiently and appropriately in practice. The embodiment of a check-list concept in a technology framework allowed far more information to be available and yet the complexity was hidden from the user in such a way that it became more rather than less usable as further features were added.

VATIA did not change underlying business processes. Rather, it was a classic example of streamlining, improving, and routinizing a series of tasks. The business benefits have been considerable and the technique of intelligent check-listing to support procedural tasks was well vindicated.

Hypertext for work product management

One of the most dramatic and impressive applications of IT in the law with which I have been involved was the development of a hypertext system designed as a central repository for work Masons was undertaking in relation to a very large piece of litigation.

Involving many claims over several years, the international dispute in question required the attention of a team of lawyers up to fifty people in size. As our work continued, it was clear that a major challenge would be that of maintaining a first-rate filing system to allow our lawyers and the clients to dip into our past research and advice. We needed a work product management system (one of the rarer categories of litigation support system and case management system—see Section 5.6).

A substantial hypertext system was evolved to meet this purpose and I say evolved advisedly, in that it developed in ways no one could have foreseen at the outset. Here, one can immediately see a major advantage of hypertext which can support the establishment of an information system whose content and style of usage does not need to be specified in detail at the beginning of a project. Rather, new structures for the information and uses of it emerge and change over time. This is not treated by design teams as a problem. Changes in direction and approach in large-scale litigation are common and so our technologies should not just accommodate this, they should enable it where appropriate.

At the core of our original system was the full text of the contract over which the dispute had arisen. This was held in typical hypertext layers so that, on entry, the user was originally presented with a list of contents of the clauses and schedules. Upon clicking on these, the lawyer could be taken down to the text itself.

As we wrote letters of advice, reports, and analysis, we loaded these into the system as well. The contents level then appeared to the user with occasional 'buttons', being the logo of our firm, whose presence next to a clause number indicated that some written work had been prepared by the firm on that clause. By clicking on that button, a list of materials was presented and the full text of each could be retrieved immediately. This was developed further by loading the text of documents from other parties, the decisions of the various hearings which were conducted across the years, and other source materials. All these were cross-referenced and so emerged a vast but usable, information system which allowed users, at the touch of a button, to locate all the materials relevant for individual parts of the contract, all of which had cross-references to other parts of the system. Although originally the point of entry to the system was the contract, as more information was entered, various further contents papers were created, including listings of decisions, points of law, and key non-contractual documents.

The power of the system became apparent to us one Friday when a dozen or so lawyers, new to the case, were each given formidable work packages to complete over the weekend. Each was immediately trained on the hypertext system (which took about ten minutes) and so had access to a unique and highly structured filing system and to a historical analysis of the legal advice given to date. Conventional methods would have been woefully inadequate in comparison.

This work product system was also installed at the client's site and this gave rise to greater participation and appreciation of the work being undertaken by our firm, gratitude for which was regularly and frankly expressed.

In this way an otherwise unmanageable process was rendered controllable and the firm's work product was more readily accessible and reusable by the client. That said, the system automated rather than innovated, in that it did not fundamentally change the nature of the service we provided on the overall course of the litigation. Rather, this powerful technology automated the document and file management challenges which traditional, reactive legal service spawns. The underlying, enabling technique of hypertext was used also as a form of groupware. It created a culture in which the cumulative legal advice was genuinely directed towards the client and it supported the development of an invaluable reference source for ongoing use in the dispute.

The Latent Damage System

My final illustration of automation again relates to expert systems, but this time as a tool for legal analysis.

When the Latent Damage Act 1986 was passed in England, it became clear that this legislation had radical implications for those involved with the manufacturing, construction, and supply industries. It also affected all professional advisers (solicitors, accountants, consultants, and so forth). The difficulty with the law on latent damage was that of the Act itself. Its provisions were impenetrable and detailed, expressed in a web of cross-references. Even for the most competent legal practitioner, this piece of legislation was formidable and could not be understood without considerable knowledge of other relevant pieces of related legislation and case-law.

A taste of this branch of law is given in section 1(2) of the Act which reads: 'Section 2 of this Act shall not apply to an action to which this section applies'. It would be natural to think that the reference to 'this Act' means the Act in which it appears—in reality, it is of application to another Act.

Only a few individuals had mastered the legislation when it came into force. The challenge with which I was involved was to seek to find a way of using IT to make some of this rare expertise available to the many who required it. Our answer was to develop an expert system in law, which subsequently became known as the Latent Damage System. The legal expertise was provided by Professor Phillip Capper, then Chairman of the Oxford University Law Faculty, currently a partner in Masons, but formerly trained by IBM. Author of the first book on the 1986 Act, Phillip was an acknowledged expert at that time. With my own interdisciplinary background, I was the knowledge engineer for the project, that is, the chap responsible for mining the gold nuggets from Phillip's head and transferring this expertise into a system which non-experts could consult. In a national daily newspaper, I described this as equivalent to having Phillip sitting on the desk of every lawyer in the land.

The system itself offers advice and draws conclusions in relation to the Latent Damage Act 1986 and related statutes and judicial precedents. It is designed for use by lawyers and legally informed persons. The system advises on the law on latent damage, dealing fully with the Latent Damage Act 1986 and the complex context of tort, contract, and product liability law in which that piece of legislation operates. The purpose of the package is to assist and identify, in latent damage cases, when a breach of duty occurred, on what date a cause of action accrued, and when the wronged party will be taken to have had knowledge of the loss suffered. The implications of fraud, deliberate concealment, contractual liability, personal injuries, product liabilities, successive ownership, and many other related matters are also taken into account. The key piece of advice offered by the system is the date after which a claimant can no longer commence proceedings. The discovery of this date is the result of a sophisticated reasoning process.

While a competent lawyer would take about five to ten hours to understand the Act and its implications and to apply that understanding to a particular case, by using the system a lawyer or legally informed person is able to find a solution within five to ten minutes. And yet, there are over two millions paths through the system. The system guides you through *all but only* those legal rules that bear on the problem at hand, concealing unnecessary complexity and obscurity along the way. The user need have no knowledge whatsoever of computer science because the system offers friendly, prompt guidance and explanation. It can clarify questions and will indicate what lines of reasoning it is exploring. It also provides facilities to examine extracts from judgments and legislation, and the option of requesting a printed summary of any consultation.

Our purpose in developing the Latent Damage System was to demonstrate that commercially and socially significant expert systems in law could in fact be built; and that this could be done without offending any jurisprudential principles of legal reasoning. In 1988, we wrote an extended case-study of the development process, in *Latent Damage Law—The Expert System*, and we packaged the book together with a complimentary version of the system tucked in the back. We believe this was the first commercially available expert system in law and do not know of systems which have been marketed since then which match that one in genuine expert performance.

In assessing the system, it is important to ignore the particular area of law in question and concentrate instead on the underlying principle of developing and using computerized legal problem solvers. I think it is clear, on reflection, that despite its power and sophistication, the Latent Damage System remains an example of automation. It greatly streamlines the underlying task of legal analysis but it was designed for use by lawyers and does not challenge or reject the conventional legal reasoning process. Systems like it may give rise to quicker and better service but still very much in today's legal paradigm. So our project suggests that it is technically possible and jurisprudentially feasible to build diagnostic systems in law. Whether it is commercially affordable or culturally tolerable is another question (see Section 7.4).

Judicial use of IT

My final illustration of automating and streamlining focuses not on any single system but on the cluster of applications which have begun to exert considerable influence on judges, especially in the United States. (Interestingly, lawyer for lawyer, judges in the UK seem more enthusiastic about computers than solicitors—this is apparent from conference statistics, research surveys and public debate—although they have suffered from lack of financial support—see Section 7.4.)

Word processing has become important, of course, both for taking notes at trial itself as well as for the preparation of judgments—here judges have recognized that technology both enhances the document production process but can, through advanced features such as outlining, help

The Practicalities

structure and organize judgments and so even change judicial methods (so there is some innovation here too).

Electronic mail, databases, and spreadsheet packages have also been used regularly, as have more advanced technologies such as 'computer-aided real time transcription'. This is a first rate example of automation in so far as the systems convert words spoken in the courtroom, and as taken down in the shorthand of stenographers, into text that appears almost instantaneously on the judge's monitor. Additionally, there is a facility to annotate text as it appears. Studies have shown that this one application can reduce the time consumed by judicial note taking and in turn lessen the cost of trials. With the advent, in the future, of continuous speech, large vocabulary voice recognition systems (see Section 4.8), this process will be automated still further.

This upsurge of interest in computers by judges directly affects solicitors and barristers. Some judges have already directed parties to use litigation support databases to manage documents in preparation for trial; others require the delivery of materials in specified word processing formats; while, in the Official Referees Courts in England, the judges regularly require parties to use the ORSA Protocol (see Section 3.1), and so exchange information about one another's preferred formats for the storage of documents. The Official Referees Courts have also pioneered a facility whereby judgments can be downloaded directly to the machines of solicitors and barristers.

Judges are gradually becoming better equipped to deal with hyperregulation, as more and more legal information retrieval systems are made available on CD-ROM and on-line, through legal electronic networks, the Internet, and so forth. At the same time, major revamping of the courtroom itself has taken place in some jurisdictions and is anticipated in others, as a veritable cornucopia of new facilities are introduced. These have included the use of litigation support systems in court, not just for document management but also for the presentation of evidentiary material on appropriately positioned monitors.

Automation appears likely to continue to dominate the judicial function over the next few years. Lord Woolf's report, *Access to Justice*, predicts and encourages more ambitious and socially significant uses of IT by judges and the courts in England. As judges become more proactive in progressing the flow of cases, the use of appropriate case management systems will follow naturally. And in this and other contexts, enhanced communication with parties will be enabled by desktop video conferencing. And looking further ahead still, from what has happened so far, it is not fanciful to suppose that future automation will also include sentencing databases (already used in

202

Canada and Australia), more widespread delivery of judgments in machine readable form directly into legal information systems, the remote retrieval of case documentation (as images as well as text, as telecommunications improve), and the use of expert systems, such as a recent prototype which assists in bail decisions.

6.2. Informating and Exploiting

Informating may be a new term and concept for lawyers but there is no shortage in the legal profession of powerful illustrations of its value. In many ways, informating can be regarded as giving rise to opportunities for further exploitation of potential—even if unintended—benefits of particular applications of IT. The challenge in informating is to exploit the lucky breaks which the informating effect sometimes generates.

Accounting and management information systems

One of the earliest illustrations of informating in a legal context arose from lawyers' use of accounting systems, which dominated law office technology in the 1970s through to the mid-1980s. Although strictly a back-office function and not of direct use in the delivery of service to clients, accounting systems nonetheless had an informating function which was to dominate practice management for many years and later came to redefine the way in which lawyers used IT to manage the financial side of their businesses.

When accounting systems were originally introduced, the overriding purpose was to automate manual techniques of bookkeeping and accounting and to assist in the preparation of invoices. Central to the assessment of the amount clients were to be charged was the notion of hourly billing, whereby the invoice rendered was calculated on the basis of the number of hours spent on a particular matter, as multiplied by a specified hourly rate of the lawyer whose time was expended. Thus, if lawyers could record all the time they spent on their various tasks and this data was entered into the accounting system, it was child's play for an accounting system to calculate bills; and this was and remains invaluable when many different lawyers are working on the same matter.

On the face of it, accounting systems were all about automating. However, it rapidly became apparent that in capturing data about time spent by lawyers, as allocated to particular matters, a very useful by-product was thereby created.

The by-product was a form of management information because the data held about lawyers' time gave rise to crucial information about the business—how many chargeable hours each lawyer was working; levels of discounting by practice area and across the firm; profitability of individual parts of the operation; the value of particular clients in monetary terms; analysis of work across industries; geographical spread of work; and so forth. And so, in entering data for accounting purposes, valuable new information was created and here was a fine example of the informating function.

Later accounting systems were designed to exploit this informating phenomenon such that the information created as a by-product could be more easily accessed and manipulated. And today, very few accounting systems for lawyers are without some management information module or functionality.

Document management and know-how

A further illustration of legal informating comes in the context of what have come to be known as 'document management systems'.

In the early days of word processing for lawyers (in the 1970s through to the late 1980s), the dominant underlying architecture was that of a central minicomputer attached to which were a collection of 'dumb' terminals. On this model, all the word processing files were held on the central system and all the processing and computing was also undertaken centrally. The terminals were simply the means by which text could be viewed, created, deleted, amended, and later printed, with the screens offering a view on the current state of the text file as held centrally.

With the advent of networked personal computers, new options arose. Now the text files and the processing did not need to be held and undertaken on the central machine (commonly referred to as 'the file server') but could be stored, as they say, 'locally', on the personal computers themselves.

Whichever of a variety of options were deployed, systems administrators very soon came to realize that in gaining flexibility users could far less easily be constrained by the disciplines of early WP and minicomputers. Whereas the filing and 'housekeeping' were performed automatically on the minicomputer, on the early PC networks there was far greater responsibility and onus on the users themselves to save and organize their files in a structured and systematic way.

On large PC networks, housekeeping soon became wildly out of control and the position became untenable. Files were inadvertently being deleted, overwritten, lost, or, more generally, named and stored using esoteric labels and locations, such that users (even the authors themselves) were unable to find and retrieve files that had previously been created.

Document management systems were designed to overcome these runaway file management problems. Ironically, these document management systems recreate and impose the housekeeping and file control systems characteristic of the bygone days of minicomputers. Again, at first glance, here we have an aspect of the lawyer's business being automated. Yet this automation spawned a further illustration of the informating effect, of more dramatic impact to the practice of law.

In operation, document management systems require their users, when creating documents, also to enter some information about the nature and content of these materials. Where those document management systems require some précis or keywords to be input, this has had a remarkable side effect.

Where originally this information was required for housekeeping purposes, it transpired quite quickly, for more imaginative users, that this same information could be invaluable in what has come to be known as 'work product retrieval'. Consider a lawyer who is preparing a letter of advice on the concept of 'best endeavours'. With a document management system, it should be possible for that lawyer to retrieve all previous letters, advice, and reports on that topic (all past work product) by entering these keywords and instructing the system to perform a routine search function. Although this information was originally required for housekeeping purposes, the informating effect is such that it creates a key approach to internal know-how retrieval (see Section 5.4).

Once again, developments have progressed on the back of the success of this informating phenomenon—later versions of document management systems encourage and facilitate the entry of information about documents being created to make for easier retrieval by later users; so that one of the express goals of using document management systems today is to make work product more easily accessible.

Much, of course, depends on the willingness of those creating documents to provide adequate descriptions and keyword characterizations of their work. A shift in mind-set is required here, consistent with the successful implementation of most know-how systems, in that lawyers should now recognize a new duality to their work. While in the past most of their written documentation served a single advisory purpose, lawyers should now be oriented towards thinking they are not only advising clients, but they are also contributing to the central 'institutional memory' or 'corporate know-how' of the firm, so that other lawyers and clients can benefit from this initial thinking without unnecessary duplication of effort.

Electronic mail and know-how

A related display of the informating effect derives from imaginative use of electronic mail systems which are now increasingly common in law firms in the United Kingdom. Although originally conceived as a convenient and effective way of passing messages and documents to one another, legal users of electronic mail within large organizations very quickly found that they can obtain prompt responses to legal queries by sending questions of law to all lawyers on the system.

While it would be possible for the lawyers benefiting from the various replies to such requests to use the information gleaned for their purposes only, many firms now seek to capture responses to questions of this kind and build up an in-house know-how capability on the back of the responses tendered.

Here, therefore, is the automation of the distribution of a request creating a valuable by-product in its own right and so illustrative of the informating effect.

And here, once again, the benefits derived from informating have helped developers design or redesign systems to accommodate the effect that was once unintended—bulletin board and conferencing technology, for instance, take the process just described one step further.

Litigation support and document management

A final illustration of informating can be found in the field of litigation support. In large-scale litigation conducted in the traditional manner, upon instruction legal advisers often must visit a variety of geographical locations to assess the extent and nature of the load of documents which may bear on the case to hand.

In particularly large construction disputes, for example, it is not uncommon to find thousands of lever arch files containing millions of sheets of paper (indeed, I was recently involved in a case with over 20,000 lever arch files and around ten million pages).

Where technology is brought to bear in such cases (see Section 5.3) some massive document loading or document indexing project is often initiated to transfer the documents, or information about the documents, from paper into machines. Where a legal team has requested that the full text of documents be available in searchable form, the cost of such an exercise can be vast—the process can cost around £2 per page, which for large construction disputes, can easily give rise to an initial litigation support investment of many millions of pounds (this assumes the technology is used on all the documents, which is not necessarily prudent—see Section 5.3).

On some projects, however, the scenario is quite different. I have in mind those projects for which sophisticated paper and document management procedures and systems (often text and image based systems) are established at the start of the project with a view at that stage to more effective control and management of the project itself.

In the event of a dispute relating to such a project, however, legal advisers may be delighted to find themselves being offered access to a system in which many or most of the documents are already indexed and stored and so are ready for searching, sorting, and retrieval.

The informating here is the unintended assembly of a litigation support system. What can be agonizing and frustrating, however, is that such document management systems may not provide all the functionality which a litigator would prefer to have when managing and controlling documents using IT.

The lesson here, from informating, is that some attention to the potential by-product at the outset and perhaps some modest tailoring or refining of the document management system could result in a—albeit dormant—fully functional litigation support system being available for consultation should the unfortunate need arise. There is scope for a consulting service here, in that project managers should take advice from litigation support specialists at the start of their projects so as to ensure that their document management systems can easily be extended for use as litigation support systems. A party which can have its litigation support system up and running from the outset should enjoy a major strategic advantage in the event of a dispute.

6.3. Innovating and Re-engineering

At the heart of this book, especially when projecting many years ahead, is the claim that legal practice and the administration of law will undergo fundamental change with the introduction of ever more advanced technologies. I have in mind here the deployment of IT in *innovating* and so transforming tasks, processes, and even organizations.

The Practicalities

This approach to IT overlaps with much that is being said by the currently fashionable management school of business process re-engineering (or BPR, as it commonly known). Pioneered and popularized in large part by Michael Hammer and James Champy, in their book, *Reengineering the Corporation—A Manifesto for Business Revolution*, re-engineering is defined as 'fundamental rethinking and radical redesign of business processes to achieve dramatic improvements in critical, contemporary measures of performance, such as costs, quality, service, and speed' (page 32). Managers are enjoined to stop tinkering at the edges of their businesses, to take no assumptions for granted, and to obliterate practices and processes of the past, where this is in the overall interests of their organizations.

They extend their message into the realms of IT and give short shrift to automation which, they say, 'simply provides more efficient ways of doing the wrong kinds of things' (page 48). Their case-study of photocopying is very convincing, pointing out that the joy of the Xerox photocopier has not been in creating a replacement for carbon paper but in radically changing our document management practices (for the worse, many senior barristers and judges would say). In any event, they suggest that '[t]he fundamental error that most companies commit when they look at technology is to view it through the lens of their existing processes . . . Instead they should be asking, "How can we use technology to allow us to do things that we are *not* already doing?"' (page 85.) The message is clear and it is one that is on all fours with my own arguments about innovating through IT.

The examples I have given so far in this study suggest that re-engineering in a legal context can extend both to individual legal processes as well as to the legal process generally.

As illustrations of individual processes, I have mentioned *non-lawyers* being guided by electronic prompts and intelligent check-lists; intelligent agents monitoring and reporting back on relevant changes in the law; law firms offering access to their know-how databases on a commercial basis; judges making their decisions immediately available through some central electronic reporting service; and legislators drafting in a way which is amenable to direct translation into an information system. More prosaically perhaps, I have also suggested that even a tool such as word processing can enable considerable change when deployed as a drafting tool which helps structure and organize materials and is not just confined to glorified typewriting. And in the procurement of legal services, I have hazarded some likely consequences of electronic legal networks—lawyers loading materials which demonstrate their expertise in the hope of attracting instructions, which, in turn, will lead to the distribution of formal invitations to tender and to competitive tendering on these networks.

Where the changes extend beyond relatively distinct processes and affect the way the law is administered generally, this can be regarded as a re-engineering of the legal process itself. My prime example here is the major shift which I foresee in legal service changing from being an advisory service to becoming some kind of information service. The realization of *the latent legal market* and the resultant structural changes in the legal profession are further hints of legal process re-engineering on the grand scale.

My purpose in this section, however, is to do more than offer a hint and glimpse—through discussion and case-studies, I hope I provide some in-depth insight into innovating and re-engineering in the law, as these apply both to individual processes as well as to the legal process itself. I am also keen that readers recognize that innovating demands a different mind-set, one which enables creative leaps beyond the boundaries of our current ways of providing legal service. It calls, at least, for the 'upside down' thinking which Charles Handy advocates and the 'lateral thinking' championed by Edward de Bono. We must divest ourselves of current paradigm thinking; liberate ourselves of the 'mind-forg'd manacles' (as William Blake put it in his poem, 'London') which certainly seem to inhibit our imaginations when thinking about the future of law.

Repackaging the law

There is nothing especially new in the notion of repackaging the law for direct consumption by non-lawyers. Indeed early efforts to do so were delivered through print and paper.

Print-based repackaging

The beginnings of innovative legal information systems can be traced to the 1970s and 1980s, when several lawyers wrote a number of books which were thought by some to be radical. These books offered 'do-it-yourself' guidance on a number of legal matters. Regarded by many practitioners as laughably inappropriate, these texts sought expressly to demystify the law and to encourage non-lawyers to undertake a variety of tasks, all of which were previously thought to be the exclusive province of duly qualified legal advisers.

Thus, the lay person was guided through the intricacies and pitfalls of domestic conveyancing (moving house); tax planning and diagnostics; and the preparation of wills. These books, iconoclastic at the time, were the forerunners of today's more sophisticated and focused efforts to repackage the law in a fashion which renders it accessible to any lay person who is prepared to put some work and effort into performing some legally oriented tasks.

In leading bookstores of today, for example, law packs can now be purchased; and these are designed to pass legal know-how along to the non-lawyer. Unlike their predecessors, these packs have been stripped of background information and explanations of legal niceties. Rather, they are of a fiercely 'how to' nature, providing appropriate forms, instructions, and check-lists, all in remarkably usable and readable formats. The law packs are not published and bound as legal textbooks but are of a loose-leaf flavour, complete with non-formidable instructions, glossaries, and forms which are ready for completion and execution.

These packs cover, for example, landlord and tenant agreements, the recovery of debts, making small claims, as well as revamped and more useful last will and testament, taxation, and conveyancing guides.

Where the early texts spent some time dismissing conventional wisdom and practice, the later packs, in style and format, are honed and tuned towards getting a specific job done.

These are early steps in the evolution towards the repackaging of legal service, corresponding also to a slight movement from left to right along *The Legal Information Continuum*. More recently, interactive software has been bundled along with these packs. These invite their users to respond to a series of questions, and in the spirit of document assembly, the responses lead to the selection of templates and the generation of appropriate documentation. In this way, wills and tax returns, for example, can be assembled automatically in light of users' replies.

IT applications in business

Further still along my continuum, legal guidance systems have already been developed for the business user. For example, in the UK, the National Westminster Bank released its Pharos system in 1992 on floppy disc. This package was intended to assist its users in assessing how their businesses were affected by the creation of the single European market; and in deciding on what strategic and management decisions should be made. The system was designed for use by UK businesses, especially for companies with an annual turnover of between £0.5 million and £150 million. Here was an important set of legal issues for small and medium sized businesses who, it transpired, were generally not taking advice on the legal impact of European directives and other regulations. Here was a *latent legal market* being awoken to legal risks and opportunities; but not, it should be noted, by lawyers.

In operation, Pharos elicits a profile of the user's company and its activities. Using its knowledge of single market legislation and the market in which the company operates, the system draws conclusions and makes recommendations specific to the company and the obligations imposed on it by the emerging regulations. It goes further and clarifies the relevance of pieces of legislation for the business being considered and suggests possible courses of action as well as other information sources to which the user might usefully refer.

The debate over repackaging

There is a standard reaction to such systems and to packs and books as well, and it is one which has been evinced with some conviction by lawyers over the last two decades. The reaction has two parts, the first a concession, the second a warning. The concession is that many legal tasks can indeed be routinized and reduced to a step-by-step procedural guide or system. But the warning is that in one case out of ten (or one of twenty, or one of a hundred, depending on the legal matter and the lawyer in question) a difficulty, anomaly, confusion or unforeseeable occurrence can render the routine model inappropriate or invalid and so lead the user dangerously astray and exposed perhaps to some extensive liability, especially if the model cannot itself help identify when its limits have been reached. It is concluded, on this account, that one instructs lawyers largely to cover this kind of exposure to liability, or at least to pass on the liability to the legal adviser.

One variant of this line of argument runs a stage further and advocates that lawyers themselves use debt recovery, conveyancing and other case flow management software, the savings and benefits of which can accrue to both the lawyer and the client. Technology here brings cost reductions and productivity improvements but keeps the lawyer in the loop to cope, where necessary, with the eventuality of the routinized model being inadequate or inappropriate.

In one of its most convincing renditions, this entire line of argument is supported by the concerns I expressed earlier (Section 2.5) regarding the limitations of IT—the all-important qualification that computer systems do not perform well in recognizing their own limitations. One consequence of this is that the routinized models will not, themselves, always be able to identify when the limit of the guidance has been reached.

However, there is perhaps a far more persuasive argument which challenges this line of reasoning. It comes from the direction of pragmatism and realism. For the reality is that the guides, packs, and systems which are now available are often used *not* as a substitute nor as an alternative to legal advice, but are employed in situations when the legal risks would otherwise not be managed at all. This is what the notion of *the latent legal market* is all about. A central theme of this book is that the integration of law with business and social life requires its earlier input into all manner of activities, tasks, and projects. Yet it is also recognized that if the only form such earlier input can take is the direct consultation with lawyers in the traditional reactive manner, then this will often be either prohibitively expensive or impractical, or both. The great social advantage of guides, packs or systems which seek to offer legal counsel is not that they will match the performance of human legal practitioners. Rather, it is that many social and business situations will have the benefit of some legal input. And even if this input does not offer complete protection and reduction of risk, it will nonetheless be considerably more beneficial than no input whatsoever. A nine out of ten hit rate is, I would have thought, grossly preferable to a zero out of ten scoring. (For further elaboration of this argument, see Section 8.3).

As one moves along *The Legal Information Continuum* towards more focused and helpful legal information systems, the policy and social objective is not to eliminate lawyers but to empower citizens with legal information and guidance which in the past would have been in written legal sources which were unmanageable (due to hyperregulation), inaccessible (due to lack of promulgation), brought to bear too late in some proceedings or process (the paradox of traditional legal service), and too costly (in a pressurized legal market-place). This is a very different form of legal service than that which is offered today.

Court kiosks and beyond

For more general public access to legal information, another innovative illustration is provided by the use of 'court kiosks', dispensing machines which generate legal guidance rather than cash, but whose impact, some would want us to believe, will be as pervasive for law and society as cash dispensers have been for revolutionizing domestic banking.

Pioneered commercially in the United States, and now used to some extent in Australia and Singapore, these self-service court kiosks are said to be easy to use, accessible, and designed to streamline complex legal procedures (and not as a substitute for complex legal tasks). Located in or near court buildings, citizens stand before these kiosks in the manner of those who use cash dispensers, and are faced with a computer screen and a simple alphanumeric keyboard. Available for usage on a twenty-four hours a day, seven days a week basis (and in this respect contrasted in marketing materials with lawyers and courts), the citizen is provided with user-friendly, multi-media, and touch-screen information about the law.

Using this basic keyboard or by touching appropriate parts of the screen itself, the non-lawyer can be guided through legal issues by a mixture of video recordings, colourful screens, and the recordings of a patient human voice (multilingual). One system, for example, allows the public to pay their traffic violations, register for traffic school, schedule a court appearance date, and obtain information on small claims procedures and other court services. Another provides information about upper court services and can produce completed (laser printed) legal documents after an interactive consultation with the user. These include the forms necessary for the filing of an uncontested divorce or for obtaining a forcible detainer (eviction). Once printed, the output is ready for signature, authorization if appropriate, and then for filing with the court. Information is also provided about matters such as the nature of the court system, alternative methods of dispute resolution, and landlord and tenant law.

As citizens become more comfortable using such technology, the idea is that court kiosks or their equivalent may provide basic guidance and support to non-lawyers who would otherwise be reluctant or simply unable to instruct lawyers. The technology, in principle, will help realize *the latent legal market.*

While court kiosk technology seems set for introduction across many jurisdictions in the world (investigations are seriously under-way in the UK as well), the future of this approach should not be overstated. The fundamental motivation behind court kiosks is, in my view, unassailable, namely that non-lawyers (for whom, it will be recalled, ignorance of the law is no excuse—see Section 1.2) should have greater, easier, and cheaper access to legal information and guidance. And IT, on the face of it, offers an appropriate vehicle for the delivery of this information.

Yet it is far from obvious that court kiosks are the best enabling technique for this purpose. First of all, there is something rather bizarre about having the kiosks situated only in court buildings. If the thrust of the exercise is to render the law less forbidding and more congenial, insisting on a trip to the formidable environment of most court buildings may rather defeat that purpose. More than this, to require citizens to make special trips to special locations for their consultations is precisely to miss the opportunities which telecommunications afford. Why not harness the power of electronic communications and make the information available at other less daunting and more popular sites, such as public libraries, legal advice centres, post offices, and shopping malls?

Second, I question the assumption that legal guidance will be most easily digested and assimilated if dispensed through kiosks in the manner of cash. I can see that the original designers of kiosks sought to offer access to the law through a medium with which, they judged, most lay people would be comfortable. Given the uptake in usage of cash dispensing machines, there must have been attractions in using that same general approach to human/machine interaction. But looking just a few years ahead, I think we can be confident that there will be a far more pervasive and dominant mode of interface with technology and that will be the personal computer with some graphical user interface. The likely avalanche of purchase and use of computers for domestic purposes (as PC/TVs become as common as video recorders) will result in a level of comfort and familiarity with PC technology which will surely displace cash dispensing technology as the most convenient way of dealing with machines. In the IT-based information society, when even social engagements are secured on the Net, and the Web takes over from the bookcase as the major information source, it will eventually become natural to turn to the PC for guidance on legal matters.

In any event, it is likely that cash dispensing technology itself will fade away in due course, as paper money is used less frequently and banking transactions are conducted by telephone, and also, I have little doubt, across the Internet or some other national or even global information service. Standing before or in a kiosk will become a thing of the past and so no longer a natural way of interacting with some machine-based service.

It is likely, then, that the legal information and guidance which is currently delivered through court kiosks will, in but a few years, be directly accessible from machines located in homes. This will extend the multimedia computer technology underlying the kiosks to embracing and exploiting telecommunications technology in the delivery of the information. This further innovation would be invaluable for citizens and provide a more manageable, accessible, less costly, and less daunting way of establishing legal rights and responsibilities.

Finally, in my assault on kiosks, I am concerned that court kiosks of today generally suffer from being too firmly tied to the proprietary technologies of their manufacturers and developers. To a large extent, this tends to leave the control over the process of loading legal information in the hands of these suppliers. In turn, this could greatly inhibit the development of legal guidance systems for non-lawyers.

If some mechanism is established for delivering legal guidance to citizens we should want to encourage as many organizations and agencies as possible to load useful information. Law societies, academic law faculties, legal advice centres, welfare groups, law firms, and many others should all be encouraged to contribute, sometimes with commercial objectives in mind, but often on some *pro bono* basis. To have commercial organizations, which use their own techniques and systems, in charge of the selection of the fields of application, of the modelling of the areas of law, of the implementation of the systems, and of the marketing as well, can lead to an unacceptable monopoly—information could only be made available at their say-so.

Instead, I suggest that legal guidance and information systems should be deliverable on industry standard, multi-media, personal computer or generic information appliance technology, in accordance with independently agreed standards and protocols. Otherwise, we will move from a society in which lawyers are the exclusive interface between the people and the law to one in which commercial information service providers assume that constitutionally dubious role.

Document assembly

Some time ago, I was approached by the head of legal services in one of the UK's largest companies. She explained to me that their company employed 4,000 new employees each year but that a recent audit of the adequacy of their standard form documentation revealed that over ninety per cent of the employment contracts being drafted were defective. She explained that their employment lawyer was not able to oversee the production of employment contracts because his time was more than amply consumed by dealing with cases of alleged unfair dismissal and by appearing before employment tribunals. Instead, he had prepared about twenty standard form contracts (in respect of the twenty most likely categories of new employee) and had assembled three lever arch files full of guidelines. These had been designed to help personnel officers, who had duly been given the task of generating the contracts. In so doing, they had to cope with the thirty or so variable parts of each contract which needed specific attention for each individual employee.

In practice, the personnel officers found this process to be cumbersome and the audit results confirmed that it was simply not working in practice.

She went on to explain that the company had no intention of instructing external lawyers to draft each contract afresh. This would have been the traditional, reactive, one-to-one, advisory legal service and would have been prohibitively expensive (balanced against the likely losses which could have resulted from the defective contracts).

Instead, she was interested in the viability of using some kind of expert systems technology to automate the generation of the employment contracts. Expert systems used in support of production of documents, as I said in Section 4.3, is often referred to as document assembly. Having spent many years being perfected in the research laboratory, document assembly is now firmly in the commercial market-place, with a number of software packages now available to support the design and development process.

Armed with a document assembly system, the personnel officers of the company in question would legitimately be able to dispense with their guidance folders and instead would engage in an interactive consultation with a custom-made computer system.

Designed with the assistance of employment law experts, such a system would hold large numbers of standard templates of text, together with a representation of the expert's knowledge of how, where, and when these various standard words, sentences, and paragraphs should be used or disregarded. In operation, the personnel officers would be asked a series of questions about a proposed employee (for example, full-time or part-time). And the responses would result in the insertion or deletion of appropriate words, sentences, and clauses. The model of expertise would ensure that the final text matched the employment profile and details of the employee in question.

Although many lawyers may be surprised that this project is technically possible, and has been on personal computers for more than a decade now, it was, for me, the implications of the commercial terms of the proposed arrangement which were far-reaching and revolutionary.

We were being invited to systematize our knowledge and expertise and make that available in a reusable form. Rather than charging for each occasion on which the system was used, which would be to follow the charging structure of traditional reactive advisory service, it was suggested that we provide this document assembly system for an initial fixed sum with an annual fee for keeping the system up to date and reflecting changes in the statute and case-law (a procedure was also anticipated to allow for immediate changes where crucial legal developments had taken place).

Many months' work of employment specialists would therefore be rewarded by a fixed fee which may indeed have been commensurate with the fees that would have been charged on an hourly basis, but which would be in no way related to the cost of the service had lawyers been instructed to draft 4,000 individual contracts. A considerable fee would also have been due for the work of the specialist knowledge engineers, those whose task it would have been to develop the models of expertise which would underlie the generation of the documentation.

Here was the revelation. For long, I had been confronted by a standard reaction to expert systems technology—lawyers could see it was technically possible to develop these systems but within their own practices there was rarely a document drafting task which was so recurrent and yet for which expertise was so rare that the development costs could be shown to be commercially justifiable. The limitation of that thinking, however, was to think that expert systems were to provide an automating function, simply to computerize the traditional way of providing document drafting services.

In stark contrast, in the employment contract scenario, we can see the objective is not to automate some existing commercial arrangement. Rather, the proposal would fundamentally change the nature of traditional legal service, from one-to-one advisory in nature to a one-to-many (one legal assignment to satisfy many legal cases) information service. Lawyers would be packaging and productizing their knowledge and experience, thus rendering it reusable, rather than deploying it afresh in respect of each new separate matter which arises.

Here, then, is an illustration of a fundamental re-engineering of the legal process, with technology enabling an entirely new commercial basis for the delivery of legal service.

Legal products

Another exciting example of innovation through IT, and one that supports several of this book's central themes, can be found in the work of the Australian law firm, Blake Dawson Waldron. In their pioneering initiative, led by Elizabeth Broderick, the development and marketing of a suite of legal products has been achieved. The systems in question are designed expressly to help with the management of legal risk and to promote compliance with complex regulations.

Packaged and sold on floppy or compact discs, the systems provide focused, legal guidance in a variety of ways. One application is a compliance check-list for the insurance industry; another offers a detailed set of summaries of environmental legislation; while a further system takes the form of multi-media trade practices training software. These and their other systems use sophisticated enabling techniques (such as advanced text retrieval and hypertext) and the emphasis is very clearly on commercially usable end-products which offer practical guidance for non-lawyers. The systems are not put to market simply to differentiate the firm from others and to attract traditional legal work. Instead, they are conceived principally as offering a revenue stream and profitable return which climbs rapidly as each copy is sold.

Here, then, is perhaps the clearest contemporary example of practising lawyers venturing into the information age, embracing advanced technologies, and moving quite unambiguously from right to left along *The Legal Information Continuum* in providing this innovative, one-to-many, pre-packaged, proactive, legal information service.

But the story does not end there. In 1995, as this book was being completed, Blake Dawson Waldron launched a joint venture with CCH Australia, a large law and accounting publishing house—the law firm will greatly extend its potential market through this move, while the publisher will now have products which complement their existing, conventional legal information systems.

Thus, as predicted (see Section 3.3), we see a traditional legal publisher travelling forcefully from left to right along *The Legal Information Continuum* and indeed meeting a law firm at a point on the spectrum which, but five years ago, we would scarcely have imagined either would inhabit. It is revealing also, and no doubt ominous for legal practitioners, that publishers are at the heart of marketing this new category of legal service (see Section 8.1).

IT in support of legal risk management

To be proactive in the delivery of their services, lawyers must not only be consulted and become involved earlier in the life cycle of transactions and disputes. They must also use different methods and techniques, if the proactivity is to be both useful and cost effective.

In my view, there should be two central pillars which support proactive legal work—legal risk assessment and legal risk control. Together these components must be at the core of any acceptable legal risk management regime. Legal risk assessment involves identifying the legal risks to which a client is exposed; and legal risk control builds on this initial exercise by advocating methods by which the substantial and manageable risks are to be addressed. The risk analysis and risk control exercises need to be conducted in a structured and methodical way and, as the following case-study shows, IT can play an innovative and invaluable role in the risk control process.

For several years, I worked on a number of legal risk management assignments, with a variety of different clients. Each has taught me significant yet different lessons. To illustrate the range of issues which arise, I have synthesized these projects into one consolidated but, taken as a whole, fictitious case-study. What is described here is a combination of features of various pieces of work rather than a description of one project for one client, although, for ease of presentation, I present the study as though it were.

Have in mind a medium to large private sector organization. Driven from the management board of this organization, a legal risk management project was launched in response to one major piece of litigation which had resulted in the client being held liable for a considerable sum. It was felt by the board that repetition of such an occurrence was avoidable if the legal risks were better understood and appropriate preventative measures were taken well in advance.

The first phase of our work was to analyse the activities and operations of the organization and to identify where the main sources of legal risk lay. This legal risk assessment exercise distinguished between risks which arose from the nature of the business in which the client was involved and the way in which it conducted that business. It become rapidly apparent that as long as the client continued in its mainstream business, then many of the risks were, frankly, unavoidable. However, many other risks—including those that had given rise to the previous problems—could indeed be controlled if good legal practice were to be injected into the organizational procedures and working practices of the client.

The business of the client required a great deal of negotiation and drafting and the team of in-house lawyers was insufficient to support the mainstream operational staff on a one-to-one basis at every stage of every project. The dilemma, however, was that legal input of some sort was needed in respect of virtually all of the client's activities. To have provided this input by provision of traditional, one-to-one, reactive legal service, could have occupied the entire complement of lawyers of an average City firm on a full-time basis.

Our challenge, therefore, was to find some legal risk control mechanism which enabled sufficient legal input for the operational staff without the direct participation of lawyers on all occasions and without the expense as well. In other words, we recognized with the client that there was a considerable and vital *latent legal market* within the organizsation, one which could not be realized in full through the provision of conventional legal service.

How, then, could we inject sound legal practice into the everyday activities of the operational staff? Given it was neither financially viable, nor practicable, to make traditional legal advice available, we turned at an early stage to fairly conventional legal information systems, both print-based and IT-based. However, the textbooks and databases which we examined, and that to some extent were already used, suffered from all the problems that accompany methods of legal guidance which reside towards the left of

The Practicalities

The Legal Information Continuum. Most importantly, their successful use presupposed that their users already had some considerable knowledge of the legal issues with which they dealt; and the guidance they offered was too general in nature, providing information which related broadly to problems rather than offering practical, focused help on how to resolve them.

In the end, we found the most effective means of delivering legal guidance was through on-screen prompts and intelligent check-lists. We identified the principal activities both of operational staff and of management and, once we had stipulated which activities should be allocated to appropriate levels of staff, we set about developing step-by-step guidance on each activity. For example, we developed prompts and check-lists which embodied sensible legal practice in activities such as preparing for and attending meetings; making and taking telephone calls; handling correspondence; producing promotional material; and managing projects. We intentionally used such everyday categories as a starting-point rather than using legal concepts and terminology (such as making representations or assuming liabilities) as our point of departure. To have done otherwise would have taken too much legal knowledge for granted (we had the paradox of traditional reactive legal service fully in mind—see Section 1.3).

Because all employees of the organization already had personal computers on their desks, this gave them the vehicle for immediate access to the sound legal guidance we systematized. The on-screen prompts provided no more than simple, step-by-step lists of points to remember and precautions to be taken. For more complex tasks and processes, we used the more advanced techniques of intelligent check-listing whereby the users could be led through matters of complexity, by interactive consultation. In light of the user's responses, the system determined what information should be presented to the user and in what order. These intelligent check-lists also had document generation facilities.

But the question of documentation itself raised its own considerable challenge. The client had developed and sought to rely upon an extensive suite of standard form agreements which were originally conceived, of course, as a means of controlling legal risks. When first drafted, it was intended that these agreements would be printed and signed but not varied or altered. And so it was hoped that considerable protection would be afforded through the solid work of the original draftsmen who had framed the agreements in a variety of ways designed to minimize the client's exposure to liability. In practice, however, either as a result of negotiation with others or through the whim and stylistic preferences of the operational staff, very few of the agreements which were eventually signed remained faithful to the original standard forms.

Again, we found that IT could be used to help control the risks that arose from this document creation practice. Whereas the standard forms had previously been stored centrally on the network in a format which allowed the staff to make any alterations which they pleased, we instead introduced a document assembly system which effectively rendered crucial clauses unalterable and yet, at the same time, permitted variations of less material and risky terms and conditions. Intermediate categories of clauses, which could give rise to significant but not overwhelming risks, were sometimes supplemented by an optional range of variations and alternatives; and often gave rise, at various points in the use of the system, to warning notices that legal advice should be taken in relation to any alterations which had been made. We could have taken the further step of automatically generating an electronic mail message to the legal team to notify them that significant alterations had been taken, but this was felt to be unduly draconian and, in any event, the overall document assembly system was very quickly seen to control the risks arising from the use of the standard form documentation without further measures.

The final set of refinements which we considered involved integrating best legal practice with the existing automated project management system. When we looked at a number of the central processes and projects with which the client was involved, we found that these were already subject to fairly rigorous project management and each had been divided into standard stages, phases, tasks, and sub-tasks. The project managers followed detailed guidelines for the execution of each step and this had been well routinized. Our recommendation was to inject the law into this existing method, so that project managers would quite naturally come to handle legal issues at the most appropriate times in the life cycles of their projects. Discharging legal tasks and taking legal precautions in this way would become one further aspect of project management. The project managers already relied upon fairly sophisticated project management software and systems and so our task was to analyse the life cycles of the projects and processes involved and integrate practical, usable guidance into the existing systems.

Our rigorous approach to document management and our integration of legal knowledge with the project management systems led us to recognize one powerful, future direction in proactive legal service. Using expert systems techniques, it is possible to develop diagnostic systems which can operate in parallel with project management and document management systems of the sort described. In operation, such expert systems can constantly monitor the activities of these management systems and recognize combinations of circumstances which give rise to legal questions or

The Practicalities

demand legal precautions. Thus, applications will themselves be able to draw attention to the legal implications of the tasks they are performing and even take remedial actions, seemingly (but not really) of their own volition.

7

Critical Success Factors

How can we give ourselves the best chance of success in realizing the vision of this book and in introducing systems of the sort just described in the case-studies of the previous chapter? This chapter deals with the fundamental steps which I believe must be taken. An overview of the topics addressed is presented in Figure 7.1.

In light of my own consulting and management experience, and countless insights from other specialists as well, I deal with the all-important trinity of strategy, planning, and management. I follow this with my *'Triple A' Formula*, which stipulates that success can be achieved only if proposed applications are available technically, acceptable financially, and achievable culturally. Finally, I map out education and training requirements for lawyers, taking account of the entire spectrum from school education through to the edification of the most experienced legal practitioners.

But first I must clear the way by disposing in advance of a number of potential terminological confusions.

7.1. Some Basic Concepts Clarified

I used to think it was only lawyers who could disagree interminably over definitional questions such as 'what is law?' and 'what is a legal system?' but I now realize that the legal fraternity has no monopoly over this kind of debate. Thus, when I turned some years ago to immerse myself in management theory, I felt at home when I found little consensus over the nature and scope of various basic concepts.

Figure 7.1 An Overview of the Critical Success Factors

Strategy and Planning
        The context of strategy
        Basic strategic questions
        IT in smaller organizations
        IT strategy across the justice system
        Planning
Management—Ten Keys to Success
        Strategy and planning
        Top management support
        Measuring performance
        Project management
        User involvement
        Hybrid management
        Expectation management
        Relentless training
        Not re-inventing the wheel
        Technical sophistication
The Triple 'A' Formula
        Commercial acceptability
                The poverty of the traditional business case
                Business cases for judicial systems
                Measurable if not quantifiable commercial benefits
        Cultivating the culture
                Appreciate the four levels of faith
                Strive for improvement rather than perfection
                Accept that legal organizations are changing
        Too secret a service
                The quest for competitive advantage
                Domestic issues for the legal profession
                International positioning
        The American experience
        Education and Training
        IT as a distinct discipline?
        Undergraduate IT
        Professional examinations
        Initial training
        Ongoing exposure

In particular, the concepts of strategy, planning and management, although vital in practice for those involved with IT in the law, are defined and analysed quite differently even by leading management authorities. For present purposes, I have resolved not to enter any debate on such matters and have opted instead for giving, simple working definitions of each. Readers may not care for my definitions but should at least know what I mean when I use certain, fundamental terms.

When I talk of *strategy* in relation to IT in the law, then, I am referring to an understanding and expression of *why* some investment in technology is being made and *where* the investment is intended to lead after a significant and specified period of time. I use the term *planning* to refer to the task of creating and articulating a statement of *how* the investment is to be made and *what* applications are expected. And when I speak of *management*, I have in mind the process of directing and controlling resources (mainly human and financial) over the given period, in implementing the plan.

These working definitions combine with earlier observations of the book to support my recommended model: pursuit of agreed benefits should inspire the strategy which should be embodied and pursued in the planning that should, in turn, be implemented by management to deliver the applications enabled by the appropriate technologies!

7.2. Strategy and Planning

Many lawyers have limited time for strategy, planning, and management. They say they would prefer to get on with the job rather than talk about it. This is reminiscent of the lumberjack who refuses to stop cutting and to sharpen his blunt and ineffective axe because, he says, he does not have the time; or of the short-tempered patron of a bar, who refuses the bartender's offer of a tray to carry the six drinks just purchased and adds 'can't you see I've already got enough to carry?'

By launching into the procurement or development of systems without strategy, planning, and management, the likely result—experience, common sense, and research suggest—is technology which is unrelated to the business in question; wastage of money and insufficient payback; applications which are usually delivered late; and are either irrelevant or do not do what was actually wanted in the first place. So it is worth a reflective look before an ill-considered leap. And this is so whether the systems in question are for direct use by lawyers or produced by lawyers for others to deploy.

I also well understand the strong inclination of action-oriented lawyers who want to make rapid progress and are dismissive of strategy and benefits which are promised for some years hence. It is but one aspect of what the great Scottish philosopher, David Hume, identified as human beings' preference for the 'contiguous' over the 'remote'. I would counsel against this impetuosity. If it is any consolation, I never cease to be amazed how quickly the remote becomes the contiguous.

The context of strategy

Why is some investment being made and where is it leading in the medium to long term? Strategic thinking should address such questions. Although these are surely entirely reasonable questions, lawyers can display a variety of negative attitudes towards strategy. For some, it conjures images of formidable yet fruitless cerebral activity with a management team closeted in some distant retreat and adopting the posture of Rodin's Thinker; for others, it means retaining expensive transatlantic consultants with apparently glamorous lifestyles; while still others reject it as airy-fairy indulgence which eats unacceptably into otherwise chargeable time. Gradually, however, as lawyers have become more businesslike in the management of their affairs, there has also been recognition of its relevance and worth.

It is often said that the formulation of strategy is a relatively straightforward task for law firms; the real difficulties lie with implementation. However, this represents a rather limited perspective on strategy and is akin in many ways to the observation that a suggestion is fine in theory but not in practice. Just as one should immediately respond that theory is about practice and if something fails to operate in practice then the related theory is defective, then so too with strategy—if implementation fails, this can often in itself be attributed to incomplete, inadequate or inappropriate strategy. Strategy is not just about abstract theorizing. It also entails the formulation of procedures, management structures, and an infrastructure generally, which will support implementation. The formulation of strategy and implementation overlap and interrelate with one another.

Another conventional view—one which was held for many years by conventional management theory—was that the role of IT was exclusively to support wider corporate strategy (which stipulates what business or businesses a firm should be in) or business strategy (which determines how a firm should position itself relative to competitors in its chosen markets). Once these broader strategic issues had been settled and articulated, the view in question suggested that only then should management turn to technologists and invite them to suggest ways in which available technologies can support the bigger corporate and business picture.

Over the past decade, this role for IT strategy has been recognized as inadequate because it restricts IT to an automating function—on this analysis, technology is there to automate, streamline, and improve existing processes. Here, IT strategy has a unidirectional relationship with corporate and business strategy, being there to support rather than in any sense influence.

Once IT is acknowledged as an enabler of change, a source of innovation, and a tool for re-engineering, this relationship will become bi-directional: IT and IT strategy will actually influence, shape, and even determine wider corporate and business objectives. Those who enjoyed saying disparagingly, through the 1980s, that various technologies were no more than 'solutions looking for problems' must now revise their thinking—imaginative, innovative use of IT in the 1990s often now derives precisely from matching existing techniques to previously unconnected challenges.

Telecommunications technology, for example, has been a major enabler and agent of change for law firms pursuing programmes of internationalization, because the ability to set up links between offices and so establish one 'virtual' office has encouraged law firms to establish outposts which would otherwise have been rejected as inappropriate or impractical because the geographical differences may have been regarded as conducive to loss of control and remoteness from corporate culture. Law firm strategists who would reject the establishment of foreign offices and do so without cognizance and recognition of the role that IT could play, clearly lose the opportunity of deploying IT in its innovating role.

Basic strategic questions

In my experience, three basic strategic questions arise or should do again and again in strategic discussions and decision making. The first relates directly to my earlier discussion of benefits (see Section 2.2). Why is the investment being made? Is it to save money? Or to deliver a higher quality service? Or to make money? Or to be different? In many organizations which I advise or visit, when I ask this question of senior management in respect of a programme of expenditure which has already begun, I am mortified to find there is no unanimity of view. Decision makers often do not agree why they are authorizing vast investment. Frank discussion of this issue simply must be conducted before a single penny is spent.

My second basic question relates to a running theme of this book. Is the investment intended to automate, streamline, and improve what already goes on or is IT intended to change and re-engineer tasks and processes? Related discussion here should focus on whether the intention is for the focus to be on the back office, front office or connecting to the client office; and whether technology is to support reactive or proactive legal service.

The third question is a matter of method. Is the point of departure for the strategic thinking to be a vision of the future to which the organization aspires? Or should the thinking be constrained primarily by where the organization is today (driven by the 'legacy'). I strongly favour vision-driven over legacy-driven approaches to strategy. The former inspires imaginative and creative thinking and the vision is often realized, through enthusiastic management, in the manner of self-fulfilling prophecies. The latter is generally depressing and stultifying and gets hampered by endless discussion of reasons why certain ideas and recommendations cannot be taken forward.

IT in smaller organizations

Upon hearing presentations from the largest of law firms, managers and lawyers from small and medium sized firms often say to me to 'it is all right for the huge firms with all their resources but not nearly so easy for the smaller firm'. While I had full sympathy with this view three years ago and more, I am now convinced that smaller firms (and barristers' chambers and in-house legal departments) should today enjoy a number of advantages over large firms in their introduction of IT.

From a technical point of view, we have now moved beyond minicomputer systems and early generations of personal computers which in the past required the availability of extensive technical skills for setting up and running the systems. Personal computer networks of today (the dominant infrastructure) can reliably and inexpensively be set up by local PC suppliers and are, in any event, becoming increasingly 'plug and play', which means that computers can be connected to one another and to printers, for example, as easily as we set up consumer products such as televisions, video machines, and hi-fi systems (although I accept that even these domestic products should be easier still to get going). Local suppliers and consultants can also help with the tailoring of off-the-shelf packages that tends to be needed to integrate these systems with the working practices of users. And operationally, as lawyers and support staff have become increasingly familiar with the graphical user interface and basic applications, again there is less need for extensive technical help in making the systems work.

If the reason for a smaller firm's hesitation over IT is that teams of technical specialists are needed, then that view is now misplaced.

If it is accepted that there are now few technical barriers to the exploitation of IT by smaller firms, we can turn instead to one very substantial advantage which they have over large firms. I am referring here to the question of manageability. It is striking that the very scale of large firms' introduction of IT requires that new systems take many years to bring in successfully. I know several of the largest City firms, by necessity, have embarked on five year projects for the introduction of personal computer networks with graphical user interfaces. It seems, in relation to IT, that far from there being economies of scale for large firms, in practice the reverse is the case—close examination of large City law firms and the even larger accounting practices suggests that there may indeed be serious diseconomies of scale. The processes of analysing and specifying requirements, negotiating with and procuring from suppliers, implementation, and training seem to throw up enormous management challenges for the largest of professional practices, mainly, it seems, because of the very substantial number of individual users involved. Internal IT teams of over 100 people are not uncommon in City law firms, each attesting to the supertanker syndrome, whereby any change in direction becomes a formidable task indeed.

Contrast this with the smaller firm, whose past investment in technology may well have been small and so has no antiquated, expensive IT legacy. Add to this the prospect of introducing new systems for all in a small number of man-days or man-weeks rather than man-years. It all sounds immediately more attractive. The overall cost of technology per fee earner in smaller firms certainly seems no more than in large firms, and if I am right about the diseconomies of scale, may indeed work out less expensive. But the payback may be quicker, given that full implementation can come about so rapidly.

Culturally, there can also be major advantages for the smaller practice in that a vision can be realized so much more quickly, which itself brings greater confidence and 'buy-in'. New technology can be geared more specifically towards individuals and yet the whole process can be managed more rigorously. Training can happen over a weekend rather than through involved modularized programmes which extend over many months, even for medium sized firms.

Already, I have seen a number of two or three partner firms whose use of technology is more advanced and imaginative than the largest of City practices. I expect many more such firms will forge ahead similarly. This will give rise to a fascinating democratization within the legal profession, with law firms of all sizes having equal rights and opportunities to participate in, and lead, the legal market-place. On the information superhighway, for example, the trappings of larger firms (for example, impressive buildings) are hidden from the user who may instead judge the worth of a firm solely on the quality of the information flowing from it.

Generally, smaller firms will have access to much improved information processing capabilities and will be able to compete on equal terms with larger firms more than ever before. With litigation, for example, larger firms with teams of paralegals to manage large document loads will now have to cross swords with smaller firms using litigation support systems and external bureau services for the loading of their documentation. Small law firms will also be able to band together as single, 'virtual legal practices', under one 'virtual' roof and put together on a one-off basis for an individual project. Electronic communications and groupware will enable this collaboration and give rise to working relationships as effective as those that subsist in large firms.

However, none of this eliminates the need for small firms to develop strategy, articulate their plans, and to manage rigorously. On the contrary, if the opportunity for democratization is not to be lost, it is incumbent on these firms and their professional bodies to conduct their investment in IT with the greatest of care and rigour.

IT strategy across the justice system

In passing, it is worth noting that the same strategic issues which I have identified for law firms apply also, on a macro scale, to the justice system as a whole. When government decision makers and policy formulators give thought to the future of law and the court systems, they too should consider the role of IT and ask why investment is being made and where that investment is leading.

I am not yet confident in the UK, however, that sufficient thought is being given in this direction. With the notable exception of Lord Woolf, in his report *Access to Justice*, and a number of senior judges on the ITAC committee (the Information Technology and Courts committee set up by the then Lord Chancellor in 1985) there is little evidence of genuine strategic thinking or of any vision of the future emanating from the government of the day or its supporting executive.

Who is systematically monitoring new techniques and technologies and considering their impact on the component parts of the legal system and across the justice system generally? No one that I can see. Yet this is surely vital not just for improving service and reducing costs within the courts, for example, but also, more generally, for seeking to achieve competitive advantage internationally for the UK's legal systems. To maintain this country's pre-eminence as a forum for international dispute resolution and to maximize opportunities for English law as the standard currency underlying international trade, the legal system must continually be refined and optimized and open also to radical change where that is beneficial to individuals and to society. A legal system which relies on hand-crafted methods of the past and is seen in the international community as averse to the deployment of technology runs a severe risk of entering into rapid decline.

If a concerted effort is made in any jurisdiction to embark on a major IT programme, the social and commercial benefits are best derived, as on the micro scale with law firms, if there is a coherent approach to strategy, planning, and management. The activities and investments of all relevant agencies and professional bodies should be co-ordinated and standards agreed upon. Without this, any IT investment is destined to be piecemeal and *ad hoc*. A co-ordinated approach should lead to an overarching IT strategy for the entire justice system, requiring all key agencies and bodies to refine and realign their current IT plans.

Planning

I like the tale of the man from the city who has lost his way in the countryside and stops his car to ask a passing farmer for guidance on how to get to a particular town. The farmer responds with a sigh of regret: 'well, I wouldn't start from here'.

It often seems to be like this for large organizations investing in IT, especially for those influenced by legacy-driven strategists. Their focus tends to be primarily on the existing, outdated systems which invariably seem incompatible with one another and apparently preclude any easy route to future, more attractive options. Unlike our lost traveller, however, the legacy-driven strategists often have only a vague notion of where they might be heading. All they are sure of is that they would like to be setting off from elsewhere.

The great advantage of being vision-driven and not legacy-driven in formulating strategy is that the current position neither dominates nor overrides the creative process of thinking and projecting ahead to what might be. Clearly there must always be realism and so the existing environment must establish some kind of general backdrop for sensible debate but the vision for, say, five years ahead, can and should be devised with far greater devotion and attention to longer term corporate and business issues than the often obsolescent technologies of the day.

The process of planning should, therefore, be invoked either to lay out how a vision might be achieved, or, we must accept, to reveal that the vision itself simply cannot be realized given available resources. In the latter event, the vision is often seen to be so attractive that greater resources are made available by decision makers (whereas there is little chance of this happening when the thinking is legacy-based).

IT planning focuses on how some investment is to be made and what applications are expected. I find it helpful, for the purposes of analysis, to go further and distinguish between *strategic planning* and *tactical planning*. In practice, any adequate IT plan for lawyers embraces both strategic and tactical issues and invariably the two are found intertwined. Nonetheless, it is helpful to understand the difference between the two, if only to ensure that the right personnel are allocated to each.

A strategic plan should articulate the underlying strategic thinking and prescribe the broad framework within which the strategy is to be pursued. Thus, I would expect to see the following, in writing, as a result of strategic planning: a crisp mission statement, capturing the overall vision and the spirit of the venture; an indication of the anticipated business benefits; a clear linkage to broader corporate and business strategies; an IT management structure with explicit allocation of responsibilities; a statement of market positioning in relation to IT, covering clients, competitors, suppliers, and the economic state of the market-place generally; the required human resources and budget, the likely payback, expressed quantitatively and qualitatively; the deliverables, expressed in broad terms; target timescales; crucial milestones; an indication of how performance will be monitored and measured; and a summary of current attitudes and expectations together with change management plans, if appropriate.

A tactical plan should delve into further detail, and must be developed with considerable input from technologists. I would expect tactical planning to deal with issues such as: target projects and applications; enabling techniques; software development methods and standards; project management methods; preferred programming environments, operating systems, and user interface; hardware and telecommunications infrastructure; staffing and organization; training; support; maintenance; marketing; security; confidentiality; and research and development.

The temptation not to write down an IT plan, dealing with these strategic and tactical matters, is almost overwhelming for most lawyers. But investing heavily in IT without a detailed plan is like constructing one floor of a building and only then turning attention to the number of storeys given there was an initial view it should be quite high. Some will say about strategic planning that they have thought through their strategy and that was the important process; not its commitment to print. This is often a rather feeble rationalization—most will find that the very task of articulating strategy in text often reveals that the original thinking was vague and insufficiently refined. As for tactical planning, this is a vital management tool: it lays out the basis of what is intended to happen. Ideally, all stakeholders (partners, for example) should read it and sign up to it, giving shared commitment, shared responsibility, and shared vision.

7.3. Management—Ten Keys to Success

With the strategy and plan in place, it is then effective management which matters most. This, as I have said, is the process of directing and controlling resources (mainly human and financial) over the periods specified in the IT plan.

For long, management was something of a dirty word in the legal community. The good manager, for many lawyers, is the individual who would have been tidying the chairs on the Titanic.

It is probably fair to say that lawyers succeeded in the 1980s in spite of, rather than because of, a somewhat cavalier attitude to management. If anything, this was a decade for fair weather managers. So lawyers who now look back nostalgically at that time, when their business did not seem to need the management baggage carried today, are in danger of missing a vital point. In the pressurized legal market-place, all the signs are now indicating that sound management is not a luxury; it is a prerequisite for solvency.

And IT has emerged as a phenomenon which needs particularly astute and tight management control. For most managers who work in a legal environment, this has called for some reskilling, as they grapple with the challenges of strategic planning (business and IT), with the management of highly talented and yet non-legal professionals, with changing working practices, and with challenging basic assumptions about the nature of legal service. Above all else perhaps, lawyers must come to terms with investing so extensively in something of which they will never have full understanding—unlike other areas of management (for example, marketing, human resources, and quality) which many lawyers think (often wrongly) that they can grasp in short order, they find in IT a discipline more profound and involved even than their own and they must resign themselves to reliance on specialists.

The Practicalities

This does not mean that lawyers should abdicate responsibility for IT management. On the contrary, it calls for more cautious and controlled management style than in other areas. Although this may seem daunting for the lawyer-cum-manager, who is already dismayed by the extent to which management is impinging on fee earning work, there are many lessons to be learned from others who have pioneered in this field over the years. I have identified ten such lessons and believe they offer a useful set of keys to success.

Strategy and planning

Consistent with the earlier messages of this section, the management of IT ought not to be conducted in a vacuum. Instead, it should be driven by well understood strategy and conducted in pursuance of a clearly articulated plan. In other words, IT is too important to leave to an IT director or manager or partner unless they are guided and constrained by agreed objectives. Without strategy and planning, investment in IT is destined to be ill-considered, haphazard, and disappointing in its results.

Top management support

Top management commitment to IT is a vital ingredient of success. The leading figures in an organization should personally take a firm hold of IT and stay continually in touch with all major operational systems, upgrades, and new developments. The leading applications discussed in this book are precisely the kinds of systems of which top managers should be aware. The function, price, capabilities, limitations, strategic significance, and organizational suitability of systems can and should be appreciated at the highest level within an organization. In terms of costs and benefits, there is often so much at stake that there can be no justification for passing exclusive responsibility down to the basement or along to the back room. Nevertheless, top management will need technical and administrative advice and support.

The role for top management will be a mixed one, involving: the establishment of policy; the resolution of priorities; the provision of overall guidance; the creation and promotion of a culture in which IT can flourish; personal use of IT and so leading by example; and the communication of the IT strategy to all members of the organization.

Measuring performance

Top management should also insist that the ongoing performance of IT is monitored and measured. The benefits which accrue must be noted, not just as they relate to particular projects but as they come about from the investment as a whole. It is important for management to approve criteria against which the performance of any project or system can be measured at specified times in the future. This performance can be in terms, for example, of costs savings, increased fee income, productivity gains, acknowledged improvements in quality, the number of new clients attracted on the strength of some system, the extent of promotional payback, or, with legal information systems being sold or licensed, the number of sales of a system. These performance measurement criteria should be articulated in the IT plan, while specific targets should be incorporated in any project plan. Failure to measure performance can lead to the unjustifiable continuation of disappointing projects—with no agreed points for taking stock, it is not easy to stop an initiative.

Project management

The management of IT must reach beyond the direction and control of an organization's general investment into the conduct of particular projects. Tactical planning is important here, in that it should lay down sensible standards and guidelines for the management of individual projects. At the very least, every project (whether relating, for example, to procurement, requirements analysis, system development or to training) should be allocated a budget, set time-scales for key deliverables and completion, and should stipulate who will be doing the work involved. Above all else, each project should be led by one single and identifiable project manager. If anyone is worrying about the project as they go to sleep at night, it should be this project manager—the problem holder, in difficult circumstances.

Although this may seem rather obvious, many organizations prefer to manage IT projects collectively as one monolithic initiative. Too often, however, this seems to lead to problematic projects being ignored or left to decay. Project management, as enabled by an IT plan, should ensure that an appropriate level of attention is paid to each project.

User involvement

Another crucial factor is user involvement. The appearance on the desktop of many professionals of a '16 megabyte RAM, 1.2 gigabyte hard disc machine with a pentium processor' is, for instance, not necessarily a development that regular mortals are likely to (or should) get excited about. To reap the rewards from technological innovations, users should not be swamped in technical minutiae; rather, they should be trained and educated to understand and accept the benefits that can accrue. More than this, management should strive for a culture in which users actually want the systems. To this end, users must be consulted regularly and their opinions should be respected as well. Management and technical specialists must actually listen to the preferences expressed and be prepared to act upon them—their requirements must be implemented (if it is commercially, technically, and organizationally feasible to do so). A marvellously designed system that no one uses is as much a failure as one that does not work at all.

Early involvement of the user and, if possible, clients who will benefit from systems, is strongly recommended. Not only will this enable the establishment of trust and confidence, but users who provide valuable input into system design are also more likely to approve of, and so use, the final version. This can be a difficult balance, however, because if users are invited to participate too early and before management and technical staff are clear about their broad objectives, projects can become derailed at the outset. When consulted too early, some users are also tempted to reject proposals rather precipitously. The gut reaction that 'we don't need that because we've never done things in that way in the past' is very common and can be avoided if sufficient preparatory groundwork is done. (It is often a remarkably blinkered reaction and can be countered light-heartedly by suggesting that the same might have been said of a proposal to introduce fax technology—'we don't need a fax machine because we don't get sent any faxes . . .'.)

Hybrid management

A pervasive problem in the legal profession is the lack of appropriately qualified IT managers to take on and run the technology function. This human resource problem is symptomatic of much of European industry's use of IT. In important work conducted over the last few years, it has indeed been forcefully argued that exploitation of IT will always be modest until 'hybrid managers' are in place in IT departments within medium and large organizations. These hybrids will not only be technical experts (like most IT managers today), but will also (quite unlike IT managers today) have comprehensive understanding of the business which they are supporting, as well as the necessary organizational, interpersonal, and management skills needed to maintain the interest and respect of people within their company. In a law firm, for example, the IT director or manager should therefore be intimately familiar with the idiosyncrasies of professional partnerships and be sufficiently impressive, articulate, and convincing to motivate the majority of partners.

It is unclear whether today's hybrid manager in the legal environment should be a lawyer turned technologist or an IT specialist with particular experience of the legal market. The lawyer who is the enthusiastic, evangelistic IT amateur (see Section 7.4) can wreak havoc if not contained. On the other hand, very few IT professionals are able to sustain the culture shock in embracing the ethos of the legal profession. Tomorrow's hybrids will be a very different species, armed as they will be with interdisciplinary education and experience. But we will have to wait some time before our educational system produces these individuals in sufficient number (see Section 7.5).

Expectation management

A challenge for hybrid managers, IT managers, and top managers alike is what I call expectation management. While the applications discussed in this book may be regarded as attractive and likely to realize substantial commercial benefits, it is crucial, prior to their introduction to any particular organizations, that the expectations of potential users are managed realistically, bearing in mind that computer systems are never the universal panacea that marketing specialists want the world to believe. Accordingly, the challenge here for managers is to manage everyone's expectations cautiously, to remain enthusiastic and forceful about the systems but frank and firm about what can reasonably be achieved given the time and finance available. In this context, managers who themselves are fairly sophisticated users must continually strive to recall what it is like to be a novice. Too often IT managers and advanced legal users fall into the trap of rejecting proposed systems because they see no use for them personally. In so doing, they run the risk of neglecting fine opportunities for less experienced colleagues.

Prior to the introduction of new systems or the adaptation of existing applications, packaging the perception of the impending change is actually more important than the eventual reality—in many ways, bringing change in IT is an exercise in marketing. The expectations of users are all-important. Demonstrations of early versions or prototypes of systems can be helpful, in offering an advanced taste. But audiences can be cynical and so the focus should be on applications which are useful and not just interesting and those which make some past process easier and not more onerous.

Perhaps the most difficult issue of all is to convey the message—to stakeholders and to users—that there is no finishing line in the world of IT. Instead, it is an ever-evolving environment, where upgrades, enhancements, improvement, and changes are par for the course. The investment is never over; knowledge in systems is never complete.

Relentless training

A further, formidable organizational challenge is that of training. Although I deal with the substance and need for ongoing training later in this chapter (Section 7.5), for now it is important to put training firmly on the management agenda. For there is a tendency across industry and commerce generally, as well as in the legal world, to fail to make the most of IT investment precisely by skimping on training.

There is, unfortunately, a common assumption that once an application has been installed and signed off as technically operational then the foreseen benefits will flow immediately and as a matter of course. There is, then, a strong tradition of neglecting to invest sufficiently in training users to feel comfortable with the technology given to them. An uncomfortable and unenlightened user is never a productive user. It is essential, therefore, that project managers are encouraged to budget for the time and finance necessary for training. Top management should readily see the wisdom of this—in due course, having technology in place of itself will be commonplace rather than a source of competitive advantage. The edge will come from developing a body of users who have been trained more thoroughly than the competition. They will make the most of the systems which will reap rewards for their organizations.

Not re-inventing the wheel

There is often a temptation amongst technical staff, when invited to introduce new applications, to want to embark on work that involves writing programs from scratch. However, on most occasions, except if an organization is pioneering, this temptation can and should be resisted, because there are often readily available off-the-shelf packages which can be used directly or tailored, with little need for involved programming. Managers should be aware of 'NIH (not invented here) syndrome' which bedevils IT departments: it results in technical staff being cynical about all developments not originated from their own groups; and calls for the launch of projects to create systems which will allegedly be great improvements over what can easily be purchased, plugged, and played. To be firm, there is rarely any commercial justification for this kind of re-invention of the wheel.

The main emphasis of system development in law, whether of applications for lawyers or non-lawyers, should be on modelling legal guidance and knowledge and embodying this in usable legal information systems. The technology should not drive but be driven.

Technical sophistication

On those rarer occasions, however, where more ambitious technical work is needed, perhaps for those who are pioneering and bringing products from the research laboratory to the market-place, managers should encourage this to be undertaken in a disciplined and professional manner. Given the complexity of the systems, it is important, for example, that they are developed in accordance with well proven methods and standards of system development. In the early days of programming, the development of systems was haphazard and *ad hoc*, with facilities and features being added and removed rather arbitrarily as projects progressed. More recently, however, there has been a move to the introduction and usage of fairly formal system development methodologies (so-called), which offer detailed guidance on how to structure and manage complex development projects. In the area of legal information systems, where so much is at stake when their guidance is relied upon, it is particularly important that such methodologies are followed. It is equally vital that such systems are fully documented so that they can be modified and updated by individuals other than the original developers.

Finally, a further useful technique is the development of what are known as small prototypes or 'samplers', which can give users, clients, managers, and lawyers some strong indication in advance of what systems will 'look and feel' like in operation. On the basis of just a few days of preparation of such samplers, more sensible judgements about the viability and usability of proposed systems can be made. There is a potential pitfall here, however, and that is of committing the 'fallacy of the successful first step'. A demonstrator system knocked up in a few days may lead those to whom it is shown to believe that the fully operational system will take but a couple of weeks more to polish off—there is a particularly acute need here, therefore, for expectation management.

7.4. The Triple 'A' Formula

Whereas the ten keys to success laid out in the previous section are directed mainly at managers, I have developed a simpler and more memorable model for lawyers and technologists. This I call *The Triple 'A' Formula* and it stipulates that any proposed investment in IT for lawyers must satisfy a three-prong test. Again, this applies not just to applications developed for lawyers but also to those put together by lawyers as legal information systems, for *the latent legal market* perhaps.

As to the Formula itself, first of all, the technologies which underlie any proposed applications which are envisaged must be *Available*, from a technical point of view. It must be possible to develop the systems in question (there can be no room for 'vapourware', in the words of the development community). Second, the applications, and the projects which are to lead to them, must be commercially *Acceptable*—the costs must be justifiable. Third, the implementation and eventual usage of the systems must be *Achievable*, from a cultural perspective.

The first requirement, the technical one, is rarely a source of difficulty today; although, in contrast, many of the applications which were sought by lawyers as little as five years ago could not be delivered then because of constraints in underlying technologies or even absence of technologies altogether (the ability to run on PC networks, for example).

The second prong, which relates to costs and benefits, continually exercises the minds and patience of business managers and I explore various aspects of this issue before moving onto what is, for me, the biggest obstacle to the development of legal applications of technology—I refer to the third dimension and the problems lurking in the murky depths of the issue of culture.

Commercial acceptability

One of the most fraught tasks in the management and introduction of IT is the development of what is often called 'a cost/benefit analysis'. The underlying motivation here is both clear and sound—that the costs of investment should be unambiguously identified and then considered critically in light of the anticipated benefits.

The poverty of the traditional business case

In practice, costing the expense of IT should be a relatively straightforward exercise although seasoned practitioners will usually suggest a handsome uplift on initial budgets to cover the realities of implementation. This will take account of the invisibles such as productivity losses and opportunity costs incurred during periods of change.

What is immeasurably more challenging, however, is assessing the likely benefits. The natural inclination of many harder-nosed managers is to demand a 'business case' which demonstrates in quantitative terms that the benefits palpably outweigh the costs. In the public sector, for example, this is what the Treasury hankers after in relation to government systems. In the private sector, the same spirit prevails. In fact, this is largely the ethos of back-office automation, where costs savings through streamlining are the order of the day. In law firms, where the costs of IT, as it is often said, come straight out of the back pockets of the partners, there is often fierce opposition to any spend unless the benefits are clear; and the particular benefit which is invariably the target is none other than an increase in monthly drawings. Advantages which are seen as more remote, such as increased market share, engender less zeal.

I have seen dozens of business cases. They generally make interesting reading but they are concocted on the strength of so many unwarranted assumptions that I treat many of them as fictional in genre. I do not blame the authors of such documents because they know that unless they can show some impact on the bottom line which is directly attributable to the technologies under scrutiny, then there is no chance of the investment being sanctioned. But I do question the presupposition of top management that all relevant future factors can be identified, put under the microscope, and then quantified in monetary terms. In our so rapidly changing society, I am amazed, for example, that the Treasury in the UK can accept and is appeased by, say, five to seven year projections for breaking even on some proposed IT investments within government departments.

The Practicalities

More than this, experience does not support the optimistic projections of savings through office automation. In the legal world, for example, it does not seem to be the case that administrative and practice management systems have reduced costs, despite the original hopes of those who authorized expenditure. As elsewhere in society, teams of filing clerks have been replaced by data entry staff and by analysts with no major dip in headcount. Word processing has not generally reduced the paper bill; it has increased it with more drafts than before, but with final work product, it should be noted, of greater quality. Yet the traditional business case has difficulty reflecting qualitative improvements.

Electronic mail offers an even more powerful illustration. The managers and bean counters who welcomed its advent as a way of reducing the costs of postal and courier services have been dismayed to find a major increase in communication. Far from automating conventional methods of the past, e-mail has changed the communication patterns of organizations which have embraced it—they communicate more regularly, more widely, and they respond more quickly as well.

Here we find a major problem with the traditional business case. It is not just that it is unrealistic but it can sometimes discourage innovation. Where there has been significant change in the underlying processes, as with e-mail, the before and after are simply not commensurable. They cannot be compared in purely quantitative terms. Where the result is better and different rather than cheaper, we find the poverty of the traditional business case. It may discourage the possibility of change and qualitative improvement through IT because fund-seekers will know that the prospects of gaining support are minimal if they cannot be expressed in the conventional parlance of quantifiable cash benefit exceeding original cost.

It would be misleading to suggest all forms of change are discouraged, however, because many of the most fundamental shifts anticipated in this book, for example the delivery of information services instead of advisory services, can sometimes be accommodated quite comfortably in the traditional model. My case-study of selling document assembly systems (in Section 6.3) would be amenable to the traditional approach—the fixed fee for the work could easily be balanced against the expense of the legal specialists and the development staff.

However, from the client's perspective, even the traditional approach may not be acceptable, for it might fail to reflect the achievement of managing legal risks more effectively. An in-house legal department which seeks to introduce IT as a mechanism for improved legal risk management across its organization should surely not always be prevented from doing so because the cost of doing so would exceed the old, less adequate, and riskier form of legal service. The business case must be able to reflect and not reject uses of IT which bring about the benefit of risk management, where the risks involved are, for example, agreed to be in urgent need of management.

Business cases for judicial systems

Judges in the UK also have a problem with the traditional business case and their dilemma further highlights the difficulties in striving to be too quantitative in approach.

A key challenge perceived from within the judiciary, given the wide range of applications available to them (see Section 6.1) is to continue to encourage government investment in courtroom technology. As in the private sector, the tendency in the past has been for back-office administrative functions to be the subject of the lion's share of IT rather than for technology to be used at the cutting edge, which in this context is IT for judges in the courts. Until recently, insufficient attention in the UK has been paid to the ways in which judicial work could be automated or perhaps changed through IT. If ever the tail wagged the dog, it has been here. The judicial system exists to perform a clearly identifiable set of functions—to generate vital decisions by way of judgments, verdicts or orders—all of which should continually be analysed in the light of IT. Instead, the administrative infrastructure has been the focus of attention, resulting in useful systems such as court listing and scheduling applications, all no doubt important but surely not penetrating to the heart of the legal system and supporting the very purpose for which the judiciary exists.

Enthusiasm amongst judges is far greater than might popularly be supposed, but they themselves have no executive or purchasing power and are constrained by their position from demanding greater investment too stridently. In moving beyond the promising pilot projects, a key obstacle facing UK judges has been their inability to convince the government purse-string holders of the case supporting the introduction of advanced technologies or even basic IT infrastructure to the court system. The difficulty has been that the case in question only seems to have force if it falls into this dreaded category of 'business case'.

Other options beyond public expenditure on courtroom IT are feasible, such as encouraging the parties to pay for some courtroom technology when the costs would be recouped through the reduction in court time, and hence expense, that would result. And, in the UK, the recent Private Finance Initiative also provides the promise of alternative sources of funding.

But in the absence of more imaginative schemes such as these, the business case requires fairly conventional cost/benefit analyses. Now, these are never easy in the world of IT, but they are particularly challenging (if not wrong-headed) when many of the benefits are so irreducibly qualitative in nature. While there is certainly great importance in the various government initiatives which are seeking greater value for money and cost conscious-ness within the public sector, any naive reductionist analysis that rejects IT in the courts on purely monetary grounds will surely result in throwing the baby out with the bath water. No one can sensibly place numerical values on benefits such as speedier recourse to the courts, enhanced quality of judicial decision making, and increases in substantive justice. These factors suggest that social and constitutional values are at stake and not simply economic variables. The judges and courts cannot be exempt from having to justify investment in IT but it is to miss the point in a spectacular way to evaluate the court system as no more than an administrative system.

More than this, excessive attention to the financial issues at the expense of the less quantifiable social and constitutional benefits could also preju-dice the English legal system as a competitor in the international market-place. It must be important that England can be seen to offer a cost effective and high quality forum for the resolution of disputes (whether by litigation, arbitration or other alternative means) and a clear commitment to the use of technology could well enhance this profile.

Thus, the whole question of judicial use of technology can perhaps have a political flavour as well. In times of reducing public faith in the legal sys-tem, might the government of the day not find it attractive to be seen to be investing in a judicial system supported by well proven and leading edge information technology, providing a quicker, less costly, and more just product than in the past and thereby fortifying its competitive positioning internationally at the same time?

Measurable if not quantifiable commercial benefits

A far richer model is needed, therefore, not just in the legal context but across the business world and the public sector as well.

I advocate a model which looks in any IT investment for commercial 'acceptability', a term I use advisedly because it can extend beyond the tra-ditional approach which seeks purely quantifiable benefits. Acceptability in business, I believe, should hinge on the achievement of the various cate-gories of commercial benefit introduced in Section 2.2. Although several of these defy immediate quantification, I insist instead on setting and moni-toring clear performance measurement objectives.

Let me give some illustrations. One category of benefit is that of enhanc-ing the performance of users in their given fields. For lawyers, this may mean higher quality of work which in turn sits comfortably with the legal profession's recent interest in the introduction of quality systems—such as BS5750 and TQM (Total Quality Management)—to legal practice. For some firms, attainment of certification under some quality standard has been set as a strategic objective in its own right. If IT can be a vital building block in seeking such certification, then that of itself offers some commercial justification even if it cannot be translated into cash value. My only qualification is that if expense on IT is authorized on this ground, then the extent to which technology is actually achieving its purpose must be monitored at agreed milestones. If it is failing to fulfil its purpose, the investment should cease.

Also on the question of quality, as just discussed, many of the systems which have been designed for judges fail to meet the requirements of the traditional case because no costs savings result; but they do nevertheless lead to higher quality of judicial decision making or greater access to justice. I believe these social benefits can and should be factored into the cost/benefit analysis, even though it may be hard (but by no means impossible) to establish performance measurement criteria.

A further example of a benefit of IT for lawyers which is not quantifiable in monetary terms is that of differentiation. Here it is hoped to achieve competitive advantage on the strength of using technology in imaginative and relevant ways—applications which differ from others and establish unique positioning in the market-place. I maintain that appropriate differentiation can of itself justify expense on IT but again performance must be measurable. This requires imagination but indicators can be found. For instance, a firm can set and monitor an objective of specified levels of media coverage relating to their use of IT. Or it can require a minimum number of new pieces of work won to be directly attributable to the differentiating use of technology.

As for risk management, where that is the commercial benefit which is sought, once again an adequate model of cost/benefit analysis should be able to accommodate this objective even if, as tends to be the case, the value of reducing risk defies immediate quantification. Here, performance can still be measured if, for instance, procedures are put in place to identify and report on occasions where loss which previously would have been incurred has been averted because of the new risk management regime.

Cultivating the culture

While it is possible to agonize over costs and benefits, there is, in my view, a far bigger issue lurking in the wings; and that is the cultural one. There are many aspects to this topic, some of which I touched on previously under the heading of 'expectation management'. At the heart of this matter, for my money, is whether or not lawyers (as users or developers of legal information systems) work within an environment in which IT can flourish as a core part of the business in question. Is the commitment to IT mere lip-service, a grudging concession to a variety of unsavoury pressures? Or is there an atmosphere in which IT is almost universally acknowledged and embraced as a cornerstone of future legal service?

These are questions which raise profound psychological and emotional issues and it is possible to theorize extensively about them. For example, some might want to argue that lawyers' conservatism is the key factor here, an inertia which extends well beyond that of most professionals and, it might be said, is institutionally enshrined and bolstered in the legal psyche by precedent, the very lifeblood of the common law. On the other hand, it can be shown that some lawyers buck this alleged trend and innovate profitably.

At the risk of monumental oversimplification, and to leave the debate open for another day, I believe we can focus on one basic underlying question which, for practical if not theoretical purposes, can greatly clarify matters. That question is—for any project or initiative involving IT and the law, do the managers and lawyers in question really and truly want it to work? (Or do they hanker after technological failure and a reversion to the time-honoured methods of the past?) Answer that basic question about an organization and one is helped considerably in predicting the likelihood of success.

If the answer is positive, I suggest that it is also helpful to bear in mind the following three further factors.

Appreciate the four levels of faith

The first is that four levels of faith can be discerned in most organizations and each gives rise to its own challenges and drawbacks—I suggest that in any law firm one can always find a distribution of individuals whose views on the relevance of IT allow them to be categorized as one of: atheist, agnostic, believer, or evangelist. (Readers may like to pause and indulge in a spot of self-categorization.)

On the face of it, it might be thought that a firm full of evangelists would be a recipe for success. However, as a manager, I have to say this has not been my experience. The enthusiast (who often likes to write programs as a pastime or has a home packed with obscure accessories) is the unguided missile in the law office. He tends to be poorly placed to judge the requirements of the average user and his predictions on cost and time-scales are often wildly inaccurate.

Instead the best supporter of IT in a legal environment is the individual I call the 'unlikely champion', of whom it might be said 'if X is taking IT seriously, there really must be something in it'. Invariably an agnostic turned believer, the conviction of the unlikely champion will tend to be more plausible than that of the evangelist, being one born of recent, personal experience rather than long-standing hobbyism.

The general lesson which flows from the four levels of faith is that we are mistaken when we talk of users as though they were a homogenous collection of persons. In fact, in most organizations, there tends to be great diversity in the extent of belief in IT and so great variation in commitment to its use. Management of the workforce should be configured accordingly. There is no point, for example, in imposing interesting little add-ons upon the atheist community; equally, the believers generally do not appreciate being preached to on the merits of staple uses of IT such as that of portable computing.

Still finer distinctions must also be drawn. Within the believer grouping, for instance, there will be the so-called 'power users' who are sophisticated and confident in their usage. They can be contrasted with many others of that same group who, notwithstanding their belief, are continually feeling their way.

In all, as we design and introduce systems for lawyers, we must be sensitive to and strive to accommodate the diversity of users and resist the temptation to squeeze or stretch everyone into the procrustean bed which often travels under the name of 'the user base'.

Strive for improvement rather than perfection

A second factor in the general context of culture is lawyers' tendency to subject change to inordinate critical analysis against idealized models of progress. While they may be ideally placed, by training and temperament, to undertake such study, it is often counter-productive.

In particular, I have noticed repeatedly that lawyers' hankering after perfection often inhibits improvement of any sort. Whether it be in marketing, IT, training, organizational structure, or many other topics of regular discussion within the legal profession, projects or initiatives are often rejected not because they would fail to offer improvement but because they would fail to meet a level of perfection that many lawyers believe is attainable.

While it is admirable to seek the best, I believe the management of change, where the law and lawyers are concerned, is best undertaken through evolution and not revolution. Partnerships, for example, should encourage gradual, incremental improvement in introducing new applications of IT and not, rather unrealistically, expect major changes overnight and the immediate realization of some kind of management and operational utopia. (Fax technology succeeded in the legal profession—even if IT gurus now reject it as antediluvian—because it followed so comfortably from lawyers' working practices with no fundamental changes needed.) This is not to deny that there should be a vision or that major upheaval or re-engineering is appropriate. Instead, it is to say that the achievement of such change cannot happen overnight and that intermediate progress should not be rejected because it falls short of some more distant mission.

In the legal profession, perfection is too often the enemy of improvement and IT often suffers from this. It is, of course, not easy to change the culture or ethos of law firms but it would be, I believe, immensely beneficial if we fostered an atmosphere in which improvement short of perfection was welcomed rather than condemned. We must move from an atmosphere where there is what I term 'a presumption of incompetence' (the view that those involved with IT management are probably getting it wrong) to a more supportive and even exploratory spirit where, once again, the users really want technology to work.

I do not pretend that inculcating this new set of attitudes is a trivial task. It is tempting to follow in the footsteps of the CEO, who, one Friday, attended a conference on the practical difficulties of short-term culture change programmes. At the end, he instructed his assistant to introduce 'a new corporate culture by Monday'. Even if we resist that temptation, I fear the changes needed will take longer than even the patient amongst us would want to allow.

Accept that legal organizations are changing

In amongst all this technological change confronting individual lawyers, there is the further complication that legal organizations themselves are also set to undergo major transformation in years to come—this is my third and final cultural factor. Although my observations focus, as they have tended to, on the private law firm, some of what I say can also be applied to in-house lawyers, to barristers in chambers, and even to the judiciary in the courts.

In the first place, IT is challenging some of our fundamental assumptions about where we should physically locate our organizations. E-mail (and for some, video conferencing as well) has already enabled massive improvements in internal communications for firms with offices across the world, for the first time bringing an entire, geographically dispersed workforce under the one—albeit virtual—roof. And this progress has combined with successful external delivery of service to clients to encourage some large firms to question whether legal work need be originated from the traditional workplace: the plush urban building; leased at great cost, perhaps for another 20 years or so; premises which are paid for and serviced for 168 hours per week but generally used for only about 70 of these hours. Do the documents really need to be prepared and transmitted from there or is major relocation of staff possible? In the IT-based information society, it is hard to imagine carrying on the way we do, clustering so intensively in but a few centres. Geographical focal points for face-to-face meetings, camaraderie, and court appearances, will remain important, of course. But we can safely expect some considerable spread and dispersal, as clients and lawyers alike recognize the potential savings and benefits.

At the same time, we read that the very nature and structure of the majority of organizations is likely to change. The very largest, in both the public and the private sectors, are already being counselled to decompose into more loosely related, strategic business units, linked in something of a federal fashion. And large, international law firms are taking note.

It is also being predicted that the full-time staff of other organizations will shrink radically and yet they will retain their market share and productivity by hanging on to a high-powered core of owners who will make use of a projected floating capability of skilled, professional subcontractors. This model has caused a stir within legal partnerships, some of whom envisage that law firms will flatten out, leaving the pyramidical structure of 1980s behind (when there were many junior fee earners per partner). Instead they will have a group of highly motivated and legally expert partners— supported by IT, and paralegal staff—who will resource their workloads, as a matter of course, by securing the services of skilled lawyers. These will include part-timers, telecommuters, academic consultants, as well as regular practitioners who prefer to stay on what Charles Handy calls the 'contractual fringe' (in his superb books, *The Age of Unreason* and *Beyond Certainty*).

Project management skills will be vital for this latter approach, ensuring that all the diverse work product of the various human resources is brought together (no doubt with the aid of IT) on time and cost effectively. Project management skills will also be imperative for that other approach, referred to earlier as the 'virtual legal practice', whereby smaller firms which are connected electronically, may collaborate, on a project basis, and match the resources and capacity of larger firms (see Section 7.2).

On any of these models, for firms to profit in this coming era of change, they will need to make significant shifts in emphasis in their approaches to practice management. The style, for instance, of successful management is more likely to be inspirational rather than authoritarian. A firm's source of strength will not, as it was in the past, be in its rigid adherence to structure and stability; rather it will be in its flexibility and adaptability and its ability to take the organization through these times of continuing change when there will be less obsession with market share and more concern with creating new markets for innovative products and services. Crucial also to continuing success will be greater respect for its people, not as components of a hierarchy but as individuals with their own individual career aspirations and plans. And the threat of professional negligence litigation may also bring a shift—towards the incorporation of legal practices, which itself will bring still further upheaval as lawyers wrestle with the demands of shareholders, the prospects of aggressive take-overs by other professional services companies, the ever more onerous obligations of directorships, and the altogether less clubby corporate culture which is likely to develop.

Too secret a service

A further illustration of the importance of the cultural and organizational prong of *The Triple 'A' Formula* is found in what I sometimes rather flippantly refer to as lawyers' covert use of IT—many solicitors in the UK wrap their use of IT in a veil of secrecy and this has profound implications for the legal profession.

Some cynical commentators on the world of computers and law argue (or perhaps hope) that this secrecy is no more than a ploy to conceal either an embarrassing lack of success with technology or indeed a complete absence of computers altogether.

But this rather uncharitable explanation will not do—many law firms in the UK have invested heavily in IT, do have fairly impressive systems in place, and yet, at the same time, remain reluctant (unlike US attorneys) to discuss their uses of IT beyond the confines of their practices. Why should this be?

The arguments normally marshalled in defence of this covert use of IT invariably have one unifying theme, namely, that any public knowledge of a law firm's usage of computers will inevitably result in some loss of its competitive advantage. But this belief in likely loss of competitive advantage can be challenged on two counts: it is a view frequently rooted in muddled thinking about competitive advantage; and, more than this, it is a conviction that could of itself give rise to significant problems for our legal profession, both domestically and internationally.

The quest for competitive advantage

Turning firstly to current thinking about competitive advantage, not only is there doubt over what this overworked concept is all about (some see it as the very stuff of modern business, others dismiss it as nebulous rhetoric), there is also some considerable ambivalence over whether it can be realized by anyone at all through their use of IT. In law, however, it does seem that most senior managers suspect there is some basis in IT for gaining competitive advantage (although the more pragmatic may consider the reality to be that of pre-empting competitive disadvantage).

In any event, management theory speaks of two basic strategies for achieving and sustaining competitive advantage—maintaining lower cost than the competition or differentiating one's organization from competitors. The first strategy is not common amongst the major legal users of IT: those law firms that have invested heavily in IT are not renowned for cut-price services. Most firms would point to another commercial benefit and say that their use of IT is intended rather to enhance, uniquely, the quality of their client service. This leads to the second strategy, that of differentiation, a strategy which can surely succeed only if all points of differentiation are made unambiguously clear to clients and potential clients alike. But how can this happen if lawyers are too secretive? It cannot. (Few management consultants would champion secrecy as part of the so-called marketing mix.)

Beyond failing to promote and exploit sources of differentiation, there is a further weakness in the view—if too strictly construed and applied—that public knowledge prejudices competitive advantage. The weakness is to think that it is but a short step from learning of an envied use of IT to introducing that use elsewhere. In fact, it is a vast chasm. To translate an idea for an application into a significant operational system requires: initial assessment of technical feasibility, commercial viability, and organizational suitability; approval of the project by stakeholders and some IT committee; followed by design, development, training and implementation. While management are wont to bemoan the time consumed in the software development life cycle, the silver lining here for innovators who can maintain progress is that by the time competitors catch up, they will be too late to regain any advantage. These innovators should take comfort in the fact that there is no such management product as 'off-the-shelf competitive advantage' (no matter how much lawyers believe or wish otherwise).

The Practicalities

The lesson in all of this is to remain circumspect about applications under development but to talk much more freely about working systems (remembering too that excessive secrecy can inhibit appreciation of what *others* are doing).

Domestic issues for the legal profession

The second general concern about secret usage of IT is that until there are a significant number of advanced and non-secretive lawyers using IT, the UK legal profession will fail, domestically, to achieve many potential benefits; and, worse, may prejudice its competitive positioning internationally.

On the domestic front, if use of IT amongst lawyers is to be successful, it will need to be fairly widespread—progress will depend on most lawyers using similar or compatible systems. There is no mileage today in being the equivalent of yesteryear's first but only user of the telephone. The challenge is to be the best and not the only user. If lawyers use litigation support databases in discovery or in listing documents, for example, or if they use computers to assist in drafting contracts, then these activities can generally (although I accept not always) be greatly enhanced if the other side also make use of IT—photocopying, retyping, faxing, and other such time consuming and costly tasks can be avoided. It is usually a joy for the lawyer who favours IT to deal with kindred spirits. Also, clients will benefit by receiving a quicker and higher quality of service and one if not actually less costly than before then at least better value for money. Clients will soon expect such use of IT from their legal advisers (and this expectation will, as I have said, more than any other perhaps, accelerate lawyers' uptake of IT). Additionally, the quality of supply and suppliers of IT products and services will also improve the more lawyers there are embracing the technology.

There is, in short, a minimal threshold below which it is in no lawyer's interests for her colleagues in the UK to fall. For technology to succeed throughout the legal profession in this country, advanced users of today should share experience with the less knowledgeable so as to achieve the critical mass of advanced users that will be necessary for full exploitation of IT in the future.

International positioning

Internationally, as I have also mentioned (in Section 7.2), one major cause for concern is perception—if the UK law firms most effectively using IT are not seen from abroad to be actively promoting and publicly discussing their usage, then the profession in this country could quickly (even if wrongly) be regarded as neither equipped nor sufficiently forward-looking to manage the emerging challenges of the international business world. For example, in relation to the resolution of international disputes and the identification of the most favourable jurisdictions to pursue legal actions ('forum shopping'), unless the UK is seen to have a legal profession that uses IT in support of litigation (in case preparation and in the courts), then the UK may well not be looked upon as a cost effective forum for litigation and arbitration, much in the same way as, within the US, litigators who do not use IT are often, for that reason alone, regarded as unsuitable advisers on major disputes.

A further problem in the international context is brought into focus by recent and highly influential research on management and international competition by the US management guru, Michael Porter. His work (and that of others as well) suggests that the most outstanding commercial organizations in the international arena are those that are grounded in highly competitive domestic markets with demanding customers and formidable competitors. It is reasonable to suppose that the best law firms internationally will have similar domestic profiles. In that event, law firms seeking to be the best in the world market should want to have (but outperform) very strong local competitors. Outstanding firms that are major users of IT, and regard it as central to their success, will surely therefore be serving their own best interests by urging their competitors to use technology; for IT will strengthen these competitors, reinforce the domestic market, and thereby encourage the best firms to flourish internationally.

So there are significant dangers in lawyers remaining too secretive about their use of IT. This does not mean that firms should be explicit in all details of their applications of technology, particularly those under development. But it will be to the benefit both of the profession and of individual practices if leading users help encourage the use of technology within the UK and also promote internationally our profession's successes with information technology.

The American experience

On this international note, it is revealing that lawyers in the UK do often express an interest in the nature and extent of attorneys' use of computers in the United States. (Soon they will perhaps evince even greater interest in Australia—see the discussion of 'legal products' in Section 6.3.) They generally assume that the US legal system is far more computerized, that lawyers are more computer-literate and sympathetic to new developments, and that insight into attorneys' activities with computers today could guide UK lawyers for the next three to five years.

There are, of course, significant differences between the US and UK legal systems, differences that no doubt affect the selection of supporting technology. For example, the greater use of juries in the US has led to a larger industry in 'graphics for the courtroom' than is likely ever to emerge in the UK.

Nonetheless, there is a great deal to be learned from our American counterparts (although there should be no wholesale acceptance of the technologies, methods, and ethos to be found there). Personally, I have been greatly assisted in my understanding of the potential of computers for lawyers through both informal visits to law firms as well as through more sustained field research that has been conducted in North America.

To increase UK lawyers' understanding of US attorneys' use of information technology, the Centre for Law, Computers and Technology at Strathclyde University obtained permission from the Chicago Kent College of Law to distribute their highly regarded Large Firm Survey of 1992 in the UK. We also supplemented that survey with a study, which highlighted the key similarities and differences between the US and UK by way of broad comparative analysis.

Very quickly, we saw a difference—greater usage, for example, of PCs by US lawyers, more exploitation of on-line and CD-based services, wider adoption of litigation support, and more ambitious work on document assembly systems. Indeed, overall, as a broad generalization, our comparative assessment and my later visits to America suggest that US attorneys are two to three years ahead of UK lawyers in their exploitation of IT. While there are many dimensions to this—strategic, technical, commercial, and cultural—in my view the greatest areas of disparity remain, once again, in the all-important cultural dimension.

Where most US lawyers now seem completely comfortable with technology, many UK lawyers—even though some of the most advanced and impressive technologies are developed locally—remain nervous and distrustful. Where most US attorneys regard IT as a strategic business resource, many UK lawyers look upon computers as a necessary evil imposed by the demands of clients and the legal system generally.

The comparison lends further support for my view that the future of computers within the legal professions of the UK—and, therefore, I would strongly argue, the future of the legal profession generally—will depend on a cultural shift. Above all, prosperity will hinge on whether lawyers here genuinely *want* computers to work for them and for the benefit of their clients.

7.5. Education and Training

In 1990, I visited the Washington office of a law firm widely recognized to be one of the most advanced and committed users of technology in the American legal community. The director of IT talked a lot about the culture that they had managed to engender within the firm. Here certainly was an atmosphere within which IT could flourish. By way of illustration, she recalled a telephone conversation that she had had on that very morning, a chat with a new recruit, fresh from Law School. That individual had called to say that there seemed to have been some kind of mistake, in that there was no machine on his desk awaiting his arrival.

I reflected, with some irony, that in the UK it would be more likely that a fresh trainee solicitor would contact the computer support department to indicate that there had been some kind of error only if a machine was indeed on his desk on arrival. Were it not so amusing, we would all immediately see this as tragic. Here, no doubt, is one reason why the US legal profession may have years of strategic competitive advantage over UK lawyers—their students are more comfortable with IT.

It is said that over eighty per cent of US law students have their own machines. I do not know if anyone has had the nerve to survey the UK position but I would hazard a guess, from my travels and chats to colleagues in the academic community, that less than five per cent of British undergraduates have computers they could call their own. And so, although it is commonly conjectured that the lack of IT uptake by UK lawyers is but a short-term concern, merely a blip because all law graduates today have surely been using technology while at university, this is almost certainly not so. In fact, few law schools in universities in the UK provide adequate encouragement and training in IT today, and even those that do are often regarded as idiosyncratic, hobbyist or self-indulgent.

If the administration of law is to be improved and changed through technology, it is axiomatic that lawyers should have a far deeper appreciation of IT, gained throughout their careers from a blend of education, training, and awareness raising (thus, genuine 'hybrids' will emerge—see Section 7.3).

IT as a distinct discipline?

Although each phase in the legal career requires and deserves a different educational perspective and approach to IT—my model is outlined in this section—there is a fundamental theme common to all phases, which I deal with first of all. It relates to the temptation to treat IT as a distinct discipline.

There are many ways in which law students and legal practitioners can learn about IT: for example, by relatively formal, conventional education; or by on-the-job training; or through awareness raising exercises. Whichever method is chosen, it is wrong-headed, in my view, to regard IT as a distinct discipline and something which should be taught as though it were a separate legal subject. To hold IT out as an entirely independent field is almost as misleading as identifying reading or writing for lawyers as distinct disciplines in their own right.

Instead, if the power of technology is to be exploited by the profession, IT should be projected as something that is an integral part of the way we research into the law, learn about new legal developments, advise our clients, and provide them with information.

To insist on separating IT from how it is applied, for the purposes of education and teaching, is at best to miss the opportunity to be exposed to practical, everyday uses of technology. At worst, it perpetuates a legal mind-set dominated by print and paper, with technology available only for those who feel so inclined or interested; rather than recognizing it to be indispensable for the legal profession of the future. The paper and print mentality will have no place in an IT-based information society, in which, for example, there will be hundreds of millions of people on the Internet. Lawyers must be trained to work digitally in a digital world or they may as well shut shop tomorrow.

Undergraduate IT

During the past two years, in the context of my own children's schooling, I have had cause to visit a large number of primary and secondary schools and have quite naturally inquired about the extent to which IT plays a part in the lives of pupils. As one might expect, I found varying degrees of commitment and interest. Generally, however, I was surprised and refreshed by the level of enthusiasm and support. The result is that most ten year olds today have more 'flying hours', as it were, than adults over fifty. And it is fair to conclude that our schools are increasingly producing students who are comfortable with computers and telecommunications and for whom the regular use of IT in learning is the norm. The National Curriculum for UK schooling unambiguously endorses the relevance of IT for the education of our young and indeed requires programmes of study and attainment targets for IT throughout the school career. Rightly, in my view, there is emphasis on the use of IT in practical situations and on appreciation of its impact on the workplace and society.

It would surely be scandalous if this solid foundation created during schooling were to be followed by a dip in exposure to IT for all university students when they progress to legal undergraduate studies. Sadly, in the already overcrowded curricula of most university law faculties, some legal academics have become exasperated with the thought of having to introduce one further subject, in the shape of IT, even though most do recognize its significance.

In the past, when it was thought appropriate to teach a separate course with some such title as 'Computers for Lawyers', those law faculties which made such a module compulsory certainly found it eating into the core legal subjects of an already packed curriculum. But those who took the alternative route, of making such a course optional, found that they were attracting only the eccentrics and the enthusiasts, those who were already committed to and interested in IT. In contrast, in the latter scenario, the mainstream law student regarded the whole subject as peripheral and tended to take a rain check on technology.

In retrospect, this was something of a nebulous dilemma, in that the future careers of these students should not have demanded any detailed knowledge of computing and telecommunications. Instead, creating a comfortable disposition towards technology and a familiarity with its impact on practical tasks would have had a more lasting and useful impact.

This positive disposition towards IT can be achieved in large part by using IT in actually teaching, and learning about, the law. This can help to highlight the relevance of technology, to illustrate its practical relevance, and bring its usage to the heart of legal understanding. Moreover, encouraging students to use technology in studying the law—whether in writing essays using word processors, using retrieval systems to undertake legal research, or communication systems to download external information—exposes law students to benefits and results, rather than abstract information about, say, the architecture of computer hardware or the basics of computer programming. Law students who have experienced IT as a teaching tool and a mechanism for generating their own work product, are well placed to progress to the next stage of their technical education.

Law tutors and lecturers should not aspire to any technical detail in their treatment of IT. They must forget about programming, operating systems, fifth generation architectures, and the like and instead instil an attitude which has for long been inculcated into students of the applied sciences. Law students should therefore be like undergraduate engineers or nuclear physicists who quite naturally turn to IT and take it on board as an invaluable tool which supports the pursuit of their core disciplines.

Thus, significant parts of the legal curriculum should be delivered through electronic law tutorials, computer-based law 'courseware', computer-assisted learning or computer-assisted instruction (known, respectively, in the UK and US, as CAL and CAI).

Distance learning should also gain acceptance, following the lead of Law Schools such as that of Strathclyde University, with whom an LL M in Legal Informatics is being taken by students all over the world, who are given remote access to 25 megabytes of teaching material and participate in on-line, group tutorials.

Above all else, our law schools must avoid the temptation to transfer responsibility for teaching IT to those who preside over later stages in the educational process. 'It's best to wait and see how your future employer will want you to use IT' is rationalization of an unhelpful variety. Claims that the proper place for IT education for lawyers should be during law school, bar school or training contracts constitute unacceptable abdication of responsibility. It is not just that we now live in a world where missing out on IT for three or four years is folly (although this is certainly so), it is that the teaching of law in absence of IT is gradually becoming a misrepresentation of legal practice and legal process.

Those academic lawyers who have accepted all of this have been confronted, however, by the very practical problem that UK law schools are severely underfunded for IT. The current level of government support still seems to be based on law students requiring little more than book-based library services rather than the IT-based information services to which some law schools are rightly now aspiring. As a matter of urgency, a high profile, coherent case must be made by the academic legal community, with the support of the professional bodies, to the various state funding authorities. This should show that law undergraduates' need for laboratory resources is now akin in many ways to the requirements of students of, say, the applied sciences, and that a minimum technology capability is as crucial as an agreed baseline for conventional library holdings. The appeal for more funding can be tempered, however, by savings which commitment to IT will bring, for example, in providing access to a vast, 'virtual' law library across the world which should make some materials available without needing to be purchased in the conventional manner.

But I do not underestimate the challenge here, in times when increase in public funding for universities seems to be anathema to the prevailing government ethos. The topic also raises many other fundamental issues about academic lawyering, not the least of which is the related need, in my view, for work on the development of appropriate, legal information systems to be recognizsed as worthy academic research and accredited with the same status as conventional publications.

Professional examinations

Once students have graduated and progressed to their professional examinations (legal practice courses for solicitors and bar school for barristers), the impetus should be maintained. The emphasis here should be less on tutoring systems and applications for student work, and more on the kinds of technologies to which these individuals are likely to be exposed when they enter their chosen branch of the profession. With their strong accent on the law in action and practical lawyering, these courses must pay more than lip-service to technology if the insights and experience gained as legal undergraduates are not to be lost. Again, technology should be portrayed as a feature of legal practice and not a discipline in its own right.

In this context I have been asked by various institutions to suggest a check-list of software packages to which the law student should be exposed during their professional studies. To be concerned about packages, however, is of little assistance and limits users' thinking and perspective. The emphasis should instead be at the level of applications (for example, litigation support or electronic communications) rather than enabling techniques and particular software packages.

It has also been put to me by providers of legal practice courses that no law firms in England have yet expressed a preference for recruiting individuals with experience of IT; and so they have said they have had little encouragement to cover IT. This problem is a circular one, however, because very few firms are themselves motivated by having actually reaped the benefits of genuinely and thoroughly IT-educated law graduates who from the very start of their traineeships can add value. In fact, most firms are not yet themselves suitably placed, in any event, to take advantage of the experience which IT literate trainees may have to offer. Until legal practices have invested in front and client office systems, they are unlikely to see the relevance of junior staff using IT. When they have such systems in place and have some experience of how trainees can contribute, I suspect firms will then clamour for more and the level of demand may shift. For now, the imaginative course providers should see that exposing their students to appropriate IT is likely to help hasten the general uptake across the profession and, in due course, to increase the interest they feel is lacking today.

Initial training

Once these graduates progress to law offices or chambers, one would hope that they would be expecting that IT will be at their disposal during the course of their traineeships or pupillages, as the case may be. Here again, the early investment in training must continually be topped up and many young lawyers have been rather disillusioned to find that otherwise seasoned practitioners either ignore technology altogether or use their machines for a very narrow set of purposes. They have been miffed even more when told that they do not get machines for their own use until they qualify some two years later. Once more, continuity is vital and there should be no period during which the trainee or pupil barrister should be without access to a computer.

Optimistically, trainee lawyers can, as I have said, be a major source of impetus for IT within an organization and there is an opportunity here for their own experience and understanding to be passed on to their senior colleagues.

Realistically, however, it cannot yet be assumed automatically that younger lawyers are more sympathetic and enthusiastic about new technologies than their more senior colleagues. In practice, I have not found this to be the case. Indeed, my most receptive audiences tend to be the most senior of lawyers and judges who contrast markedly with many recently qualified lawyers who are prone to being cynical and rather closed minded about IT. This is a temporary phenomenon, however, because this prevailing attitude today is probably a function of an IT-free earlier legal education which has not prepared them for the use of technology.

Ongoing exposure

Perhaps the most challenging of all aspects of IT education for lawyers is the provision of training to well established, senior practitioners who have never been taught about IT and whose awareness is low. While many such lawyers hope that they can hold out until retirement without having to immerse themselves in technology, the challenge for management in firms is to create an environment in which keeping up to date with IT is as natural as monitoring legal developments.

One-to-one training in the comfort, security, and seclusion of lawyers' own offices works very well, and avoids the inhibitions and embarrassments which may arise for senior colleagues in group training sessions.

Moreover, for the busy, practising lawyer, there seems to be no better way of introducing new technologies than to have the trainer introduce applications in the context of live work which the lawyer is currently progressing. On one model, the trainer asks the lawyer what tasks he has before him for the day and then they work together in completing these tasks. It may be drafting a letter, for example, in which case they will use the computer and prepare the communication from beginning to end.

In this way, technology training for lawyers should focus on the accomplishment of tasks and the achievement of results rather than running a lawyer through the features of particular packages or describing the various capabilities of some system. Lawyers, like all users, absorb more from training when it is provided in the context of everyday work and not when it is served up in a vacuum of technical chit-chat. Lawyers need to see IT in action. They must learn about text entry (by keyboard or voice), hypertext browsing, project management and electronic communication by seeing it work in familiar surroundings and in relation to their specific workloads.

Looking beyond basic training, an enduring dilemma is whether to be paternalistic or libertarian in helping lawyers to make the most of their investment on a day-to-day basis. The paternalists commit to spoonfeeding and continually seek to top up their users' IT know-how. The libertarians let their lawyers explore for themselves and encourage self-reliance and a working environment in which IT will flourish without training programmes. The reality is that some lawyers react well to one approach and others favour the opposite. In an organization of size, both approaches must be adopted if widespread and successful exploitation is to be achieved.

Only then will all lawyers in the entire workforce gradually see themselves as information managers in the business of information processing. They will also come to feel comfortable with the notion of providing information services and not just advice. Ultimately, they will want IT to work for them.

PART FOUR—THE VISION

8

Law's Future

And so we come now to look to the future—of law, lawyers, and legal service.

It is hard to know where to begin when thinking ahead about the future of law. What might our legal institutions look like in, say, one hundred years' time? In other aspects of our life, we perhaps feel more comfortable about guessing. Manufacturing, we tend to hazard, will be dominated by advanced robotics. Travel will become quicker, smoother, and sleeker no doubt, relying on less offensive energy sources than are used today. Education and learning will be transformed by hugely enhanced information flow and distance learning, dominated we suspect by simulated experiences delivered through virtual reality. Remote diagnosis in medicine seems inevitable as does on-line domestic purchasing without crossing the physical threshold of a shop or store. Above all perhaps, we anticipate that technology will release our descendants from many of the excesses of work to enable fulfilment in a society where leisure activities will play a more prominent role. And so we could go on.

But what of the law? Will lawyers still congregate in offices, chambers, and courts, the only group with mastery of the law? Will this prime source of social control retain the traditions of the centuries gone by? Three-piece suits, dusty law libraries, wigs and gowns, pomposity, arrogance, and aloof disposition—will perceptions of these stereotypes prevail? Change is surely likely.

One way of tackling the challenge of predicting the future of law and legal service would be to draw up a list of the various techniques, technologies, and applications that have already been successfully but not yet extensively exploited by lawyers across the world and to combine this with an inventory of the most promising laboratory developments (which at any given time can give us at least three years' reliable, commercial foresight).

We could make a couple of assumptions along the way about hardware and communications, namely that the overwhelming majority of lawyers in the land, very early in the next millennium, will have lightweight, high-powered, multi-media portable machines capable of communicating locally within offices and more widely across countries and continents, courtesy of some global information infrastructure (some of which will be wireless).

We would surely also create a vision of vastly more user friendly systems, with unimaginably slick adaptive user interfaces, fully integrated with voice recognition and synthesis. Hypertext, document assembly, expert systems, conceptual retrieval, and document image processing would probably figure as the key enabling techniques, putting personal and internal know-how as well as externally published information at the fingertips of lawyers. And for dispute resolution, one could comfortably envisage as a matter of course that huge quantities of documents (many millions) will be loaded and readily accessible in a variety of ways in preparation for hearings; ready also for use by all participants in the courtroom together with all manner of graphical, no doubt multi-media, ways of presenting evidence.

But to dwell on this type of prediction would be to miss the point dramatically. Although these prognostications may prove to be accurate, it is to let the tail wag the dog to think about the future of law and lawyers as being led by IT. Rather, the starting-point in this kind of speculation (and, in turn, in long-term strategic planning within the profession) should be the shifting demands of the market-place for legal services combined with the shortcomings of current legal practice. IT in this context then comes into play as a management tool, an instrument of change, improvement, and response rather than technology for technology's sake.

This bears directly on what is perhaps the greatest management challenge facing lawyers grappling with IT, that of moving beyond successful *automation* of existing practices to *innovation*, so that IT changes—cost effectively and qualitatively—the way legal practice is undertaken and the manner in which legal services are delivered.

A new vocabulary is needed if we are to face the future squarely. This is not playing with words. Our use of language often reveals our understanding and assumptions and the introduction of new terms and concepts can help shift our perceptions and help ease us through difficult transitional periods. We should be thinking less of clients and of lawyers but instead in terms of users, legal information engineers, and providers of legal information. We should be redefining the role of lawyers. We should be facing the most difficult questions head on. We should be trying to understand what tomorrow's legal paradigm will be like. In this final chapter, I try to make a start in these general directions.

Before doing so, however, I should say just a few words by way of classification of the future. It should be clear from this book that IT will affect the practice of law and the administration of justice in a variety of ways. The leading applications, supported by the key enabling techniques, will give rise to automation and streamlining of legal processes as we know them today, as well as to innovating and re-engineering of various parts of the legal system, as legal service becomes a type of information service.

More specifically, in the *short to medium term*, during which we will be in the transitional phase between the print-based industrial society and the IT-based information society, the order of the day will be automation, streamlining, optimizing, and improvement of current practices.

In the *longer term*, after this transitional phase, there will be a fundamental shift in paradigm, from advisory to information service. Then, innovation will dominate and new working practices will emerge.

But what is the future of law in the *very long term*, well after we are firmly ensconced in the global information society? The further one seeks to predict the future, the more unsure one's footing becomes. My guess would be that once we progress fully into the information society, the dominant enabling techniques will be multi-media (systems incorporating combinations of text, video, animation, graphics, and sound) and developments in that branch of information systems.

I have made no attempt here to seek to explore the changes in the nature, structure, and delivery of law in a world dominated by multi-media. The only sustained attempt to do so (at least that I know of) has been by Ethan Katsh in his recent book, *Law in the Digital World*. In a brave attempt to speculate about the likely transformation in the law on the back of multi-media, Katsh anticipates fundamental change but remains tantalizingly sketchy on detail. My own inclination is that while multi-media is likely to change the ways in which we represent the law and package it for consumption, I do not believe it will bring yet another shift in legal paradigm. Multi-media will enhance legal service as an information service and will render the law still further accessible but I have read or seen nothing which suggests it will bring change so far-reaching as that which I predict for law in its movement from advisory to information service.

For what it is worth, I believe the next shift in paradigm for the law (after the current one) will not occur until several centuries hence, at the end of the information society when, through enablers such as nanotechnology, man and machine become one and supplementary information and knowledge will be genetically encoded in human beings.

In the meantime—and it will be a long meantime—the foreseeable future of law (the basis of a more accurate but less snappy title for this book) lies in the law becoming a form of information service. And it is to a further and final exploration of this notion—of what I have called *the longer term*—to which I devote the remainder of the book.

8.1. Users, Legal Information Engineers, and Providers

Once the current shift in legal paradigm has come about, I claim, legal service will become a form of information service in two broad ways. First, as enabling techniques and leading applications are refined, much of today's conventional legal work will be routinized and proceduralized and then made available on the information infrastructure as a consultative service. The second dimension is potentially far more significant and this is the realization of the vast, *latent legal market*—the countless instances in domestic and business life which would benefit from legal input but where this has been impractical or too costly to achieve in the past.

In both instances, there is a major change in the underlying relationship between those who are involved in delivering legal advice and those who receive it. On the traditional model, we have had lawyers and their clients, with the contractual commitment upon the legal adviser to offer some kind of advisory-based service, to their individual clients alone, on the basis of some more or less agreed charging structure (invariably, in the past, charging by the hour or day). When legal service becomes information service, there is a change, but not simply from the delivery of advice to the provision of information. Much more, a new set of relationships are established, under which those who are guided become *users*, the lawyers who analyse and organize the material become the *legal information engineers*, and the organizations who develop and market the legal information products and services become the *providers*. The key relationship in this scenario is between the users and providers of the information service, with a secondary arrangement between the provider and the engineers. (I have left, for another time, more detailed analysis, in information terms, of the *originators*—the legislators and the judges.)

Users of legal information

The users of legal information services of the future will consult, navigate about, and be empowered to apply legal information made more readily accessible and financially acceptable than in the past. Legal information will be but one of countless sorts of information available on the global information infrastructure, although the compartmentalization of information into legal and other such conventional categories will itself fade away in time. The information products and services available—and available, in due course, to all citizens—will be packaged and oriented towards providing practical and directly implementable guidance with little or no distinction between the disciplines from which the final information product has been derived. A user who has a problem which traditionally may have needed, say, accounting and banking expertise as well as legal, may consult a service which provides a synthesis of these three sources of guidance; but there will be no particular need or benefit in the overall guidance being broken down into units which reflect their original structure. This kind of compartmentalization may be a practical necessity of today but will have less place in the IT-based information society.

The basis for charging users for legal service will shift from being fixed in the number of hours expended by the lawyer towards a fee that is more likely to reflect the overall market value of the information to the user.

The number of such users will be vastly greater than the number of conventional clients of today; and the frequency with which these legal information services will be consulted will greatly outstrip the frequency of consultations with lawyers today. The difference will lie in the emergence and realization of *the latent legal market*, as innumerable situations in domestic and business life are enlightened by the law when this would or could not have happened in the past. For example, when a citizen crashes his car, purchases faulty goods or considers taking out a loan, he will have at his fingertips practical, focused, and applicable guidance which, it is likely, would not have been realistically available in absence of some IT-based information service. Similarly, in the commercial world, in preliminary negotiations, in on-the-spot procurement or in business planning generally, a layer of legal counsel will be available when previously it may have been regarded as too cumbersome or costly to obtain legal input.

And so to those lawyers, and there will be many, who will say 'Ah, but my clients don't just benefit from our legal advice, they need a shoulder to cry on, a confidante, and so a personal, one-to-one service which no IT-based information service can provide', I have a firm response—those who belong to *the latent legal market* will generally have the plain option of legal guidance through some information service or no legal guidance at all. They do not, and will not, have the luxury of choosing between the personal service and the information service. By definition the former is not available. Thus, the objection collapses.

Legal information engineers

At first glance, this may seem like tragic news for the average lawyer and be thought to be a harbinger of the end of the legal profession—asking the legal practitioner to buy into this model of the future may seem akin to inviting the proverbial turkey to vote for an early Christmas.

In fact, it will mean fundamental change and a very different market for legal knowledge and expertise will emerge. Those lawyers who fail to recognize and plan for the shift in legal paradigm may well cease to trade profitably; whereas those of vision and entrepreneurial flare are already planning today for an exciting commercial future.

The systematization of work which is done manually today, in my transitional phase, will be yet one more source of strain and reason for shrinkage in the pressurized legal market-place. In contrast, the liberation and emergence of the hitherto *latent legal market* will create a range of opportunities for lawyers to package and sell their expertise in innovative ways.

What, then, might the lawyer's role be as an engineer of legal information? The main task, in the first instance, will be that of analyst—it will be for the lawyers, with their unparalleled knowledge of the legal system, to interpret and repackage the formal sources of law (legislation and case-law) and articulate it in structured format suitable for implementation as part of a legal information service. Trained lawyers will continue to have unique insight into the law and legal process. In the information society, they will repackage this insight and sell it not through one-to-one advisory work, but in the creation of legal information products and services.

Intellectually, many lawyers may find this extremely difficult because it involves thinking about the application of law at a higher level of generality than is familiar to most practitioners. Traditional legal service requires legal advisers to concentrate on the very specific details and circumstances of their client's cases. The legal reasoning and problem solving processes involve subsuming these particulars under the more general categories in legislation or case-law. In contrast, in developing legal information systems, the legal mind must work at a higher level of generality, expressing guidance and counsel which is intended for wider application and use than the specifics of particular cases. The discipline involved is no less rigorous but is broader brush in orientation and product than conventional legal analysis.

There is, potentially, a very significant and attractive role here for legal academics, whose work, as commentators and theoreticians, has always been at a more general level than practitioners. In fact, it is the general findings and observations as held in academic lawyers' writings which are often, in practice, the basis of conclusions and recommendations of lawyers in practice. Yet as practitioners are faced with the formidable challenge of operating at a higher level of abstraction than that with which they are comfortable, then legal academics aspiring to join this particular information revolution have the equally daunting task of supplementing their formal legal analysis with the experience of what actually works in practice. This practical business know-how often refines and sometimes even overrides the law in books.

There is a natural opportunity here for collaboration between the academic and practising branches of the profession, although both will need to be adaptable and flexible in working together.

Who are the providers?

In the legal advisory paradigm of the print-based society, lawyers have enjoyed a dual role, combining that of being legal information engineers as well as providers. In fact, the two functions have become intertwined as one—those who gained expertise in law, in a world based on print and paper, were the only individuals who were in a practical position to apply it in particular circumstances in providing advice.

In the IT-based information society, in contrast, the process of analysis and formulation of information can and will be separated from that of the provision of legal information service. Knowing the law and being able to articulate legal information will no longer necessarily lead to domination in the sale of that information.

Lawyers will by no means be the only workers affected by this break from the past—many of the middlemen known as brokers or agents or intermediaries or the like who have also enjoyed their monopoly over various information services (estate agency, insurance broking, and travel agency, for example) will find they may no longer dominate their markets. Where the service being delivered is essentially information-based, other imaginative providers will enter the markets and strive to use IT to deliver greatly improved service on the information highway. 'Disintermediation' will be the order of the day and the middlemen will need to find new, imaginative ways of adding value.

In this, we see perhaps the greatest commercial challenge of all for lawyers, because with the shift in paradigm of legal service comes their loss of a monopoly over the provision of legal services. While at first glance, today's lawyer may be most apprehensive about moving from an advisory role to that of an engineer and analyst, the far graver and fundamental challenge is actually that of retaining market share in the provision of legal information. In terms of *The Legal Information Continuum*, lawyers should promote a shift from the right of the spectrum (where the legal advisers sit) to the left (towards the formal sources), as IT enables the provision of legal service in other than its traditional, advisory form.

In the past, conventional legal publishers have been positioned towards the far left of the continuum, delivering products which clarify the formal sources and put them in their wider legal, business, and social contexts. The market for these products was confined mainly to lawyers themselves, as the nature of printing (as discussed in relation to the information services substructure, in Section 3.4) imposed a natural constraint on the range of individuals who could directly derive benefit from books and articles. In short, legal publishing was for lawyers because no one else could really understand law books.

However, as legal publishers have diversified into electronic legal publishing and are gradually exploiting crucial enabling techniques such as hypertext, document assembly, enhanced text retrieval, and groupware, then the products they produce demand less legal expertise on the part of the users and so appeal to a wider user base. As these techniques are refined, legal publishers will progress slowly rightward on the legal continuum and vie with practising lawyers in the market for legal information. It is entirely conceivable, for example, that a leading legal practitioner may be invited to collaborate, even on a permanent basis, with imaginative electronic legal publishers who may retain the services of this lawyer at rates which could match or exceed the fee income which would be generated by traditional work on an hourly billing basis. At the same time, innovative lawyers will package their conventional work product, such as a well drafted document, in electronic form using techniques such as hypertext to enhance and clarify contractual and other materials and to provide ready access to relevant legal sources. Thus, lawyers will gradually themselves move leftwards on the continuum.

As publishers and lawyers move towards each another on *The Legal Information Continuum*, both must also look beyond this one dimension if they are together to dominate the market for the provision of legal information systems. For they are likely to have to confront and avert threats in the commercial world far graver than one another. I have in mind the large accounting and consulting firms, whose vast information systems resource will prepare them far sooner for the delivery of professional services on the information infrastructure. It is entirely conceivable that the recruitment of legal specialists to act as sources for information service providers is as likely to occur at the instance of these multinational players as from the legal publishers. With mastery of the information services market which will outstrip the most technically advanced of lawyers, it is entirely conceivable that an accounting and consulting giant could cultivate and then dominate *the latent legal market*. On this model, lawyers would be relegated to the role of back-room technician, while the other professionals enjoy the glamour and profit of delivering the information service to society generally.

Equally, the same *latent legal market* may be recognized by the increasingly powerful telecommunications providers whose great experience of the information infrastructure would stand them in splendid stead to exploit the legal market. While the telecommunications industry may be less attuned to the nature of professional services than the accounting and consulting firms, it may be that professional service, as we know it in the industrial print-based society, may be superseded by some other ethos and organizational infrastructure in the IT-based information society.

The development of the legal information services market will, of course, constitute a major challenge to the legal profession itself, a profession which has its roots in a well understood body of knowledge and which until now, but not for much longer, has enjoyed legal protection over its work through regulation that has required certain kinds of legal tasks in society to be discharged exclusively by suitably qualified lawyers.

8.2. The Province of Lawyers Determined

It follows from the arguments in this book that, in the future, there will be two broad ways in which legal risks will be managed, legal problems will be solved, legal guidance will be offered, and legal disputes will be disposed of. On the one hand, as legal information services and products are developed and marketed, the market will require that all manner of legally oriented tasks and processes will be systematized, proceduralized, and made widely available across society. While much of the demand for such legal information services will come from the hitherto *latent legal market*, many conventional legal advisory services which are provided today will also be routinized and delivered in this way. To this extent, the conventional legal market may shrink, although there will still be work opportunities here for lawyers (in England, especially for solicitors), as legal information engineers or providers.

On the other hand, an important legal market for service delivered in the traditional way will remain (although streamlined through IT), because there will be a variety of situations in which it will not be possible or appropriate for legal information systems to supplant or replace the conventional approach. It is also likely that some traditional legal work will itself arise from *the latent legal market*—in those cases where legal advice would not have been sought in the past but when it transpires that the available legal information services cannot offer sufficient guidance.

In all the excitement of anticipating a shift from advisory to information service, it is vital not to overlook these areas of legal life which will remain the province of lawyers—for these will often be of great social significance and commercial value. This province itself can be divided into two: the specialist function and the judicial function.

The specialist function

Both for commercial reasons and because of the nature of law, there will still be a need for specialist lawyers in the information society. The strongest candidates for assuming this role in England are barristers and specialist solicitors.

Commercial imperatives

From the commercial point of view, there will still be many situations where the value of a transaction, dispute, project or activity will be so high that the stakeholders will inevitably be prepared to invest in a second opinion. This will be so even if the scenario at issue is one which seems to be routine and well proceduralized and systematized in readily available legal information services. Where the guidance offered by legal information systems supports the position of the stakeholder involved, then consultation with a specialist may either be a matter of prudence and caution ('belt and braces') or another layer of legal risk management. When, however, the legal input offered by information systems inclines the other way and is potentially or actually contrary to the stakeholder's substantial financial interest, then direct consultation with human specialists will be with a view to investing in expert legal advice which either challenges the guidance of the information system or argues that the stakeholder's particular circumstances are not so straightforward as to be covered completely by the routinized rendition of the law.

It is realistic and not cynical to anticipate this latter deployment of lawyers, because this is precisely what happens today. When there is enough at stake, the services of the very best lawyers are invoked either to challenge and destroy the arguments of others, or to suggest there has been a category error and that the client's circumstances are actually governed by other rules and principles (inevitably in their favour).

Moving beyond the commercial imperatives which might drive users of legal information services to call upon specialists, there are a further set of compelling reasons why the services of conventional legal specialists will still be in demand in the future. These have their roots in the very nature of law.

A jurisprudential digression

To address this issue, we need to make a minor philosophical digression and delve briefly into issues which properly belong to the discipline of jurisprudence (legal theory or legal philosophy). Jurisprudence is concerned, amongst many other issues, with the nature of the law and of legal problem solving. The issues here are complex and I have dealt with them at some considerable length in an earlier book, *Expert Systems in Law*.

For present purposes, it is important to clarify one particular topic, that of the impossibility of creating a legal information system which can cover all eventualities and so have no gaps. My view is that this is impossible for four reasons, no matter what enabling techniques or applications are used to package the law.

The first is to do with language. Because the law and legal information is expressed in natural language (see Section 2.5), there can always be doubts or arguments over whether the particular circumstances of one's case fall within a category presented by some information system. If a system makes it clear, for example, that a user is not permitted to drive a vehicle in the public park, does this rule extend to skateboards? In this, and many other instances, because language is indeterminate, we are not given watertight help. Sometimes there may seem to be little doubt—it seems to be clear, for example, that I should not take my ten-ton truck in this recreational area.

A second kind of gap is where there does not seem to be any law or legal information governing particular circumstances. This is to be expected because legislators, judges, and legal information system developers have limited foresight and cannot anticipate all situations which may arise.

On some occasions, legal information systems (like lawyers) might seem to provide a series of suggestions, some of which contradict one another. In this third eventuality, the uncertainty with which the system speaks can be regarded as another sort of gap.

Finally, there will be gaps in any legal information system due to the possibility of any guidance being subject to implied exceptions. No representation of the law can be regarded as fixed and static, but can always be refined or disregarded in the context of a particular case because of some overriding purpose of the law or because of some legal principle. For example, the ten-ton truck in the earlier illustration may transpire to be acceptable for the park in the light of the future information that the purpose of its entry is by way of some war memorial gesture. In these circumstances it might be said that the *purpose* of the regulation was to promote a harmonious community facility and the memorial gesture may be construed as supporting rather than defeating that purpose. An instance of the application of legal principle is the legendary jurisprudential example of the man who murdered his grandfather to inherit under the latter's will. Although the rule of testate succession seemed to point to the murderer as the rightful inheritor, the courts found this rule subject to the implied exception that 'no man may profit from his own wrong', a legal principle inherent in the legal system in question. Similarly, when enough is at stake, I have no doubt that clever lawyers will always contrive to find similar such countervailing principles and bring these to bear in opposition to any unacceptable guidance offered by legal information systems.

This dip into legal theory suggests that on those occasions where the language of a system is indeterminate, or there is an absence of relevant information, or there is a conflict in the information or there is a realistic prospect of some exception being implied, then the legal information system may not be sufficiently powerful to help the user and recourse to the specialist adviser would still be necessary.

The judicial function

Speculation about the future of computers and the law often leads to debate on the impact of IT on judges. There are three distinct questions here. First, will the more widespread use of legal information services reduce the number of cases which come before the courts? Second, will IT help judges in the conduct of their work? And, third, can computers replace judges? The second question, I have already dealt with elsewhere in the book: in Section 6.1, by way of case-study, I outlined the leading, current and likely future applications; while in Section 7.4, I suggested that, in the UK at least, obtaining funding is an ongoing challenge.

Let me now deal with the first and third questions.

The new 'living law'

As legal guidance becomes readily available and increasingly usable and useful, it may well be, in the future, that recourse both to lawyers and to the courts will be made less frequently. On this view, legal information systems will of themselves reduce the number of formal disputes before judges. If legal risk management does indeed become the order of the day, then this will lead, more generally, I believe, to a culture where dispute pre-emption is pervasive rather than dispute resolution.

It may be that only a subset of those cases which, for the commercial or jurisprudential reasons just discussed, would be handled by specialists, may thereafter require the attention of the courts.

Yet, this has extremely profound implications for the law. It is possible, for example, that the information which will be accessible on the global highway will guide our social, domestic, and working lives more directly than the primary sources (legislation and case-law) themselves. In a sense, this legal guidance itself may come to be regarded as the law itself and not just a representation of it. This may indeed become the prime illustration of what the legal sociologist Eugen Ehrlich, earlier this century, called the 'living law'—the law which actually reflects and conditions behaviour in society.

That such a representation could ever assume this status (as a quasi-legislative source) may challenge the constitutional purist who will say that valid law can only emanate from a properly elected legislature or a duly appointed judiciary. Yet there is some precedent, in Scotland at least, for commentators' writings becoming the law itself: the so-called Institutional Writers were scholars whose analysis and synthesis of the law came to be treated later as authoritative and binding sources.

Certainly if legal information systems were regarded by non-lawyers as constituting the law itself, then this should encourage legal institutions to seek to set standards for legal guidance being widely available in this form and perhaps also to establish some central body or to appoint individuals (perhaps judges) with responsibility for reviewing and even endorsing materials of sufficient quality.

Can computers replace judges?

What, then, of those cases which do seem to call for resolution by some impartial authority? Might computers ever assume the judicial function? Can judging, in large or small part, be mediated by machine? Is this just fertile ground for science fiction writers or can we expect automated justice dispensers?

First of all, it is clear that the jurisprudential limitations of legal information systems as discussed in relation to specialists apply equally to the concept of judicial systems. In fact, it is precisely when there are gaps in the law (in the senses identified) that judges are most urgently required today and no doubt tomorrow as well. The technical limitations of IT (see Section 2.5) are also relevant here because the problems of natural language processing and common sense reasoning are at the heart of our current inability to program computers to display the creativity, individuality, intuition, and common sense that we expect of judges acting in their official role.

And moral issues come into play here too. The considerable disquiet that Joseph Weizenbaum (see Section 2.5) expressed in relation to the notion of the computer judge is, at root, a moral claim which might be extrapolated to run as follows: so long as we accept the primacy of human beings as the basic moral unit in society (mainly western democracies) then we would have difficulty in justifying certain sorts of conflicts between human agents being resolved by non-human forces. Even if it were possible, therefore, to program computers to exhibit, for example, moral, religious, social, sexual, and political preferences akin to those actually held by judges and applied in their dispensing of justice, we may reject it as morally undesirable. We might do so because this may require the design of systems which would generalize in these various dimensions where the judicial system has always presupposed uniquely human, empathetic focus on the part of judges in dealing with very specific details of particular cases.

Yet the jurisprudential, technical, and moral arguments cannot be stretched too far, because there are no doubt all sorts of legal dispute to which they do not apply; there are many cases with no significant moral dimension which may, in principle, be disposed of more effectively by some form of system, even if the techniques and technology to enable this are not yet sufficiently refined.

Existing research in artificial intelligence and law does hold some promise of systems which will help choose between diverging accounts of the facts of cases—by applying probability theory together with the rules of evidence, for example. And, using diagnostic expert systems techniques, systems are also able to apply complex bodies of rules to the facts presented to them. Systems which can solve legal problems and choose between competing arguments under some sets of circumstances are entirely conceivable, although I suppose we might come no longer to regard the process of handling these situations through IT as judicial but may instead look upon them as a matter of public administration instead.

Looking ahead, the judicial function may then largely be confined either to what computers cannot do, or (on one view) ought not to be doing. And today these two categories seem to coincide in the functions of making moral and ethical judgements about the circumstances of individuals or the interests of society more generally. Such decision making will no doubt continue to involve human beings of integrity, knowledge, and experience acting as impartial arbiters in relation to related disputes over fact or law.

Additionally, it may be that judges will also come to have a vital new role to play in reviewing the 'living law', the content of the legal information systems used in society; and in hearing appeals resulting from the operation of these systems.

8.3. Two of the Most Difficult Questions of All

I would be the first to admit that this book is an upbeat portrayal of IT and its application in law. I do recognize that a plethora of challenges, objections, and dangers could be levelled at the information society which I anticipate. I suspect I would accept many of these and I do harbour concerns myself about excessive reliance on IT, morally objectionable applications of emerging technologies, and the general lack of high level discussion on the ethical and social impact of IT in the future. However, my purpose here has been to sketch out the changes which I believe are both possible and likely.

That said, I do have two particularly nagging doubts of a fairly fundamental nature. One concerns the distinction between those legal matters which can be handled by legal information systems and those which require human specialist attention. The other relates to the impact of legal information systems on the traditional route to becoming a legal specialist.

For the system or human specialist?

Explicitly and implicitly, I have distinguished regularly in this book between legal questions and circumstances which can be disposed of or handled through the use of legal information systems and other situations when, for commercial reasons, or because of the nature of law, specialist human legal input is required.

The distinction is, of course, an oversimplification because there will be some borderline situations and so we should allow for a grey area between these two categories. The far more fundamental problem, however, is that everyday circumstances do not come neatly packaged or labelled as capable of disposal by a legal information system or requiring the attention of a human specialist or belonging to the grey area. A citizen or business person (as distinct from a lawyer) who uses a legal information system as his first port of call may not receive guidance on this initial question of classification. Can the system offer me sufficient guidance or do I need specialist human help?

On some occasions, on the strength, for example, of the extensive financial implications of the users' position, it may be fairly obvious that a specialist is needed. However, in other situations, profound financial implications may not be apparent to the non-specialist or the considerable legal complexity, equally, may not be obvious. The net result here may be the use of legal information systems on occasions which are contrary to the interests of the user.

I find this an extremely vexing issue and it is similar, in many ways, to an issue over which I agonized in my doctoral research in the mid-1980s. Then, I was concerned only with expert systems in law and I had concluded, for theoretical reasons, that these systems could solve 'clear' but not 'hard' cases (this distinction of case type having been a major object of study in the field of jurisprudence). The expert systems under discussion were rule-based (the law was represented as a complex body of interrelated rules) and, in operation, were interactive, proceeding by a question and answer session, led by the system itself. The Latent Damage System is an example of such a system (see Section 6.1). I argued that although rules were at the core of the administration of the law, nevertheless rules alone often offer insufficient or unacceptable guidance to those involved in legal reasoning.

Given that rule-based expert systems were being said to offer guidance of a similar nature, I concluded it crucial that users of the systems had to be sufficiently conversant with the legal and court systems to be able to recognize the circumstances under which rule guidance was either insufficient or unacceptable. To be used responsibly, I claimed that the user had to have knowledge of legal principles, of the role of purpose in legal reasoning, of the presuppositions of compartmentalizing the law, and have the ability also invariably to recognize the limitations of his research tools and be able to recognise those occasions when the system does not seem to be probing to the heart of his problem (an ability to 'smell a rat' or 'hear alarm bells', when things do not feel quite right).

I concluded that only the competent lawyer or legally informed person could fit this bill. By the latter I had in mind the quasi-legal professional adviser or the commercially aware person who had made it his or her business to make a study of the operations of the legal system. I took the view, then, that only these categories of person were legitimate users of expert systems in law and that the systems would assist these users in solving problems that were easy for relevant experts but hopelessly difficult for non-experts.

I have to say that my approach was not universally accepted. Some argued that the enterprise was entirely misconceived because representing the law only as rules was to oversimplify the law and would result precisely in such dilemmas as that of putting on the user the onus of recognizing the limitations of the system. Others embarked on projects to develop systems which themselves would be able to differentiate between those problems they could solve and those that were beyond their scope—this approach was fascinating because it addressed the fundamental problem of computers not knowing their own limitations. These debates are directly applicable to the kinds of legal information systems discussed in this book, but the systems considered here raise an even more difficult problem because I have not anticipated here that the projected users would be limited to the categories of lawyer and legally informed person.

If we cannot rely on the users themselves to recognize the limitations of the systems, is the whole enterprise then not fatally flawed? Is this the IT-based version of the paradox of reactive legal service?

I believe there is a challenge here to the social utility and reliability of legal information systems but not a devastating one. In the past, I have distinguished between the 'pragmatists' and the 'purists' in the world of computers and law and have always positioned myself an even distance between the two camps. In this context, however, my position is highly pragmatic and inspired by my earlier notion of seeking 'improvement rather than perfection' in introducing information systems (see Section 7.4). I also gave notice of my views earlier in Section 6.3 in the context of the putative limitations of law packs.

My conviction rests largely on what I believe to be the most socially significant impact of IT on law in the information society—the realisation and emergence of *the latent legal market.* With numerous legal information products and systems widely available, I have suggested that in our social and working lives we will readily and easily be able to obtain legal guidance in circumstances—and this is vital—where in the absence of IT we would find it impractical or too costly to seek traditional legal advice.

We can, therefore, summarize the dilemma as follows. Do we embrace IT and the information society and develop legal information products and systems which will guide us far more extensively than would otherwise be possible but may fail, on occasions, both to notify us that more complex issues may be at play and that human specialist advice is needed? Or do we reject the new technology on the grounds that even although the law will be invoked far less frequently, on those fewer occasions we can nevertheless then have complete confidence in the reliable, expert disposal of our problems?

Even more crudely, if tendentiously, should we prefer a society in which the law is fully integrated with our lives but not applied correctly on all occasions to a society in which the law remains alienated from our social and working lives but is correctly applied on the rare occasions it is invoked?

The issue clearly requires further debate but, as a crude utilitarian on this occasion, I would favour the adoption of IT. However, if I had to identify a line of inquiry which might lead to a more sophisticated rendition of my position, my starting-point would be writings on the economic analysis of law and justice, especially those of Richard Posner.

The dilemma does also point to other fruitful areas for further research and practical development, for it is surely crucial that we develop and implement techniques to enhance our systems' ability to help users classify their problems as appropriate for disposal by system or not.

It is a striking thought, in any event, that the widest use of legal information systems, even on occasions which are more properly the province of lawyers, could itself create a culture in which the application of the law is assumed to be straightforward rather than subject on all occasions to endless debate of legal minutiae.

Of itself, this could engender a culture which is driven less by literal interpretation of highly detailed rules and adversarial attitudes than by legal guidelines pitched at a higher level of generality where confrontation is exceptional. In the end, the availability of legal information systems for *the latent legal market* could begin to align the legal method of common law systems with that of civil jurisdictions where today they are already more liberal and broad-brush in their approach to interpretation and less inclined to launch into combative legal dispute.

How does one become an expert?

The other very challenging issue, again premised on a legal world dominated by legal information systems and supported by specialist lawyers, is
whether or not the route to becoming a specialist lawyer is cut off when routine legal work is undertaken by systems rather than junior lawyers.

Traditionally, lawyers have developed their skills and evolved to the
status of specialist by apprenticeship and then ongoing exposure to problems of increasing complexity. By natural selection, it seems, whether as a
solicitor or barrister, lawyers are allocated legal problems of complexity
consistent with their level of knowledge. On this model, the main emphasis
on becoming a specialist is on experience of the law in action rather than
exposure to the law in books.

Given that this book suggests IT would automate, streamline, and proceduralize increasing amounts of conventional legal work, does this not eliminate the very training ground upon which all lawyers cut their teeth and
rely upon in progressing through to specialist positions?

It follows from my arguments that the traditional legal advisory service
will be the province only of specialists. So how can lawyers become fit to
grapple with the most challenging of legal issues if the methodology of legal
problem solving has not been inculcated during their early careers through
regular exposure to the resolution of more mundane and prosaic legal
problems? Even if we felt inclined to advance the argument that a different
set of techniques and methods are applied to mundane as opposed to
thorny legal problems, it seems contrary to our intuitions as lawyers that
judges and specialists will be able, in the future, to leap-frog from designing
legal information systems to resolving the most testing of legal matters.
Surely they will need some intermediate experience to help them along the
way to becoming expert?

I have no pat answer to this dilemma, but I can see two broad approaches
that might be taken. On the one hand, if one accepts that the only way of
becoming a specialist is by gaining experience of routine matters of increasing complexity, then it could be argued that the province of lawyers should
be extended so as to retain a slice of routine traditional advisory work,
largely as a training and development facility for lawyers as they progress
through their careers. (There must be a debate here, however, over just how
many repetitions of routine work are required to press the message home.)

In some ways, this would need to be institutionalized to ensure sufficient
usage of these trainees in circumstances where users/clients may be
more attracted to legal information systems. While users may accept the

argument that referrals to trainees are vital in order to sustain the social essential of human specialists, the cost would need to be commensurate with that of legal information systems and so the services of these trainees may be very modestly costed indeed by today's standards (it may be in the legal information providers' interests to help fund the shortfall). Although this approach may seem contrived, if market forces demand pervasive legal information systems, I find it hard to think of an alternative approach if we accept that lawyers can only become the kinds of specialists that we need through gaining experience of routine legal work.

The alternative approach is more radical and would seek to challenge the perceived wisdom about how lawyers become specialists (although I should stress that we would be helped in our deliberations here if more formal work was undertaken on the profile and specification of the human legal specialist). In my experience, the best solicitors of today tend to deny, in true macho fashion, having any extensive knowledge of the law and will ascribe their popularity to their adopting a highly commercial approach, to understanding the businesses of those they advise, and to superior client handling generally. Barristers may be different in tending to have greater specialist knowledge of the law but the attributes of the successful barristers tend, in large measure, to include powers of persuasion, formidable memories for detail, and the capacity to bring enormous effort to bear in short bursts at vital times in the course of their case-load.

While I suspect these will remain the hallmarks of specialist lawyers in the information society, it is not obvious that aspiring specialists can only develop these talents through exposure to repetitious routine legal tasks. Indeed, some might argue that this exposure is of little benefit in their development and would prefer to grow by working alongside the gurus while in their most challenging roles. If exposure to, and emulation of, specialists transpired to be as effective a training and development tool as routine legal work has been thought to be, it may be that the profession could structure itself to encourage what might amount to a return to the genuine apprenticeship approach to legal education. This might be supplemented by junior lawyers' involvement with the other main dimension of legal service, namely, the development of legal information systems. Although specialists would also be heavily involved in the design of these products and services, there will be formidable tasks of analysis required of many non-specialists who are trained in the law. Junior lawyers may, therefore, become a fundamental part of the development process, maybe as those individuals who would undertake a preliminary analysis and transcription of the formal sources, perhaps for later refinement by specialists.

Here there would be exposure to routine legal work but of a very different sort. My experience in the field of legal knowledge engineering suggests this form of analysis would be more intellectually stimulating than the conventional work of junior lawyers; and it would also demand far more penetrating and rigorous legal analysis than is generally required of them.

This, in turn, may help encourage an intellectual curiosity and a thirst for understanding which would lead to fuller appreciation of the law and perhaps also to the development of personal problem solving methodologies.

It is too early, in my view, to be dogmatic in selecting either of the above approaches over the other, but the debate does raise pressing questions for those involved in formal legal education. Should legal studies focus on providing a basic legal education with a view to producing graduates equipped to discharge routine legal work? Or should the emphasis in the future shift towards a new breed of law graduate, equipped more as a legal analyst who will start work as a legal information engineer on legal information system development projects? Might it be that only specialist lawyers, ironically, are capable of developing the legal information systems themselves? Or can we train our general practitioners of today to model their know-how and embody it in IT-based systems?

These will be central questions of policy and strategy for legal academics in the future. And they should be a matter for fascinating debate today.

8.4. Tomorrow's Legal Paradigm

It is said that an author never finishes a book and has to be content with abandoning it instead. I thought it best to abandon this study by returning to my suggestion, in the opening chapter, that we are on the brink of a shift in legal paradigm; and, that after this fundamental change has come about, many features of legal service and legal process of today will be displaced by a new way of legal life underpinned by a fresh set of basic assumptions about the law and lawyers.

I have argued again and again that this shift in legal paradigm can and will only happen when we emerge from the transitional confusion in which we find ourselves into the fully fledged IT-based information society. Only then will *The Technology Lag* be overcome and will our capacity to manage legal information be more than equal to our ability to create and disseminate it.

As to providing some detail of the shift to this new legal paradigm (as summarized in Figure 8.1), I use as my starting-point the twelve central features of today's legal paradigm which were introduced and laid out in Section 1.6. And again, my analysis is divided into the two general categories of legal service and legal process.

Figure 8.1 The Shift in Legal Paradigm

Today's Legal Paradigm	Tomorrow's Legal Paradigm
Legal Service	**Legal Service**
advisory service	information service
one-to-one	one-to-many
reactive service	proactive service
time-based billing	commodity pricing
restrictive	empowering
defensive	pragmatic
legal focus	business focus
Legal Process	**Legal Process**
legal problem solving	legal risk management
dispute resolution	dispute pre-emption
publication of law	promulgation of law
a dedicated legal profession	legal specialists and information engineers
print-based	IT-based legal systems

Legal service

In Section 1.6, I analysed legal service by describing its prevailing characteristics under seven headings. I have followed the headings below in an attempt to capture the shift in paradigm which I anticipate.

From advisory to information service

If this book has any single, unifying theme, it is that IT will eventually enable and encourage legal service to change from being a form of advisory service to a type of information service. While most of the work of the lawyer in today's paradigm is advisory and consultative in nature, the emphasis will shift radically in the information society as many lawyers assume the role of legal information engineer and devote much of their professional lives to the design and development of legal information services and products. With the exception of specialist lawyers and judges, the work of lawyers will move gradually in a leftwards direction along *The Legal Information Continuum*, both serving and liberating *the latent legal market*. The ultimate deliverable will be reusable legal guidance and information services pitched at a level of generality considerably higher than the focused advice which characterizes legal advisory work of today.

From one-to-one to one-to-many

As legal service becomes a form of information service, and lawyers package their knowledge and experience as information services designed for direct consultation by non-lawyers, the work product of individual lawyers will no longer be devoted only to one case and to one client. Instead, the legal information will be reusable and for that purpose cast in a form well suited to repeated consultation. It will be applicable in many circumstances and for many different users. In this way, far more citizens will benefit from the intellectual efforts of individual lawyers.

From reactive to proactive service

Once it becomes practicable and financially viable for non-lawyers quickly to obtain usable legal guidance, earlier legal input in the life cycles of transactions and disputes will become commonplace. For lawyers to be proactive, they will no longer need to be instructed and involved themselves at the start of all projects, for example. Instead, they will develop suites of legal information products, the embodiment of proactivity, which will expressly overcome the paradox of traditional reactive legal service. For these systems will help non-lawyers in identifying those situations in which specialist advice is required and, crucially, will assist them in identifying when to instigate any specialist advisory process. (I am conscious that critics could argue that this could lead to an infinite regress. As a practical matter, this does not worry me.)

From time-based billing to commodity pricing

When the work product of lawyers becomes reusable and the time and effort expended cannot sensibly be allocated amongst those who are paying for the service, there can be no question of hourly billing. This regime, which I have said can penalize the efficient and reward the indolent, will have no place in tomorrow's legal paradigm. Many commentators assume hourly billing will be displaced by some form of value billing which entails charging for the value of some service to the client. Others go further and

287

suggest lawyers will be able to charge for time saved rather than for time spent (although I have never heard a client accept this suggestion with relish). Value billing may, however, prevail during the transitional period between the print-based industrial society and the IT-based information society, but I doubt it will survive in its pure form in the new legal paradigm when it is more likely that legal information services will be akin to commodities, for sale in *the latent legal market* and subject to the more prosaic economic models of supply and demand which apply to physical goods today. Gradually, access to legal service packaged as information service will sell in high volumes for mass consumption at low prices.

From restrictive to empowering

With the demystification of the law and its far wider availability will come the perception that the law does far more than set up obstacles in the path of domestic, social or commercial aspirations. Instead of regarding the law as restrictive, users of legal information services will gradually appreciate that the law can be a source of empowerment and a powerful weapon which can be marshalled in support of the exploitation of opportunities and the attainment of all manner of objectives. While the business person would characterize this future feature of the law as empowering and catalysing, the citizen should come to regard this as meaning the law has become more helpful and supportive.

From defensive to pragmatic

One of the great debates which awaits us is over the extent to which legal liability can be attached to those who develop and market legal information services. While the courts have not indicated where they will draw the line, in liability terms, on *The Legal Information Continuum* (see Section 3.3), as a matter of public and social policy it is likely that the state will want (or want to be seen to want) to promote and encourage the development of legal information systems and the realization of *the latent legal market*. But uncertainty over liability could well inhibit the growth of legal information services.

In any event, by their very nature, legal information services are pitched at a higher level of generality than legal advice. And so, while it may be reasonable for users to rely on the guidance offered, we have to accept that on those (rare) occasions where the guidance is inappropriate and gives rise to problems, the pragmatic social compromise will be not to attach liability to the developers other than in exceptional circumstances. Otherwise, all services would be emblazoned with disclaimers warning that the guidance should not be relied upon without taking conventional, professional advice. The essence of liberating *the latent legal market*, however, is precisely that such additional professional guidance is not sought.

The availability of legal information services will give rise to improvement but not perfection in making the law more usable and available and the market-place itself will establish mechanisms for drawing attention to unreliable or defective services (perhaps allowing users—both disgruntled and content—to leave accessible evaluations on the service for future users to peruse). Legal information engineers may not often be held liable in the future but they will find their market severely eroded if their systems fail to do the job.

From legal focus to business focus

The successful information services of the future will be those that provide legal guidance which is packaged and integrated with more general commercial assistance. While I would not go so far as to suggest that the 'man of affairs' will mutate into some 'information system of affairs', it will surely be both beneficial for users and commercially astute for legal information engineers, to embed some street wisdom and business acuity into the legal services they provide. On this model, legal advice will be bundled with and embedded in more general business advice; other than for the legal specialists in their advisory role, who will probably retain the mantle of ivory tower legal analysts.

Legal service as information service will also have far greater business focus in another sense. The products and packages which will be developed will not be devoted exclusively to the conventional areas of law, as taught in today's law schools, or practised within individual departments of law firms. Nor will the services correspond to the subject matter of today's legal textbooks. Rather, the business focus will require that the guidance transcends many of our conventional legal boundaries and, no doubt, into other disciplines as well. Even if multi-disciplinary practices do not come to fruition, multi-disciplinary information systems most certainly will.

Legal process

Lastly, looking now at the administration of justice rather than legal practice, I have once more used a structure that corresponds with the model laid out in Section 1.6.

The Vision

From legal problem solving to legal risk management

While legal problem solving will not be eliminated in tomorrow's legal paradigm, it will nonetheless diminish markedly in significance. The emphasis will shift towards legal risk management supported by the proactive facilities which will be available in the form of legal information services and products. As citizens learn to seek legal guidance more regularly and far earlier than in the past, many potential legal difficulties will dissolve before needing to be resolved. Where legal problems of today are often symptomatic of delayed legal input, earlier consultation should result in users understanding and identifying their risks and controlling them before any question of escalation. Those legal problems that do slip through the net will be handled either by dedicated legal information products or, where complex or of high value, will be the province of specialist advisers and then perhaps judges.

From dispute resolution to dispute pre-emption

A corollary of effective legal risk management is an overall reduction in the need for formal dispute resolution. The effective control of legal risks prior to their escalation and realization as problems will mean that disputes will be pre-empted and avoided and so will not progress to any formal or alternative resolution process.

Furthermore, in a society which sustains the social compromise of not attaching liability to defective legal information systems, users will tend, on the first time round, to follow and accept the guidance offered by the 'living law'. The broad, generic representations of the law as embodied in legal information systems could themselves create a culture in which there will be little incentive to pursue legal matters at the high level of specificity and in the strictly literal terms which are so characteristic of today's legal paradigm. For all practical purposes, the law in action will be the law as held in legal information systems; less rigorous, less formal, and less adversarial than contemporary, common law jurisdictions. By a quite different route, and following entirely different principles, common law jurisdictions of tomorrow may come in line in spirit with civil law jurisdictions of today.

From publication of law to promulgation of law

Despite the apparent reluctance to make both legislation and case-law freely available on the Internet, international trends, political pressures, and relentless lobbying from within and beyond the legal profession will, in due course, convince the government of the day in the UK to reverse its policy. Far from endorsing the commercially oriented publication of primary sources which is characteristic of today's legal paradigm, the state will then play a far more positive role, in supporting promulgation in the future. All primary and secondary legislative sources, eventually as the tail-end of the legislative process itself, will be placed, as a matter of course, on the Internet or its successor. As for case-law, when it is commonplace for judges to prepare their judgments in electronic form, specific electronic communications facilities will be provided to them by the state to enable and encourage the establishment of far more extensive and current bodies of judicial decisions than are available today. And, eventually, it will barely make sense to speak of 'unreported cases'.

To help guide lawyers and non-lawyers through this far larger, projected mass of legal sources, a major legal information services industry will spring up. These providers will develop systems, products, front ends, filters, and agents, using a wide range of enabling techniques, which will take the user to all but only the relevant sources relevant to her purpose. Expert commentary, analysis, and practical prompts will also be packaged alongside the primary sources of law, building up the legal guidance which is set to become the 'living law'.

From a dedicated legal profession to legal specialists and information engineers

The information society will always need access to legal knowledge and expertise. What will not be sustainable is any continuation from the position in today's legal paradigm whereby the legal profession enjoys an exclusive position as the interface between individuals and businesses on the one hand and access to the rule of law on the other.

In place of lawyers at this interface, will lie ever more flexible, powerful, and accessible IT-based information systems serving both *the latent legal market* of the past and other areas of law amenable to systematization. For problems of great complexity or high value, legal specialists will continue to operate in their traditional advisory role. But they will represent a relatively small fraction of the legal profession of tomorrow. A far larger number of lawyers will have reoriented their careers and will become the legal information engineers whose knowledge forms the basis of the legal information services. Thus, the legal profession of the future will be constituted of two tiers, not the solicitors and barristers of today, but the legal specialists and legal information engineers of the information society. Whether or not the profession has sufficient entrepreneurial talent and general foresight to be involved in the third discipline, that of marketing, as providers of the legal information services and products, is a great unanswered question of today.

From print-based to IT-based legal systems

Finally, and in summary, legal practice and the administration of justice will no longer be dominated by print and paper in tomorrow's legal paradigm. Instead, legal systems of the information society will evolve rapidly under the considerable influence of ever more powerful information technologies. We will no longer suffer from the excessive quantity and complexity of legal material. There will be mechanisms in place to give everyone fair warning of the existence of new law and changes in old. Legal risks will be managed in advance of problems occurring and so dispute pre-emption rather than dispute resolution will be the order of the day. Our law will thus become far more fully integrated with our domestic, social, and business lives.

In all, then, I am optimistic about the future of law.

Bibliography

I have divided this bibliography into two parts. For the first part, I have selected the works which seem to me to have had the greatest impact on the thinking underlying this book. In the second part, I have provided lists of further reading, on a chapter by chapter basis. Readers will notice that there is some duplication, in that a few references appear in both parts of the bibliography and some occur several times in the second part.

1. Selected Bibliography

The central arguments of this study belong to the fields of law, management and information technology. The following books are those which have tended to influence me the most in each of these disciplines.

Law

Bentham, J., *Of Laws in General*, edited by H.L.A. Hart (The Athlone Press, London, 1970).
Dworkin, R.M., *Law's Empire* (Fontana, London, 1986).
Ehrlich, E., *Fundamental Principles of the Sociology of Law*, reprint edition (Arno Press, New York, 1975).
Frank, J., *Courts on Trial* (Princeton University Press, Princeton, 1949).
Harris, J.W., *Law and Legal Science* (Clarendon Press, Oxford, 1979).
Hart, H.L.A., *The Concept of Law*, 2nd edition (Clarendon Press, Oxford, 1994).
Kelsen, H., *General Theory of Law and State* (Russell & Russell, New York, 1945).

Management

Drucker, P.F., *The New Realities* (Harper & Row, New York, 1989).
Drucker, P.F., *Managing for the Future* (Butterworth-Heinemann, Oxford, 1992).
Kay, J., *Foundations of Corporate Success* (Oxford University Press, Oxford, 1993).
Hammer, M., and Champy, J., *Reengineering the Corporation—A Manifesto for Business Revolution* (Nicholas Brealey Publishing, London, 1993).

Bibliography

Handy, C., *The Age of Unreason* (Hutchinson, London, 1989).

Maister, D.H., *Managing the Professional Service Firm* (The Free Press, New York, 1993).

Peters, T.J., and Waterman, R.H., *In Search of Excellence* (Harper & Row, New York, 1982).

Information Technology

Amdahl Executive Institute, *Business Success and Information Technology: Strategy for the 1990s* (The Amdahl Executive Institute, London, 1988).

Boden, M.A. (ed.), *The Philosophy of Artificial Intelligence* (Oxford University Press, Oxford, 1990).

Gore, A., and Brown, R.H., *Global Information Infrastructure: Agenda for Cooperation* (US Government Printing Office, Washington, 1995).

Dreyfus, H.L., and Dreyfus, S.E., *Mind Over Machine* (Blackwell, Oxford, 1986).

Morton, M.S.S. (ed.), *The Corporation of the 1990s: Information Technology and Organizational Transformation* (Oxford University Press, Oxford, 1991).

Negroponte, N., *Being Digital* (Hodder & Stoughton, London, 1995).

Zuboff, S., *In the Age of the Smart Machine* (Heinemann, Oxford, 1988).

2. Further Reading

The following works are either referred to explicitly in the specified chapters of the book or are especially relevant to the subject matter of the chapters in question.

Chapter One   A Law Unto Itself

Allen, C.K., *Law in the Making*, 7th edition (Clarendon Press, Oxford, 1964).

Bentham, J., *Of Laws in General*, edited by H.L.A. Hart (The Athlone Press, London, 1970).

Booker, C., and North, R., *The Mad Officials* (Constable, London, 1994).

Coopers & Lybrand, and The Lawyer, *Financial Management in Law Firms 1995* (Coopers & Lybrand, and The Lawyer, London, 1995).

Cross, R., and Harris, J.W., *Precedent in English Law*, 4th edition (Clarendon Press, Oxford, 1991).

Ehrlich, E., *Fundamental Principles of the Sociology of Law*, reprint edition (Arno Press, New York, 1975).

Fuller, L.L., *The Morality of Law*, revised edition (Yale University Press, New Haven and London, 1964).

Griffiths, C., 'Whose law is it anyway?' (September 1994) *Legal Business* 46.

Hart, H.L.A., *The Concept of Law*, 2nd edition (Clarendon Press, Oxford, 1994).

Kuhn, T., *The Structure of Scientific Revolutions* (University of Chicago Press, Chicago, 1970).

McCormack, M.H., *The Terrible Truth About Lawyers* (Collins, London, 1987).

MacCormick, D.N., *Legal Reasoning and Legal Theory*, paperback edition (Clarendon Press, Oxford, 1994).

Maister, D.H., *Managing the Professional Service Firm* (The Free Press, New York, 1993).

National Consumer Council, *Seeking Civil Justice—A Survey of People's Needs and Experiences* (National Consumer Council, London, 1995).

Ogus, I., *Regulation* (Oxford University Press, Oxford, 1994).

Reed, R.C., *Beyond the Billable Hour* (American Bar Association, Chicago, 1989).

Robbie, G.G., 'Primary Legal Materials—The Other Side of the Coin' (June/July 1995), 6, *Computers and Law*, 3.

Saxby, S., 'Public Sector Policy and the Information Superhighway' (1994), 2, *International Journal of Law and Information Technology*, 221.

UNICE, *Releasing Europe's Potential Through Targeted Regulatory Reform—The UNICE Regulatory Report 1995* (UNICE, Brussels, 1995).

Woolf, Lord, *Access to Justice* (Woolf Inquiry Team, London, June 1995).

Chapter Two   The Advance of IT

Dreyfus, H.L., and Dreyfus, S.E., *Mind Over Machine* (Blackwell, Oxford, 1986).

Gates, B., *The Road Ahead* (Viking, London, 1995).

Lenat, D.B., 'Artificial Intelligence' (September 1995) *Scientific American*, 62.

Morton, M.S.S. (ed.), *The Corporation of the 1990s: Information Technology and Organizational Transformation* (Oxford University Press, Oxford, 1991).

Negroponte, N., *Being Digital* (Hodder & Stoughton, London, 1995).

Patterson, D.A., 'Microprocessors in 2020' (September 1995) *Scientific American*, 48.

Rheingold, H., *The Virtual Community* (Addison-Wesley, Reading, Massachusetts, 1993).

Rheingold, H., *Virtual Reality* (Secker & Warburg, London, 1991).

Searle, J.R., *Minds, Brains and Science* (BBC, London, 1984).

Sheil, B., 'Thinking about artificial intelligence' (1987) *Harvard Business Review*, 91.

Tapscott, D., *The Digital Economy* (McGraw-Hill, New York, 1996).

Weizenbaum, J., *Computer Power and Human Reason*, with new preface (Penguin, Harmondworth, 1984).

Winston, P.H., *Artificial Intelligence*, 3rd edition (Addison-Wesley, London, 1992).

Zuboff, S., *In the Age of the Smart Machine* (Heinemann, Oxford, 1988).

Chapter Three   Law as Information

Capper, P.N., and Susskind, R.E., *Latent Damage Law—The Expert System* (Butterworths, London, 1988).

Chicago-Kent College of Law, *Chicago-Kent 1992 Large Firm Survey*, UK edition (Chicago-Kent College of Law, Chicago, 1993).

Dretske, F.I., *Knowledge and the Flow of Information* (Basil Blackwell, Oxford, 1981).

Bibliography

Harris, J.W., *Law and Legal Science* (Clarendon Press, Oxford, 1979).

Hart, H.L.A., *The Concept of Law*, 2nd edition (Clarendon Press, Oxford, 1994).

Hoebel, E.A., *The Law of Primitive Man* (Harvard University Press, Cambridge, 1961).

Katsh, M.E., *The Electronic Media and the Transformation of Law* (Oxford University Press, Oxford, 1989).

Kelsen, H., *General Theory of Law and State* (Russell & Russell, New York, 1945).

Leith, P., *The Computerised Lawyer* (Springer-Verlag, London, 1991).

Mander, M., 'The Judith Report' (1993), 1, *International Journal of Law and Information Technology*, 249.

Mital, V., and Johnson, L., *Advanced Information Systems for Lawyers* (Chapman & Hall, London, 1992).

Niblett, B. (ed.), *Computer Science and Law* (Cambridge University Press, Cambridge, 1980).

Official Referees Solicitors Association, *The ORSA Protocol* (ORSA, London, 1991).

Ong, W.J., *Orality & Literacy* (Routledge, London, 1988)

Robson Rhodes, *The Robson Rhodes 1995 Legal IT Survey Report* (Robson Rhodes, London, June 1995).

Society for Computers and Law, *Computers and Law* (all issues).

Susskind, R.E., *Expert Systems in Law* (Oxford University Press, Oxford, 1987).

Woolf, Lord, *Access to Justice* (Woolf Inquiry Team, London, June 1995).

Jenkins, B., Susskind, R.E., Warburg, M., and Carrington, J., (eds.), *Focus on IT in the City* (Worshipful Company of Information Technologists, London, 1995).

Chapter Four   Enabling Technologies

Ashley, K.D., *Modeling Legal Argument* (The MIT Press, London, 1990).

Bing, J., *Conceptual Text Retrieval*, NORIS (77) (Norwegian Research Center for Computers and Law, Complex no. 9/88, Oslo, 1988).

Bing, J., 'Legal Text Retrieval and Information Services', in Bing, J., and Torvund, O., (eds.), *25 Years Anniversary Anthology in Computers and Law* (Tano, Oslo, 1995).

Bing, J., and Harvold, T., *Legal Decisions and Information Systems* (Universitets-forlaget, Oslo, 1977).

Brooks, S.M., *Computerizing for Personal Productivity* (Butterworths, Toronto, 1989).

Capper, P.N., and Susskind, R.E., *Latent Damage Law—The Expert System* (Butterworths, London, 1988).

Communications of the ACM, *Special issue on Intelligent Agents*, Vol 37, No7, July 1994.

Drexler, K.E., 'Hypertext Publishing and the Evolution of Knowledge' (1991), 1, *Social Intelligence*, 87.

European Commission, *Report on Europe and the Global Information Society* (ECSC-EC-EAEC, Brussels, 1994).

Gardner, A.v.d.l., *An Artificial Intelligence Approach to Legal Reasoning* (MIT Press, London, 1987).

Gore, A., and Brown, R.H., *Global Information Infrastructure: Agenda for Cooperation* (US Government Printing Office, Washington, 1995).

Hafner, C.D., *An Information Retrieval System Based on a Computer Model of Legal Knowledge* (UMI Research Press, Michigan, 1981).

Johnson, D.R., 'Building and Using Hypertext Systems in the Practice of Law', in Braeman, K.M., and Shellengberger, F., *From Yellow Pads to Computers*, 2nd edition (American Bar Association, Chicago, 1991).

Mital, V. (ed.), *Advanced Litigation Support & Document Imaging* (Kluwer, London, 1995).

Negroponte, N., *Being Digital* (Hodder & Stoughton, London, 1995).

Sharman, R.A., 'Speech Recognition in the Office: How the Technology Supports Dictation' (1994), 97, *The Computer Journal*, 735.

Shneiderman, B., *Designing the User Interface*, 2nd edition (Addison-Wesley, Reading, Massachusetts, 1992).

Susskind, R.E., *Essays on Law and Artificial Intelligence* (Tano, Oslo, 1993).

Susskind, R.E., *Expert Systems in Law* (Oxford University Press, Oxford, 1987).

Swaffield, G., 'THUMPER—An Expert System for Stamp Duty', in *Proceedings of The Third International Conference on Artificial Intelligence and Law* (ACM, New York, 1991).

Tapper, C.F.H., *An Experiment in the Use of Citation Vectors in the Area of Legal Data*, NORIS (36) (Norwegian Research Center for Computers and Law, Complex No. 9/82, Oslo, 1982).

Tapper, C.F.H., *Computers and the Law* (Weidenfeld and Nicolson, London, 1973).

Chapter Five   Leading Applications

Blair, D.C., and Maron, M.E., 'An Evaluation of Retrieval Effectiveness for a Full-Text Document-Retrieval System' (1985), 28, *Communications of the ACM*, 289.

Braeman, K.M., and Shellengberger, F., *From Yellow Pads to Computers*, 2nd edition (American Bar Association, Chicago, 1991).

Broderick, E., 'Technology on Trial: Project Managing the Litigation—A Solicitor's Perspective' (1993), 24, *Computers and Law* (Journal for the Australian and New Zealand Societies for Computers and the Law) 8.

Brooks, S.M., *Computerizing for Personal Productivity* (Butterworths, Toronto, 1989).

Perritt, H.H., *How to Practice Law with Computers* (Practising Law Institute, New York, 1988 (Supplement, 1990)).

Perritt, H.H., 'Mapping the Information Superhighway' (1995), 3, *International Journal of Law and Information Technology*, 200.

Society for Computers & Law, *The Future of Electronic Communications for the Legal Profession* (SCL, Bristol, 1995).

Staudt, R.W., and Keane, J.I., *Litigation Support Systems*, 2nd edition (Clark Boardman Callaghan, Deerfield, 1992).

Susskind, R.E., 'Electronic Communication for Lawyers: Towards Reengineering the Legal Process' (October/November 1993), 4, *Computers and Law*, 4.

Bibliography

Sveiby, K.E., and Lloyd, T., *Managing Knowhow* (Bloomsbury, London, 1987).

Terrett, A., 'Neural Networks—Towards Predictive Law Machines' (1995), 3, *International Journal of Law and Information Technology*, 94.

Venables, D. *Guide to the Internet for Lawyers* (Venables, Lewes, 1995).

Waite, T., 'The Crisis in Litigation Support' (1995), 3, *The International Journal of Law and Information Technology*, 63.

Woolf, Lord, *Access to Justice* (Woolf Inquiry Team, London, June 1995).

Chapter Six   Case Studies

Capper, P.N., and Susskind, R.E., *Latent Damage Law—The Expert System* (Butterworths, London, 1988).

de Bono, E., *The Use of Lateral Thinking* (Penguin, Harmondsworth, 1967).

Hammer, M., and Champy, J., *Reengineering the Corporation—A Manifesto for Business Revolution* (Nicholas Brealey Publishing, London, 1993).

Handy, C., *The Age of Unreason* (Hutchinson, London, 1989).

Harbidge, M., and Catchpole, M., 'Technology Report: PHAROS: Business Adviser' (1993—1994), 2, *Artificial Intelligence and Law*, 69.

Hassett, P., 'Can Expert System Technology Contribute to Improved Bail Decisions?' (1993), 1, *International Journal of Law and Information Technology*, 144.

Hutton, N., Tata, C., and Wilson, J.N., 'Sentencing and Information Technology: Incidental Reform?' (1994), 2, *International Journal of Law and Information Technology*, 255.

Mander, M., 'The Judith Report' (1993), 1, *International Journal of Law and Information Technology*, 249.

Morris, J.E., 'It's Already Tomorrow in Australia' (September 1994) *The American Lawyer*, 88.

Plotnikoff, J., and Woolfson, R., 'Replacing the Judge's Pen? Evaluation of a Real-time Transcription System' (1993), 1, *International Journal of Law and Information Technology*, 90.

Susskind, R.E., and Tindall, C., 'VATIA: Ernst & Whinney's VAT Expert System', in *Proceedings of IV International Conference on Expert Systems* (Learned Information, Oxford, 1988).

Chapter Seven   Critical Success Factors

Bloor, R., *Corporate Computer Strategy* (ButlerBloor, Milton Keynes, 1993).

Chicago-Kent College of Law, *Chicago-Kent 1992 Large Firm Survey*, UK edition (Chicago-Kent College of Law, Chicago, 1993).

Collins, H., 'The Place of Computers in Legal Education' (October 1994), 3, *Law Technology Journal*, 6.

Grindley, K., *Managing IT at Board Level*, 2nd edition (Pitman, London, 1995).

Hammer, M., and Champy, J., *Reengineering the Corporation—A Manifesto for Business Revolution* (Nicholas Brealey Publishing, London, 1993).

Handy, C., *Beyond Certainty* (Hutchinson, London, 1995).

Handy, C., *The Age of Unreason* (Hutchinson, London, 1989).

Kay, J., *Foundations of Corporate Success* (Oxford University Press, Oxford, 1993).

Maister, D.H., *Managing the Professional Service Firm* (The Free Press, New York, 1993).

Morton, M.S.S. (ed.), *The Corporation of the 1990s: Information Technology and Organizational Transformation* (Oxford University Press, Oxford, 1991).

Paterson, A.A., and Susskind, R.E., 'Technology, Lawyers and the Atlantic Divide' (May 1994), 3, *Law Technology Journal*, 43.

Porter, M.E., 'The Competitive Advantage of Nations' (1990) *Harvard Business Review*, 73.

Scott, C., and Widdison, R., 'Law Courseware: The Next Generation' (May 1994), 3, *Law Technology Journal*, 7.

Terrett, A., 'Hypertext—New Paradigms in Legal Education', in Bileta 9th Conference Pre-proceedings, *The Changing Legal Information Environment* (Bileta, Warwick, 1994).

Widdison, R., and Pritchard, F., 'An Experiment with Electronic Law Tutorials' (May 1995), 4, *Law Technology Journal*, 6.

Woolf, Lord, *Access to Justice* (Woolf Inquiry Team, London, June 1995).

Chapter Eight   Law's Future

Asimov, I., 'The Next 70 Years for Law and Lawyers' (1985), 71, *ABA Journal*, 57.

Katsh, M.E., *Law in a Digital World* (Oxford University Press, New York, 1995).

Kennedy, P., *Preparing for the Twenty-First Century* (HarperCollins, London, 1993).

Posner, R.A., *Economic Analysis of Law*, 2nd edition (Little Brown, Boston, 1977).

Purcell, T., North, R., Truda, P., *Tomorrow's Legal Services* (Law Foundation of New South Wales, Sydney, 1994).

Staudt, R.W., 'Law Office Automation Approaching the Millennium' (1993), 1, *International Journal of Law and Information Technology*, 59.

Tapscott, D., *The Digital Economy* (McGraw-Hill, New York, 1996).

Toffler, A., *Powershift* (Bantam Press, New York, 1990).

Widdison, R., 'Virtual Law School' (1994), 8, *International Yearbook of Law Computers and Technology*, 185.

Index

Index

construction disputes
  litigation support 171
costs
  hours spent, on basis of 173
  litigation support, of 172–3
court kiosks
  access to law through 214
  positioning 213–14
  technology 215
  use of 212–15
court system
  dissatisfaction with 11
  finite resources of 33
  pressure, under 32–4
courtroom
  use of IT in 167
critical success factors
  overview of 224
  Triple 'A' formula 240
customers
  needs, focus on 1

data processing
  application areas 57
  artificial intelligence, progress to 57–8
  number crunching, progress from 56–7
desktop publishing
  text creation and production 164
diagnostic systems
  purpose of 121–2
dispute resolution
  legal advisers, role of 45
  modes of 45
document assembly systems
  employment contracts, drafting 215–17
  purpose of 123
  text creation and production 165
document image processing
  basics of 126–7
  case loads of documentation, loading into
    portable format 129
  challenges of 127
  character recognition 127–9
  components 126
  development of 125
  images converted to text 128
  motivations 125–6
  reasons for 126
  recognition hit rate 128
  scale of systems 126
  searchable text and retrievable images,
    documents available as 128
  technology, use in litigation support 169
document management systems
  development of 204–5
  informating, use of 204–7
  nature and content of materials, informa-
    tion on 205
  work product retrieval 205

documents
  drafting
    hypertext *see* hypertext
  systems 77, 81
  management 82
  systems *see* document management
    systems

education
  IT, benefits of 54
  IT, in
    approaches to 255
    distance learning 258
    distinct discipline, as 255–6
    professional examinations 259
    schools, in 256
    undergraduate 256–9
electronic communication
  basic uses of 151–4
  documents, transmission and reception of
    153
  e-mail 152
  external information, access to 153–4
  information on particular matters, access
    to 154
  innovation through 160–1
  internal know-how, access to 153
  lawyers, approach of 150–1
  legal networks
    failure, reasons for 155–7
    future of 161–2
    innovation through 160–1
    Legal Information Network (Link) 158–9
    LEXIS Counsel Connect 157–9
    ownership and control 159–60
    poverty of 155–7
    progress 155
  messages, transmission and reception of
    152
  other users, discussion with 154
  universal mailbox 161
electronic legal networks
  failure, reasons for 155–7
  future of 161–2
  innovation through 160–1
  Legal Information Network (Link) 158–9
  LEXIS Counsel Connect 157–9
  ownership and control 159–60
  poverty of 155–7
  progress 155
electronic mail
  increase in communication, leading to
    242
  know-how, obtaining 206
  systems, use of 152
employment contracts
  drafting, expert system for 215–17
enabling techniques
  background to 106

302

Index

Index

Index

Index